This book is dedicated to the people who just want their mobile phones to make phone calls – SMD

To Sascha and his lifelong companion, the late Bert – SJD

And to our family and friends who once more wondered where we went this time, and why we stopped answering our calls when we bought those shiny new phones – SMD & SJD

# e-marketing
## theory and application

**Stephen Dann**
and
**Susan Dann**

First published 2011 by
PALGRAVE MACMILLAN

Palgrave Macmillan in the UK is an imprint of Macmillan Publishers Limited, registered in England, company number 785998, of Houndmills, Basingstoke, Hampshire RG21 6XS.

Palgrave Macmillan in the US is a division of St Martin's Press LLC, 175 Fifth Avenue, New York, NY 10010.

Palgrave Macmillan is the global academic imprint of the above companies and has companies and representatives throughout the world.

Palgrave® and Macmillan® are registered trademarks in the United States, the United Kingdom, Europe and other countries.

ISBN 978–0–230–20396–9

This book is printed on paper suitable for recycling and made from fully managed and sustained forest sources. Logging, pulping and manufacturing processes are expected to conform to the environmental regulations of the country of origin.

A catalogue record for this book is available from the British Library.

A catalog record for this book is available from the Library of Congress.

10   9   8   7   6   5   4   3   2   1
20   19   18   17   16   15   14   13   12   11

Printed and bound in China

# Short contents

**Short contents**

# Contents

Contents

### Section 3 Applications

# List of figures and tables

## Figures

## Tables

# Preface

Writing a book on e-marketing is a challenging process of second guessing the future, monitoring the past and hoping the present will hold still long enough to stop the sentence you're writing about the Apple iPad from becoming obsolete.

For the most part, we've spent the duration of the project trying out new content, new frameworks and a host of new websites to the point that if you've got the same name as one of the authors, you're not going to have any social media sites left that will accept it as a valid username (which we discovered when one author's namesake friended them on Facebook and permanently confused everyone).

In order to put the book together, we made a few decisions at the outset. First, we'd name brand names so people knew what sort of websites, hardware and technologies matched the generic home-brand marketing theories. Secondly, that merely naming a brand wasn't going to be an endorsement any more than naming the Ansoff matrix was grounds to automatically assume a business growth strategy. Thirdly, that this was e-marketing, so we'd bet on the marketing theory ahead of the technology since marketing's older, more robust and runs in online, offline, mobile and in-flight mode. Finally, we also decided to go for the first person marketer approach of using less third person (apart from the odd cut scene) and more author integration. The only rule we had was to keep the authors anonymous (so you can't say for sure which one of them has the contemporary games habit, and which one believes gaming perfection was reached with Tetris).

## Design decisions

Writing a print book about e-marketing is like using time-lapse photography as a navigation tool. The past looks pretty and it's a good field guide to what's been there previously in the same area. However, as with something as unstable as the Internet, there's room for change, upgrade and new concepts. That said, the last time the authors wrote an offline marketing book, the AMA definition of marketing changed in the same year the book was published (and that was offline marketing).

We're used to change being a constant and have factored that into the book's frameworks – including putting in some technology predictions that might come to pass if marketing students were to invest their time, effort and energy into developing and using these new areas (hint, hint). At the same time, we're also keenly aware that change doesn't negate history, and the cyclical nature of human endeavour is one of action and reaction. Build a distributed network and someone will compete with a centralized structure that in turn will find a distributed network showing up a while later for a rematch.

## Old theory, new technology

There's a deliberate strategy behind our selective mixture of antique theory and cutting-edge content. Back in the early days of the Internet there was a propensity for self-proclaimed and actual experts to declare all of the old rules of business dead and that the Internet changed everything so fundamentally that new rules were needed. This turned out to be wrong, and the old rules of profit, loss, revenue and consumer satisfaction still applied (along with the rest of the notes). Fast forward to a new decade, social media and a new batch of proclamations about the old rules being dead, and we're suffering a serious case of *deja Google*. So we elected to run with the rules, models and frameworks from the 1990s to showcase the idea that fundamental principles of marketing outlive software, hardware and self-proclaimed experts. We may not be using dial-up modems (just the mobile wireless laptops and smart phones), hopping onto the Internet to check mail on CompuServe and AOL (Google and Yahoo!) or talking to our friends in IRC (Twitter) or USENET groups (Facebook groups) but we are still using the new technology for same old communications outcomes.

## Learning from history

By far and away the most surprising reaction to the Internet has been the opportunity to abandon the social constraints imposed by the Industrial Revolution. Prior to industrialism (the manufactured goods superhighway), cottage industries dominated the production landscape as small producers serviced local and niche markets. With the development of factory systems and the high demand for manual labour, society recalibrated to cluster workers around their employment sources (factories) in order to expedite the production processes by getting employees to work as fast as possible. Cities, suburbs and whole towns were based around geographies that suited the physical locations of factories, shipyards and other industrial activities.

As the Internet has gradually moved information production into the forefront of contemporary employment, a 'revolution' has taken place. Separation of employees from the production location is touted as new and revolutionary despite having been the dominant industrial model several centuries prior to the Internet. The development of temporary businesses, loose coalitions of individuals who cluster together for the duration of a project then spread out into their next projects, sounds just like the sort of thing the Internet was designed to support. Said model of 'temporary companies' is the operational model of Hollywood and the film industries, where the break up of the big studios was driven by the 'Company of Strangers' model, some fifty years prior to the Internet being little more than a back-of-a-napkin idea.

The lesson for the Internet is to accept that the use or development of a new technology does not negate the lessons of history. Anyone sold on the idea of the Internet as a 'revolution' should be reminded (with varying degrees of force) that revolution does mean 360° rotation and going around in circles as much as it means the overthrow of established order.

Plus ça change, plus c'est la même chose.

## Notes for the readers

There are a couple of points we'd like to highlight about the book.

### Cross-linked content

The chapters are sufficiently cross-wired that you'll probably try to click the (chapter) references out of habit. As soon as we're doing this in an e-book, that'll work. For now, we've heavily cross-linked and cross-referenced the content so you know where it first appeared and when it's next likely to appear. When you reach the far end of the book, the cross-referencing increases dramatically as we're drawing together a whole book's worth of the content to showcase how to use the concepts, theory and notes in more practical examples.

### It's a trap

There's one thing we should warn you about this book – it's loaded with links to highly interesting places that will capture your attention. If you're easily distracted, buy a kitchen timer and ration your online research time into short units. That said, we'd also like to point out that we had to field test our research in Facebook games, which meant playing around in addictive Flash gaming *as a form of work*. It's the only time procrastinating about our homework resulted in a book chapter being written.

## Cats

The Internet is powered by cats. We don't know why, but if you're a dog person (or chicken person), then it might be a bit annoying to constantly have cat references littered throughout the online world. You'd have our sympathy, but we're cat people, and the plethora of captioned cat photos is quite relevant to our interests.

Oh my god, it's full of cats
*Source*: http://xkcd.com/262

## e-introduction (aka Chapter 0, the Web chapter)

The dead tree edition of the book comes with an online chapter that is variously known as Chapter 0 (since it's the precursor to Chapter 1), e-introduction or 'that web chapter'. The chapter covers the sign up and registration details for a range of e-marketing activities, and since the Internet is considerably volatile we figured a chapter full of screenshots, URLs and recommended web companies being printed out was just asking for trouble. The chapter will probably go through a few revisions over the lifespan of the printed book since web pages change, companies, brands and products come and go, and all the screenshots will fall victim to the passage of time and web design fashions. The e-introduction is available on the Companion Website: www.palgrave.com/business/dann.

# Acknowledgements

The authors would like to acknowledge the ongoing support of the backroom workers of the Dann & Dann publishing machine. Thank you to Jean Shepley, Michael Dann, Peter Dann and Jennifer Gearing for their ongoing support. Thanks also to the team at Palgrave Macmillan who shook hands with us and said, 'Call when it's done'. Since we're still figuring out that bit of our phones, we e-mailed them instead.

Stephen would like to thank his colleagues at the Australian National University for their contributions, suggestions and assistance over time, and the IT team at the College of Business and Economics, who steadfastly refused to ask what precisely he was doing with that computer (it's been much appreciated and heavily documented). Thanks go to everyone who has contributed to this book by being part of Stephen's online life through USENET, IRC, Facebook, MSN, Twitter, e-mail and the many hundreds of hours logged in game servers. It's the people who make the Internet, especially the thousands of you who will never read this dedication because it's printed on a dead tree. Susan and Stephen would like to thank Randall Munroe of XKCD.com for providing us with the opportunity to use his cartoons throughout the text. XKCD has been proof that the Internet can bring together the extremely potent combinations of awesome observation and stick figures into a powerful force for good (even if mouseover text is impossibly hard to render in print).

Finally, Susan and Stephen would like to thank you for reading this page.

# About the authors

There are two authors. Neither remembers who was lead author and since they're both Dann, S., it doesn't actually matter. For the record, their parents never expected them both to work in the same field, co-author books and generally have copious confusion when the letters addressed to Dr S. Dann arrive at the mail box (which is one reason they both like e-mail).

## Dr Stephen Dann (BA, B Com (Hons First Class), GCHE, MHE, PhD)

Dr Stephen Dann's Avatar logo

Stephen Dann is a senior lecturer at the Australian National University in Canberra, Australia. Stephen's research specializations include social marketing, strategy, consumer behaviour and Internet marketing. His ambition is to collect one of each qualification available in post-secondary school education.

*URL: www.stephendann.com*

## Dr Susan Dann (BA, MPubAdmin, PhD, FAMI, CPM, MAICD)

Dr Susan Dann's Avatar logo

Dr Susan Dann is Professor of Marketing and Deputy Head, School of Business, Australian Catholic University. Susan combines an extensive career in academia with a role as an independent company director, bringing marketing expertise to a number of boards and as a member of government tribunals. She first taught an e-marketing subject in 1994 where students complained about having tutorial exercises e-mailed to them, and asked why they couldn't come to class to get the notes instead. Susan's research specializations are in the non-commercial applications of marketing, including social marketing and corporate-level marketing strategy, and she has a publication background in business strategy, marketing and public policy. Her ambition is to find out the best three laws people would pass if they were arbitrarily made ruler of their local area.

*URL: www.susandann.com*

# Background and planning

Section 1 of the text includes the first five chapters of the book, which cover the groundwork for e-marketing from the background history of the medium, marketing and the role of strategy, planning and consumer behaviour. Chapter 1 is the history lesson on where the Internet and e-marketing have come from, and how this shapes the direction and development of where it can (and should) head in the future. Chapter 2 brings together a background briefing on marketing theory from the usual suspects of the marketing mix to some of the more influential marketing models and ideas that recur through the advance stages of the book. Chapter 3 introduces strategy to e-marketing with an emphasis on thinking through the practical decisions needed to be addressed, and the questions that need to be answered before any of the tactical elements can be considered. This leads directly to Chapter 4, which outlines the procedures for documenting the decisions of the previous chapter through a range of different plans and planning processes. Finally, Chapter 5 delves into the consumer behaviour aspects of the Internet with a review of the common models, assumptions and insights into how people use the Internet to set the context before Section 2 reviews the implementation issues of addressing consumers through e-marketing.

# CHAPTER 1

# Introduction to e-marketing

## Learning objectives

By the end of this chapter, you should:

- understand the basics of e-marketing and the distinctive styles of using technology for marketing purposes

- be conversant with different perspectives of the Internet, including a brief history of the medium

- appreciate how different social, technological and economic influences have shaped the Internet

- understand where some of the services mentioned in the e-introduction (setting up for e-marketing) fit into the bigger picture of the Internet.

## Welcome

Welcome to *e-marketing: the book* (the musical is under contract negotiation). This chapter will briefly introduce you to e-marketing, give you an overview of the nature of the Internet, fill in some of the history of how a Cold War weapon system evolved into a global communications framework and set the scene for some of the ideas expressed later in the book. This chapter is more focused on the Internet than marketing. Chapter 2 is more about marketing and less focused on the Internet. Combined, Chapters 1 and 2 lay the groundwork for getting into the e-marketing frame of mind before you start the strategy (Chapter 3) and planning (Chapter 4).

A word of note: the authors write in a cross-referenced style, pointing out the connections between ideas in the current chapter and other information in the book. As e-marketing makes copious use of hypertext and linking to relate content, the authors use the nearest print equivalent, which is the bracketed (Chapter) statement, to point out where the related ideas reside. It's also worth noting that marketing and the Internet are equally self-referential and that circular logic applies to both areas – marketing is an ongoing cycle of measurement, action, measurement and reaction (and more measurement). At the same time, the Internet has the capacity to generate an infinite loop of cross-links, cross-references and cyclical activity.

## Marketing with an e

e-marketing is any type of marketing activity that needs some form of interactive technology for its implementation. Throughout the book, the term e-marketing is used as an umbrella definition to describe a range of means, mechanisms and approaches for making the best use of technology for delivering marketing. That said, it's worth defining the different styles of e-marketing that sit under the central definition, much in the same way that cricket has a core set of rules which translate into the stylistically different test matches, Twenty20 and the one-day series whilst all still being cricket. The same deal applies to e-marketing – there's a core set of rules (electronic, interactive, marketing) which can be applied in a range of interesting ways to make the best use of the features of the particular technology. There are three different forms of interactive marketing to examine:

o  marketing over IP
o  interactive marketing
o  mobile marketing.

### Marketing over IP

'Marketing over Internet protocol' (MOIP) is our term for all forms of marketing that make use of any part of the Internet. If the marketing requires an Internet connection to take place, then it's MOIP in nature. MOIP is the dominant theme of this book and will be the mainstay of most of the chapters (Chapter 13, m-commerce, being the obvious exception). The book takes a slightly broader approach to MOIP to avoid limiting marketing thinking to just web-based campaigns and product delivery to include: Internet-based systems such as social networks and virtual worlds (Chapter 9); non-web technologies such as peer-to-peer file sharing, instant messenger chat, IRC channels, FTP sites and even e-mail (Chapter 14); and Internet-connected devices such as the Xbox, Wii, Playstation and Internet fridges (Chapter 14 again). All are considered in relation to what their specific technical merits can contribute to marketing.

### The Internet fridge: TCP/ IP + cold storage

Somewhere around 2002, the refrigeration industry was going to be revolutionized by providing Internet connections straight to the refrigerator door. This was, and may yet remain, one of the most improbable ideas concerning Internet access. Adding an LCD touch screen to a cold storage device was supposed to revolutionize food ordering, with pull-down menus of ingredients, automatic reordering of food, barcode scanning and a whole host of concepts that look okay on paper but fail miserably in practice. The fridge wasn't smart enough to tell the difference between an empty and full milk bottle, the (few) users trying out the barcode service usually forgot to scan in or scan out the empties and the on-screen touch screen ordering of food from a website ran into the problem that it was usually quicker and cheaper to head to the shops for whatever you needed to restock the fridge. In short, it turned out that you could put a fridge on the Internet, and the Internet on a fridge; it was just not that useful. As such, the term ' Internet fridge' is occasionally used to describe a technology that's technically feasible but utterly useless in practice.

## Interactive marketing

Interactive marketing excludes any MOIP devices to focus on the use of non-Internet, non-mobile, interactive systems. This allows marketers to consider options outside of the standard Internet or mobile phone frameworks to make use of other technologies such as sample media (e.g. DVD, CD), pre-loaded demonstration devices (e.g. iPods, USB sticks), in-store devices (electronic kiosks, CD printers, iPod docks) and even the interactive capacity of digital television. Interactive marketing is the older sibling of Internet marketing, and whilst the Internet can handle dynamic interaction and small-to-medium-sized file distribution, there's still no faster way to place content in the hands of a customer than a physical object. A single, standard 4GB USB or DVD can hand over several hours of downloadable content in mere seconds. Interactive marketing devices will periodically show up throughout the book where they can be used to augment the e-marketing thinking. (They'll feature in Chapter 14 and make cameo appearances in Chapter 13 as means to augment mobile marketing.) Interactive marketing also features the use of some conventional cinematic and television devices such as product placement in video games or sponsorship of downloads, content or data (Chapters 7 and 14).

## Mobile marketing

Mobile marketing (m-marketing) uses a distinctive suite of communication protocols and tools such as wireless access, Bluetooth devices, multimedia messaging (MMS) and short messaging systems (SMS). Whilst the average mobile device seems capable of Internet access, accessing the Internet by a handheld device doesn't necessarily mean the use of MOIP. (Consider the distinction being whether the user needs an e-mail address or mobile number to sign up for the offer.)

If you send a product announcement out by e-mail, tweet it and post it to the company website, you're probably thinking MOIP even if all of the above can be read on an iPhone. However, if you use the native mobile technologies to send out an SMS, or have an interactive billboard broadcasting a Bluetooth downloadable voucher, or send content through the GPRS networks, then you're definitely using m-marketing. M-marketing as a distinctive approach within e-marketing is covered in depth in Chapter 13.

## I can't believe it's not e-marketing

The chief boundary line that determines whether the marketing is conventional marketing or e-marketing is whether or not the marketing process fits within the Hoffman and Novak (1996) one-to-many-to-one communications model. Back in the dawn of the commercial Internet, Hoffman and Novak put forward a simple model of computer-mediated communication in an interactive environment, which basically asks whether the recipient of the communication (consumer) can interact with the sender (company) in a way that links both customer and consumer (Figure 1.1).

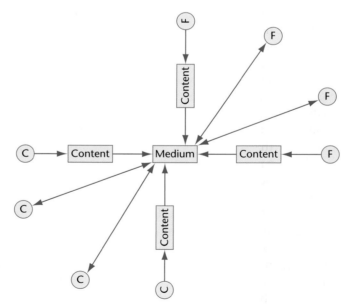

**Figure 1.1  Hoffman and Novak's model**
*Source*: http://jcmc.indiana.edu/vol1/issue3/hoffman.html

One-to-many-to-one communications are those computer-mediated communications that are published by an individual into a public sphere, such as Facebook, and are read and responded to either directly (to the individual by direct message) or indirectly (to the Facebook group) by other readers (Hoffman and Novak, 1996). Computer-mediated communications (CMC) is the use of computers and computer networks as communication tools by people who are collaborating with each other to achieve a shared goal that does not require the physical presence or co-location of participants and which can provide a forum for continuous communication free of time constraints (Kaye, 1991). Hoffman and Novak's (1996) house rule didn't require actual interaction, just the capacity for interaction if desired between consumer and marketer.

This approach neatly isolates television and radio into non-electronic marketing due to the lack of interactive capacity (print media loses on the grounds it's not electronic) whilst preserving a role for the interactive television broadcasts such as the 'red button' voting system on Sky News (news.sky.com). There's a grey area over SMS voting for reality television shows and the live phone call request lines on radio counting as interactivity – thankfully, that's resolved by neither of them being marketing.

## Defining e-commerce

e-commerce forms the broader business domain of using electronic-mediated systems for commercial activity and is the parent business activity which contains e-marketing. It encompasses all electronic business models, including those which operate between customer and provider through the Internet as well as the direct electronic exchange of data between business-to-business partners. e-commerce provides commercial frameworks for organizations to manage customers and partners for profit.

e-commerce and e-marketing are often used interchangeably to describe e-marketing activity. For the purpose of this book, e-commerce is the broader platform of commercial activity conducted using electronic systems (Gilmore, Gallagher and Henry, 2007). When a customer uses an ATM to withdraw cash, e-commerce covers the electronic data interchange (EDI) that occurs between the ATM and the customer's bank. As an ATM terminal is displaying adverts for additional products or services, e-marketing is also taking place. The core differentiating factor for e-marketing is the involvement of a targeted customer rather than just the use of a network to facilitate a commercial transaction.

e-commerce can, and does, occur without e-marketing. Radio frequency identity (RFID) tags can be used for inventory management through automated systems that maintain and update accounting records (Chapter 14). The supermarket checkout scanner's automated data systems provide inventory control, accounting and auditing as they validate the transaction and adjust stock levels to enable just-in-time ordering systems to function. Although these systems may be used for marketing, they function independently of an e-marketing programme. Just as an organization can engage in commerce without using marketing, it's entirely possible to forgo e-marketing and still be in the e-commerce business. The importance of isolating e-commerce from e-marketing is the recognition that e-marketing is not the be-all and end-all of commercial activity on the Internet. e-marketing has the distinctive focus on the marketer–marketplace–society trifecta for value creation that is part of the larger e-commerce agenda but only one aspect amongst many (no matter how important we might want to see ourselves as being).

## The Internet

The Internet is a giant network of interconnected networks which combine to host a virtual economy, a massive virtual infrastructure and the dynamics of the interactions of real people around the world, all off the back of cables, servers and a lot of electricity generation. Back at the start of the commercialization of the Internet, the American Federal Networking Council (FNC) (www.itrd.gov) produced a definitive statement outlining the Internet as a multi-layered platform consisting of separate yet connected distinct components which covered the hardware, software, intellectual and social infrastructure which produced the Internet as recognized by the end users.

### Component parts of the Internet

For the purpose of this book, and based on the FNC's original definition, the Internet is divided into four equal component parts: infrastructure; exchange; interaction and environment.

### *Infrastructure*

Technical infrastructure covers the hardware infrastructure such as the computers, cables, power lines and power supplies that provide the backbone through which the Internet is housed and accessed. If you emphasize this aspect of the Internet, you probably think of it as a 'network of networks' where the priorities are the computer and software issues. At the same time, the physicality of the Internet as a set of machines, cables and servers is also connected to viewing the Internet as a place and emphasizing the virtual geography of the medium (particularly if you play online as game servers become their own pocket universes).

### *Exchange*

Interactive exchanges are the second aspect of the Internet which covers both the interactivity of Hoffman and Novak's (1996) computer-mediated communication and the software infrastructure of the Internet. The software infrastructure is the veritable alphabet soup of communication protocols that govern how the interconnected network of networks actually exchange data. This covers aspects such as TCP/IP protocols, IP addresses, packet routing, HTTP, FTP, bittorrent traffic, VOIP, SMTP and any other future protocols. For the most part, this level of the Internet is almost invisible to the end user insofar as the computers go about their business largely without human intervention or human observation. If this is your dominant way of thinking about the Internet, you'll either be at the network of networks approach or considering the user experience of the Internet as a service delivery platform.

## Interaction

Social interaction is the social infrastructure that relates to the human-to-human, human-to-business relationships that are conducted via the medium of the Internet. This also incorporates an intellectual infrastructure of online content that was created by and for other Internet users. If you think of this as the Internet, you most likely consider virtual presence as a key issue for e-marketing. The combination of virtual goods, services, experiences and knowledge forms economic goods of value for a virtual economy and provides the required shared goods of value to create the basic community framework for interpersonal interaction (see Chapter 9 for more on shared goods of value).

## Environment

Virtual environments are the culmination of the human need to conceptualize the unfamiliar with the nearest metaphor that almost fits – hence, on the Internet where nothing is remotely real, the metaphorical terminology relates to the physical world in terms of 'home page', 'site', 'virtual world' and 'virtual economies'. The virtual environment is a way of collectively understanding how the infrastructure, social interaction and seamless exchange of data and human interaction results in an economic and social structure. If you focus on this aspect of the Internet, then your interests are likely to lie in the development of virtual worlds and the virtual geography as an exploration of the spaces of the Internet. Alternatively, if you're interested in the meta-level results of the dynamic interaction of people, places and exchange, you're probably captivated by the virtual economy. Figure 1.2 outlines a visual representation of the conceptual boundaries of the Internet.

Figure 1.2 intentionally locates each of the four categories at the mid point between their respective defining terms as there are no absolutes within the model. For example,

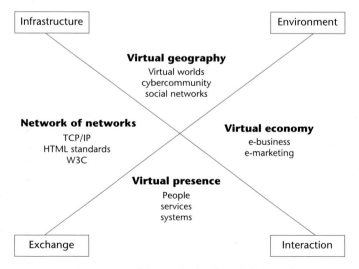

Figure 1.2 Conceptual boundaries for defining the Internet

there are no pure infrastructure applications in that either the infrastructure does something (network of networks) or is something (virtual geography). Similarly, environment facilitates virtual geography or the virtual economy (or both). The following section outlines how the network of networks, virtual geography, virtual economy and virtual presence classifications can be used to encapsulate different types of e-marketing activity, websites and non-web activity.

## Network of networks (infrastructure + exchange)

The Internet is a legacy of a much different world. Borne out of the later part of the twentieth century, the Internet was designed to augment the capacity of the American military-intellectual infrastructure to survive a series of direct nuclear hits in the event of the Cold War turning into a nuclear war. The original design of the Internet was based on combining the principles of load sharing with a distributed infrastructure that avoided implementing a vulnerable central command point that could be targeted for destruction. Consequently, the schematics for the Internet included the capacity to function without a central hierarchy, withstand massive damage from the loss of various nodes without collapse and still contain most of the useful stuff you'd want in the event of having to exchange nuclear missile fire with another nation. The practical reality of the Internet's infrastructure includes a realistic chance of an Internet Brownout if you combine peak demand with the loss of a large slice of any nation's power grid, and the geographic reality of isolated chokepoints at various points on the map – notably, the undersea cable that connects each continent and island to the rest of the grids.

However, as the Internet was designed to function as a decentralized system, it also invoked a sense of distributed responsibility within the system's administrators and programmers. The principle of network neutrality was paramount when networks were limited and demand could easily exceed supply on one pipeline. Network neutrality solved the infrastructure issue by allowing unfettered carriage of information between the various networks as a distributed (and mutual) load-sharing scheme. Any data packet can use any network equally to avoid blockages with the overall system, meaning that all packets can seek the most efficient path from A to B. As the nature of digital transmission and replication is relatively lossless, the decentralized sharing of carriage also created an unexpected by-product in the form of a mindset of information sharing for the human operators of the networks. As the Internet demonstrated the technical feasibility of near-limitless replication of data, it led people to challenge the applicability of physical world economic models of scarcity within the new environment.

One particular point to be noted here is that the Internet's 'blockage as damage' approach to shifting data combined with the lack of scarcity to generate a notion that 'information wants to be free' where 'free' meant 'able to move about the network'. (The 'free' bit is sometimes co-opted as 'information wants to be distributed without charge'. It's not strictly true since information pretty much enjoys the journey as much as the destination.) As the Internet needed to be able to seamlessly re-route around broken, blocked or destroyed nodes in the network, and be able to reconcile and replicate dozens of different redundant systems, it was custom designed to create value through duplication and multiple redundant copies of information. This is absolutely counter-intuitive to the conventional physical world model of commerce where value comes from scarcity. Understandably, if you invert the physical models of value from scarcity, it requires some serious recalibration of commerce, intellectual property law and property rights. The recalibration is currently under way in a range of legal, practical and social manners which are discussed further in Chapter 15. Similarly, network neutrality is also an unusual framework from a physical world perspective and is periodically challenged by organizations that try to apply a physical world model of scarcity to the online world's surplus model (Chapter 15).

From an e-marketing perspective, there are a few reasons to take an interest in the network of networks. First, it allows you to understand the physical constraints that limit the capacity of the Internet to deliver on promises of value. Secondly, it ties back into virtual geography (Chapter 9) and encourages an expansive view of the Internet beyond the Web (Chapter 14). Finally, it's also thoroughly fascinating (if you have the slightest geek propensity) to be able to appreciate the logistical feats that underpin how the Internet actually functions at the code level. (If the section on HTML in the e-introduction (setting up for e-marketing) sparked any interest, it's worth pursuing the network of networks view further in your own research.)

## Machinery and the Internet

The Internet is both the machinery and the machinations of technology, software and systems interacting with each other as much as the interactions that take place between the human members of the community. Predictions of intelligent shopping agents who scour the Internet for the best bargains, deals and prices are perpetually in the process of 'coming soon'. Ultimately though, digital agent (and related systems) still report back to human masters. Only when computers are capable of applying for their own credit cards and earning their own incomes will marketing need to focus on the computer-to-computer transactions that are currently the domain of the engineers (even if the equipment in NASA's space programme has its own Twitter account, it's still a human operator typing up the mission output in human-readable format). Marketing strategies remain aimed at human interactions for the majority of Internet transactions, with the possible exception of the search engine optimization strategies.

### Computers as customers: the case of search engine optimization

Search engine optimization (SEO) is an odd area of marketing that is ostensibly business-to-business in nature, but bordering on business to computer in actual conduct. SEO marketing attempts to develop the optimum mix of content and metadata to improve the search engine's automated review of the site's content. Although SEO is formally considered a form of advertising and promotion, there is a possibility that it may have become the first foray into a human-AI barter programme. If you consider the search engine's computer as a customer, SEO is about swapping ease of indexing for the computer for a decent result in the computer's automated report. The process of SEO involves placing a range of formalized structures such as metadata information into websites, videos, Flash animations and other elements which are in formats that are easiest to read for the automated search systems that build the search engine databases. What complicates the issue beyond mere administrative Internet paperwork is the nature of something like the Google Index which has a consumer behaviour style 'black box' complexity to it. In an eerie parallel to CB theory, the Google Index is approximately 200 known variables, with a range of unknown elements including the differing priorities, importance and weighting placed on each variable. In marketing terms, the process of SEO revolves around developing a product that offers superior performance in meeting the varying needs of the automated search engine software programs. If satisfied with the data product, the search engine software exchanges a good placement in the search engine rankings for ease of search, indexing and 'optimized' information. Although it is still mostly discussed as an advertising issue (Chapter 7), there's still a sense of value for value swap between marketer and automated system that may just make this a new form of marketing.

## Virtual geography (infrastructure + environment)

Virtual geography is the ways and means in which the Internet can be subdivided in regions, zones and locations based on a range of different factors. Geographic metaphors dominate the market with their ability to make the intangible, ethereal nature of the Internet into something that at least feels real (even if it's only a model). The value of thinking of the Internet as a physical place is examined throughout the book with a strong emphasis on the value of 'place' in the formation of cybercommunities (Chapter 9) and the role of virtual geography in e-marketing distribution (Chapter 6). The book focuses on a microcosm of ways of thinking about the Internet as a physical location through:

○ cyberspace
○ marketspaces and marketplaces
○ virtual geographic boundaries
○ virtual worlds.

### Cyberspace

No discussion of the Internet as a virtual space can avoid mentioning cyberspace. That said, the word 'cyber' tends to rank alongside 'information superhighway' as a term to avoid using unless you're hosting a 1990s retro party. Cyberspace as a concept talks about the Internet as a place, environment or thing that's just there at the back of the computer screen. The best (and prettiest) forerunner to the discussion of the Internet as an inherently physical place comes from William Gibson's (1984) definition of 'cyberspace' as physicality created by shared understanding. Gibson (1984, p. 51) wrote:

> Cyberspace. A consensual hallucination experienced daily by billions of legitimate operators, in every nation, by children being taught mathematical concepts...

A graphical representation of data abstracted from the banks of every computer in the human system. Unthinkable complexity. Lines of light ranged in the non-space of the mind, clusters and constellations of data. Like city lights, receding...

Gibson's cyberspace was purely fictional playground for his novels which, as part of the cyberpunk movement (another 1990s concept gone awry), provide a large amount of inspiration for the graphical visualization of the Internet (partly because most of us early Internet fans were also reading Gibson's work). In addition to the notion of the Internet as a physical structure, the development of the Internet also borrowed heavily from the lexicon of libraries with the use of terms such as index, directory and searching. The next wave of metaphors came from the interlinked structural diagrams of the World Wide Web, which looked like some form of bizarre spider web. Bad puns and in-jokes about spiders and web crawlers took over a little slice of the language. Finally, and noticeably coinciding with the rise of Web 2.0, the language of the Internet is increasingly evocative of interpersonal ownership aspects (my*, you*, face* etc.). Cyberspace, however, remains a conceptual framework that allows the end user to place a familiar mental model of the physical world over the top of the incredibly unfamiliar Internet infrastructure. It also gave the world the comparatively less popular concept of 'meatspace' to describe the physical world.

## Marketspaces and marketplaces

If you consider cyberspace as the end-user's metaphor for the virtual landscape of the Internet, then marketspace is the business world's way of converting its familiar frameworks for understanding how the Internet functions. The 'marketspace' is the parallel digital world that accompanies the physical world of the marketplace as a conjunction between ideas and exchange, where goods, services, ideas and money can be exchanged as items of value (Weiber and Kollman, 1998). The marketspace–marketplace continuum demonstrates that value chains of product services, procurement, distribution and production can be found and solved in both online and offline environments.

Marketspace is independent of the Internet in that it exists at the local shop with the scanner data feeding into the supply chain network that allows Tesco, for example, to automatically re-order stock based on actual sales figures. At the same time, marketspace also encompasses the entire e-commerce world where payments move from end users (consumer or businesses) through the retail networks to suppliers, distributors and producers (Chapter 4).

## Virtual geographic boundaries

The geography of the Internet also indicates the ways and means of accessing the content. For example, the multiple web browsers featured in the e-introduction (setting up for e-marketing) can all access the front end of the World Wide Web for viewing and interaction, whereas the FTP clients access specific parts of the back end of the Internet. Similarly, virtual worlds exist isolated from the Web (Chapter 9) through the need for specific-purpose pieces of client software (Second Life, World of Warcraft), or operate as closed catalogue environments (iTunes, Steam) for content distribution

(Chapter 14). Appreciating that there are issues of geography within the Internet aids the development of e-marketing distribution strategies (Chapter 3), market segmentation (Chapter 4) and the understanding of online consumer behaviour (Chapter 5) as virtual boundaries also arise from the development of cybercommunities (Chapter 9).

Geographies of the Internet also provide useful metaphors for understanding social clanning behaviour and shared interests – and great visual metaphors for webcomic cartoonists (Figure 1.3).

Much like the physical world, the geographies of the Internet present their own, different operating conditions. Online interaction is usually classified as lean or rich media depending on the extent to which you have more than just text or static images at your disposal. Lean media environments are communications media that tend to strip away non-verbal cues and information otherwise available in a face-to-face environment – usually by relying mostly on text-based communication (Montoya-Weiss, Massey and Clapper, 1998). For the record, the textbook is semi-lean media in that we get away with images, links and sending you off on quests, but do so without the benefit of rich media engagement. Similarly, if you consider the visual differences between Delicious (http://delicious.com) and Flickr (www.flickr.com), you can see how the infrastructure of a website influences the users and how they interact. Delicious is for tagging,

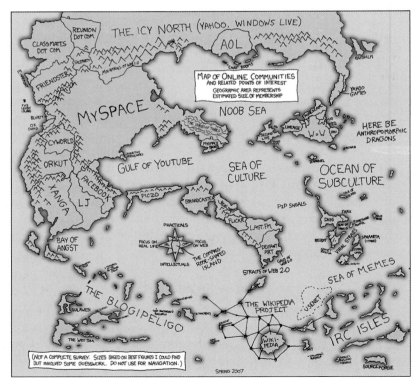

**Figure 1.3** The XKCD map of the Internet
*Source*: http://xkcd.com/256

organizing and adding commentary to saved web addresses (like an oversized annotated phonebook), whereas Flickr is the family photo album or scrapbook. Both use tags and annotations, and have community capacity – the primary differentiation is in the purpose of the system (discussion of the URL and its contents versus looking at pictures). Delicious's community structure is less intra-site focused than Flickr and doesn't tend towards Flickr's 'friends and family'-style community.

At the other end of the spectrum are the rich media environments which cover sites where the Internet medium extends itself to capturing the visual and verbal nuances of the conversation through audio (podcasts), video (YouTube) and graphical elements (Flickr). If you look at YouTube's capacity to publish video responses to allow people to talk at each other (rather than to each other), you'll notice that you can capture nuances of sarcasm and humour through the non-verbal cues. You'll also find that the text comments below those videos lack any such nuance since they're lean media responses to rich media content (it's a partial excuse for the sad state of YouTube text commentary).

Each of these 'regions' within the Internet has also functioned in a manner reminiscent of the geography for creating regional characteristics, traits and social norms. The 'physical' features of various Internet environments help shape the cultural norms of the cybercommunity structures that form around these virtual environments (Chapter 9). Even the choice of web browser can shape the physical experience of the Internet – compare the look of the Flock browser, with its constant reminder that there are other real-life people on the other end of the Internet, with the more impersonal lines of Internet Explorer, Google Chrome or Firefox. Facebook (www.facebook.com) and Gmail (http://mail.google.com) constantly remind you that other people exist (and they can see you) within their own networks through their chat status updates on the side of the page.

## Virtual worlds

Virtual worlds are the text-based, two-dimensional and three-dimensional self-contained environments that exist in isolation from the rest of the Internet. The most widely known virtual worlds are usually gaming orientated with World of Warcraft (www.worldofwarcraft.com), EVE Online (www.eveonline.com/) and City of Heroes (http://eu.cityofheroes.com/en/) being high-profile entrants in the genre. In the non-gaming universe, Second Life (www.secondlife.com) remains the highest profile virtual environment that's not linked to some form of video game. The distinguishing features of these virtual worlds are the need for a specialist piece of software to access the environment (client software) and their status as pocket universes that support real-time interaction with both computer-generated characters and other human participants (Chapter 9). There's also a case to argue that the Xbox Live (www.xbox.com/en-GB/), Sony Playstation Home (uk.playstation.com/psn/pshome) and even the Nintendo Wii's (uk.wii.com) Internet channel are all virtual worlds by virtue of their pocket universe status – access requires specific hardware, and the hardware is linked to persistent, ongoing worlds. For instance, you can't transfer between the hardware worlds – a Mii character from the Nintendo platform can't migrate to an Xbox. The same Mii character can, however, travel from one Wii to another across the Nintendo network. Consequently, it's possible to consider the consoles as the gateway devices to virtual worlds (Chapter 14).

## Virtual economy (interaction + environment)

The virtual economy is the consequence of a supportive Internet environment for commerce and interactions that occur within that commercially orientated side of the Internet. It's vitally important to realize that the commercial and commercialized side of the Internet is a small and absolutely replaceable part of online life. The Internet functioned just fine without commercial interference and, with the development of Internet2 (www.Internet2.edu) as a non-commercial Internet infrastructure, it may well function just fine without us again. Whilst e-commerce has added some useful elements to the online environment, it wasn't the foundation or cornerstone of the development of the technology. Consequently, it needs to retain a sense of perspective as to how commercial activity fits within the broader socio-political landscape of the Internet. From our perspective, there are three aspects worth considering: the e-business environment, e-marketing and the virtual product.

### e-business environment

Most of the focus of this book is on business-to-consumer (B2C) and consumer-to-consumer (C2C) activity. However, an entire level of business-to-business (B2B) activity exists on the Internet in terms of product acquisition, sales, catalogues and even the shipping and logistical infrastructure that underpins the ability of companies to offer seamless B2C services. For example, while Zazzle (www.zazzle.com) and Lulu (www.lulu.com) both provide print-on-demand solutions with the consumer market in mind, they also function as brokers, printers and distributors in a B2B context. For example, when celebrity geek author Wil Wheaton (www.wilwheaton.typepad.com) used Lulu as a print-on-demand distribution system for his book *Sunken Treasure* (http://stores.lulu.com/wilwheaton), Lulu took on an e-business role for the author and functioned as a B2C transaction hub for buyers of the book. Further, as Lulu operates as a virtual business, where the content is digitally uploaded to the server for printing and physical shipping, the company also handles the logistical issues of integration with Amazon.com, ISBN acquisition and cataloguing, and related publishing tasks of printing, shipping, warehousing and order fulfilment.

### e-marketing

Given the nature of this book, most of the discussion of e-marketing happens within the next fourteen chapters. However, from the perspective of understanding how e-marketing fits into the Internet framework, it's worth noting three things. First, the market research and metrics aspect of e-marketing is a natural by-product of Internet web server capacity to handle mass documentation of interaction with end users. Originally developed to assist the debugging of broken systems, server logs have become valuable marketing metrics as they explain, classify and categorize different users visiting the sites, where they're from, how long they stayed and which was the last page they viewed on the site before leaving (Chapter 10). Secondly, e-marketing exists in the open as part of the Internet landscape of downloadable products, embedded advertising, advertorial content and a range of overt commercial activities, including everything from the shopping cart at Amazon (www.amazon.co.uk/) to the very nature of Paypal (www.paypal.co.uk) as a means to send money for goods won on eBay (www.ebay.co.uk/) auctions. Finally, e-marketing is less visible and the ethereal touch when it comes to using the knowledge of the marketplace to develop better user experiences, improve product performance and quietly reduce the time, energy or effort requirements of engaging with an online experience.

## The virtual product

The third aspect of the virtual economy is a brief detour into the development of product theory (Chapter 6). Figure 1.4 introduces a visual representation of the four different categories of the virtual product (this gets a more detailed exploration later in Chapter 6).

The unusual nature of e-marketing is that it can be dealing with movement of physical goods (atoms) facilitated by e-commerce and e-marketing activity. For example, the printed book purchased from Lulu is an atom-based product that requires physical-world logistics to move it from the point of production to the point of consumption. At the same time, you can also buy a virtual good – a PDF version of the book – which requires virtual logistics to move from the point of production (the server) to the point of consumer (you) whilst being semi-tangible in that it takes up storage space on your

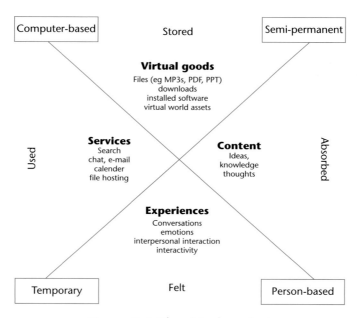

**Figure 1.4** The virtual product

computer (or iPhone, iPod, Kindle, etc). In contrast, content delivery such as YouTube videos (which occupy an amazingly large amount of server space somewhere in Google's Volcano Fortress) never reside on your own devices (or at least, not without third-party assistance). Similar issues arise when you read a blog, the online news or Wikipedia (en.wikipedia.org) – the ideas are stored in your head rather than on the computer. Much in the same way, the experience of virtual life in a three-dimensional game is temporary, internalized to you (the rush of victory, the annoyance of defeat, the conflicting desire for a pizza versus staying in the raid) and non-retrievable after the event. Finally, to really mess things up, if content, virtual goods and experiences weren't enough, there's also a whole slew of virtual services such as online calendars, cloud computing, file hosting, chat and even online banking which do little more than move data flags in some remote computer based on whatever you're doing at your computer. It's also worth noting that none of the four components is 'real' in the sense of being tangible goods. An iPod is the tangible product that contains the virtual goods (audio book) which were purchased through a virtual service (iTunes) which are then consumed to create experiences (happiness) and content acquisition (learning).

# A brief history of the Internet

According to a consensus of opinion across a range of Internet history websites, it appears that the launch of Sputnik in 1957 was largely responsible (or to blame) for the development of the Internet. The launch of Sputnik created the America–Soviet Union arms and technology race, which in turn was responsible for the creation of DARPA (Defense Advanced Research Project Agency). Following a series of developments in computers, information technology, communications systems and university science labs, Internet 1.0 emerged as a recognizable form in 1969 as the ARPANET. From there, it linked universities, government and military agencies and was restricted to these agencies. Between 1969 and 1990, the development of Internet technology contained many milestones of significance to the IT/ Internet community that are best read through the Internet Society's history pages (www.isoc.org/Internet/history).

## Dawn of e-marketing

The first significant milestone for e-marketing occurred in 1990, as the Internet changed from a private network between academia, government, the military and select industry groups to become part of mainstream society. The World Wide Web made its debut in 1990, courtesy of Tim Berners-Lee and his web server software. What happened next is a complicated explosion of web-related software and popularity with Mosaic (www.ncsa.uiuc.edu/SDG/Software/WinMosaic), then Netscape (browser.netscape.com), Internet Explorer (www.microsoft.com) and Lynx (lynx.browser.org), providing easier access to the Internet.

The first major wave of commercial Internet access arrived in 1995, when a significant spike of Internet and web-related users appeared from outside of the university and government sectors. From there, the rapid expansion of the Internet has seen an unheralded march of technology, people and ideas using the Internet for commercial and non-commercial purposes.

## The World Wide Web (Version 1.0)

Strangely enough, there never was an official Web 1.0 statement when the concept rolled out back in the 1990s. The World Wide Web is the graphical, user-friendly end of the Internet, which came to prominence in the mid-1990s following the success of a series of web browser software programs. It has remained the most accessible element of the Internet for self-publication because websites can be created, published and accessed without reference to a centralized broadcast authority. The Web is based primarily on hypertext mark-up language (HTML) protocol and a series of programming languages such as Java, Perl and common gateway interface (CGI). For a comprehensive list of the web technologies, see the World Wide Web Consortium website (www.w3.org). Away from the alphabet soup of programming, file types and *.htm, *.asp, *.php and *.shtml file extensions, the most significant aspect of the Web is the hyperlink. The hypertext system allows the user to navigate to, from and through websites providing an almost seamless journey through the graphical front end of the Internet (one small step for code, one giant link for webkind).

For marketing, the Web is the place to be conducting business, hawking the company wares and developing an effective customer interface. Even in the early days of the commercialization of the Internet, the Web was seen as the 'official' venue for electronic commerce, and it is conceded by even the non-business Internet purists as a place to allow commercial endeavours. The ease of access for publishing websites, the speed of updating and near ubiquity of the 'Web as Internet' mindset in the general public makes the Web a viable venue for conducting business.

### Boom

In the late 1990s/early 2000, the siren call of the Internet also led to a significant and short-lived economic boom based around investments in the Internet and the promise of future rewards that were just around the corner for the company with the largest market share. The first dot.com collapse was almost inevitable as the attitude of the day was summarized as 'the old rules don't apply' when, really, those rules about profit, funding and economic return were fully armed and operational.

### Kaboom

As with most economic booms, the economic bust that followed led to recriminations, allegations and a range of venture capitalists dusting themselves off and looking for somewhere else to invest to recoup their losses. The difference for Internet marketing and Internet marketers is that commercial realities had finally arrived to a sector that was prepared to invest money on the basis of a good idea, rather than on the basis of business plans, market research and financial forecasting. While some might bemoan the end of the dot.com revolution, the final result brought a level of realism and stability

home-based workers to trade their wares. Finally, the global financial crisis may be an extended period of self-correction by the open market which proceeds to reboot and resemble the previous economic environment with slightly faster lead times and a few additional lines of code to prevent some of the excesses that caused the last crash. With all of these scenarios as possible outcomes, the emphasis in the book is on higher time cost ahead of higher financial cost investments (where there's a choice, we'll aim for the lower of the two costs – there's no economic sense in spending less money if the resultant savings are consumed by the time cost of your hourly rate).

## The parameters of the book

The Internet, like any other process, is prone to cycles of boom and bust. The Internet (along with the world economy) is loitering around the edge of the downward-trending business cycle and whether Boom 2.0 happens depends a lot on accountants and economists. (Try not to feel doomed.) Consequently, there are a few safety measures that we need to take as authors. First, when you're writing a paper-based version of an electronic medium, there are certain challenges associated with picking the future. For one thing, it's a lot harder to update than a wiki page once the book has hit the shelves. Secondly, as an author, you have to bet on success of a technology, service or corporation with the secure knowledge that the only permanency involved is your record of endorsing a company that may no longer exist. Finally, there's also the future-proofing approach of producing a textbook that could survive even the catastrophic loss of Google (although, if Google sinks, we might be hard pressed to find anything on the Internet to write about next time). To deal with these problems, the authors have taken a few liberties and made a few assumptions about how the book will function and the role the reader will play in helping deal with written history versus contemporary reality.

### Liberty City: Population – You

One chapter in and you've been drafted to participate in the process already. Here are the assumptions we're making about you so you know the sort of role you have to live up to when reading the book and the liberties we're taking in assuming you're reading this with a desire for the conversational style of writing, a bit of knowledge about your computer and a love of novelty seeking adventure.

### Liberty 1: You, yours and ours

This book is for you. Instead of talking of the mythical marketing manager on the Clapham omnibus, the text addresses you directly with instructions, comments and observations. There are two reasons for this approach. First, the Internet is a really good place for live, hands-on, get-things-done education, and giving instructions gives you the option to get involved. Secondly, the new model of the Internet and e-marketing evolving into the 2010 decade is more of a model of conversation than ever before. Saying 'we did' and 'you should try' is the language of the Web 2.0 conversational market.

There's also this significant piece of marketing theory called 'customer co-creation of value', which is where we (the marketer/producers) provide the platform that you (the consumer) can use to make something that's specifically valuable to meet your personal needs and wants. (Customer co-creation gets a detailed explanation later in Chapters 5 and 7). We liked the theory so much, we've implemented it in practice in this book.

## *Liberty 2: You know something about your computer*

We're going to place some faith in your technical prowess with your own computer (be that a favourite seat in the lab, a laptop or a home machine). e-marketing is a computer-mediated business practice, and the unavoidable elements of the process are the words 'computer' and 'practice'. Knowing how to do medium-level complex tasks with your computer will also assist your sense of self-confidence, self-efficacy and comfort zone when trialling new ideas on the Internet.

If you've never wondered how the pieces of the Internet fit together, you're probably not alone. The nature of being around the Internet since 1994 and working in the e-marketing field has meant looking under the hood of Internet technology, and one of us usually finds it fascinating even if it is thoroughly beyond our grasp to actually program or control. We acknowledge that most e-marketers need to know very little about the deeply technical issues of Internet protocol addresses, domain name servers and the ever-present shuffling of information through the TCP/IP protocol. This entire aspect of the Internet exists at the meta level and is of less importance to marketing (so long as it's functioning – as soon as it stops working, it becomes very important, but we don't know enough about it to do anything useful to fix it). That said, it's worth pushing the boundaries of your own knowledge of the software, systems and code as a development exercise for your own competitive advantage over the less curious e-marketers. Although you may never need to code your own cascading style sheet, fix a buffer overflow error or compile your own kernel, knowing what these things are (and more) gives you a certain level of credibility amongst those who you will need to rely on for the technical solutions. If nothing else, it's nice to be able to smile along with 'There's no place like 127.0.0.1' because it means something to you.

## *Liberty 3: You're up for a bit of innovation*

The biggest assumption and liberty we're taking with this book is that you're ready, willing and able to handle the level of innovation that will come your way in the course of reading this book. Consumer behaviour theory often discusses innovation-adoption theory in a very abstract manner, and talks of ideas such as 'innovation-resistant consumers', early adopters and late-majority adoptions in terms of them being something that happens to other people. This book is going to push a range of new ideas, new practices, new software and new websites at you in a relatively steady stream of new things to learn, new behaviours to try and yet another login e-mail and password to remember. We're not fans of innovation for the sake of innovation. The book was written in part using Word 2002, on machines running Windows XP. We're innovation resistant to a certain extent, and we respect that in our readership – you're not being asked to do new things just because they're new. You're usually being asked to try new things because e-marketing is an incredibly young field of endeavour which is still in the rapid growth phase (remember the product lifecycle curve from your introduction to marketing textbook?). The infrastructure supports a rapid process of development, and e-market maturity is measured in weeks or months, when the average person is just hoping it all slows down and settles for a bit so they can catch up. However, until that happens, you'll need to be mindful of how your own innovativeness (when it comes to the Internet) will impact on your willingness and desire to keep up with the new ideas and exercises in the book. (Chapter 5 has a section on Domain Specific Innovativeness, which will help.)

## Authorial assumptions

Having told you what liberties we're taking with your role in the book, it's only fair that we also explain where we stand on a few key issues that impact on how the book is written.

### Assumption 1: You're going to read something marked 'READ ME FIRST'

If you're reading this, we assumed correctly. If you're not reading this, we don't have much to say to you now, do we?

### Assumption 2: Safety-first e-marketing

We're working on an assumption that this text has to back more established technologies, sites and systems over the exceptionally cool but potentially short-lived alternatives. This means a certain level of conservative, safety-first marketing which may not necessarily suit your personal style. More stable options can provide the basic grounding that allows you to try out the higher-risk option later in proceedings. To achieve this, the authors have split their respective roles to have one covering the high-risk options, and signing up to every new thing that they find, whilst the other author holds back to observe which of the several hundred new options is stable enough to join the ranks of recommended e-marketing equipment.

We're also working on the assumption that if Twitter (www.twitter.com), Facebook (www.facebook.com), Google (www.google.co.uk), Yahoo! (www.yahoo.co.uk) and Delicious (http://delicious.com) all collapse in the global financial crisis, and, if there's still an Internet left after these behemoths depart, someone else will step up to the plate and take over from them. Google replaced Infoseek, which dethroned Lycos, which succeeded (briefly) where Hotbot failed. Someone in a garage in Basingstoke or Jaipur or New Orleans is working on a project that could fill the void if Google (or Facebook et al.) went away. From an e-marketing perspective, the behaviours are the key – people want to search, communicate and play games whilst looking busy or talking with friends. Where there's a market, there's going to be an entrepreneur with enough venture capital to look after our needs for free for a while.

## Assumption 3: Things will go wrong

The book contains a series of strategies that can maximize opportunities, boost chances and still backfire and fail outright. The beauty of the Internet is that the 'ready, fire, aim' mentality allows for a certain level of improvisation and rapid backpedalling when the 'perfect on paper' plan meets an unfortunate outcome in the reality of the Internet. Be willing and able to react swiftly to replace a broken service, fix a dead link or completely rethink the strategy when a central cog in the service-delivery platform goes away. We're used to it. You should see what happened when one of the technologies we picked as the next big thing failed (then again, maybe you shouldn't and we should maintain the mysterious air of predictive accuracy). Stuff breaks, things change and marketing rolls on regardless.

## Assumption 4: Mistakes will be made

The Internet is both extremely forgiving and thoroughly ruthless. Whilst the technical nature of the medium would lend itself to the ethereal nature of data going away, history and practice have demonstrated that data on the Internet has a half-life to rival nuclear waste (and it's every bit as toxic when it spills into the environment). As a gigantic interconnected network of people, the Internet suffers from human error in a way that hasn't been fully addressed by society yet. Whilst the strategies of learning by trying, failing, analysing and having another crack at it are highly endorsed, those early mistakes will hang around, be archived, show in Google cache or reappear unexpected off an old backup tape somewhere at some time.

Similarly, as an interconnected series of people, the Internet's capacity for human error being spread far and wide is unprecedented. Human error, on the other hand, has massive precedent, and the standard operating procedures of offline life should be considered for online conditions. Namely, you will make mistakes and your mistakes will be known and visible. It's how you handle the post-mistake recovery, apology and learning opportunity that determines how badly the mistake will impact on you as an e-marketer (and online person).

- You will make a mistake. Everyone will get it wrong, and depending on how you cope with error and recovery, you may get it wrong multiple times over the one issue. Own your error. It's yours, you made it and you own it. Denying the error, blaming others or trying to escape the error just highlights the original mistake (and makes life harder for you to recover).
- That mistake isn't going to go away. The digital world is surprisingly permanent, searchable and prone to echoing off into the distance. Similarly, the number of people willing to copy, save and preserve your mistake will rise in direct response to your efforts to make those people (and the record of the mistake) go away. Address the root cause of the mistake, address the mistake and fix the problem in a timely manner. This is where ownership of the problem comes into play – if you step up and say 'My mistake, I own it', you get to keep some control. If you say 'That mistake isn't mine' and deny ownership, then people will hand it around until they find the owner (or someone willing to take ownership and step up with a solution).

# CHAPTER 2

# Foundations of e-marketing

## Learning objectives

By the end of this chapter, you should be able to:

- outline the business considerations for engaging in e-marketing
- identify the inhibitors and facilitators of e-marketing
- understand the different definitions of marketing
- recognize the unique features of the e-marketing environment.

## Introduction

Marketing is an adaptive 'smart' technology. As a consumer-orientated approach to business, it must learn and evolve in response to changes in the environment, and must constantly adjust its practice, preferences and techniques to maintain its value to the organization. The rise of consumers' willingness and ability to communicate with organizations, suppliers and each other to build a network of shared experience outside of traditional market boundaries has driven many of the recent developments in marketing theory and practice (Kiani, 1998). Interactive communication technologies have increased the capacity of marketing to reach and communicate with consumers, and for consumers to communicate with marketers and the marketplace. To meet this new challenge both marketing theory and practice have undergone significant developments since the advent of widespread access to the commercialized Internet in the mid-1990s.

The Internet and the associated e-technologies of distributed information systems, 'smart' products and networked technologies have created a massive market for ideas, information and communication. e-marketing represents one of the business ideas to arise from the convergence of technology, marketing and the consumer marketplace. However, e-marketing is not a standalone application, and as such, is dependent on core marketing principles and frameworks to provide the means, mechanisms and market understanding to address the consumer.

## Marketing

There is no single universal definition of marketing. Marketing is a living discipline that adapts and evolves on the strengths, weaknesses and operational foibles of the marketplace. At the same time, marketing is both a business practice and an academic science, which means that any definition of the discipline is required to be descriptive, comprehensive and encompass what marketing looks like in reality and what it should aspire to become in the future. Some definitions of marketing focus on what marketing can (or should) do for the organization as a means to set the limits and expectations for the organization and marketer. Other definitions focus on what marketing is as a discipline, and what philosophical world view it occupies when compared with accounting, economics and other social sciences. Either way, all attempts to define marketing are crucial to the functionality of the discipline and its application in e-marketing. Whilst it may seem pedantic to focus on the definition of marketing, it is vital that an agreement as to the role and purpose of marketing is settled upon before trying to implement it in practice. This also connects marketing back to itself by using the principles of marketing practice, such as product definition (Chapter 6) and positioning strategies (Chapter 7) to establish the core brand for 'marketing'

Marketing has always had international applications and a global focus with the export and adaptation of products and business practices to fit with local, cultural constraints. Different business practices and market expectations have shaped regional understanding of marketing and have led to the rise of region-specific marketing groups and meanings of marketing. As part of the regionalization of marketing, the American Marketing Association (AMA) and the Chartered Institute of Marketing (CIM) have each issued an official definition of marketing to guide their members. The CIM represents marketing practitioners and academics in the United Kingdom and, to some extent, also represents some of the European marketing community. The AMA is the chief body for marketers in the United States and geographically related regions.

Given the interconnections in the world of marketing and the importance of cross-cultural understanding, both the US and UK definitions of marketing are being used to guide the structure of this book and direct the operational issues of implementation, practice and design. The AMA (2007) definition is focused on orientating marketing to customer needs, whilst the CIM (2005) definition addresses meeting the long-term survival requirements of the organization. Individually, each definition is a functional application of marketing. Combined, the definitions represent complementary forms of the marketing world view of meeting the needs of the market and serving the organizational goals of profit, stakeholder value and organizational longevity.

## Customer focus: the AMA definition of marketing

The AMA (2007) defined marketing as:

> The activity, set of institutions and processes for creating, communicating, delivering, and exchanging offerings that have value for customers, clients, partners, and society at large.
>
> (Keefe, 2008)

The definition reflects the growing trend of consumers to prioritize intangible experiences over the ownership of physical objects, particularly with regard to new technologies such as the iPhone and iPod (Lovelock, Patterson and Walker, 2007). Consumers are more interested in what the product can do for them rather than focusing on a list of features and component parts – the ability of an iPod to fend off idle conversation on the London Underground is more valuable in practice than 4GB or 8GB of storage. As concepts go, the idea of feature versus benefit harks back to the 1920s and a great quote from Charles Revson saying, 'Perfume is made in the factory, "hope" is sold in the store' (MacInnis and de Mello, 2005). 'Hope' is probably now available for download from iTunes (at US$0.99), as online marketing has seen a shift from the promotion of features (gigabytes of space, RAM, numbers, stuff) to the promotion of benefits (connect with friends, embarrass family members, look busy at work). The rise of services marketing has helped push the emphasis from physical goods (stuff is bought by you) to experiential marketing (stuff happens to you).

The rise of the experiential marketplace has also been influenced by the growth of Internet access and widespread acceptance of the non-physical services provided across the Internet. Interpersonal exchange brought about by Web 2.0 and the social media marketplace has also created an awareness of the value of the consumer to consumer connection for marketers, society and the consumer. The key value of Facebook,

MySpace and Twitter is the interconnection with other people; it is not the social software that's used to make the connection happen. The same outcomes apply for online communities that can spring up from the worst implemented protocols if a group of interesting enough people hang out there together for long enough (Chapter 9). As society increasingly accepts the role of non-physical products in everyday life, ranging from cash-free shopping to digital music collections, the emphasis of marketing becomes more focused on the value a product or service will provide rather than the product or service itself.

The AMA (2007) definition addresses the intangible approach to marketing by viewing the role and purpose of marketing as having three core elements:

○ activities, processes and institutions
○ creation, communication, delivery and exchange of offerings of value
○ exchange between marketers, marketplace and society.

### Marketing as a set of activities, processes and institutions

Any organization, website or individual can engage in marketing practice by implementing the philosophy, tools, techniques and methods of marketing practice (Dann and Dann, 2004). Seeing marketing as an applied process frees it from the requirement to have a formal marketing department attached in order to be 'real marketing' (although it doesn't hurt to have a formal recognition). We're focusing on marketing as an activity and process in this book, with activities such as market research and planning (Chapter 4), using the marketing mix for value creation (Chapter 7), engaging in relationship marketing (Chapter 8) and measuring the impact of the activities (Chapter 10).

### Marketing creates, communicates, delivers and exchanges offerings that have value

Value creation is a literal technique of making something useful for someone else so that everyone involved in the process gains from the experience. It's a semi-formal process of developing an offer and releasing the offer to the market, so the consumer can use it to solve a problem, fill a need or satisfy an urge (Chapter 6). The phrase 'offerings that have value' is the all-inclusive term for anything (goods, services, ideas or experiences) that an organization is delivering to the marketplace that can be used by the customer for the customer's benefit (Dann and Dann, 2007). Communication of value is the process by which the organization can alert the potential (or actual) customer as to the existence of the offer and how that offer can benefit them (Chapter 5). Delivery of value is about making the value offering available where the customer can access it, and ensuring that the components of the offer (e.g. product features and price) can be used by the customer (Chapter 6). Exchange of value can be simple and direct trades of benefit (usually money for something, cheques for free) or exceedingly complex benefit exchanges such as time, support or loyalty (Chapter 7).

*Marketing involves exchange between marketer, marketplace and society*

The recipients of marketing activities, processes and institutions are divided into four clusters:

- customers
- clients
- partners
- society.

Customers are the targets of the commercial marketing exchange of value and usually pay cash (or nearest equivalent) as their value exchange with the organization. Customers buy things, pay bills, purchase subscriptions and are usually on the paying end of the words 'monetize'. Clients are the recipients of the marketing offer from non-profit, social marketing, political and other non-commercial marketing applications in that they do not engage in a traditional financial trade. That said, the Internet is putting non-financial client exchanges firmly in the commercial marketing camp as e-marketers trade content for viewership to sell adverts, advertorials and other funding arrangements. Customers and clients shouldn't be considered mutually exclusive categories. If there's direct cash, it's a customer and if it's indirect (and leads to cash or non-cash benefit), think in terms of client. For the purpose of this book (and to make life easier), the term consumer is used where customers and clients are interchangeable. Partners are those involved in the organization's marketing activities as employees, suppliers, distributors or indirect contributors through any other aspect of the marketing process. This has also been interpreted to incorporate the component elements of the marketing organization to ensure that they have a role in the exchange of value (Dann and Dann, 2007). Society represents the broader community in which the consumer and the organization exist. This element represents the requirement for marketing to engage in ethical practice and to consider issues of corporate social responsibility such as sustainability, environmental impacts and the possible social impact of marketing activities.

Since marketing is a cyclical process which involves interactions of consumers, marketers and society, offerings are constantly updated and refined to meet the changing needs of the marketplace. Whilst there's a physical world time lag between product development and the next generation of iPod hitting the shelves, e-marketing has a faster idea-to-market cycle (that said, let's not mention the lag between ideas and delivery for video game development). e-marketing is well suited to the shared value creation that comes from marketer, marketplace and society working together for a mutual gain. Posting to a blog creates value for the author, reader, and if done well, broader society, if the blog provokes new ideas, thoughts or developments. Similarly, posting your photos of the weekend trip to Brighton on Flickr (www.flickr.com) under a creative commons licence aids parents on the other side of the planet who are helping their children with a primary school project. Flickr benefits by being useful; you gain by using Flickr to store your photos, and the world gains in general gains from the benefits flowing around the planet. No money swaps hands, but exchange is present, value is created and the planet gets that little bit smaller, neater and better off for a day.

## The CIM definition of marketing

The second definition of marketing we're using in this book places a greater emphasis on the organization's role in the marketing process, and is reflective of the need to include the long-term goals and objectives of survival as part of the marketing process. The CIM (2005) defines marketing as:

> the management process identifying, anticipating and satisfying customer requirements profitably.

The CIM (2005) definition emphasizes the managerial and commercial aspects of the marketing process and presents a tighter focus than the AMA's (2007) 'activities, institutions and processes'. Abimbola and Kocak (2007) regard the CIM definition as the connection between innovation, inventiveness and the capacity of the firm to create an offer of value for the organization whilst maintaining the focus on organizational outcomes. Similarly, Helgesen (2006) notes that the strength of the CIM definition is the explicit recognition of the duality of focus inherent in marketing through the need to satisfy the customer and achieve organizational survival through profit. As with the AMA definition, the CIM definition of marketing breaks into three sub-elements as management process, customer-centric checklist and profit prompt.

### Marketing is a management process

This element recognizes the role of marketing as a management tool within the organization and the use of the marketing planning process to guide organizational goals, objectives and outcomes (Adeyoyin, 2005). For an e-marketer, the definition brings home the need to keep the company objectives in the frame and to work with the management structures to make marketing happen through the strategic (Chapter 3) and operational levels (Chapter 4). It's a touch different in focus from the AMA's 'we're all in marketing together' approach of exchange happening between marketer, marketplace and society. The CIM is slightly more reserved (*quelle surprise*) in its view of the role of marketing in the organization than its US counterpart.

### Marketing identifies, anticipates and satisfies customer requirements

From an e-marketer perspective, the CIM definition of marketing brings a fantastic three-piece suite of 'identify, anticipate, satisfy' as a guiding hand for shaping e-commerce activity. It's a fast, light and thoroughly viable way to evaluate any Internet, e-commerce or mobile technology for marketing purposes. For example, if you're still wondering why Twitter (www.twitter.com) is in the e-marketing toolkit, think in terms of 'Can it be used to *identify* customer requirements?', 'Can it be used to *anticipate* customer requirements?' and 'Can it be used to *satisfy* customer requirements?' If you can answer yes to any one of those three questions, then the technology can be used for e-marketing purposes. (If not, then don't worry about adding it to the toolkit. Not everything is about marketing.)

The CIM framework also does a great job of bringing a holistic view of marketing in three words – identify, anticipate, satisfy. The identification of customer requirements is related to market research (Chapter 3), new product development (Chapter 4) and consumer behaviour analyses (Chapter 3). Anticipation of customer requirements is connected to the distribution of value insofar as it represents the operational aspects of having the value offer in a location that can be accessed by the customer (Chapter 7) and managing the various logistics that ensure peaks in demand can be met successfully and profitably (Abimbola and Kocak, 2007). It also includes the predictive elements of planning in emergent markets and understanding consumer needs (Chapter 3) throughout the product or market lifecycle. Finally, satisfying customer requirements is the value creation aspect of the AMA (2007) definition (Chapters 4–6) in conjunction with the implementation of marketing strategy (Chapter 10).

### Marketing is profit-driven

The profit orientation of the CIM (2005) definition may seem at odds with client target market and the non-profit, non-commercial capacity of the AMA (2007) definition. For the purpose of this book, the profitability element of the CIM definition is seen as recognition of the need for return on marketing investment (Abimbola and Kocak, 2007). This can be measured either financially as reflected through traditional measure of cash, profit, revenue and shareholder value, or non-financially in terms of the 'social profit' generated by the organization's activities.

Non-financial 'profits' can be considered a form of return on investment where organizational goals of social change, community participation or other non-financial costs are at least covered by the success of the campaign. For example, where a web-based community relies on active forum participation by members which is facilitated by staff participation, the participation level of the community would be the return on the investment of the staff member's time and salary. 'Profit' arises where the benefit gained from the interaction is greater than the effort spent on the process – an active community bulletin board with a healthy range of discussions is a profitable investment of the time of the moderators. The impact on the bottom line of the organization is indirectly measured through the success of the brand, the longevity of customer relationships and the conversion to customer lifetime value created through the community into sales over time. Although non-financial profit doesn't pay the bills directly, it is an investment by the firm and needs to be considered in terms of the influence it has on the direct revenue streams rather than just being seen as a cost.

## Core concepts refresher

e-marketing is an applied form of marketing and works on the assumption that you're conversant with a few basic marketing ideas and activities. This section briefly covers a few basics of marketing to ensure that author and reader are on the same wavelength for the rest of the book.

## Business orientations

There are four classic business orientations that are used to describe ways of thinking about business: the production; product; selling and marketing orientations. Each of these represents a particular world view of the respective role of the consumer and the organization in the development of product offerings for the masses.

*Production orientation* is based on the belief that there is demand for your product and that the way to success is to be the cheapest, most efficient producer of the product. Production orientation emphasizes the 'faster, cheaper, more' approach; that bulk saturating a market will win against making less of something that's more expensive and more targeted. Best summed up by Henry Ford's assertion that customers can have the model T Ford in any colour they like as long as it's black, this approach often is very successful at the early stages of the product lifecycle when demand for a product outstrips supply and people are willing to put up with the inconvenience of a less than perfect match just as long as they have something in that particular product line.

*Product orientation* is summed up in the catchphrase 'If you build it, they will come', from the ancient film *Field of Dreams* (back when Kevin Costner was relevant. You may have to ask your parents.) Those who subscribe to product orientation obsessively focus on upgrading the product offering for the marketplace on the assumption that more features, more options and more will lead to the product being more relevant for more people. This isn't a bad method, and more than enough of the Internet exists simply because someone had an idea, built it and it turned out for the best for everyone. That said, once you've started with the product approach, it's really easy to move over to a marketing orientation if you want to customize and tweak the product to better suit the audience who just found you. Neither the product nor the production approach asks the customer-focused questions of 'What features does this product need?', 'What do consumers want?' and 'What don't we need to cram into the product?' Both orientations are evident in Zawinski's (1995) *Law of Software Envelopment*, which notes that 'Every program attempts to expand until it can read mail. Those programs which cannot so expand are replaced by ones which can.'

The *selling orientation* is based on faith in the power of price discounting and heavy promotion to shift excess product onto the market. This approach tends to talk at customers rather than to them and combines the faith in the product with a need to communicate frequently, loudly and with every integrated marketing communications (IMC) tool in the kit. As with the previous orientations, the selling approach doesn't check in to see if what is being sold is what the customer was hoping to buy. Sadly, the low cost of information distribution, combined with the relative ease of message broadcast, made the Internet the ultimate selling orientation device – with a large enough market (the Internet) and a saturation-style message offence which cost virtually nothing to implement, it was possible to turn a profit from the bulk mail and the spam message campaigns. This is also why Google has an active spam filter on Gmail (http://mail.google.com) and why we rarely see these messages in the really good mail clients of the modern era (and why e-mail is a dead-end for IMC – Chapters 1 and 7).

The *marketing orientation* is our show. This is the implementation of the marketing concept, which balances the needs of the organization (profit, long-term survival, goal achievement) by reviewing the needs of the market and developing offers that satisfy the marketplace and meet the organization's goals. The key for the marketing orientation is that customer and company have to come out ahead – if the customer dominates and the firm fails, that's no better than the firm dominating and failing the customer. The marketing orientation uses the CIM framework (anticipate, identify, satisfy) and the AMA framework (create, communicate, deliver, exchange) to meet the needs of the market, create the value and walk away with a profit (or at least a break even that lets you come back and do this again next time). The marketing orientation can be the starting point for an organization (e.g. market research-driven product development) or it can be an upgrade from the selling, product or production orientation once the initial success of those strategies has worn off.

## The marketing mix

The marketing mix is the short-hand method of creating a value offer by being able to address four important factors – price, product, place (or distribution) and promotion – to make a good offer to the market.

*Price* is the total sum of what the customer is prepared to give up to get the product. Price starts with the money – what cash value is placed on the product? Beyond that, and significantly for the Internet, are the non-financial factors such as time, effort, pride and social costs. Time costs are a serious consideration as you consider adding yet another social media site that you would need to update plus the social cost of being the only person you know on that network (and not on the network with everyone else you know). There's also the time needed to be invested in making sense of it all, customizations and tweaking. Eventually you start pining for the day when it was just a question of when 'How much is it?' was answered with 'Ten pounds!'

*Product* is the offer you make to the market, and what you and the market come up with together that leaves both of you satisfied with the transaction. In less esoteric terms, offline, products are usually goods, services and ideas. Online, products get to be a little more complex (and fun) in that you can sell goods (to be shipped to the physical world), virtual goods (to be stored on the hard drive), really virtual goods (stuff in a video game server somewhere), ideas (contents of a blog post), experiences (YouTube video clips, video game experience, music), behaviours (super-poking in Facebook, conversations in MSN Messenger), services (online banking) and access to other people (community memberships). The key is not to think of product equating to physical goods, particularly in e-marketing where physical stuff (sandwich) makes up a much smaller portion of the business than the virtual stuff (invisible sandwich).

*Place* (or distribution) covers the mechanisms for moving the product from the point of production to the point of consumption. In e-marketing terms this means 'the Internet', which is the single largest distribution channel in history but so often completely misunderstood as a logistics channel. Delivery of value is highlighted in Chapter 6. The multifaceted role of the Internet as product, distribution and promotional channel makes more sense when you view value as the outcome of the combination of the marketing mix, rather than arising from a single element.

*Promotion* covers all forms of audio and visual communication between the marketer and the marketplace, and handles message distribution to the market, plus engagement in the new Web 2.0 conversation with the consumer. Promotion is covered in Chapter 7, which also examines how the integration of marketing communications is also dependent now on how a company performs at all levels (from the legalese in contracts to the CEO's personal life) given the hyperconnected world and the ease of comparison between the promises in the marketing messages and the actual behaviours of the organization.

There are two important considerations for using the marketing mix as a mental checklist for value creation. First, if you can't answer each of the questions 'What is it?' (product), 'What does it cost?' (price), 'Where do I get it?' (place/distribution) and 'How do I explain this to my friends?' (promotion), you haven't thought the offer through clearly enough. Secondly, whilst there is a range of really good criticisms of the marketing mix, the purpose of the exercise is as a starting point to figure out the bits that you, the marketer, have a say over and control before you put the product into the marketplace and let the consumers take over. Value comes from the interaction between the marketer, marketplace and society. The marketing mix is the identify/anticipate side of the CIM definition of marketing, and the 'create, communicate, deliver' side of the AMA definition. Without using the mix, the marketer abdicates too much responsibility for his or her own performance, outcomes and success to the consumers who were only supposed to be assisting in the first place.

## Innovation adoption

Innovation adoption theory is a fundamental framework for understanding how consumers deal with the constant flow of new stuff from the Internet. The short version of the theory is that every person has a varying level of ability to cope with new ideas, information, products and activities. The level to which you can cope with new ideas will influence how quickly you can pick up on new trends, technologies or fashions. The complication for e-marketing is that innovativeness is an inherent personal character trait which varies between people, and it's also related to specific areas of activity. You'll find people who are intensely innovative users of the latest websites but who prefer older mobile phones, and people who crave the most up-to-the-moment new mobile phone but who still listen to the same bands they heard back in the first year of high school. Innovative behaviour is specific to certain areas, and we cover this in more depth in Chapter 5. For now, the key insights to understand are:

○ not everybody is innovative
○ relative advantage, which is the extent to which the new thing is better than the old ways; is the key to success
○ people can and will say 'no' to new things.

### *Not everybody is innovative*

Not everyone will want the newest product. Only 2.5 per cent of a group of people will be innovators who are interested in new things for the sake of their newness. (The

**Figure 2.1** Cutting edge
*Source*: http://xkcd.com/606/

Internet, being a very large place, has a lot of innovators who are into new things.) After the innovators come the early adopters, who make up 13.5 per cent of the group. Once you have the most innovative people around all on board with your product, you still only have a market share of 16 per cent. The next category, the early majority, who hold back and wait a bit to see if this new thing rates highly amongst their innovative friends, consists of about 34 per cent of any given group. Whilst innovators and the early adopter are fun targets for marketing, they're not always the bill-paying crowd, and the early majority outweigh them 2 to 1. The late majority (33 per cent) will only adopt your product once a critical mass of a majority of all potential users have, so as not to be left out. Meanwhile, 16 per cent of the population, the laggards, will never adopt a specific product or technology. Keep this in mind when deciding whether or not to develop a brand new product or a me-too product in a developing market – very few people are innovative (Figure 2.1).

### Relative advantage for the win

There are five consistent features that impact on whether people will like or dislike an innovation: relative advantage; compatibility; complexity; ease of trial and visibility (Chapter 5). The relative advantage factor is critical – the new thing must be better than the current options otherwise there's no point in giving up the older version. This could affectionately be called the Microsoft Curse, given the number of times the company's most recent operating system release fails to demonstrate a relative advantage over the currently installed, existing and mostly just-working products the customers already have available to them.

That said, the other four factors can defeat relative advantage if the new option is simply incompatible. High-definition DVDs, CDs, Blu-ray discs and every other new format that doesn't play on the older technology is asking for a compatibility problem. The first platform that plays the brand new format and cheerfully accepts older formats tends to win out in this situation. People who own large DVD libraries, having already replaced their large collection of VHS video tapes, are far less likely to want to buy yet another format (and restock the library again).

*People can and will say 'no' to new things*

Rejection of new ideas is an acceptable outcome. Not everything new is better than what it sets out to replace. Similarly, there are going to be times when the relative advantage battle is decided in favour of the older method you're more comfortable with using rather than the new approach which promises great future rewards as a trade-off for short-term confusion. The only problem you face in e-marketing from an innovation–adoption perspective is ensuring that you track the innovation acceptance/rejection of your target audience and prioritize it over your own preferences when it comes to delivering value. If your audience doesn't think the Internet is much use, then e-marketing isn't the method to reach them. At the same time, if your audience is shifting en masse to m-commerce, and you're still using the first mobile you ever bought, you might want to consider upgrading (or trading markets with someone else).

One of the reasons for having so many new technologies in the e-introduction (setting up for e-marketing) is to give you the self-confidence to say 'no' to technology. You do not need five web browsers for day-to-day operations but you will need access to all five when you get into product testing just so you can see what, if anything, goes wrong between the intended design and what the browser does to your blog layout. At best, most people have a primary browser, a back-up plan and a complete lack of desire to fire up a third web browser if the website failed to display on the first two attempts (relative advantage test failed). Similarly, some of the e-marketing technologies you'll see in this book won't appeal to you – no relative advantage, no compatibility, too complex (or not complex enough) or you get 'that look' from your friends whenever you mention it, and you don't want them knowing you use it (observable). Rejecting the technologies on offer in this book is fine. You may need to test-drive a few of them for assessment purposes or to answer end-of-chapter questions or class exercises (trialability). After the course is over, it's okay if you decide not to continue using the accounts.

## Using marketing theory for e-marketing practice: Stages of Change model and Twitter

As one of the few recent disruptive innovations, making the decision to use the Internet, or any given technology available through the Internet, requires users to adopt certain changes in behaviour. In the social sciences a number of models have been developed to explain how a person moves from the point of total ignorance about a behaviour to forming a habit. These same models can be used to effectively explain how a consumer moves from knowing nothing about an innovation to learning an entirely new consumption behaviour and making the innovation part of their everyday life.

One of the best known of these behaviour change models is the 'Stages of Change' model proposed by Prochaska and DiClemente (1983). This model is based on the idea that, rather than jumping in at the deep end and checking it out whenever someone comes across a new behaviour or product, most people will observe and think about changing before trying it out (unless you are an innovator).

Twitter (www.twitter.com) has been a great success in rapidly getting large numbers of adopters to commit to their new tweeting behaviour in a very short time. There are a number of ways of explaining this success, but when it comes to the actual behaviour change that is involved, the Stages of Change model provides a quick and simple framework to understanding the phenomenon.

Stage 1: Precontemplation. This occurs before the potential user has even heard of the product or behaviour. If you don't know it exists, you can't use it. For some segments of the population, Twitter still falls into this category.

Stage 2: Contemplation. At this stage you've heard of the product but don't really know what it is or what it does. Those people who have started to see Twitter featured in traditional news reports and magazines are at this stage. They are aware that the phenomenon exists and are now sufficiently interested in it to find out more.

Stage 3: Preparation. At this point you know it exists, it seems like a good idea and you want to try it out but, in the case of Twitter, you need to find out how to set up an account and how to send out a 'tweet'. Currently there is a massive market of would-be tweeters who are getting ready to take the plunge.

Stage 4: Action. Action is similar to trialling or sampling. At this point you try the behaviour for the first time and, in the case of Twitter, send out your first tweet. Depending on the reaction and effort involved, you may never do it again.

Stage 5: Maintenance. This stage is roughly comparable to the post-purchase relationship-building activities of commercial firms. Maintenance is when you reinforce, reward and encourage users to keep using. For consumers to stay with Twitter it has to offer sufficient perceived benefits to become a permanent fixture in people's lives, not just this year's fad.

Stage 6: Termination. At this stage the behaviour has achieved its objectives and generally 'had its day'. This could be because lifestyles have changed and everyone's moved on or because a newer, brighter, shinier behaviour has hit the market and superseded Twitter.

## Features of the e-marketing environment

The unique practices of e-marketing have evolved in light of the environment in which it operates with computer-mediated communication, mobile technology, electronic data interchange and other neat network-based technologies. There are ten characteristics of the e-marketing environment that are central to understanding how it functions in practice (and online). These characteristics are grouped according to their impact on consumer behaviour, accessibility and product characteristics.

## Consumer behaviour impact

The three features of the e-marketing environment that impact on the ways in which consumers behave, both towards the e-marketing organization and to maximize the benefits of e-marketing to themselves, are:

o  interactivity
o  mass customization
o  the interest-driven nature of the Internet.

### Interactivity

Interactivity refers to the degree of two-way communication which occurs between the organization and its clients (Wang, Xu and Gao, 2005). Traditional marketing communications allowed for one of two models: communication was either conducted on a mass level (advertising) with a single, one-way message to many recipients, or as a two-way, interactive, face-to-face sales presentation. The selling orientation grew out of the ease of one-way broadcast communication with the rise of radio and TV networks – standing on the rooftops and shouting loudly was never easier. Computer-mediated communication over the Internet has changed the balance back in favour of the marketing orientation because the conversation between market and marketer is much easier in the age of integrated interactivity of one-to-many-to-one communication (Hoffman and Novak, 1996). (See Chapter 3 for the one-to-many-to-one model in detail. And again in Chapter 7 for its use in practice.)

Hoffman and Novak (1996) identified two main types of Internet-focused interactivity: person interactivity and machine interactivity. Person interactivity is the ability of a person using the Internet to communicate with other people. This forms the central platform for what has been described as the killer application of the Internet – the capacity to reach out and interact with people (Bray, 2007). Manifestations of person interactivity vary from one-on-one e-mail queries to facilitated online communities such as Apple Discussions (discussions.apple.com) and social networking sites such as Facebook (www.facebook.com) and MySpace (uk.myspace.com). Person-to-person communication is also why this book has a consumer behaviour-dominated theme – even if you're in the B2B marketplace, it's you (a person) in communication with another person at the other company. The basics of human nature still count when it comes to decision making by people on behalf of their organizations.

The second type of interactivity identified by Hoffman and Novak (1996) is machine interactivity, or the ability for the individual to be able to access hypermedia content such as searching through Google (www.google.co.uk) or reading pages in Wikipedia (en.wikipedia.org). Manifestations of machine interactivity also include any interaction with automated online functions, such as paying through PayPal (www.paypal.co.uk/uk), searching online archives via the Wayback Machine (www.archive.org) or using the online booking facilities at EasyCar (www.easycar.com). Machine interactivity can occasionally give rise to Brogan's (2009) 'plastic human problem', where visitors to an online community (hint: this may mean you) forget that the avatars on the screen represent real people and interact with those real people as if they were computer-generated characters. Of course, given the number of genuinely false people on the Internet, including the NASA Mars robots on twitter (@MarsRover and @MarsPhoenix) and a variety of twittering cats (@sockington), it's understandable that people may feel detached from the sense that it's a real person on the other side of the monitor.

While interactivity is not a purely Internet-based phenomenon, a special feature of online interactivity is the ability of the individual to personalize the situation and control the extent of interaction (Merrilees and Fry, 2003). There are a number of opportunities available to organizations to facilitate interactivity in the e-marketing environment, such as the use of feedback systems and self-service functions. Consider, for example, online seat allocation and check-in at British Airways (www.britishairways.com), downloadable entertainment content via the BBC's website (http://bbc.co.uk), discount vouchers via e-mail from WH Smiths (www.whsmiths.co.uk) and, of course, reading the hyperbolic rantings of Jason Scott's cat (@sockington).

### Mass customization

In a case of form following function, customization follows on from interaction since the Internet is capable of producing personalized user experiences. Customization ranges from simple choices made on an ad-hoc basis to view pages within a website, such as reading a blog in chronological order or following tags and links of interest, to the heavy customization of the look and feel of a user interface on social networking sites. The ability to customize the flow of information from marketers has significantly increased levels of consumer empowerment in the marketing relationship. However, it should also be recognized that taking the time and effort to customize a web page requires a degree of motivation and commitment on the part of the consumer (Wang, Xu and Gao, 2005). Just because an organization provides the capacity to customize, it should not be assumed that customers will take advantage of this benefit. All those sites you signed up to in the e-introduction (setting up for e-marketing) contain customization options ranging from uploading icons/photos as avatars to setting privacy and publicity options. Similarly, even without a Gmail account, Google lets you break out the customization toolkit (safe search on, safe search off, etc.).

Should you want a really customized experience, sign into your Gmail account and work over the settings functions. You'll be able to generate your own unique G-product form by bundling together a range of feeds, widgets, gadgets and content from a variety of digitized component parts. For example, iGoogle (www.google.com/ig) offers a range of preset custom elements such as weather, news, sport, joke of the day or Flash games. Similarly, Google Reader (reader.google.com) can be used to create a customized stream of relevant information by tracking RSS syndication feeds from around the Internet. From the marketer's perspective, while consumer empowerment inevitably leads to a loss of control at one level, the incorporation of sophisticated tracking technologies allows marketers to better understand what choices different consumers are making and what elements of the organization's communications strategies are sparking people's interest.

### *The interest-driven nature of the Internet*

A third important consumer behaviour-focused feature of the e-marketing environment is the fact that consumer interactions with the e-marketing organization are interest driven (Dann and Dann, 2004). To some extent, all active consumption activity is interest driven – all consumers shopping for products, whether in a traditional or online retail environment, will be driven by their needs and desires. At the same time they will be passive recipients of the ambient marketing messages of the media, outdoor advertising or other messages. Although passive media consumption is still an option on the Internet, it is considerably easier to use the Web as an active media where links are clicked based on whether they look interesting to the reader. Similarly, Google searches are active consumption behaviours that are interest driven in that the consumer is using the search engine to find an answer to a question or to locate more information (or to do something totally irrelevant to what you're supposed to be doing – TV Tropes (http://TVtropes.org) demonstrates that locating more information is interest driven, and thoroughly counter to any form of productivity.)

Interest-driven consumption of the Internet can be an advantage and disadvantage to the marketer. Potential consumers actively seeking out information on specific topics or about particular products are a bonus for the marketer as these motivated consumers are more likely to interact with the company. On the downside, being interest driven relies on knowing what you are looking for rather than finding out about a product or service by chance. This becomes an issue of broader consumer behaviour with awareness sets and evoked sets (Chapter 5). That said, the fact that consumers initiate interactions with marketers significantly increases the level of consumer control and empowerment. It's also a promising sign from an engagement and involvement point of view – active pursuit is active interest, and that usually helps with the sales and innovation adoption (Chapter 5).

Marketing has three roles to play in an interest-driven environment. First, the marketers need to have something of interest which relates back to the anticipation and satisfaction of customer requirements and the creation and exchange of value (CIM, 2005; AMA, 2007, Chapter 6). Secondly, they need to generate sufficient interest and awareness of the organization to drive traffic to the website via searches, conventional media advertising, word-of-mouth or link referrals (Evans, 2007; Chapter 7). Finally, once the consumer reaches the website, the functionality and value of the website need to be sufficiently attractive to retain interest and deliver on the promised value in order to maximize repeat purchase, repeat visits and the possibility of word-of-mouth recommendations (Di Ianni, 2000; Chapters 4–7).

## Accessibility

Access is the centre point of the second set of differentiating characteristics of the Internet. Consumers have unprecedented access (whatever surpasses the Internet for global reach has the Internet as precedent) to information and services against the world's largest digital distribution outlet. The impact on marketing and e-marketing falls across three areas:

- global access
- time independence
- ubiquity.

### Global access

The world is much smaller than it first appears. The Internet is a global network of networks which was designed to interconnect. Sure, there are limits to the practicality of the interconnection of the people on the Internet – language, cultural and literacy barriers abound. Unlike a traditional marketing environment bounded by geographic reach through physical locations, shipping or operating hours, the Internet lets you access your version of it (language, content, culture) from anywhere on the planet. The Internet has created a near-borderless marketplace with instant global access to information, digital products and services, and real-world goods (although the physical objects still have shipping times to consider). Consequently, there are attempts from government, individuals and enterprise to build digital boundaries and borders and to impose barriers to the free flow of information. The network may be capable of unilateral information movement, but that's not to say that the world is ready to handle such radical notions of global human interconnectivity.

The Internet creates an opportunity for companies to play in the international arena without having to qualify through the traditional route via local, regional and national market success. The capacity to buy and sell online using PayPal (www.paypal.co.uk/uk) for international transactions has meant that it is possible for any organization to sell nearly anywhere in the world that has an Internet connection (Melewar and Smith, 2003). Borders in the global marketplace and the limitations of the global playing field are discussed in Chapter 15. International small-trader marketplaces such as eBay (www.ebay.co.uk) facilitate small-scale international transactions on a level not previously possible – particularly in the provision of niche services and information-based exchanges. Personal organization sites such as Remember the Milk (www.rememberthemilk.com/) offer a global product of task-list management that appeals to a sufficiently broad international market, and which may not have been able to survive a series of elimination rounds in finding sufficiently viable niches in its local marketplace.

The impact of the global nature of the Internet on markets extends beyond e-marketing to emerging business models. It is now feasible, and increasingly common, for businesses of all sizes to be 'born global', necessitating an international approach to e-marketing from inception (Forsgren and Hagström, 2007). Global access is also addressing the nature of human interaction, whereby communities are able to form around shared interests rather than shared geography (Chapters 9 and 10). By lowering the transaction barriers for interpersonal interaction, the Internet has also increased the geographic diversity of friendships, social networks and consumer alliances. From a marketing perspective, this also increases the size of the potential stakeholder group of 'society', from those in the local region to active consumers on the Internet. Being socially irresponsible in a foreign marketplace may now lead to consequences in the domestic market as consumers communicate across national and international boundaries. In short, Disney had serious prescience when it released *It's a Small World* back in 1964.

## Time independence

The Internet is always open, always on, and costing the planet a lot of sleep. One of the most appealing aspects of the Internet is time independence (Arnott and Bridgewater, 2002). Time independence facilitated by the Internet can mean true 24/7 access through a combination of online tools and information and the use of international call centres. Greater time independence is possible in those industries that encourage self-service, such as online banking (www.lloydstsb.com/) and data purchasing (www.apple.com/itunes), or which have the capacity to digitize routine operations such as purchasing (www.amazon.co.uk/), tracking shipments (www.usps.com/) or feedback (www.ebay.co.uk) (Di Ianni, 2000). The downside is that the Internet does not shut down (nor does it take kindly to websites that shutdown for the weekend or go offline for a public holiday maintenance day).

## Ubiquity

Access to the e-marketing environment is widespread in the majority of first-world nations and increasingly available in nations with developing economies. Internet access through mobile systems equipped with GPRS (general packet radio service), such as global positioning systems, are allowing for the mobility of a technology previously tethered to a phone cord and power cable (Chapter 13). Similarly, logistics-tracking technologies, such as the Radio Frequency Identification (RFID) tag, which was designed as a warehousing and logistics solution, are rapidly being deployed into everyday life as part of smartcards and biometric systems. In 2006, the Soccer World Cup used RFID tags to validate and authenticate tickets and potentially track ticketholder locations (privacy issues relating to ubiquity are examined in Chapters 14 and 15). Existing commercial applications of RFID are rapidly being normalized as an integral part of everyday life (Srivastava, 2007). The false Latin *ubiquitous Internetous* is likely to be the catchphrase of the 2020 period once the problems of battery life are overcome or wireless recharging reaches the mass market.

The second aspect of ubiquity is that the Internet makes it possible for media to cross geographic boundaries instantly in direct contrast to the regionality of the traditional channels. The breakdown of traditional international barriers with respect to information dissemination has ensured that e-marketing has acquired a ubiquitous point of presence around the world. Regardless of personal location, if users can access the Internet, they can access their version of it with limited filtration based on their locale (Di Ianni, 2000). For the most part, accessing Google from any Internet connection in the world will bring up the Google.com home page. That said, certain countries have various restrictions on Internet content and block various sites, IP addresses or content (which usually means a ban on YouTube and filters on Google search results). Some sites also attempt to be overly helpful and offer customized regional content based on the user's IP address. Numerous airlines provide region-specific websites, which can be problematic when trying to book an intra-country flight from outside of that country. Although perfect ubiquity of access is unlikely, the Internet is less prone (but not immune) to regionality than other media sources (Dann and Dann, 2004).

## Product characteristics

The third cluster of characteristics that define the e-marketing environment and its impact on marketing practice relate to four specific characteristics that shape the value offering created by the Internet. These are:

o intangibility
o mobility
o portability
o volatility of the Internet as a service product.

### Intangibility

e-marketing focuses on the communication and delivery of intangible benefits which cannot be experienced using the physical senses. As weird as that is, it's also the way the world is moving by focusing on the sensory experience of physical goods and the emotional-experiential outcomes of 'real' objects. Similarly, the major benefit of e-marketing is the intangible value created by providing a combination of convenience and access. Traditionally, intangibility has been the key defining characteristic of services, with the consequence that there is substantial knowledge in the services marketing field as to how to overcome the issues associated with the marketing of an intangible product (Lovelock et al., 2007) and how to make considerable use of intangibility as a selling point (Vargo and Morgan, 2005). Whilst many of the value offerings in e-marketing can be classified as services, a majority of e-marketing activities are focused on digitized information products. Information products differ from traditional goods and services in that not only are they intangible, but they also have a number of additional unique characteristics that stem from the fact that regardless of method of transmission, all are underpinned by a mathematical form which allows for digitization, replication and the creation of additional copies without depleting the resources of the original product (Frieden et al., 1998). (Some of these issues came up in Chapter 1 in the discussion of virtual goods versus virtual services.) Intangibility, the characteristics of information products and the implications for e-marketing are discussed in more detail in Chapter 6.

### Mobility

Mobility is a rapidly expanding aspect of e-marketing that is evolving and adapting to new developments in the related technologies of portability, power management and wireless communications. As e-marketing can be delivered at any time and any place through multiple distribution networks, it does not need to depend on fixed channels for message delivery. Improvements in battery technologies, processor sizes and mobile phones have helped to create devices capable of receiving a variety of communications formats, from simple text messages, multimedia messages, video calls, Internet connections and GPS signals through to the old-fashioned voice phone call. The combination of processor power and mobility has radically transformed the e-marketing landscape.

e-marketing mobility covers a broad spectrum of access issues that have arisen from the use of the mobile phone as the e-marketing platform for television (Ali, 2007) or as a mobile credit card (Amin, 2007). It also incorporates the liberation of the Internet from the last tether of geography by removing the need for a device to be connected to a network of cables to access it. The consequences, opportunities and limitations of engaging in business through m-marketing or e-marketing in a geographically distributed multipoint communications network are examined in Chapter 14.

## Portability

Portability is split between information portability and data portability. Information portability deals with the nature of digitized information as a product that can be replicated exactly with no theoretical limits to the amount of duplication and without any degradation to the original data source (Frieden et al., 1998). This provides multiple ways and means for information to be transferred through various digital channels that cannot occur with physical products that depend on limited and finite resources (see Chapter 1's section on scarcity versus surplus discussion). The opportunity for marketing exists in the development of distribution functions that give value to the customers by letting them access their information products in a variety of ways across a range of devices. For example, Gmail is available as a web service or on mobile phones via GPRS, WAP or Internet access, or as a specific application on the iPhone.

Further, as information can be replicated without degrading the source copy, replicated information can be translated into a range of alternative formats. The software engineering application of this approach to information is known as the API (application programming interface), which is a form of source code provided by a website, or software developer, that allows other developers to create products to interact with the site. Twitter (www.twitter.com) offers a range of API functions that have been used by developers to create software that includes desktop clients such as Twitteroo (www.rareedge.com/twitteroo), dynamic posters (http://twitterposter.com/), world maps of Twitter usage (www.twittervision.com) and to-do list management through Remember the Milk (http://twitter.com/rtm). Surplus-driven economic conditions are addressed in the delivery of value, where value is no longer determined by scarcity (Chapter 6).

Data portability is the level of ownership that individuals can exert over the data trail they create in the use of a social media site, including content they have uploaded, relationships and network connections, plus historical data of instant messages, communications or other notifications (Dataportability, 2008). This issue is increasingly important in the context of social media systems such as MySpace, Facebook and Twitter, or social bookmarking sites such as Delicious (www.delicious.com), where users contribute content and may or may not be able to extract their data to take it to another site (Chapters 12 and 15).

## Volatility of the Internet as a service product

The Internet is thoroughly unstable. Its volatility has been absolutely brilliant for the rapid development and growth side of the equation but completely off-putting for the large portion of the population that likes a bit of calm and consistency in its technology. Technological capabilities are still expanding rapidly, with developers aiming for faster, smaller and more powerful devices despite plateaus in the Moore's Law prediction of exponential growth (Srivastava, 2007). Thankfully, as processor capacity stabilizes to a relatively finite environment (where finite is still massively powerful), programmers can adapt and adjust their code to maximize what power they can draw from the existing technology. Nowhere is this better demonstrated than in the difference between the quality of games developed for the launch of PlayStation 2 and the last generation of games before the launch of PlayStation 3 ruined everything. As the processor power of the platform did not change, the developers pushed their insight of the system and started being able to maximize the capacity of the device. Similar opportunity exists for the development of software-driven efficiency once a physics hard limit is reached in areas of processor power, bandwidth and data storage. The reach of information is still growing, and the ease of data collection, processing and storage is still in the early growth phase.

One of the hardest aspects of e-marketing from an implementation perspective is the volatility of the environment. New tools, technologies and expectations are developed on a daily basis. Keeping up with advances, and sifting for those that are of commercial use and value, is an ongoing task for e-marketers. Not only is it important to keep up with technical innovation and decide what to adopt and what to reject, it is also important to keep up with social innovation and expectations. As many organizations have discovered to their cost, not all new tools are appropriate for commercial or other marketing purposes due to the expectations of other users and the emergence of new e-ethics and standards of behaviour.

Large-scale innovation and significant jumps in technology mean that the implementation of e-marketing strategies may change rapidly from year to year. At the same time, the consumer behaviour constructs of innovation adoption and the usual patterns of diffusion of innovations indicate that there will be a portion of the market who are content with their 'old' technologies and 'yesterday's innovations'. The challenge for the marketer is to determine how best to satisfy the target market. Is it the constant churn of innovation or the stability of established technology that will create the best fit between the needs of the market and the capacity of the organization?

## Business considerations for e-marketing

There is only one reason to use e-marketing strategy in business – to create value for the organization by providing a superior way for the organization and then customer, client or partner to achieve their goals and objectives. Determining whether the organization will benefit from going online and being engaged in various online activities is a matter of balancing the pros and cons, costs and rewards, and coming to a conclusion based on the specifics of the organization, its markets and target consumer. To help in the decision-making process, six reasons for being online and three critical potential inhibitors to e-marketing have been identified.

## Six reasons to be involved in e-marketing

There are six reasons why it's worth the time and effort to engage in e-marketing activity. These are: the financial question of cost reduction; overall improvements in organizational performance brought about through effectiveness and efficiency; improved access to the marketplace; promotional and communications options; competitive pressures and the organization's corporate image.

### Cost reductions and financial considerations

Money is the lifeblood of the organization, and e-marketing as a means for reducing costs to increase cash flow, bolster profits or improve savings has been a central motivator for many organizations and industries. Cost saving is an organization-centric focus that sees the move online as a sound investment in long-term financial goals. Goodman (2004) outlines several areas of common cost savings in moving to e-marketing:

o  Perceived savings on promotional materials by moving from print to electronic brochures
o  Savings on postage by converting mass mail-outs to database-focused e-mail campaigns
o  Reducing the need for staff as consumers move from direct, personal interactions to online self-service
o  Reducing market research costs through the use of tracking software to determine actual rather than reported consumer behaviour
o  Savings in developing customized products through the user-driven amalgamation of component digital parts.

### Effectiveness and efficiency considerations

The strategic use of online information systems can drive whole-organization changes to business structures and models leading to greater overall effectiveness and efficiency (Hassan and Tibbits, 2000). Resource allocation in e-marketing, coupled with the customization of websites and the development of customized marketing messages and digital products based on screening criteria, means that less time and resources are wasted on developing unwanted products. Access to large-scale databases which are constantly being updated and expanded has significantly increased effective collation of information from multiple sources. This in turn has resulted in increased efficiency and effectiveness in a range of business activities, from shared online access to group/company resources such as HR manuals and other internal policies, to better invoicing and payment systems between organizations and their clients (Chapter 11).

### Wider access to clients, customers and partners

The global nature of the Internet makes it intensely attractive to anyone seeking geographically dispersed audiences or a voice in the global marketplace (Arnott and Bridgewater, 2002). Search engine optimization, specialist and niche-driven word-of-mouth recommended products are more likely to find and service their customer base online than in limited geographic or regional markets. Broad access to national and international markets through the Internet combined with micro segmentation can create viable business models from niche offerings of value.

Information and digital experiential products also benefit from the lowering of traditional export barriers through cost-effective, simple distribution logistics over the Internet and cost-effective, international mail and courier services for smaller shipments of physical products (Chapter 6). The relative ease with which global commercial activity can take place via the Internet is particularly attractive to the operations of small-to-medium-sized businesses which normally would not attempt international expansion.

### Promotional value

The Internet offers unprecedented capacity for organizations to showcase and promote their products, services and ideas through third-party providers and the organization's own website. Understandably, this is a dual-edge sword – positive promotional material travels fast, but nowhere near as fast as negative word of mouth. Documented actions speak far louder than IMC claims in the contemporary world. Traditional media such as print, radio and television all have technical limitations which limit the type and length of message that can be delivered (and all have strengths in that respect as well). Websites can be tailored to the message structure, giving the Internet the combined benefits of all three media. Text-based messages can be as simple as 140 characters (www.twitter.com) or as detailed as complex explanations (multiple posts on a blog, a whole wiki), written instructions (pdfs, wiki) and video demonstrations (YouTube, http://uk.youtube.com). Customer-based customization can also assist e-marketing messages in that the reader of the site can choose to seek more information by clicking on the embedded links, by accessing video on demand or by simply skimming the content. Putting the control of message consumption into the hands of the recipient means that the most appropriate mix of personal preference and message delivery can be simply and effectively delivered by providing a suite of options for the marketplace to roll out their own solution.

### Competitive pressures

One of the main motivators to create an initial online presence was fear of being left behind (Dann and Dann, 2004). The pressure of not having an online presence once competitors started to adopt the medium meant that many organizations made early, and often ineffective, forays into the world of e-marketing. Today, that particular concern is at the forefront of half-hearted or ill-conceived forays into the social media environment. Consumer expectations of the ubiquity of the Internet are such that most people now expect to see URLs on product packaging and advertising and at the very least a basic, static, information-based website or something hosted on MySpace. At the same time, whilst competitive pressure might be an incentive to recon the terrain in the new social media, it's no excuse to blindly create an ill-conceived, poorly supported or half-hearted effort just because someone else was in that marketspace. You're better off doing nothing than doing something badly if you're driving your strategy based on the actions of your competitors.

### Corporate image

There are two aspects to creating a positive image on the Internet. First, early use of new technologies and e-marketing techniques may present a public image of that company as being up to date, innovative and at the cutting edge of social and technological trends. Of course, being annoying or making a serious social media *faux pas* in an innovative way will hurt more than it helps. Secondly, e-marketing impacts on the corporate image of the organization. Increased interest in sustainability, green marketing and corporate social responsibility has been used to justify the movement from traditional paper-based communications to the online sphere by repositioning the move in terms of environmental responsibility whilst still reaping the financial benefits of reduced printing and mailing costs.

## Mission-critical inhibitors

Despite the many benefits of creating an online presence, e-marketing has not been universally adopted and there are still several inhibitors which limit its application in different business situations. It's also worth considering these inhibitors when examining any specific form of e-marketing practice – for example, when deciding if the organization needs a blog, a MySpace profile, a presence on Facebook or whether or not to shift the entire client contact database over to Highrise (http://highrisehq.com/).

### Financial viability

The counterpoint to the question of cost reduction is the question 'How much will this cost?' e-marketing is not cost-neutral. Free does not mean cost-neutral; it means no charge for the service. If the service costs time or requires extra staff or investments in training and development, then you're looking at a set of costs that need to be equalled or exceeded by the benefits from the exercise. If the costs outweigh the potential benefits, bail out. If they break even, it's worth a try to see if efficiency with the technology will bring profit (with an eye to abandon ship when icebergs appear on the horizon). Engaging in e-marketing is not recommended on its own merits – you need to have a reason, a rationale and a purpose for getting involved in the technology. For this book, most of the reason and rationale is a training exercise for you to learn how to do e-marketing. Cost-benefit scenario says you'll learn more by guided trial and discovery than you'll learn by not doing anything.

### Organizational capacity

Not all products and services are suited to e-marketing nor are all organizations equipped to implement an e-marketing strategy. If the resources available to the organization (money, skills, technical capacity) are limited then attempting to implement an e-marketing strategy may be counterproductive. Doing e-marketing well involves conforming to consumer expectations with respect to services offered online, frequency of updates and the currency of online information. If the organization cannot meet these expectations, doing e-marketing badly is worse than having no online presence. Whilst a lot of people on the Internet will give great and valid reasons for getting connected, they're also connected because there was a benefit to them (if nothing else, then there was the benefit of being able to give the advice to be online). There are plenty of grounds for you not to commit resources where the expected return on investment is fairly small. A small business with limited capacity to service more than a small number of clients, for example, may be able to operate effectively and profitably by simply relying on traditional word-of-mouth referrals. Alternatively, the cost of implementing a full e-marketing strategy, including online purchases and ordering, may be prohibitive if the products being sold have tight profit margins and sell in low volumes, or if adding the international shipping cost will kill off any chance of competitive pricing.

### Customer capacities

Not all target markets will be effectively reached using e-marketing. Before adopting e-marketing the usual market research on consumer preferences needs to be conducted, in this case specifically focusing on preferred methods of communication and delivery of products and services. If the electronic alternative is less attractive to the market than the traditional market then investment in a complementary or alternative e-marketing strategy is likely to be wasted. Gilmore et al. (2007) examined barriers for small and medium enterprises using the Internet and found a significant barrier to e-marketing existed where the organization was too far in front of the target market or suppliers when it came to technology adoption. Although the organization could handle the various online tasks and requirements, its marketers or suppliers were not sufficiently adept to use the systems, and as such, the organization still needed to use 'older' approaches to deal with these markets.

## Level of involvement in e-marketing

The extent to which any given business engages in e-marketing will vary according to three factors: resources; relevance and requirements.

*Resources* are the capacity of the company to implement an e-marketing programme which incorporates planning, HR and IT implications, and the implementation issue of 'Can we do this with what we've got?'. Resource issues are addressed in Chapter 10.

*Relevance* is the value of e-marketing and is largely dependent on consumer behaviour considerations (Chapter 5), marketing strategy (Chapter 4) and whether or not you can deliver value with the technology (Chapter 6). e-marketing is a field full of incredible devices, amazing technologies and wonderful toys that are meaningless and useless if the target market isn't going to want to use them or isn't even online. e-marketing has the challenge of creating relevance through identifying, anticipating and satisfying consumer needs when it comes to the how and why of online interaction (Chapter 5).

*Requirements* are the features of the product or service being sold and how well these adapt to e-marketing. Information-based products can be delivered directly online, physical goods ordered for later delivery and services booked in advance. Specialist and niche products which are sought out by consumers are more suited to e-marketing than fast-moving consumer goods which are widely available in the offline distribution channels. Ordering a home delivery of a single Mars bar from Tesco Online (www.tesco.com) is possible but far less satisfying than picking up the chocolate in the store (even if that does mean leaving the house to get there). Similarly, whilst reservations for personal services such as hairdressing can be made online, the customer still needs to be at the hairdresser's location for the haircut. (Haircut downloads are a way off into the future, somewhere after the pizza printer and Coffee Over IP are released.)

## Unique e-marketing issues

e-marketing shares many common issues with other branches of marketing, including those relating to strategy, segmentation and market research. The specific e-marketing environment, however, has created a number of new, unique marketing issues which need to be considered and addressed in developing an e-marketing strategy.

### Audience control

Audience control refers to the extent to which marketers are able to identify the consumers of e-marketing communications and restrict viewers of websites to the preferred target audience. Whilst all mass communication media have a degree of difficulty in audience control, traditional media vehicles are generally targeted to specific demographic and lifestyle groups, thus making the placement of marketing materials to reach a particular audience a relatively straightforward process. In the case of e-marketing, websites are often visited by individuals who have found the website indirectly via a search engine whilst looking for specific information. Consequently, it is more difficult to tailor the messages and language of the site without specific interaction and input from the consumer via some process of customization. Increasingly organizations are offering a series of alternative websites accessible from a single homepage based on user segmentation variables such as member, staff or visitor, in an attempt to address this issue. Audience control and the consequences of failing to block content, moderate access or prohibit users from seeing certain marketing messages are examined in Chapter 15.

### Information proliferation

The ability of the Internet to transmit large quantities of information cheaply and easily, combined with the increasing expectations of the market for regularly updated, quality information, means that managing information for public consumption has become a major strategic issue. As a general rule, marketers respond positively to the widespread dissemination of information about their products. However, the ease with which information can be disseminated has a negative impact in the case of errors such as the inadvertent release of confidential information. Issues of copyright, trademark protection and the means and mechanisms of distributing protected ideas across the Internet are examined in further depth in Chapter 15.

## Share of voice

Traditional broadcast media have the capacity to be bought out in controlled units and create the opportunity for a small number of influential players to restrict who shares in the overall media 'voice'. In the case of the Internet, the lack of centralized commercial control has freed up communications with the result that all individuals have the capacity to promote themselves and speak freely in the Internet arena (Dann and Dann, 2004). As far back as 1996, this was seen as the dual-edge sword for marketing – unlimited voice creates competitive environments for the underdog marketer and prohibits the overdog marketer from raising entry barriers to the marketplace (Berthon et al., 1996).

Rapid growth in the accessibility and popularity of peer-to-peer networks and social networking sites has leveraged off this capacity to create an alternative media space in which competition for share of voice is based on the desirability and attractiveness of the message rather than the capacity of the individual to purchase media time and space (Dann and Dann, 2007). Again, widespread access to broadcast tools such as MySpace, Facebook, blogs and peer-to-peer networks is dual edge in nature – the capacity to speak to the market is increased at the same time as the sheer volume of signal is also raised as everyone else has a chance to speak. Marketers have decreased ability to dominate share of voice and, therefore, become more dependent on creating messages of value rather than dominating the share of voice (Chapter 7).

## Internet time

Unlike traditional media outlets such as newspapers and magazines which have clearly defined and well-publicized regular deadlines for the submission and printing of information, the Internet is constantly open for information distribution. Marketers need to determine the timing of information release based on criteria such as the urgency of the information. For example, in a crisis, an early and speedy response is a necessity, whereas generic, press releases that raise corporate image can be flexibly timed and planned to fit into related marketing and corporate schedules. Internet time also relates to the speed at which changes can be made to data-based products. Errors in code are able to be patched, tested and released without requiring the physical recall and reissue of goods (Chapter 1's 'ready, fire, aim' approach). Similarly, idea patching and brand repairs can be conducted by fast responses, open communication and quick thinking by the e-marketer. The impact of Internet time on consumer behaviour is examined in Chapter 5, and the impact for businesses is covered in Chapter 10.

### The 'beta' factor

The last unique factor in e-marketing is the capacity to ship incomplete products to a willing marketplace of customers, who assume that the product will improve in quality over time, version numbers and revisions. As websites can be updated constantly, software can patch itself and information can be reissued in updated forms. The online marketplace is far more tolerant of unfinished goods than the physical world. The 'beta release' candidate used to be the pre-release test version of software that was incomplete and examined for flaws, failures and ineffective processes. Since the widespread deployment of a 'beta' tag on a range of Web 2.0 sites, and Google virtually championing it as a means to excuse under-optimized performance, 'beta' is almost becoming a brandmark of quality amongst software, websites and, eventually, offline services. The use of open beta testing as a form of value creation is explored in Chapter 6.

## Conclusion

e-marketing is an applied form of marketing that operates within the confines and expanses of the interactive electronic environment. This chapter began with the fundamentals of marketing, including the two operational definitions of marketing (CIM, 2005; AMA, 2007) that will form the core marketing principles for this book, followed by an overview of how these two definitions function as a co-operative unit for shaping marketing practice. It went on to give an overview of the e-marketing environment, the factors that make e-marketing a separate sub-discipline of marketing and how e-marketing interconnects with m-marketing and e-commerce. Finally, the chapter covered the features and factors of the Internet and e-marketing that form the first vital business decision – should we engage in e-marketing? Assuming the answer is 'yes', Chapter 3 takes a guided tour through the important processes, activities and institutions that can be adapted for use to enable the e-marketer to identify, anticipate and satisfy customer requirements in the interactive electronic environments.

## References

### Books and journals

Abimbola, T. and Kocak, A. (2007) 'Brand, organization identity and reputation: SMEs as expressive organizations. A resources-based perspective', *Qualitative Market Research: An International Journal*, 10(4): 416–30.

Adeyoyin, S.O. (2005) 'Strategic planning for marketing library services', *Library Management* 26, (8/9): 494–507.

Ali, S. (2007) 'Upwardly mobile: a study into mobile TV use amongst children', *Young Consumers*, 8(1): 52–7.

American Marketing Association (2007) 'Definition of marketing', http://www.marketingpower.com (accessed 2 July 2010).

Amin, H. (2007) 'An analysis of mobile credit card usage intentions', *Information Management and Computer Security*, 15(4): 260–9.

Arnott, D.C. and Bridgewater, S. (2002) 'Internet, interaction and implications for marketing', *Marketing Intelligence and Planning*, (20)2: 86–95.

Berthon, P., Pitt, L. and Watson, R.T. (1996) 'Marketing communication and the world wide web', *Business Horizons*, Sept–Oct: 24–32.

Bray, T. (2007) 'The Intimate Internet', http://www.tbray.org/ongoing/When/200x/2007/10/04/Intimate-Internet (accessed 2 July 2010).

Brogan, C. (2009) 'The Plastic Human Problem', http://www.chrisbrogan.com/the-plastic-human-problem/ (accessed 2 July 2010).

Chartered Institute of Marketing (2005) 'Marketing and the 7Ps: A brief summary of marketing and how it works', *Knowledge Hub*, http://www.cim.co.uk/KnowledgeHub (accessed 2 July 2010).

Dann, S. and Dann, S. (2004) *Strategic Internet Marketing 2.0*. Brisbane: John Wiley & Sons.

Dann, S. and Dann, S. (2007) *Competitive Marketing Strategy*. French's Forest, NSW: Pearson Education.

Dataportability (2008) 'Dataportability: Connect. Control. Share. Remix, http://www.dataportability.org/ (accessed 7 July 2010).

Di Ianni, A. (2000) 'The e-business enterprise and the 'Web-first' principle of e-marketing', *Interactive Marketing*, 2(2): 158–70.

Evans, M.P. (2007) 'Analyzing Google rankings through search engine optimization data', *InternetResearch*, 17(1): 21–37.

Forsgren, M. and Hagström, P. (2007) 'Ignorant and impatient internationalization? The Uppsala model and internationalization patterns for Internet-related firms', *Critical Perspectives on International Business*, 3(3): 291–305.

Frieden, J., Goldsmith, R., Takacs, S. and Hofacker, C. (1998) 'Information as product: not goods, not services', *Marketing Intelligence and Planning*, 16(3): 210–20.

Gilmore, A., Gallagher, D. and Hnery, S. (2007) 'E-marketing and SMEs: operational lessons for the future', *European Business Review*, 19(3): 234–47.

Goodman, S. (2004) 'A proposed marketing activity and outcome framework for marketing in the new economy', *The Internet Business Review*, 1, October: 1–20.

Hassan, H. and Tibbits, H. (2000) 'Strategic management of electronic commerce: an adaptation of the balanced scorecard', *Internet Research: Networking Application and Policy*, 10(5): 439–50.

Helgesen, O. (2006) 'Customer segments based on customer account profitability', *Journal of Targeting, Measurement and Analysis for Marketing*, 14(3): 225–37.

Hoffman, D. and Novak, T. (1996) 'Marketing in hypermedia computer mediated environments: conceptual foundations', *Journal of Marketing*, 60 (July): 50–68.

Keefe, L.M. (2008) 'Marketing defined', *Marketing News*, January 15, 2008: 28–9.

Kiani, G.Z. (1998) 'Marketing opportunities in the digital world', *Internet Research: Networking Application and Policy*, 8(2): 185–94.

Lovelock, C., Patterson, P. and Walker, R. (2007) *Services Marketing: An Asia-Pacific and Australian Perspective*, 4th edn. French's Forest, NSW: Pearson Education.

MacInnis, D. and de Mello, G. (2005) 'The concept of hope and its relevance to product evaluation and choice', *Journal of Marketing*, 69: 1–14.

Melewar, T.C. and Smith, N. (2003) 'The Internet revolution: some global marketing implications', *Marketing Intelligence and Planning*, 21(6): 363–9.

Merrilees, B. and Fry, M.L. (2003) 'E-trust: the influence of perceived interactivity on e-retailing users', *Marketing Intelligence and Planning*, 21(2): 123–8.

Prochaska, J. O. and DiClemente, C.C. (1983) 'Stages and processes of self-change of smoking: towards an integrative model of change', *Journal of Consulting and Clinical Psychology*, 51: 390–5.

Srivastava, L. (2007) 'Radio frequency identification: ubiquity for humanity', *Info*, 9: 4–14.

Vargo, S. and Morgan, F. (2005) 'Services in society and academic thought: an historical analysis', *Journal of Macromarketing*, 25(1): 42–53.

Wang, T., Xu, Z. and Gao, G. (2005) 'The model of Internet marketing program considering 2Is', *Services Systems and Services Management, Proceedings of ICSSSM '05*, 1: 451–6.

Zawinski, J. (1995) 'Zawinski's law', *Jargon Manual*, http://www.catb.org/jargon/html/Z/Zawinskis-Law.html (accessed 2 July 2010).

## Introduction

Strategy makes the difference between success and failure in e-marketing. e-marketing strategy draws its direction from the firm's broader marketing approach, which in turn is based on the overall business strategy objective of the organization. e-marketing strategies are most effective when they integrate the strength of the Internet as a marketing medium with the existing online and offline activity of the organization.

This chapter covers e-marketing strategy in four sections. First, the chapter links e-marketing to the bigger picture of corporate development options, with an emphasis on fitting your online activity in with the end-game of achieving broader organizational goals. Secondly, the chapter examines the value and necessity of setting clear and realistic objectives in e-marketing strategy so you know where you're going, what you want to achieve and can later see if you've actually achieved it. The setting of clear objectives at this point in the process will make your life a lot easier when you come to complete the metrics and measurement tasks in Chapter 10. Thirdly, the chapter tackles the hardest task of marketing – working out who is (and definitely who isn't) your ideal customer through the strategic use of market segmentation. Even if you want to believe you could be all things to all people, chances are firmly in favour of you having a group (or several groups) you really don't want reading your blog, using your site or hanging out on your server. This part of the chapter covers the strategic aspects of identifying target markets, anticipating their needs with site design decisions and satisfying your customers' needs by meeting (and exceeding) expectations. Finally, the chapter examines the role of positioning in e-marketing strategy as a key to understanding your own offering to the market and who your natural competitors and allies will be on the Internet.

## Big picture strategies

There are certain clichés in business, and the 'bigger picture' is a favoured expression amongst management – largely because it started life as a useful metaphor for explaining how the strategy plan works. If you launch Google Calendar (www.google.com/calendar) you get a brief view of how and why the big picture/small picture becomes useful. Consider the month (business strategy) view as the big picture that you can break down into a smaller, weekly picture (marketing strategy) and a daily schedule (marketing tactics). With the big picture strategy, you can see the upcoming challenges and tasks (assessment deadlines, weekends and parties). These can be dealt with by breaking them down into a weekly schedule of work, study, classes, travel, sleep and recreation. If you're then trying to co-ordinate something specific (tactical) you'd normally need to focus on a narrow section (a Tuesday) and refine the narrow section again (Tuesday afternoon, around 4pm) to find out if you are free to catch up with your mates.

Business strategy works in basically the same way – the 'big' strategic picture is the organization's plans for the next few years (or decades); the marketing strategy fits into the broader business plan and has a shorter time frame, faster goal achievement (and goal resetting). Within the marketing strategy there are tactical implementation issues (Chapter 4).

## Merging online and offline strategy

At the dawn of e-marketing there was a sense that the Internet was somehow different and separate from the rest of society. The whole thing operated under a variety of assumptions regarding the independence of Internet activity from offline activity, which can be summarized in three famous rules:

o The separation of identity from reality, known as the Vegas Rule (What happens in Vegas stays in Vegas)
o The separation of online activity from offline personal reputation, using the Tour Rule (What happens on tour stays on tour)
o The separation of actor from action, with an acknowledgement that you could talk about the action but not who was involved, by using the Chatham House Rule (Participants are free to use the information received but neither the identity nor the affiliation of the speaker(s) nor that of any other participant may be revealed).

This approach worked for the first few years of e-marketing until the relative ubiquity of access to the Internet, combined with the widespread plastering of URLs on everything, led to what can only be described as an e-business singularity – what happens on the Internet impacts on offline brands, and what happens offline is discussed online. The merger of online and offline is becoming a significant HR issue as employers start turning their attention to the online activity of their staff – usually for the express purpose of finding something that breaches a policy guideline. The blending of online and offline is also a growing area of significance, with portable Internet access increasing the ubiquity of online access in previously offline areas. This can also work to the benefit of all involved by using mobile phone-readable QR codes on name badges or business cards to link back to a much more detailed portfolio (Chapter 13).

Previously hard decisions about whether to retain existing branding and positioning strategies, whether to try to appeal to the same markets on and offline and how the online activities of the firm can be used to complement, rather than compete with, existing marketing functions became relatively moot points. The Internet is no more or less an integrated part of life than the television, radio or newspaper when it comes to segmentation decisions, targeting and marketing activity. If you're willing to assume that you can behave differently on television than you do on the radio since neither radio listener nor television viewer will find out, feel free to operate an isolated online strategy from your offline activity. Otherwise, stick with an integrated marketing strategy for online/offline, onTV/offTV, onradio/offradio and inprint/offprint.

### Blogging note: anonymous, pseudonymous and synonymous

When setting up a blog, Twitter account or any other social media device, there's the question of whether to operate under your own identity, operate anonymously or run with a pseudonym. Each option is balanced in terms of pros and cons for its branding, tactical and personal impacts.

Synonymous blogging has the advantage of being directly linked to your real-life identity, and if you're working to build a personal brand, seeking glory and fortune, this could be the path for you. At the same time, you have no privacy insofar as what you say is linked to you. You're the front and centre person for your brand that can be read by anyone with Google access. Effectively, you are the same person online and offline, so you're operating an integrated strategy where activity in both fields will contribute to your collective personal reputation.

Pseudonymous blogging is a popular approach. It creates a branded identity that is used consistently across online interactions and which is kept mostly masked from your personal life for a variety of reasons, including isolating your work environment from your blog space (quite often at the behest of the bland corporation that worked very hard to be faceless and really doesn't need someone associating your cute kitten photo blog with its soulless corporate identity). Pseudonymous blogging has a serious downside in that certain synonymous bloggers believe that they have a right to unmask your pseudonym simply because you're not using your real name. Also, as time progresses, it's increasingly hard to keep both identities isolated – you may reveal too many identifying details in either space that might unmask you (particularly if you're running a really high profile or controversial pseudonymous identity. The urge to brag must be resisted.) There are also serious consequences to be faced online and offline when the two isolated identities are eventually merged, as many will feel somehow betrayed that Identity2700 wasn't actually the offspring of Mrs and Mr 2700. This is the split strategy, which means you're doubling your workload as you maintain two isolated personal brands (and a good pseudonym needs considerable brand maintenance), with the advantage that it does allow you to pursue two independent strategic objectives that could clash horribly if you tried this under a synonymous brand.

Finally, anonymous blogging is a dual-strand strategy where you're working to avoid connecting a consistent set of behaviours (anonymous online activity) with your offline profile. There's limited value for marketers in having anonymous online activity and that's entirely market research-related. If you're going to expend effort in creating, communicating, delivering and exchanging content online, you may as well go pseudonymous for the brand consistency and reaping the rewards. If you're considering anonymity as a strategic option, be advised that the likelihood of being revealed will operate in direct proportion to the extent you're blogging anonymously to do something you wouldn't sign your name to in the offline world. Whereas pseudonymous blogging has a level of credibility from authors, musicians, actors and video gamers, anonymity has distinct problems when it comes to branding (there are so many anonymous commentators), consistent identity (which anonymous are you?) and credibility (anonymous comments are usually screened if accepted at all).

On the business side of the agenda, most corporations find themselves either in synonymous or pseudonymous arrangements, where the author is representing

> a member of the corporation, as is the case with the Zappos company which has its CEO twittering as @zappos and the various @zappos_[StaffName] employees (http://twitter.zappos.com/employees) openly identified with the brand. In contrast, 'corporate' Twitter accounts, such as the one for the Prime Minister's office, are often staffed by teams of writers who have a pseudonymous Twitter account (@DowningStreet) rather than being operated by the Prime Minister.

## e-marketing and strategy: growth options

There are three key strategic planning models that are worth revising for e-marketing:

- the classic, often misunderstood and sometimes ignored product lifecycle model
- Porter's legendary generic competitive strategies framework
- Ansoff's strategic growth options.

These planning models will be used to demonstrate how e-marketing strategies can be developed in reference to existing strategic theory, with the consequence that you can adapt and use any other strategy models you see fit.

A word of caution – all strategy is based on information, evidence and research rather than guess work, assumptions and wishful thinking. With this in mind, we're introducing the broad frameworks first then incorporating advice on analysis, research, environmental scans and related techniques into Chapter 4. Evidence-based marketing is a vastly easier form of marketing than the gut-feel, instinctive variants that seem to propagate through business (for one thing, gut instinct requires training, practice and a gut). Market research with Google, Twitter searches and half an hour on the Internet can often produce enough decent marketing information which can be fed into the systematic ways of thinking about strategy discussed in this chapter. Read this chapter to pick up the strategic thinking. After picking up the techniques in Chapter 4 (which will make sense after reading this chapter), come back and have another look at the strategic models here (then move to Chapter 5). Do not get caught in a recursive loop between Chapter 4 and Chapter 3.

### Product lifecycle model

The most vital concept in e-marketing theory is the product lifecycle model. This is a conceptual model of how the market works when a new product is introduced to the world. The product lifecycle model is the business-side view of the marketplace, which is described from a consumer perspective in Chapter 5 as the innovation-adoption curve. For the sake of connectivity we've included consumer-side statements even though you haven't covered that part yet (marketing's cyclical referencing comes into effect here).

Dann and Dann (2007) outlined the extended cycle as a series of six phases.

*Phase 1* is the introduction phase, where the product first hits the market and where the innovators buy it because it's new and therefore interesting. It's a period of low profits, high prices, cost recovery and innovative customers. Online it's also known as 'beta', where the product is (mostly) finished apart from the bits that need to be fixed after breaking on contact with the consumer. Google has at least ten services sitting in the Phase 1 beta category under the 'Google Labs' tab at any given moment.

*Phase 2* is the early growth spike that occurs when the innovators are starting to clear out in search of the newest new thing and the early adopter opinion leaders (Chapter 4) start to show up. It is important to note here that many, if not most, product innovations never make it beyond Phase 1 and into Phase 2. For those that do, prices drop, new features are added based on the experience with the beta, and version numbering starts (if it wasn't there before). This is still an era of rapid development in response to customer needs although some of the emphasis moves from constant changes to the current offering to the offer of stability (Version 1.0 is much better than Version 0.99a) with the promise of future iterations. It's a safe bet to say that the Internet in general is somewhere between Phase 2 and Phase 3. It's well established, has hit the very first version number (Web 2.0) and looks reasonably stable (for a house of cards). Services such as Twitter are definitely at this point in the process (Plurk, Facebook and others aren't quite in the same category).

*Phase 3* represents sustained growth, where a broader share of the market of early majority joins the early adopters in using the product. It's also where competition for market share increases – consider if you will that mobile Internet access on the iPhone, iPad and Blackberry is a competitor alternative to the fixed Internet access at work and at home. Strategy tends towards the market leaders locking up the marketplace, raising barriers to entry and generally preparing for the slug fest that happens when the market matures and stabilizes. Social media services such as Facebook are approaching the far end of Phase 3 at the time of writing. Facebook is the poster child for ongoing growth with the sinking sense that it's got to run out of new users sooner rather than later.

*Phase 4* is the late growth spurt, the last gasp, for most products before the curve flattens out into loyalty based repurchasing. Late growth for the Internet is where people who left a service because it wasn't useful come back now it's reached critical mass (Facebook, MySpace), or where secondary uses for a product are found (a work blog, a personal 'home' blog and a personal blog for tracking gym training and exercise). Phase 4 is the money phase for most businesses as additional copies of the product are used or paid versions of free services are acquired to make more use of the features now that plenty of experience has been gained with the basic model. In technology terms, the iPod, Xbox360 and PlayStation 3, plus every copy of Microsoft Windows after Windows 2000, sit in this camp. Late growth also ties into the late majority adopter category, who are belatedly joining the cycle as they see a need to pick up the technology or else be left behind their friends and family. MySpace is the definitive Phase 4 late-growth technology, slowly heading into decline as people migrate from the MySpace profiles to Facebook, Twitter or a self-hosted blog.

*Phase 5* is the market maturity stage, which can describe technologies such as the DVD player, CD audio, MP3 audio and televisions. Attempts will be made to introduce radical 'new' versions of the existing mature product (Blu-ray, HDTV, MP4, Ogg Vorbis). However, since the market has stabilized and product variations are widespread, the market is saturated with product offerings. It's a tough ask to break through the mature market. Realistically, a breakthrough at this stage is just moving people back to a growth phase without offering anything sufficiently radical to constitute a new product that would start the process back at Phase 1. Online searching hit a plateau before Google arrived and knocked MSN Search and Yahoo! out of the competition. Web browsing sat firmly at maturity after Internet Explorer 6 beat Netscape 6 into oblivion. Then Firefox, Flock and Chrome arrived, pushing the category back to the highly competitive, saturated marketplace.

*Phase 6* is the decline phase, where the product is retired and shutdown, sufficiently retrofitted as to move it back into one of the growth phases or farmed off into a mature market niche to live out its days as a specialist product. Currently, newspapers and newsprint seem to be doing their level best to move from maturity into decline, despite the success of a whole array of online services that resemble journalism in varying degrees. Phase 6 can also spell the end of technology as the organization orders the cessation of production and support – Windows 2000 was officially 'Phase Sixed' when Microsoft ceased any and all forms of development and support for the platform.

The product lifecycle plays an important role in calming down marketers, strategists and anyone else invested in the traditional business strategy based around the idea of growth as an indicator of organizational health. Problematically, many business strategists believe that the rapid growth at the start of a product lifecycle, steady consistent growth during the operation of the product or continuous growth through to market maturity are the be-all and end-all of strategy. The mindset was summarized as 'if you're not growing, you're failing', which was an unquestioned *modus operandi* for business prior to the global financial crisis. The product lifecycle puts paid to the idea of constant growth as a realistic strategy. In reality, continuous growth is not a sustainable business proposition – neither marketing nor marketing practice indicates that growth can or should continue once market maturity is achieved in the product lifecycle.

Similarly, traditional e-marketing was predicated around continuous ongoing growth based on the the Internet moving from the innovators (2.5 per cent) to early adopters (16 per cent) and into early majority (34 per cent). Rapid growth is possible in these market conditions since the expansion of the total possible market from 2.5 per cent to 52.5 per cent of a population is a curve with a sharp upwards incline. That said, once you've crested the wave of early majority, you've got a remaining market share of 34 per cent in the late majority available before you hit the wall of laggard-based rejection. (If none of this makes sense to you, Chapter 5 has the details on the innovation-adoption curve.)

Rapid growth can be expected at the start of any product lifecycle but the nature of maths, curves and marketplaces means it cannot continue unchecked forever under any set of circumstance known to marketing. From an e-marketing perspective, this also means that you need to calculate issues of breakeven occurring well before the peak of any one of the growth curves. Avoid dependence on perpetual growth as a business model and instead focus on a viable business model that can support sustained activity in a mature competitive marketspace.

products operating in mature markets can make effective use of online differentiation. The pasta industry is a little on the old side, yet a well-considered set of online supplements in the form of a recipe website can create differentiation within the market. Similarly, whole foods, health foods and quasi-niche products such as low allergen food can augment the physical product with additional online advice, support and the opportunity to order directly from the wholesaler.

In terms of developing an e-marketing differentiation strategy, you can push for an objective or subjective differentiator. Objective differentiators are features that are exclusive to the product. For example, exclusive titles for the Xbox or Nintendo console, exclusive downloadable content (Chapter 14) for a game title (*Rockband 2, Guitar Hero World Tour, GTAIV*) or unique capacity found within a product offering – applications for the iPhone and iPod Touch (Chapter 13). Objective product differentiation is replicable even when and where protected by patents, licences and other defensive strategies. The unique nature of the iPod controls are now ubiquitous in MP3 players and the concept of downloadable content is widespread across the PC, Xbox, PlayStation 3 and Nintendo platforms. Even the television industry has moved into the DLC (downloadable content) market, with television series offering exclusive 'webisodes' to supplement the fans in the breaks between the broadcast seasons.

Alternatively, focusing on subjective differentiation allows you to treat the consumer in a way that provides a unique experience for them in terms of personalization, interaction, emotional connection or image management. By using a combination of product positioning (later in this chapter), branding (Chapter 7), service delivery (Chapter 6) and being awesome, a company can produce an uncontestable space in the heart and mind of the consumer as their differentiating factor. In the online sphere, the Zappos company dominates the sphere in terms of being caring, providing quality services and engaging in acts of outright awesome.

Maintaining a successful strategy of differentiation requires the creation of a product mix that is not easily replicated by competitors (anticipate and satisfy customer needs) and one which is valued by current and potential customers (identify needs). Think in terms of whether you can provide exclusivity of content as your differentiator (knowledge, entertainment, original art, original materials) or whether you can create a community experience that can't be replicated elsewhere. In order to make the product differentiation approach work in the online environment, planning needs to be conducted to answer the question 'How can you use the unique attributes of the Internet to add value and differentiate your product from your competitors?' Being able to answer the question requires the organization to understand the nature of the Internet, the nature of the product, the needs of the consumer and the nature of the business.

## Cost leadership: driving the dollar further

Money has been the major issue for much of the discussion concerning the Internet. Moving online has often been seen as a cost-cutting measure that ought to result in significant savings for an organization. Organizations focusing on cost leadership develop sustained competitive advantage in the longer term because they maintain greater profit margins (lower margins, higher profit per equal units of volume) than their direct competitors. It is important to remember that the focus of cost-leadership strategies is on reducing costs to the organization. While one outcome of these strategies may be price reductions as a result of passing savings on to the consumers, this should not be an assumed outcome (which is why the strategy isn't called price leadership).

In the absence of direct competitive downward pressures on price, the decision to maintain price levels and operate with increased profit margins can provide the resources to further develop and differentiate the organization and its products through strategic internal investment. For example, if the movement of the organization into online distribution results in cost reduction, a strategic decision is needed as to whether to:

○ take the profits
○ pass on the savings directly to consumers
○ use the money for longer-term investments in new product technology, or
○ cross-subsidize other elements of the product and service mix.

Low cost does not have to mean low quality, given the benefits accrued from experience and economies of scale. A cost-leadership advantage can allow the organization to position itself as a low-cost, value-for-money player in the online marketplace. The nature of the digital product and digital distribution has created an environment where an information product can become an inexhaustible supply which reduces the need for scarcity-based economic pricing (Raymond, 1999). The single greatest cost-cutting measure the Internet provides is the share of voice that can be gained by participation in the social media environments (Chapter 12) and the knowledge that can be gained for greatly reduced costs with online market research (Chapter 4). Consider time expenditure to be the financial cost reduction – time invested in communicating with other people in social media environments can be a greater return on investment than paid advertising broadcast in exactly the same space. Cost transfers from financial investment to time investment can also aid the development of the 1000 True Fans base, where you can acquire, maintain and look after your fanbase through a time-based rather than a cash-based investment in relationship marketing (Chapter 8). For example, if you're selling handcrafted materials on Etsy (www.etsy.com) whilst being available to answer questions about the products on Twitter (http://twitter.com), profiling each new product on a blog, have a fan page on Facebook (www.facebook.com) and an e-mail database of previous purchasers who you occasionally update when you make something similar to what they bought before, you're committing very limited cash investment. However, maintaining these networks is time intensive, and that factor needs to be considered when looking at time cost reduction and time pricing (Chapter 6).

## Niche marketing strategy

To some extent, the Internet was born to be a niche marketing paradise, with its origin as a network of interconnected networks. The notion of a network of networks that can be reached by searching for specific information is nearly the ideal market conditions for niche strategies. The interest-driven nature of the Internet (Chapter 2), coupled with the ease with which the consumer's search behaviour can be rewarded with finding useful information (Chapter 5), makes niche marketing a viable option from a promotions angle. Add the global nature of the Internet with international mailing, global financial brokerage through PayPal and the almost limitless categorization options of eBay as a distribution channel (when the category 'Everything Else' can break into four sub-categories including 'Other', you're dealing with a really diverse marketspace), it's entirely possible to run an esoteric niche and still turn a profit (see Figure 3.1).

Niche marketing has proven to be a popular strategy that allows an organization to develop a specialized marketing mix under a specific brand name to appeal to a narrow target market. The nature of the Internet as an interest-driven medium, coupled with cybercommunities, (Chapter 9) has allowed marketers to develop micromarkets of common interest, irrespective of geographic barriers (Chapter 6). Unlike mail-order catalogues (which have to find the consumers), niche marketing online is aided by the consumers seeking out the niche product through their search behaviours (Chapter 5).

Alternatively, market niches can be serviced through systems such as eBay (www.ebay.com), where specialist goods can be offered by hosted auctions. Traders of specialist goods, such as rare collectibles or memorabilia, can make use of these global, electronic, secondary markets instead of having to establish their own marketplaces (Arunkundram and Sundararajan, 1998). Similarly, the social media networks now allow for searchable communities so that the collectors of the rare, esoteric and downright limited interest can find each other on Facebook, Google Groups, or set up their own

**Figure 3.1** A minus minus
*Source:* http://xkcd.com/325/

niche communities on specific-purpose blogs about the things that they thought only they were interested in collecting (and if there's one truism of the Internet, it's that whatever you thought you were the only person interested in, there's at least one other and they're probably blogging it too).

The process of choosing a generic marketing strategy is similar for companies that operate predominantly online and in the traditional environment. Larger, more established firms are more likely to be able to pursue product differentiation and cost leadership. Smaller, newer firms tend to take a niche market approach due to resource restrictions, although strategic use of the Internet for targeted niche marketing can overcome some of these restrictions. Bloggers starting out are usually advised to focus on mastering the skills necessary for successful blogging in a single niche before expanding out into running multiple, small business enterprise blogs.

## The Ansoff growth matrix

When you're setting up for e-marketing, your first major strategic decision will be to determine your growth strategy from introduction to late growth phase of the product lifecycle. One of the most robust business models for strategic growth decision is the $2 \times 2$ Ansoff matrix, which focuses on the organization's markets and products. It works on the principle of having either an existing product or market or needing a new product or market. When you combine the four options (new/existing market; new/existing consumer), you end up with a $2 \times 2$ matrix (Table 3.1) and a set of developmental guidelines.

This model proposes that organizations can achieve growth based on one of the following four strategies.

### Market penetration

The first quadrant of the matrix produces a strategy that depends on an existing market and an existing product. By definition this is a strategy for the growth or maturity market, and doesn't apply to the introduction phase of the product lifecycle. From an e-business angle, this is the strategy of offering a new tier of paid-for and sponsored accounts in addition to the free services you've been offering since the beta version. A quick browse of the iTunes applications store will demonstrate the sheer volume of applications that are sold with a free limited feature to gain marketshare, trial adoption

Table 3.1 Ansoff matrix

|  | Current Products | New |
| --- | --- | --- |
| Current Markets | Market Penetration | Product Development |
| New Markets | Market Development | Diversification |

*Source*: Reproduced from Watts, G., Cope, J. and Hulme, M. (1998) 'Ansoff's Matrix, pain and gain: Growth strategies and adaptive learning among small food producers', *International Journal of Entrepreneurial Behavior & Research* 4(2):101–11.

and create a user base which can be converted with a market penetration strategy of selling a better version of the product to the existing user. Growth comes from selling more of the same product or upgraded services to the existing target market, so there's a propensity to focus on sales promotion activities such as price discounts and competitions or heavy spending on reminder advertising. If you're dealing with physical goods and services, the movement of the customer and sales online raises an expectation that existing customers can choose to purchase from their usual store or order online (from the retailer's or manufacturer's website).

Market penetration has a solid reputation as a low-risk growth strategy, since you're converting the already convinced rather than trying to build a new market or gain new customers. It also has the advantages of organizational familiarity with the product and market, and the market's familiarity with the organization and product (Chapters 5 and 6). However, an alternative viewpoint is that relying too heavily on penetration increases risk to the company as it is a strategy of 'putting all the eggs in one basket'. Google probably represents the pinnacle achievement of the online market penetration strategies as it gradually expands the number of services that the one Gmail account can provide to the consumer, and the consumer steadily moves across from competitor alternatives to the one integrated Google-based online life.

### Market development

The market development strategy probably has the greatest value when you're moving from the introduction phase and, again, when you're heading into the late growth phase as you try to gain new customers from different markets by expanding the appeal of the current product. This is also where you're looking at the movement from innovator to early adopter and, again, from early adopter to early majority as the same product solution is introduced to a new group of users. From a risk perspective, market development is considered to be a medium-level risk strategy.

This can be as simple as removing the 'beta' from the title of the service or introducing a new version number (Web 2.0), or as complex as renaming the brand with a comprehensive repositioning strategy (Microsoft Services Network to Windows Live). However it's done, the existing product is released to a new target market either by finding alternative uses for the product so that it appeals to a new market segment (Twitter as a personal status message rather than a short chat function) or by moving into a new geographic area (Livejournal in Russian; global shipping to places that aren't Canada or Hawaii). Establishing an online presence to coexist with the offline stores is, by definition, market development because the Internet represents a new region. Similarly, opening your site into a new language is the online equivalent of a new region due to the ubiquity of the Internet (Chapter 2). The growth of Internet use on a global scale and efficient international payment systems have significantly reduced the barriers to entry for smaller firms wishing to enter international markets. The geographically independent nature of the Internet has made market development a viable strategy for firms with specialist products seeking national and international niche markets.

From a blogging perspective, this may be as simple as moving from making extended status updates and notes in Facebook to hosting the same sort of commentary on

WordPress or Blogger. In a similar vein, it may also include the movement from a WordPress or Blogspot site into your own hosted domain, or the introduction of a community structure to replace your blog's comments section (Chapter 9). As long as the core product (the value offer) remains mostly the same and it's a new market of readers, listeners or viewers that's being pursued, you're looking at a market development strategy.

### Product development

The product development strategy is used when you've got an existing market and you've identified or anticipated a need within that market that you can solve with a new product. Like market development, product development is considered a medium-level risk strategy as you already have a good knowledge of one of the key variables for growth, in this case the product. Software services are probably the most obvious in this respect – Adobe started life with a small portfolio of related print design products and now offers a comprehensive suite of creative tools that cover everything from print, video, web and audio production. That said, Google and Microsoft also have a solid stake in the product development camp with their ability to maintain a current audience through an ever-expanding portfolio of products, services and ideas aimed at the same marketshare as their present products occupy. There is a downside to this strategy that Microsoft is most notorious for suffering from in that it has to compete with itself for its own marketshare. Each version of Windows faces more threat from the previous version than it does from Linux or Apple. If you like Windows XP, Windows Vista offered little incentive, and if you didn't like XP, you were probably already headed for OS X or Linux.

Whenever an organization wants to retain its existing customer base and achieve substantial growth by the sale of new products, it can develop products that are either complementary to existing products, such as podcasts from radio shows (www.bbc.co.uk/radio/podcasts), or leverage off the brand name of the product (iPod, iMac, iTunes) or the name of the company itself (GoogleMail, Google Search, GoogleGoogle). Finally, you can also leverage directly from the understanding of the current market by building specific-purpose products to serve the ongoing needs of the organization's identified target market (the sheer volume of Apple-authorized accessories for iPods). Websites can either be developed to on-sell these new products or be the new product or offering that complements the existing product. The online version of the BBC operates as a parallel product to the broadcast versions, whereas the Apple website provides a new array of information products which leverage off the company's existing brand reputation in the portable music and computing industry.

The flexibility of products and the extent to which product development represents a cost-effective growth strategy depends on the nature of the product. Digitized information-based product mixes and online service options are more flexible and far better suited to product development strategies than traditional physical products. Product development is a common feature in the blogging field when the blogger produces supplemental products in the form of group training activities such as Problogger's 31 Day Challenge (www.problogger.net), physical books such as Wil

Wheaton's *Sunken Treasure* (http://wilwheaton.typepad.com), podcasts such as Penny Arcade's downloadable content (http://feeds.penny-arcade.com/padlc) and physical merchandise like that offered by Icanhazcheezburger's Lolmart (www.lolmart.com).

### Diversification

Diversification is also known as going back to square one as you need both new market and new product. In some cases an organization may wish to set up a totally new division which draws on neither its existing customer base nor its product lines because it happens to develop a market offer that just doesn't fit into the current framework. Many technology companies end up spinning off sub-divisions that pursue diversification projects as they chase the development of a product that doesn't fit the parent company line-up.

It's understandable that diversification is usually considered the highest risk of all strategic growth options and experiences the same challenges that you're mostly likely to encounter in starting up a new blog, new company or new idea. As far as strategies go, this is most appropriate where emerging needs in unrelated markets have been identified and are not being met by existing companies. Some of the strangest diversification arrangements can be achieved – notably, Microsoft's sudden and apparently inconsistent foray into the development of hardware with the Xbox 360 (strictly speaking, despite a successful track record in keyboards, mice and joysticks, producing a fully fledged hardware solution was a massive movement from a software company).

## Picking the best option

If you signed up for the blogging services back in the e-introduction (setting up for e-marketing), you've already experienced diversification in that you've developed a new blog which will need a new audience before it's viable. The beauty of the online environment is that diversification is often that simple – sign-in to a site, upload content and start work on developing and acquiring your share of the market.

When approaching e-marketing strategy, you need to consider where your e-marketing will fit into the overall business strategy. Whilst the Internet offers substantial benefits for diversification with the speed and ease of new positioning and market development, it can equally support the implementation of any of the strategies outlined above. Existing target markets can be better served by improving channel selection, and markets can be further developed by making integrated use of the website as both a promotional tool and an online ordering system. Coca-Cola can push sales promotion campaigns through the physical media to encourage people to visit coke.com and can offer Coke fans exclusive access to merchandise options that are only available online (and of interest) to Coke's True Fans. Market penetration can be used to increase sales of the Coke brand to the loyal customer, and product development can be used to sell Coca-Cola-related merchandise and promote regional Coca-Cola sites (www.coke.co.uk) as additional information channels for region-specific promotions. Just about the only thing that Coca-Cola can't deliver over the Internet is the drink itself – and that could be arranged by the appropriate cross-promotional venture with Tesco's (www.tesco.com) or Sainsbury's (www.sainsburys.co.uk) online order systems.

Market development can occur naturally under the existing organizational structure by explicit targeting of the technologically literate with current services – for example, social media sites targeted at the early adopter markets who are looking for a way to demonstrate their social leadership and technical prowess. Given its global nature, creating a website automatically exposes the organization to potential new markets, which pretty much guarantees an organic market development strategy in amongst any deliberate decisions. That said, acknowledging and formalizing the online market development as part of the integrated strategic direction of an organization needs to be carefully managed at all levels to ensure that the right customers are serviced without placing undue strain on the organization. Minimizing market exposure to undesirable markets can be achieved with segmentation strategies, positioning and outright technical solutions that limit other elements of the marketing function such as distribution and payment systems to specific geographic regions, thus making the site irrelevant to all but the desired market (frequently known as 'America' when you're dealing with online shopping carts).

Product development is also readily achieved by moving key functions from offline service delivery into an integrated online transaction (offering financial advice during Internet banking sessions) or by providing additional services (mobile banking via an iPhone application) or information-based products to existing customers (pre-populated loan applications within Internet banking). Exclusive online products can be developed and promoted to existing customers as a product development growth strategy which can be complementary to existing products (new downloadable games for Xbox, PlayStation, Wii or PC), additional services (video rentals from iTunes), or just detailed product information, such as technical manuals for offline products.

Alternatively, new products that leverage the brand and existing product line can be developed, such as Apple's vast array of software accessories for the iPod Touch and iPhone which are available on the iTunes software (Chapter 14). The success of an online product development strategy depends upon the extent to which the existing target market is already involved with the company on or offline. New product development can be as simple as developing merchandise through print-on-demand sales via Zazzle (www.zazzle.com), collecting most popular posts from a blog into a book at Lulu (www.lulu.com) or starting a supplementary podcast. It would not be an appropriate strategy for organizations where the majority of the target market is not computer literate and does not, or cannot, access the Internet.

The beauty of the Porter and Ansoff models lies in their capacity to help marketers to focus and learn from the experiences of others who've been through similar situations in the on and offline world. Simply being involved in a new playing field such as the Internet does not negate the strategies used successfully in other environments, particularly since you're quite likely to be competing for the attention of people who are also offline customers. Embedded within each generic strategy is a guide for the development of specific objectives and, by applying these models, an integrated marketing strategy becomes easier to design.

## Objectives and goals

The purpose of any marketing strategy is to map out the game plan to move the organization from Point A to Point B. Objectives are the marker points that indicate whether you've arrived at Point B or if you're headed the wrong way toward Point C. Without a decent set of objectives, you can't tell whether your marketing strategy has succeeded or failed. The e-marketing element of any business programme must have its own specific goals and objectives that are integrated into the organization's broader business strategy. Focusing on the bigger picture while developing the technical specifics of a campaign will ensure that you actually support the organization's goals, which is how you 'add value' to the business.

### Setting objectives

The most obvious question for e-marketers then becomes 'What are appropriate objectives for companies to pursue in relation to their online activities?', with the most obvious answer being 'It depends'. If you're going to do marketing, and do marketing properly, you can't rely on off-the-shelf solutions or ready-mix goals and objectives. From developing your own objectives for what you want to achieve with a blog to setting objectives for online marketing within a major corporation, you have to custom make each objective based on the available resources, desired outcomes and current market conditions. Thankfully, it's not all bad news on this front – suitable marketing objectives are much like good recipes; there are common elements that can be used to create the customized solution you need for your own purposes. The following section explores how to put together a good set of objectives within the recommended parameters that have been tried, tested and refined over time in online and offline business.

### *The SMART mantra*

One of the favoured approaches to setting objectives is the time-honoured business mnemonic that 'All objectives should be SMART', where SMART breaks down into the five points of specific, measurable, actionable, realistic and timetabled.

*Specific* means that any objective needs to state clearly what you're trying to achieve. Spell it out in detail and be as precise as possible so that you can design and develop an implementation plan that matches the strategic objective. The more specific the objective, the easier the measurement (Chapter 10), and the easier life becomes in the tactical planning phase (Chapter 4). A little hard work here and now will save considerable time further down the road.

*Measurable* means that if you can't measure it, you can never know if you've achieved it. Every objective needs to be quantified in some way so you can at least tick it off the to-do list, and so the tracking (Chapter 10) becomes a question of assessing actual results against a measure of what achieving the objective should look like in practice. The measurable element of the objectives should tie back in with the information available or collected through market research and the marketing information system.

*Actionable* means breaking out the verbs for the objective since it needs to indicate how the outcome is going to happen as much as measurable is needed to indicate what is going to happen. Action-orientated objectives are a must so they can guide the tactics and give you some guidance for the implementation (Chapter 10).

*Realistic* means keeping the corporate ego in check and the objective within the bounds of reality. Any decent objective walks the fine line between the optimistic, ideal outcome and the much less fun, reasonable and realistic reality. By emphasizing the specific and focusing on actions that can be measured, it helps keep the reality check from bouncing. The key is to ensure that the objective can be achieved with the actions stated, resources available and time allocated. Unrealistic goals can lead to perceptions of failure, even when astonishing success has occurred in reality. If you've asked yourself to go from blogging unknown to international superstar, you'll be disappointed with national notoriety (which, in itself, is a huge achievement).

*Timetabled* is the 'when' of the previous 'where, how and what' statements. If you can't say when you want the other parts of the SMART metric achieved, it's possible those elements are missing the grounding in reality that's vital for good strategy. Timetabling the objectives also encourages honesty in the process, particularly if you've brought a calendar and calculator to the timetabling discussion. Set the due date, calculate the number of work hours required and then do the maths to see if you've left any time for sleep in the agenda.

## Packet mix objectives

Although every objective that is set in business is contextual and needs to be related to the precise circumstance the firm finds itself in, there's a broader set of generic categories of objectives that can be used as a starting point for working out what you want to achieve from being online. For the purpose of this book, several of these packet mix objectives will be useful for a blog, and others won't remotely relate to blogging in the slightest. Your challenge is to determine which of the generic categories works for you and your desired e-marketing outcomes, and which don't fit the game plan. It's also worth noting that whilst these six objectives are presented from the business perspective of what to do with the Internet, they're also revisited in Chapter 5 in terms of how consumers use the Internet. After all, the whole point of e-marketing either revolves around the creation, communication, delivery and exchange of offerings of value to the market or it's about anticipating, identifying and satisfying customer needs. Either way, the customer in the target market needs to be the front and centre priority in order to really make the Internet useful in marketing.

There are six generic objective categories.

*Cost-oriented objectives*, from an organizational perspective, are the bottom line. An organization may decide to move some or all of its activities online because there are genuine savings to be had when offline services can be reduced or replaced by a self-service website (O'Connor and O'Keefe, 1997). However, those savings only happen if you retain your customers. If the customers want offline delivery and will quit buying from you if you deny them the offline sales channel, there's no saving to be had in alienating the market. Cost cutting in the organizational sense needs to be presented

overall game plan which includes profit from revenue being greater than expenditure. Twitter may cut financial costs dramatically on the surface until you factor in employee time costs, and as such, shouldn't be used as a profit centre. In reverse, you may find the advertising expenditure on banners, billboards and television commercials could be sunk into three interns and a community manager for far greater financial return as they respond to product queries in real time.

As a note of caution, it's important to remember that the advertising industry has known for decades that awareness and liking of a product are no substitute for purchase decision. People may well love the brand and buy elsewhere because the distribution strategy let them down, or they're based outside the geographic area or the price was wrong. Same goes for free users of a website – they may never upgrade to the paid account because the benefit they're receiving is worth the price they're currently paying, and nothing more. At the same time you may not even want to consider direct financial return from the online activity because you're working towards a different goal – market analysis based on the real-time observation of millions of short messages across a giant communications network could create a self-sufficient profit centre that allows you to give away the communication channel for free.

However, the value of any communications medium is in the impact it has on the primary product. If the website plays a far greater role in developing and maintaining relationships and disseminating information than it does in generating direct online sales, it's still paying its way in the greater scheme of the organization's objectives. Some of the objectives listed are investments in long-term gains rather than potential channels for short-term profit, much in the same way advertising and promotion can be an investment in the long-term development of a brand identity.

The value of the website and its perceived success should be determined in the light of these broader functions which are likely to lead indirectly to increased sales. Some websites will serve the purpose of being online versions of window-shopping, where potential consumers browse online, compare prices, styles and product information, and then go to a traditional outlet to actually purchase the product. By doing this consumers believe that they are combining the best of both worlds. Cross-subsidization of online activities with more traditional elements of the organization is both appropriate and, in many cases, essential. Evaluation of the website's success can be undertaken effectively only if it is considered within the context of its role in the overall strategy of the organization.

## Segmentation

Segmentation is the division of a heterogeneous marketplace into smaller, more homogenous groups that can be the focus of specific marketing messages, branding and product customization. It is a complex process combining business strategy, existing positioning strategies and a good dose of current market research. It's a strategic decision that plays a serious role in shaping the whole of the marketing mix from product through to price and distribution mechanisms, as well as dictating a lot of the promotional strategy. Putting a good solid segmentation strategy in place at the start of the process reduces the risk of investing time, effort and other resources in the wrong markets.

Online market segmentation can be focused at the macro level of the Internet population, or on the micro-level development of target markets for individual websites. The value of large-scale segmentation of user types at the macro level is that it studies the Internet as a population group. Studies such as iVALS ( (www.strategicbusinessinsights. com) have proven useful for the macro-level studies of the Internet and the development and diffusion of the Internet. However, for individual companies, market segmentation is best conducted with the view to tailoring their site to their market, rather than an iVALS or equivalent user category. Sarabia (1996) outlined the four functional tasks for any segmentation strategy as being:

o describe the audience
o identify the match between market and marketer
o select the segment
o tailor to the market.

## Description

Segmentation starts off by describing the vital statistics of the segment in terms of information that can be used for clustering people into homogeneous groups and which can also be used to identify the user again later when it's time to tailor the firm's offerings to their needs. Sen et al. (1998) set out a categorization approach for identifying specific segments in an online marketplace based on usage, experience, familiarity, audience match and technical demography:

o *Usage patterns* relate to any and all online behaviours (Chapter 5), including what's being used (Twitter, Web, games, Facebook, bittorrent, etc.), duration of its use compared with average users (light, medium, heavy, excessive) and frequency of use (hourly, daily, weekly, monthly).
o *Internet experience* is the length of time the user has been online, their depth of experience with various bits of the Internet and how skilled they feel they are with the relevant technology you're planning on making them use. Be cautious with experience as a segment – just because someone is good with instant messaging doesn't mean they'll automatically be able to cope with a blog, virtual world or even Twitter. Expertise is category specific to what you've learnt to use – although the longer you've been online, the more likely you are to have generic transferable skills and the confidence to trial a new technology that looks roughly similar to something you already know (Chapter 5).
o *Familiarity* is the level of knowledge with the brand, product, service and the Internet offering (which is logically related to experience but still a separate item). Familiarity is connected to other marketing concepts such as unprompted recall, product category knowledge and the ability to mean it when you say 'I've heard of that'.
o *Audience match* is the relative usefulness of your online offering for the end user. It's a segmentation variable that's basic, working on the assumptions you have about

the same media platform. For everything you're firmly against, there's probably a site and community dedicated to supporting it (and, thankfully, vice versa if you're looking for allies).

*Economic environment* scans combine the bigger economic picture (in light of the global financial crisis, it's hard to describe it in polite terms), smaller economy issues of market segments and available disposable income, and, as you'll see in Chapter 6, the new surge of time and energy budgetary limits as people try to juggle different aspects of their work, leisure and family commitments. Time economy issues give rise to an incredible array of time-management blogs and products as people convert their personal economy scans into saleable and readable content.

*Technological environment* scanning is the most fun if you've got the slightest geek tendency in you (or a strong innovative streak). Tech blogs are a dime a dozen, with the top-end bloggers receiving good incomes, press releases and personal invitations to product launches. At the bottom end, there's a lot of competition and a lot of people rehashing the same content. Still, the technology scans are one of the easier areas to conduct, since 'tech' is usually a recognized trend category at the major search sites (which you'll examine in a few paragraphs). A subtle trend rising in the technology community (coupled with the economy) is the notion of retaining last year's model (http://lastyearsmodel.org) whilst still being either innovation prone or supportive of new technology development.

*Physical environments* are the 'away from keyboard' world around you. Physical scans link to distribution logistics, physical shipping and anything connected to the movement, ownership or storage of atom-based objects (such as this book). That said, it's well worth also considering replicating the style of physical environment scan for key virtual environments of interest (Chapters 1 and 9) to assess stability of servers, uptime for key services and longevity of a virtual world (particularly when the owner announces server merges. That's always a bad sign.)

### Input note

Scan the environment for information useful to your objectives. Randomly learning things about the world around you is fun but rarely connected to gathering research for the marketing plan.

### Throughput note

This section links to trend data, SWOT analysis and market segmentation.

### Output note

At this stage, make a note of possible conflicts, opportunities or areas for further investigation which look useful.

## Scanning the environment with trend data

One of the key methods for scanning the environment involves observing existing trend data to look for recognizable patterns or business cycles that can be (relatively) safely predicted from the methods for looking over existing trends to see which ones present the best set of opportunities to pursue. An-old school method is used by Faith Popcorn (1991) to perform 'trend scanning', a technique for looking at a range of business and non-business information sources to identify potential movements in the marketplace before they're identified by your competitors, or even by the market itself (Durgee et al., 1998). Since the Internet produces a very large volume of content that can be aggregated into trending data, life has become significantly easier for the future predictor. For your purposes, there are a few different trend aggregator sites to trial:

○ *Twitter.* Your personal Twitter stream has an aggregated 'Trending Topics' semi-live dataset published on the side bar which tracks rising trends and threads (http://twitter.com/timeline/home). Remember, Twitter is the live voice of a few million early adopters – it's biased, noisy and profitable to pay attention if you plan to address that sort of market segment.

○ *Yahoo! Buzz* (http://buzz.yahoo.com). Sign in with your Yahoo!ID (which you acquired to sign up to Flickr back in the Introduction) and not only can you monitor the breaking trends in news, you can also influence the outcome by 'Buzzing up' or 'Buzzing down' stories on the main page. You can also see the one-hour delay search results from the Yahoo!Search engine, and search Buzz in subcategories off this page.

---

### Plan input

What market monitoring will you use for your site?

---

○ *Google Trends* (www.google.com/trends) and *Google Insights* (www.google.com/insights/search). Both sites provide semi-public access to the popular search terms running across the Google servers.

○ *BlogPulse* (www.blogpulse.com). Run by research heavyweights Nielsen Online (www.nielsen-online.com), BlogPulse provides an aggregated view of popular searches on YouTube, trending posts across more than 100 million blogs and highly linked news stories.

○ *Technorati* (www.technorati.com) and *Digg* (http://digg.com). These social aggregator services have trend analysis and trend reports on popular topics, posts, links, tags and keywords. As with Twitter, there are overt biases towards certain topic areas that make these tools vary in value depending on your target market.

○ *Delicious* (www.delicious.com). This social bookmarking site (see Introduction) displays the most popular bookmarked sites and keyword tags for various recent time periods.

○ *iTunes, Steam and XboxLiveArcade.* Most of the software, used as shop-front systems (Chapter 11), will have some form of popularity ranking mechanism that's used to encourage people to buy the 'hottest' titles. It's one part social compliance mechanism (Chapter 5) and one part market data report (this chapter).

Consequently, it's entirely possible to maintain and monitor trending data on the Internet through the observation of results from several of these sites. Your challenge is to convert the trending data (popular posts, hashtags and bookmarks) into useful information which can be used to assess the general state of the Internet as part of the external analysis.

### Inputs

Search keywords related to your product, brand, blog content or rivals. Observe top trends over a period of time to look for patterns.

### Throughput

This section connects to market research, and these market-monitoring tools can be reused repeatedly with increasingly focused searches to set up information for market segmentation, metrics and other sections of the plan.

### Outputs

Note down key trends of interest. If you're working with an existing brand, see how it's already represented in the live marketspace. Write up a short list of areas for future research to set up the market research.

## Online market research

Market research is the lifeblood of informed marketing and sits squarely within 'identify' in the CIM (2005) definition. Without the support of reliable market data and carefully selected competitor and customer information, marketing becomes a patchwork of guesses, hunches and product failures. Market research is an incredibly active aspect of e-marketing – every activity performed online can be turned towards market research activity. Checking out the latest blog post from an ally or competitor blog is market research. Monitoring or engaging in conversations on Twitter, Facebook, Plurk or anywhere else about what you do is also research. Even something as seemingly mundane as a Google search can bring back a wealth of marketing information before you've even left the first page of results for one of the recommended links. It's one of the most under-recognized, underrated and totally amazing aspects of engaging in e-marketing – the constant flow of useable and useful research information. This section of the book will open up an array of new options for discovering the marketing data in the world at your keyboard.

**Plan input**

What market research will you do for your site?

That said, using the Internet for marketing-related research involves both the adoption and adaptation of traditional market research techniques. Access to global secondary data sources means that all marketers, not only those who are attempting to develop an online presence, can change the quality, quantity and type of resources investigated for marketing purposes. The Internet also provides a wide range of information regarding competitor and consumer intelligence. From a practical perspective, access to online annual reports, consolidated industry reports and trend analyses, either free or on a pay-per-use basis, means that the marketers of today have better and more up-to-date information on the competitive environment than ever before. With so many options to choose from in the e-marketing marketspace, you need the old, classic approaches to provide a good, solid framework to help you avoid information overload (aka drowning by numbers).

This section puts together some of the old and some of the new of market research. It outlines a couple of principles of online market research, including a caveat on the weakness of the Internet for data collection. Emphasis is placed on exploring the different types of market research that can be used online, and how and where these different mechanisms are most appropriately applied. This includes an examination of the process and methods of conducting online market research, including environment scanning, and the collection of market intelligence data using the Internet. The chapter gives an overview of the value of online market segmentation, both at the population level and the site-specific level, and reviews a method of conducting segmentation. Finally, issues concerning privacy, ethics and anonymity are raised because of the prevalence of online market research.

### The caveat: the Internet is not a perfect marketplace of data

There are limits and restrictions to the value of primary data collected through the Internet. Due to the limited and skewed sample that the demographics of Internet users present (not everyone is online, not everyone online is on Twitter, etc.) you have to use a modicum of caution when attempting to generalize beyond your target sample when conducting Internet-based research. That said, if you're building something for the market you're studying, don't get hung up on generalizability if you can turn a profit from the members of the unrepresentative, skewed cohort.

Even with the widespread adoption of the Internet, the online population is still skewed towards innovator, early adopter and cusp early majority markets (Chapter 5), which means they're mostly innovative, intelligent and financially secure people. Early

information you can create from the more basic end of the statistical analysis continuum. Don't forget to make use of Google during the interpretation process – if you're stuck on SPSS, Excel or any other tool, search for analysis advice, FAQs and help documents (more than enough universities keep this information in the public domain).

## 7. Convert the results and data into information

If you've done market research for yourself, you may be tempted to skip this section since you'll feel you know the answer, so it's time to get on with the rest of the process. Documenting the answer to your research question, along with the steps you took (sites used, keywords used and other useful methods noted), is the easiest path to follow at this point. Fresh from the research process, you'll be able to write up the report fairly quickly and avoid the need of having to recall what you did, how you did it and what you found out when you need to repeat the process at the next marketing planning phase (the authors assume that you'll have seen, read and done a lot more interesting things that'll be competing for the top of your mind ahead of marketing research information). Writing up your notes, results and outcomes will also help when you begin writing up the marketing plan and will serve as a reference for product development (Chapter 6), marketing metric analysis (Chapter 10) and possibly even provide content for a blog post, PDF white paper or saleable e-book, if you're really good.

## 8. Follow up the research

Market research is a snapshot of a moving target. By the time you've finished the write-up, things might have changed (if they have significantly, start again, and then write up the before–after for a blog post). It's tempting to disregard market research in a dynamic environment like the Internet, since the situation can change rapidly. That said, market research snapshots help you piece together a rough map of the terrain, and, if the follow-up research indicates limited changes, can guide you towards the more stable areas (or away from them, depending on your preference). Without the snapshots, benchmarks and baselines, you'll not be able to appreciate where the stability lies in your business environment. Some recommended follow-up techniques include:

○ automated scans through saved Google searches
○ monitor interesting hashtags through Hashtags.org
○ e-mailed weekly data reports where available from your own site server stats
○ setting up a Google Calendar reminder to perform manual monthly (quarterly, annually, etc.) research updates.

Some of the follow-up research techniques also draw on the metrics set up to review your progress (Chapter 13). Once again, the cyclical nature of marketing is a feature – market research undertaken at the start of the process leads into the marketing activity which, when benchmarked in metrics, can lead back into the market research information gathering.

## Automated Google research

Saved searches, RSS feeds and other neat tricks – Google's search engine is an inordinately powerful device with a range of bonus features tucked away on the side under 'Advanced Search' (Figure 4.2).

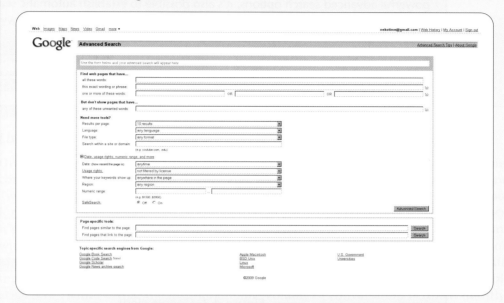

**Figure 4.2** Advanced search
*Source*: http://www.google.com.au/advanced_search

Several books have been dedicated to exploring the nuances of the advanced search, and as such, we'll just highlight a couple of tactical marketing uses:

○ File-type lists are useful in two directions: First, you can specify the type of document and so limit the type of file returned in the search. Try looking for 'Marketing budget' using the Microsoft Excel file type (Search term 'marketing budget filetype:xls') to see what can be uncovered from publicly available marketing budgets. Secondly, file type can be combined with site-specific searches if you're looking for a PDF, PPT or other file you know you've seen on a site but just can't find again.
○ Site-specific searches: 'Search within a site or domain' is a great way to find specific information within a website (and the larger your own site becomes, the more likely you are to head to this search before manually looking over the content). Try searching the CIM's site (www.cim.co.uk/home.aspx) for the definition of marketing (search term: 'definition site:http://www.cim.co.uk').
○ Under the 'Date, usage rights, numeric range, and more' are the 'Page specific' tools which offer competitor scans through 'Find pages similar to the page', and a market ally scan with the 'Find pages that link to the page'. Again, try this out with the

**Table 4.1** Segmentation matrix

|  | No Long term | Long Term |
|---|---|---|
| No short-term | Quad 1: Dead Weight | Quad 3: Slow Fuse |
| Short-term return | Quad 2: Quick Burn | Quad 4: Gold Mine |

Quadrant 1 Dead Weight: those segments which have no short-term or medium-to-long-term value to the company. Discard, abandon and avoid as they'll be a waste of time, effort and resources (trying to sell iPhone applications to Blackberry users).

Quadrant 2 Quick Burn: covers any segment where there's short-term profit and no realistic chance of medium-to-long-term sustainability (innovators might be the category du jour here – first to buy, first to leave). Segments such as these may reap initial dividends but will eventually disappear, leaving the company with a product and no market. These are good secondary markets to consider for cross funding the longer-term Quadrant 3 or for quickly recovering investment costs whilst searching for Quadrant 4. Alternatively, this might be the market that's easiest to satisfy – with the downside that once happy with their products, they don't upgrade for each and every new edition (#lastyear).

Quadrant 3 Slow Fuse: those segments with no short-term value but with medium-to-long-term value. This is probably the early majority from the innovation adoption curve in Chapter 5. Chasing Quadrant 3 requires large cash stockpiles or cross-funding from profitable products until the marketshare is attained and the segment becomes valuable. Consequently, this is rarely a primary market segment.

Quadrant 4 Gold Mine: those segments that have short- and long-term value and form the core customers upon which the majority of the company's strategies, website designs and IMC messaging should be based. (See also the 1000 True Fans model from Chapter 3.) For example, Apple would find people with multiple iPods to be its Quadrant 4 customers for iTunes, and Quadrant 3 customers for future iPods.

### Round 3: Picking the target

Once you've established a working list of possible market segments consisting of possible customers who should be relatively homogenous in their reactions to your work and relatively distinctive (so as to qualify as a separate set of target markets), the final choice comes down to you based on a few factors:

o Where do you have a strong match between what you're offering and what the market wants?

> **Plan input**
>
> Why will this value offering be suited to your audience?

○ Are you going for short-term or short-lifespan projects? Alternatively, are you aiming for the longer term and do you have the resources to support the pursuit of eventual profit?

○ Which market fits the organizational goals?

○ What can you make of the consumer behaviour information in Chapter 5 to help out with the decision?

---

**Plan input**

Who is the main audience you want to address?

---

## Strategy objectives to planned targets

Once you've picked a set of target segments, the next step is acting on the information by converting those action-orientated objectives you set in Chapter 3 into some tactical guidelines for the rest of the operations. At this point, revisit SMART guidelines to establish specific, measurable, achievable, realistic and timetabled micro-level goals, such as launch dates for the site, an editorial calendar for content provision to the site and a set of design guides for how to present the site to the world through branding (Chapter 7) and the product offerings from the site (Chapter 6). You'll feed these short-term goals into other parts of the planning process – specifically, the 'How do we get there?', which requires you to spell out the where, how, when and what of actually delivering products to the marketspace.

---

**Plan input**

What challenges are likely to prevent you from meeting these objectives?

---

**Plan input**

What opportunities exist to make the objective easier to achieve?

---

## Positioning strategy

The last 'Where do we want to go?' question to ask yourself involves setting the positioning strategy. As discussed in Chapter 3, positioning and the positioning strategy are closely related, but not identical. At this point, you're setting your corporate-side ambition (positioning strategy) for where the site should site and which sites should be considered allies, equals or rivals. The actual position the site holds in the minds of the consumer is up to the consumer's interpretation of the branding (Chapter 7), product offerings (Chapter 6), social media activities (Chapter 12) and community perceptions of the site (Chapter 9). There are seven (and a spare) generic positioning strategies to consider setting as the organizational goal. These were adapted from Belch and Belch (2004) by Dann and Dann (2004) for use online, and cover the following options:

1. *Attributes and benefits positioning*, which is where you position based on features (140-character messages, unlimited uploads, pleasing taste), that you think are important to your target market (Chapter 6). Positioning through this approach is an attribute-based categorization, describing the feature of a site such as LinkedIn (www.linkedin.com) as a network for socializing which would position it against Facebook (www.facebook.com) and Orkut (www.orkut.com). Alternatively, you can try positioning based on the benefits – such as positioning Twitter (www.twitter.com) alongside 'communicate with friends', which would position it against e-mail, Facebook messages and SMS. Or, you could position it as a microblog, which would position it below the macroblogs of WordPress and Blogger, and alongside FriendFeed (www.friendfeed.com), Plurk (www.plurk.com) and Tumblr (www.tumblr.com).

2. *Use or application positioning,* which is what the end user actually does with the product (as opposed to the components of the product, which is attribute positioning). This is the hardest strategic position to declare (Chapter 5) and, notably, it mirrors the attributes and benefits position. Application-based positioning is developed according to how the market is actually the service rather than how you think it should/would be used (benefits). Online retail stores can be associated with the weekly shopping tasks (www.sainsburys.co.uk), or a digital product can be associated with an event (www.thefa.com) or season (www.christmastimeuk.com).

3. *Product user positioning* is where you line up the site by who is using it rather than how it's being used, although the two are logically connected. It depends a bit on consumer behaviour theory and market segmentation (Chapter 5). Slashdot (www.slashdot.org) has the most blatant positioning strategy in the corporate tag line 'Slashdot: news for nerds', which clearly identifies its position among information sites by showing its relevance to a select Internet psychographic segment.

4. *Price–quality positioning* involves using prices associated with the goods and services to influence the perception of the site. This approach is a little more complicated online than in traditional environments due to the large array of services that are available for free, and 'free' isn't held in such low regard as it is offline. Price–quality positioning often relates to the charges for the premium products or extended service features. Positioning by price also requires a clear gap between the paid service and the free accounts so that higher price gives a sense of quality and value to the purchaser and the lower-end products don't compete against their premium-level companions (Chapter 6).

5. *Cultural symbol positioning* is the most complex in theory yet reasonably easy in practice as you align your position in the market through images, icons and wording at the domain name level with a regional domain (.uk), use a thistle on a Scottish site

or add the odd reference to Sainsbury's, Tesco and Manchester United in a British e-marketing text. Cultural symbols can also be used to identify your affiliation with Internet cultural clusters (Chapter 9).

6. *Product class positioning* is a sort of corporate word association game where you align yourself against competing offers from products and/or services outside of the product category. For example, airlines compete against trains, buses and other airlines for domestic travel. Online radio stations (www.last.fm) compete against other online music services such as iTunes, the user's MP3 collection and YouTube music videos (uk.youtube.com) plus the usual alternative forms of on and offline entertainment. This would be where you position a website against an iPhone app or a print magazine, or web-based versus virtual world versus standalone software (Chapter 11).

7. *Competitor positioning* focuses on a specific competitor and outlines the similarities or differences between you and them. This is subverted slightly where competitor positioning is used in blogging to create communities of blogs which are both allies (share a common theme, cause or movement) and competitors for attention, advertising and sponsorship (Chapter 9). For the most part, competitor positioning online serves the consumer more than it helps the marketer – although there are good business reasons for alliances of mutual convenience. This is one area where you can go to Google's 'related' site search to see who the search engine lines you up with – even if it feels a bit like corporate speed dating.

## Plan input

What sites are your direct competitors?

8. *Repositioning,* which isn't actually a specific positioning strategy in as much as it's an attempt to move from where the market currently sees you (or where Google related links you) by using one of the other seven options and an orchestrated dose of branding (Chapter 7).

Once you've picked a desired positioning strategy, the next step is to move through the respective tactical implementation elements of the marketing mix to act on the creation, communication, delivery and exchange with your desired market.

## Step 3: How do we get there?

Step 3 is where the fun really kicks in. Whilst the last two steps have been about lofty visions translated into less lofty and more practical goals, this is where we start to get our hands dirty and make plans for things to happen (Figure 4.4). It's best to consider this as the precursor to Chapters 6, 7 and 8 since the objectives put into place here are converted using the techniques and ideas covered in those three chapters.

Figure 4.4 Marketing interview
*Source:* http://xkcd.com/125/

## Marketing objectives (the corporate GPS)

Converting the e-marketing strategy into small, micro-level goals for use in setting tactics relies on a combination of interpretation of the strategic directions in conjunction with an established set of generic marketing objectives. Referring back to the broad categories of strategic objectives outlined in Chapter 3, these are able to be contextualized as follows:

○ *Cost-oriented objectives*, which focus on using the Internet to reduce costs and increase savings for the firm by shifting away from physical media, physical world distribution or any other use of online technology to save a few dollars. These objectives are financial in nature and come with a timeline, expected budget cut and the need to ensure that the financial costs from column A (physical world spending) are not overshadowed by the per-hourly costs that come with the increased time commitments when shifting the e-marketing approaches. There's no point saving £150K on print costs if you have to hire a web development team at £200K a year to achieve the same communications outcomes.

○ *Sales-oriented objectives*, where the Internet turns into a sales vehicle that facilitates indirect purchases through affiliates, offline sales or some other mechanism and/or the site handles direct sales. Sales objectives are measured in terms of increased volume, increased value per sale or revenue targets over a set time frame. Direct online sales objectives will also shape the type and nature of the product offering produced by the organization (Chapter 6).

○ *Behavioural change objectives,* which are where the site's purpose involves altering the way in which people behave in either their online or offline lives. It's probably best to consider most of the social media sites as having at least one set of behavioural change objectives that involve moving offline conversations, photo sharing and quick chats with mates or family, into an online framework. These types of objectives can be set in terms of increasing the number of current users, decreasing use of offline services or improving the proportion of online transactions from specific users within a set time frame (Chapter 5).

o *Information dissemination objectives,* which use the Web as a channel for distributing information, ideas or knowledge without necessarily offering something for sale or requiring behavioural change from the users. Blogging has an inherent bias towards information-based objectives as do government sites that host forms, information, FAQs and/or policy statements. Given that the aim of such sites is to maximize exposure to ideas and information, success indicators would include traffic statistics, interlinking with other sites, commentary in social media and the general dissemination of the site's content as broadly as possible. A typical objective of a site based on information dissemination would be 'to increase the number of mentions of the site on Twitter (twitter.com) by 20 per cent over the next three months' or 'to double the number of hits to the second level of information pages of the site within 12 months'.

o *Promotional objectives,* which is where the website is integrated into the promotional mix as an advertising tool. Many websites currently in existence are based around promotional or communication objectives (O'Connor and O'Keefe, 1997). There is some degree of overlap between information orientation and promotional sites although the promotional sites tend towards the persuasive rather than the straight-out informative. The effectiveness of a promotions-based website should be measured by standard promotional objectives, such as recognition and recall, satisfaction or sales inquiries generated. Sample objectives could include 'to achieve a response rate of 25 per cent within one week of mailing out a new product release to our existing e-mail list' or 'to achieve a recognition rate for the URL of 30 per cent among the target market within six months of launching the site'.

o *Conversation objectives,* which is where the organization sets up shop on various social media platforms in order to engage the broader online community and its actual (and potential) customers. Communication objectives are a new aspect of the e-marketing agenda which is where you recognize that your role online involves listening as much as speaking and where engagement in conversation with the members of the community is a serious business priority.

## The marketing toolkit

This section of the planning process is where you break out the toolkits and start applying the whole gamut of your marketing skills to figure out how to develop the product (Chapter 6), what promotional and branding methods to use (Chapter 7) and how to combine these factors to create ongoing and long-lasting customer relationships (Chapter 8). It's also where you need to consider a whole array of technical issues, such as the delivery platform for whatever you're planning on offering to the market – be it web-based, mobile (Chapter 13) or an off-web e-marketing production (Chapter 14). As mentioned in Chapter 1, this is where you need to identify your marketplace and marketspace, and prepare your tactics accordingly. This includes determining the investment in the key resources of time, effort, energy, brand reputation and cash (Chapter 1).

---

### Plan input

What steps will you take to create the content required for your site?

---

There are four different marketing mix toolkits that can be considered at this point in the planning process: the 4Ps; 7Ps; SIVA and the AMA (2007) definition mix. Each of these approaches is based around the central platform of modifying company-side controllable variables in order to meet the needs of the marketplace (even if SIVA is customer-sided, you don't get to adjust the settings on external factors such as customers as easily as you can on company-internal matters). The four mixes are as follows:

- 4Ps – price, product, promotion, place
- 7Ps – price, product, promotion, place, people, physical evidence, process
- SIVA – solution, information, value and access
- AMA (2007) – create, communicate, deliver and exchange.

### Four and seven P models

There are two versions of the McCarthy (1960) marketing mix: the classic 4P version and the extended 'services' 7P variant (as a side note, McCarthy proposed 30Ps as the first model – there has been some consolidation over the last five decades). The *Classic Edition* (4Ps) consists of 'price, product, promotion and place (distribution)' as the central checklist for assessing whether or not you've covered all the bases needed to address the market (Chapter 2).

The *Services Marketing Extended Edition* (7Ps) added three items to the 4P framework (or removed just 23 objects from the 30P framework) with the inclusion of people, physical evidence and process. *People* refers to any person who interacts with the customers, predominantly the staff (but sometimes the customers themselves). This is increasingly important when social media (Chapter 10), community (Chapter 9) and relationship marketing (Chapter 8) are key elements for success. *Physical evidence* was originally used to exclusively describe real-world objects that represented the organization, its brand and product offering. Given the development of the Internet, 'physical' evidence can also include the virtual evidence of the website, social media presence (Chapter 10) and any virtual-world presence of the brand (Chapter 11). Finally, *process* relates to the way in which the products are delivered and the interaction the organization has with the customer. It can include discussions in the comments on a blog, interactions in social media, e-mail and automated self-service systems such as web-based ordering or

SMS-based contact. The Chartered Institute of Marketing endorses the 7P model as part of its professional training and development activity for commercial marketers.

### SIVA: a customer-sided marketing mix

The customer-sided 'SIVA' model was developed by Dev and Schultz (2005a and 2005b) as an alternate form of the organization-focused marketing mix. SIVA (solution, information, value and accessibility) examines how the customer views your product offering. *Solution* represents the capacity of the offer to meet the consumer's needs, solve a problem or otherwise be useful. *Information* represents the sum total of knowledge the customer has about the product offer and whether it's come from external sources (web searches, word of mouth, marketing communications) or drawn from internal sources (memory, experience). *Value* is the cost to the consumer in terms of money, time, effort, opportunity forgone and any other factor that the consumer feels is a relevant tradeoff necessary for buying the product. *Accessibility* is the final element which handles both the consumers' capacity to get to the product to buy it (shipping, logistics, channels) and their ability to actually use the product to provide the solution based on the performance requirements of the product (complexity, time investment, additional resources). SIVA is a useful benchmark to use in conjunction with the 4P, 7P and AMA marketing mix models to assess whether the consumer-side elements have been adequately addressed by the mix.

---

### Plan input

How does this content address the needs of your audience?

---

### Marketing as an activity mix: AMA 2007

The American Marketing Association introduced a potential contender for a new marketing mix in the form of the processes for generating the 'offerings that have value' in its most recent definition of marketing. Creation, communication, delivery and exchange makes for a useful marketing mix mantra that can assess whether you're acting in a manner that's likely to result in something valuable for your target audience (Dann and Dann, 2007). *Creation of value* asks if you're doing something new, different or enhancing value. For example, simply re-blogging existing information isn't adding value, whereas repackaging information in a format that's more accessible for the customer, easier to read or comes with editorial observation can potentially be the creation of value.

*Communication of value* is where you are engaged with the audience, and where the conversation provides something useful to the end user up to and including (hopefully) the insight that owning your product will bring benefits to their life. The key point is that communication is a bi-directional process that makes use of the one-to-many-to-one model (Chapter 2) and the conversational quality of the social media environment

(Chapter 12) to enable companies to listen to the market as much as they've previously talked at it.

*Delivery of value* brings forth the supply lines, distribution issues and the capacity of the product to actually meet the needs of the consumer. Whilst the creation element builds the framework (blog, service, idea, physical goods), delivery ensures that when the consumer uses the framework for customer co-creation, they can achieve their personal goals/outcomes. (Short version: creation and communication make a promise. Delivery turns the promise into a reality.)

*Exchange of value* is the mutual gain experienced by the consumer (sense that the product did the job) and the marketing organization (Money! Profit! Survival!). Central to this part of the mix is the appreciation of what value you'll get back from the trade (cash, profit, loyalty, subscribers, whuffie, ego, karma) in return for creating and delivering something valuable to the consumer (who feels what they had to forgo for this offer was worth it).

### All for one, one for all: using the whole of the marketing mix

The greatest strength of all the different marketing mixes comes from the multiplier effects built into the model when you apply all four core elements at the same time. Consider a well-designed product sold at the right place, for the price you can afford and backed up by the right messages to introduce it to the market. How much better will that perform than a heavily promoted product that lacks a sensible pricing structure or good set of supply lines? Probably the biggest single trap in marketing is the sense that one of the four elements of the mix (ahem, promotion/communication/information) should be considered more important simply because it's the most visible. Promotion's role as the high-profile element of the mix just means it's doing the job it's designed to do – get your attention and keep it focused on the product. At the same time, there's more than enough adverts for products you'd really like but just can't justify the costs (particularly in the post-global financial crisis). Without a good grasp of price, the best product will be a footnote in Wikipedia, the greatest campaign will continue as a set of case studies on YouTube and your distribution channel will become specialist traders on eBay.

---

### Output note

At this stage, ensure that you've directly and overtly addressed all elements of your chosen marketing mix. Line up the gaps in your write-up of your planning notes to ensure you cover each element and that each aspect of the mix is given equal consideration.

---

## Where should we end up?

The fourth and final question to be asked at the planning stage is a combination of setting the results of where we're headed with the means by which we intend to get there – and producing a list of outcomes that can be used to determine if we've met with success, failure or simply need to keep going to get to the destination. For the most part, these metrics are covered in more depth in Chapter 13. What's worth noting at this point is that you'll be setting out broad measures that link back to where you're planning on going and what you set out in the marketing objectives.

## Objectives, goals and metrics

The very first task in this section is to copy and paste the goals and objectives from your overall strategic marketing planning (Chapters 3 and 4) and start looking at how these items can be converted into measurements. A good objective will come with a measurement element built into the framework – for example, the marketing objectives should mention the level of sales volume, profits per unit or cost savings incurred per activity.

> **Plan input**
>
> How will you know if you have achieved your objectives?

These automatically move into benchmarks plus yes/no statements (What were our savings over the stated period? Did we achieve the stated savings target?). If you're struggling to determine how to assess the objectives or goals you've set, now is the time to revise and revisit them. Do it before you write up the plan. If you're struggling for clarity in the measurement, you'll struggle for guidance for implementation. Revise, revisit and repeat the planning process until you're confident you've attained a working roadmap with due dates, benchmarks and guiding instructions.

## Reporting and documenting: it's all part of the plan

Once you've satisfied yourself that you've covered the bases, set goals that you can achieve and measure, and have mapped out the steps you need to take to achieve those goals, it's time for some formal documentation. A marketing plan is a living document designed to be used to guide the day-to-day activities that work towards achieving your goals. In some organizations, plans become elevated to the status of relics or artifacts that are revered objects that sit on shelves as some form of business collector's item. Just so we're clear on this – there's no secondary eBay market for 'Mint in Box', perfect, untouched marketing plans. If anything, the demand is for the battered, paint-chipped and battle-scarred plans that have seen a lot of action – and driven a lot of success. The purpose of documentation is to allow you the breathing space to not have to remember, memorize and commit the entire game plan to your head whilst trying to act on the various advice goals and tasks you've set yourself. The planning process was about

to, or Principles of, Marketing subject) you'll have enough background to produce a rough sketch so you can fill in the details later. We've left budgeting for later in the book (Chapters 10 and 11) although even at this early stage it's worth putting together rough figures of available cash (none, some, pizza money, etc.) and available time (none, some, plenty, etc.).

---

### Plan

Satisfy:

o What steps will you take to create the content required for your site?
o How does this content address the needs of your audience?
o What resources do you have available to meet your content schedule?
o What resources will you need to acquire?
o What is your available financial budget for the site?
o What is your available time budget?

---

Also at this point in the process it's worth investigating sites such as Basecamp (www. basecamphq.com), Remember The Milk (www.rememberthemilk.com) or Zoho Projects (http://projects.zoho.com) as project management systems to help guide the product development process, site roll-out and every other task that's about to mount up as you turn this project from 'great idea' into reality.

### Communications framework

We've separated out the communications from the rest of the marketing plan for the moment, since the Internet is a communications platform and because there are lots of individual elements which you can link together with the strategic objectives, goals, branding (Chapter 7) and product development (Chapter 6). The plan listed here is also just a skeleton framework which is fleshed out in Chapter 7. We've split the framework up into five segments which are:

o *The content pitch.* This takes the form of five of the most common ways in which you'll need to explain your website to someone, including Twitter posts (140 characters), the obligatory Twitter bio sentence (one sentence), the elevator pitch (the two-sentence response to 'So what do you do online?'), the full-length paragraph for the 'About you' or 'Biography' section of social media sites and the extensive self-descriptive 'About us' page for your website or blog (and if you find those 'Describe yourself in 25 words' parts of CVs and job applications tough, you'll hate this section).
o *The search engine optimization plan.* Search engine traffic is the life blood of the Internet and you'll have to pay some attention to how it all functions (even if you plan to use an organic SEO strategy). This section of the plan outlines the keywords you

want to associate with your site (and use in the site), any deliberate SEO strategies you intend to employ (and there's hundreds of options) plus the human element of thinking through how your market would normally come to find a site like yours. Do this by putting yourself into the most convenient spots for them to find you (which is one part distribution channel, one part promotion – Chapters 6 and 7).

○ *The conventional communications plan.* If you've done advertising integrated marketing communication or similar subjects, this is probably the easiest part. That said, this is the largest part of the communications section since it covers the most options, broadest bases and picks up the offline communications strategies to reinforce your online work. This covers online advertising (Google AdWords, adverts, banners, etc.), offline advertising (the outside world), conventional public relations including addressing the mainstream media, blogger relations for pitching press releases online and generating publicity through being interesting. We've split off blogger relations from social media in that conventional communications plans treat bloggers like online journalists and involve deliberate, targeted messages to entice the blogger to cover your story on their site. The social media stuff is much more organic (and much less organized).

○ *The social media plan.* Sick of planning yet? The next level ensures that you have a good plan for how you'll be using those social media accounts for the forces of good and how you'll be turning your copy of Flock (www.flock.com) into a one-stop conversation portal. The plan covers your intended social networking activity. This amounts to personal brand development through interpersonal activity (and not being annoying online), social media participation including limiting which networks you use and picking the spots as to where you will have accounts. There's also the question of when and how frequently to use the accounts, plus which community areas have the best opportunities for mutual gain through community engagement, including how to foster and develop community around your blog or site. Finally, there are the organic social media options, where you rig out your site to be easy for other people to share on their preferred social media systems (Digg Buttons, RT button, post to Facebook, etc.). The central point of the social media plan is also to be able to sit back and review what you're planning on doing to see if you're going to commit any obvious social media *faux pas*. There is no way we're going to endorse the development of a social media plan that spams accounts or turns Twitter into a string of links to 'Earn n+1 dollars from affiliate Internet sales programmes' (we really dislike those people and their misuse of the word marketing). Understandably this plan is going to run across Chapter 7 (where you set objectives) and Chapters 9 and 10 (where you pick the methods and learn to avoid making a nuisance of yourself).

○ *Technical communication issues:* This is a short list of marketing plus technology questions such as 'What's the address of the site?' and 'Can we communicate the site's address on the promotional material?' It also includes the question of what to call the site (site title, site brand name) and the branding and communication issues associated with the site's address and title (can the site address become the key brand name?).

## Introduction

Consumer behaviour is a central part of virtually all marketing decision making (with the exception of business to business, and even then, there are people making personal choices in a business context). This chapter brings together some of the highlights of the consumer behaviour field that can be applied to e-marketing, the Internet and the online consumer. The CIM (2005) definition of marketing recognizes consumer behaviour as identifying consumer needs through consumer insight (Chapter 2) and the anticipation of needs (Chapter 4) which are satisfied in the value offerings (Chapter 6). The strength of an e-marketing campaign is dependent on understanding consumer behaviour both in theory and practice (Chapter 2). Finally, the best part of understanding consumer motives and ways of behaving (and misbehaving) is that it really helps when you're trying to turn an idea from something you think will work into the something that the market really wants to use (besides just the opportunity for profit, it's a great sense of achievement to make someone else's day with a good product).

This chapter is written in three sections – innovation adoption theory, consumer psychographic characteristics and some of the ways and means in which consumers actually use the Internet. These three sections are set out to be precursors to product development (Chapter 6) and link back to some of the generic uses of the Internet from the company's standpoint (Chapter 3). It's important to note that this is the highlight reel of consumer behaviour theory. Neither space nor time permits a comprehensive view of general consumer behaviour theory (decision-making models, etc.). We've picked up on the areas that recur in social media (Chapter 12), cybercommunities (Chapter 9) and value creation (Chapter 6) to ensure that you have a refresher course before tackling these areas. It's well worth revisiting your consumer behaviour textbooks and course notes for the broader models and techniques to assist the e-marketing process.

## Innovation and the Internet

When the Internet is over fifty, and the World Wide Web is pushing thirty, it's hard to still think of the Internet as an innovative technology. At the same time, since so much of the Internet consists of entirely new-to-the-consumer experiences, it takes a special breed of innovative consumer to cope with the constant flow of novelty. Between the ultra-new and ever-changing content and the somewhat aged-to-perfection platform, the Internet serves up a range of consumer behaviour challenges. The Internet is also a perfect storm of content distribution with content seeking markets. The nature of the Web as a self-publishing-friendly medium allows for an almost unlimited share of voice to be distributed to content creators across the globe. Whereas the offline content generation market has managed to retain some of the high barriers to entry such as physical delivery costs (Chapter 6), the online marketspace was designed to be an effective (and/or efficient) mechanism for the distribution of information content, which now includes the digitized services of music, video, gaming and information delivery. The Internet is a novelty seeking person's paradise when you consider the sheer volume of new stuff available on an hourly or daily basis as a result of the massively reduced barriers to distribution for content. It's also headache inducing for anyone without a love of novelty, innovation or a vested interest in being the local opinion leader.

Innovation adoption divides into three connected blocks of ideas, some of which were first raised in Chapter 2. First, there's the innovator categories which are forms of hypothetical market segmentation (and which were also raised in the segmentation techniques in Chapter 4). Secondly, there's the detail of the market segments based on their relative innovativeness (on a sliding scale of 'very innovative' to 'not sure about this new-fangled fire thing'). Finally, there's the innovation itself and the interaction between the needs of the innovation adoption market segments and the features of the product.

## Innovation adoption curves

Most innovation adoption curves are mathematically derived models of the perfect world performance of a product in a theoretical market. Like everything else stolen from economics by marketing, the models make a lot of assumptions (perfect knowledge, perfect products, rational decision, etc.) and as such, come with the usual disclaimers of 'May not apply to reality' and 'Do not use whilst operating heavy machinery'. As noted in Chapter 3, innovation curves should be considered as the partner idea to the product lifecycle curve – they cover the introduction, spread and eventual decline of a product in a marketplace. To that end, it's useful because you'll be pitching the product in a different manner depending on where it's at in the market (innovation versus mature product) and where it's at in the product lifecycle curve (Chapter 3). For e-marketing, there are three useful innovation curves to consider – the smooth growth pattern of the 'S' curve for permanently adoptable ideas which take a few waves before hitting critical mass, the classic (albeit imperfect) fast and sustained growth model and the wonderfully named 'contagion' model of products that go in and out of use in a market.

### The 'S' curve

The S-curve model of innovation adoption describes the type of innovation which moves smoothly (and permanently) through a marketplace from innovators at the start, into the early adopters and then slowly moves through the market until it hits the tipping point and the entire market gets involved (Gladwell, 2000).

For all the beauty and maths purity of the model, it's more economics than marketing in the volume of assumptions necessary to make it fit reality. At the core of this model is the idea that the innovation cannot be unadopted – that is, once exposed to the idea, it can't be unlearned (Figure 5.1). Consequently, it works well for music, television, books and disposable products that are consumed and repurchased. It's less useful for tracking lifetime ownership, since it assumes you won't give up the product. For example, after finishing this course (barring serious head trauma) you'll now always have known about Twitter, Google and a range of other ideas and behaviours that you can't discover again for the first time. This is useful for when you start looking at the type of innovations (really new versus quite new) although the model needs to be limited to application to

success stories from the innovators allows them to hold a position at the cutting edge whilst ushering in the social credibility for their chosen innovations.

○ Opinion leadership through endorsement by use (see the Introduction) as early adopters lend mainstream credibility to a new idea and, once in use by this group, the idea becomes something for the later groups to copy and mimic.

○ Social connections, since these are the connected people who have multiple circles of friends, numerous social network structures on and offline and a fairly busy social calendar. They need these networks in part to endorse their social status, and, equally, to track and monitor the trends in fashions in the group around them.

It's no coincidence that the arrival of the early majority to the Internet also ushered in the era of social media (Chapter 9). Nothing screams 'early adopter' louder than social networking sites such as Facebook (status updates), blogging (opinion broadcasting) and Twitter (existence broadcasting). In fact, Twitter could be the perfect early adopter protocol – short messages that indicate the current status of the user, broadcast to a wide net of followers who can either be followed or ignored as appropriate. Plus, it's an established technology that was in use by the innovator crowd (who are all grumbling that it's gone downhill and are headed off to something newer). The only significant downside to the early adopter crowd is the small size of the market they represent (12.5 per cent) and their need to differentiate themselves from the masses. In short, if Twitter breaks into the mass market mainstream, the early adopters will be off elsewhere to stand out from the Twitter-using majority.

### Early majority (What's in it for me? Deliberate and calculated decisions)

The early majority represent the point where the new idea isn't quite that new anymore, which means it's time for the mass-market approaches of multiple segments, product variations and a range of competitors. It's worth noting that despite their financial value and sheer volume (double the size of the previous two markets combined), the early majority mistakenly tend not to be considered as a market for innovations. This is partly because most innovation adoption researchers and consultants are innovators (or cusp early adopters) and are long since bored with 'that old idea'. Similarly, some of the strategies for addressing this group, such as market penetration, also depend on the market's familiarity with the organization and its product (Chapter 3).

However, if you look at the marketing strategy guides for the early majority market from the corporate side you'll find the advice in market maturity is to use innovations as new ways to sell the existing idea to the market. To that end, the early majority are actually a surprisingly innovative marketplace – just as long as you're only talking about modifications and variations to an existing product. Members of the early majority can be recognized by a few distinct characteristics.

○ Risk aversion, which is both a precursor and a result of other factors in this list. Unlike the innovators, the early majority don't have the resources or desire to take chances, and they'll want security over uncertainty.

○ Calculated decision-making processes which are based on finding a very good set of arguments in favour of the product on the balance of a whole range of pros, cons, costs and benefits.

○ Slower deliberations against a greater set of options,. The calculated nature of their thought processes, combined with the need to sift through a wider array of information sources found in the mature markets (Chapter 3), means longer delays between opportunity identification and decision making.

○ Opinion seeking behaviour, which explains the how and why of the early adopters broadcasting their preferences to the early majority. Opinion seeking is used to reduce the risk of adoption by seeing what worked for the people around them and the fashion leaders.

○ Listening through aggregated information channels, which is the preference for moderated, edited or endorsed knowledge (Chapter 4). Early majority users read the editorial columns of newspapers, listen to the movie reviewers and take guidance from these endorsements as a means to reduce their risk. Public measures of popularity are useful for this group since the popularity ranking mechanisms of Top 10 lists and '101 movies you must see before you die' help with their pursuit of social compliance (Chapter 4). Popularity means security by numbers and volume of market consensus.

○ Sheer volume of the market. There's a lot of them – they're everywhere – and when you've arrived in this mainstream mass market, you'll know all about it. Since the early majority outnumber the innovator and early adopter you'll be hearing those category members complaining of the product, brand or company 'selling out'.

○ Simplicity and functionality dominate their needs since they're not in this for the novelty and, whilst they want to be like their fashionable friends, they've got a really strong pragmatic streak that stands between them and frivolous activity. Plus, risk aversion means that the innovation has to be a useful application of their limited resources.

This category of the market thinks hard about their decisions, since they're usually dealing with a wider choice of options and a more limited set of resources than innovators or early adopters. The movement of the early majority into a market completely rewrites the social dynamics of the product's user based simply on sheer weight of numbers. Access and functions will become tailored for ease of use rather than technical complexity. Optional customization functions will be moved from the front of the software to the ubiquitous 'advanced features' heading, and there's a disquieting sense that whatever the idea was originally, it's now in the 'Grown Up', settled down and looking to buy a summer home in Sussex phase (compared with the innovator products sharing a bed-sit squat in inner Manchester and the early adopter product doing up that terraced house in Camden, London).

### Late majority (If we must)

Late majority users are the last of the adopter groups to arrive at the product and they've usually been dragged here grumbling and muttering under their breath (kicking and screaming is more an innovator behaviour). For the most part, the reason people are in the late majority is due to the product and not the person. For whatever reason, the product didn't capture their attention and certainly didn't have the perceived merit that saw it picked up by innovators and early adopters. To that end, the late and early majority share a few points in common, namely that both are looking very carefully at their decisions. Whilst the early majority found a good match for their needs, the late majority didn't find a compelling reason to change – until their alternatives were dragged away from them by changes in the marketplace. This group is characterized by several features.

o Justifiable resentment towards the product since they usually only adopt this newer alternative because their older model broke, was replaced or phased out.
o Scepticism of the technology, with a begrudging concession to its necessity rather than any particular desire for the product. These are the people who liked going into the banks to talk to the tellers and couldn't see the point of the ATM since you didn't get the features and benefits of the personal contact from the machine.
o The sound of inevitability, since this market is the hallmark indicator that the product lifecycle has peaked, and if managed well, will sit in the maturity phase indefinitely. It's worth noting that quite often the late majority are the best indicators of whether a product is entering late maturity and going into decline.
o Perceptions that the product has 'jumped the shark' (www.jumptheshark.com), which is to say that the attempts to make the product fit for the later parts of the early majority category and the first part of the late majority category resulted in some bad decisions, alienation of the core fan base or inexplicable events leading to the user base moving onto a new idea. (Note: 'Nuking the fridge' is where a good but ageing franchise makes a bad tactical decision in a comeback. Jumping the shark happens whilst the franchise is still in the original run.)

Late majority members often don't want to be here, don't want this product and are frustrated that the world has changed and moved on without them. They're conservative in nature and it's this conservatism that forces them into a situation of buying into the good, service or idea that has mainstream support (add a little more radical spirit and your late majority member will turn into a laggard as they hold out against prevailing trends in the marketplace). They're often resource poor in the primary category that the product needs for adoption and have put off the purchase until they feel that they can't afford to be without it. Whilst this is often considered in terms of money (mass market discounts, end of product run-out discounts) it's also worth noting that by the time a product hits the late majority, it should be at its peak of energy efficiency and time effectiveness, and be able to be easily taught or learnt by the time poor end of the market.

### Laggards: (Want not, adopt not and/or tried and it failed)

Laggards are the most complex of the categories and are only really defined by a single, unifying characteristic – they haven't adopted your idea and they're not about to adopt it either. Technically, everyone starts in the laggard category, and your membership of another group (early adopter, etc.) is related to the speed at which you go from 'Do not want' to 'Mine' when encountering the idea, good or service. Laggards range from being extremely radical groups (leaving the innovators well behind in the risk-taking stakes) as they reject the widespread trends in the market to plot their own course, to being extremely cautious and fussy, waiting for the product to reach their exacting standards. Basically, beyond non-adoption, there's not much else that binds the group into a cohesive unit. The result is a large number of laggard sub-groups, some of which are:

o Traditionalists, who previously formed the classic view of the laggard. These are the strictly conservative, often extremely religious type of people, who are set in their ways and not about to change. Whilst they exist, their reasons for rejecting your idea are usually based on a lack of compatibility between the idea and their lifestyle and beliefs. Consequently, if the product is altered enough to be compatible, they'll leave the laggard spot. The Amish view of technology is probably the best example of this approach – they don't view technology as having an inherent merit (eliminating them from innovators) and don't believe that products should be used to create differences in the community (early adopter out). If anything, they're the prototypical perfect early majority group with their carefully calculated decision making. If the product is compatible, they'll adopt it. If not, then the lack of compatibility, not the conservative nature of the group, is the point of failure.

o Chronic Know-Nothings, who aren't so much laggards by choice but laggards by default since they're not aware of your offer to the market. They may not be your market and may never have heard of you, and that's why they're not buying into the product. People often fall into the laggards category when there's a gap between the release of a new product and news of the product reaching a market segment (of course, if the market segment responds immediately, they jump from laggard to innovator).

o Conscious Choice Rejecters are well informed, well educated, extremely well aware of the benefits and costs of your idea, product or activity and have declined your offer anyway. This is possibly the most hated of the laggard groups because they've gone through all of the same decision-making steps as the people who adopted the product but they said 'no' rather than 'yes'. Respect that and let them go (if you need them that badly for survival, you should get a better business model). These are the rebellious late adopters who didn't buckle to social pressure or the deliberate early majority who found no merit in your product.

o Cautious Super Adopters are the supremely late adopters by action despite being up there with the innovator class for discovering the concept. They've been sitting back and waiting for the idea to reach the feature-rich, cost-reduced version that's almost (if not actually) fully functional. They're best considered as non-risk-taking innovators.

If you consider the innovation adoption categories as a soccer team, the innovators are the goal keepers, the early adopters play up front in the forward line as wingers and strikers, the early majority look after the defence, and the late majority bang the ball around in the midfield. In this metaphor, the laggards are the reserves bench, including the players who train in the squad and don't make the reserves – mostly invisible, not terribly glamorous and utterly vital for the functioning of the whole side. Within the laggards category, the bench players are those who are laggards by choice because the product is insufficiently advanced, doesn't do the job yet or lacks a key feature; they will come off the bench as soon as that feature is available. Other laggards won't ever want the product, and as such, make up the groups noted in the market segmentation as people who you don't want using the product (Chapter 3).

## Interconnecting adopter attitude and innovation characteristics

Innovation adoption involves two elements: the adopter and the innovation. The development of an offering of value to satisfy the needs of the consumer needs to be measured against two innovation concepts: Rogers's (1995) innovation characteristics list and the relative novelty of the idea.

### *Rogers's (1995) innovations characteristics list*

The most vital aspect of determining the speed at which someone moves from non-adopter (proto-laggard) into one of the adopter categories is the nature of the offering of value and whether it successfully anticipated and satisfied the customer's needs. Rogers (1995) outlined five characteristics which make the critical difference in the mind of the consumer when they're assessing a new product against their existing options (Chapter 6). These are:

o *relative advantage*, which is the way in which your new idea, product or service beats its predecessor in head-to-head competition. Twitter beats blogging in broadcasting to listening audiences for speed and brevity. E-mail beats physical mail for speed. Physical mail beats Twitter and e-mail for delivering boxes of real stuff and so forth. Relative advantage gives the consumer a reason to have a go at the product. Failure to attain relative advantage (do something better than how it's already being done) is usually the main killer of new products.
o *compatibility*, which is the extent to which whatever you're offering links into the rest of the lifestyle of the customer. It also includes the extent to which the customer has to mess around with their lifestyle, daily routines and/or learn new behaviours to make the product work for them. Typewriters begat computer use for word processing which, when used for letter writing made e-mail seem just a logical step from 'print' to 'post'. Once comfortable with e-mail, other approaches that sent what you wrote on screen out into the Internet were fairly compatible with the idea of using the computer for communication.
o *complexity*, which is the relative difficulty of using and understanding the innovation. This is a dual-edge sword – intensely complex products sell to markets seeking complexity but, simultaneously, there's a massive push away from complexity towards streamlined products that are 'easy' to use. Twitter took off in part due to the low complexity (say what you're doing in 140 characters). At the same time, people insist on playing Sudoku for fun, so complexity still sells in the marketplace

(seriously, it's the same sets of maths puzzles we hated at primary school now sold as nostalgic difficulty).

○ *trialability*, which is the 'give it a go' factor that lets people try the product out without committing themselves to it wholeheartedly. More trialability means greater immediate uptakes as people use the trial to figure out the compatibility, complexity and relative advantage. Trial can take the form of beta testing, invite-only accounts or free accounts where there are paid upgrade options (Flickr, Remember The Milk, Livejournal).

○ *observability*, which is the level of visibility of the use of the product to other members of the adopter's social group. This ranges from near anonymity and just-under-the-radar activity online to the incredible visibility of joining your friends on a social media site. Gregor and Jones (1999) found that the Internet was generally regarded as a low-visibility product which relied on word-of-mouth communications for its visibility (which is why the social media networks are crammed full of early adopters who love to broadcast word of mouth, and why the Internet is a lot more visible these days).

Table 5.2 provides a brief summary of how the innovation adoption characteristics interact with the innovator categories and, as a result, require different offerings of value for each of the marketing segments (Chapter 6).

Table 5.2 Innovation characteristics by innovation adoption category

| | Relative advantage | Compatibility | Complexity | Trial | Observable |
|---|---|---|---|---|---|
| **Innovator** | Novelty | Limited | Maximum | In the alpha and beta test | Noticeable if it works |
| **Early adopter** | Trend-setting | Leadership | Status symbol | In the invite-only beta test | Used to promote their own visibility |
| **Early majority** | Followership | Fashionability | Moderate | Upgraded from a free account | Important to be seen to be fashionable |
| **Late majority** | Compliance | Forced | Simplicity | Free account | Complains it's everywhere |
| **Laggard** | No advantage | Not compatible | Too complex | Signed up, couldn't see the point, left | Noticeable by their absence |

## Relative novelty of the idea

Thankfully, not all innovations are equal, and there's a sliding scale of 'really new', 'quite new', 'not that new' and 'neither new nor improved'. These four categories are based on a combination of the relative compatibility of the product to other ideas (contemporary and historical), the audience's familiarity with the idea (Chapter 3) and their experience with other products in the same area.

- *Really new products* – RNP (discontinuous innovations). These are the game breakers that redefine an industry or marketplace. This type of idea creates new markets, defines new product categories, causes the consumer to form new behaviours and is difficult to associate with a single existing product. Really new products are exceedingly rare and very hard to move past the innovators in their first entry to the market because they bring about such a radical shift in behaviour. They threaten existing social structures (and that doesn't appeal to the socially conscious early adopter or more conservative later groups). There's also a lot of risk associated with really new products. They're usually quite complex (the bit with the learning what it is, what it does and how to create the new behaviours) and invariably highly visible (and not always in a positive way). As such, most organizations prefer to refine and revise the really new product prototype to create something more compatible, recognizable and easier to introduce to the mainstream markets.

- *Quite new products* – QNP (dynamically continuous innovations). These are the second generation of really new products and are the radical shifts or upgrades within a product category. They are significant shifts in technology, behaviour or application, with a family tree and heritage that can be traced back to a previous idea or technology. Computers track back to typewriters that follow a family tree back to the moveable type of the Gutenberg printing press (as compared to the Glutenberg sandwich press). These days, most of the leading-edge and cutting-edge developments of technology on the Internet have a 'quite new product' level of innovation as they replicate something else from offline, online or in between, in a new format. Same goes for a lot of the work on the mobile technologies (Chapter 13). Because these products have a heritage to them, they're easier to communicate to the market and can be explained in terms of relative advantage and compatibility. Quite new products are often the less complex successors to the really new products.

- *Improved products* – IP (continuous innovations). These are the products of the mature markets, where the main changes to the product are driven by reactions in the market, competition or improvements in technology and manufacturing, or by an effort to stave off the decline phase by seeking to use innovations. It's also important to note that a product cannot be new and improved. It can be new (QNP or RNP), which is where no product like it existed, or it can be improved, where it is an update to an existing product. Improved products are sold on relative advantage and are often competing against their predecessors for new sales and marketshare.

- *Continuing product* – CP (neither 'new' nor 'improved'). This is not strictly an innovation class but represents the 'me-too' products that enter an existing product category, copy the market leader and provide no new features, benefits, relative advantage or other distinguishing factor. The closest part to innovation for the product is that it may be new to the company, but it's so well established in the marketplace it can't be considered innovative or novel.

Table 5.3  Category versus class

| | Really new products (RNP) | Quite new products (QNP) | Improved products (IP) | Continuing products (UP) |
|---|---|---|---|---|
| **Innovator** | Strong | Medium | Limited | None |
| **Early adopter** | Limited | Strong | Medium | Limited |
| **Early majority** | None | Limited | Strong | Medium |
| **Late majority** | None | Limited | Medium | Strong |

It's worth noting that the four different categories of product are fairly subjective and largely based on the market's opinion. Basically, if the market's seen it all before (or it's been done before) it doesn't matter if the organization thinks the product is the newest thing ever – it's an improved or unimproved product to the market. At the same time, far too many marketers overlook the novelty of one of their old products when it arrives in a new market segment. Just because it's old hat to the firm doesn't mean it can't be sold as an innovation to the people who are seeing it for the first time (and, equally, doesn't mean you'll be going straight to the early majority if this is a new product to this market). Table 5.3 outlines the match up of the four categories of product novelty (RNP, QNP, IP, CP) with the four innovation adopter groups (we've dropped the rejection-orientated laggards. They're just not that into you.)

## Consumer psychographic characteristics of the Internet

People are complicated. The bundles of experience, opportunity, personality and resources that constitute the average person have a range of impacts on the way we conduct ourselves on and offline. Hence, there's an entire field of study (that borrows heavily from psychology) dedicated to examining the impacts of psychographic characteristics on the marketplace, purchase decisions and behaviours. From an e-marketing perspective, there's a select group of personality traits that play an important role in how the consumer copes with the online world (and approaches e-marketing offers of value). These areas are:

o innovativeness, which is the speed at which you adjust to new ideas and integrate them into your life. There are two sub-components: temporal innovativeness and domain-specific innovativeness
o novelty seeking, which is the level to which you need new stuff to keep you amused, entertained or just stave off boredom
o attention to social pressures, which is the extent to which you're prone to paying attention to social cues from the people around you (or you're the one issuing the cues).

## Innovativeness

Life is the pursuit of novelty. Due to linear time, we're constantly exposed to new experiences and it's our innate capacity to cope with these changes that's reflected in our innovativeness personality traits. Innovation is the degree to which you cope with new ideas and are willing to try out something different in terms of products, behaviours, ideas or activities. It's predicated on your speed of response (temporal innovativeness) and whether this is your area of interest (domain-specific innovativeness). It's also a learnt behaviour that can be aided by positive experiences with innovation (risks turning to rewards) or diminished by negative results (product failures, set-backs, social embarrassment). As such, it's partly an innate characteristic and partly a taught behaviour. It's also part of the generic transferable skill of having the confidence to try new technology – which we've been trying to instil in you since the Introduction (hence the gauntlet run through the browser, software services and other innovations).

### Innovativeness and blogging: putting the theory into practice

When you're developing a blog, the type of reader you're planning on attracting will shape how you approach the content of your blog. If you're looking for the highly innovative and novelty prone blog reader, your content needs to be high turnover, short and sharp, and include fresh takes on new ideas. Consider your role models to be Engadget, Boing Boing or IO9 in terms of speed of production and the short, sharp posting styles.

If you're looking at an audience who still have innovative tendencies, and are more prone to some degree of restraint for social conformity and novelty, you'll be well suited to reading the high turnover blogs and picking out your favourite articles for discussion and commentary. By taking the innovative content as your input and applying your own discussion, research and opinion, you'll be providing the sort of social endorsement sought by large portions of the market.

Finally, if you're looking at the far end of the scale for novelty seeking, low innovativeness and high social approval in your audience, then you'll be blogging Top 10 lists, 'Best of the Internet', link blogs or reviews and commentaries on classic television series that have been released on DVD. The Onion is probably the best example of the low innovativeness readership market, although these types of readers are becoming increasingly present in the market and well worth considering because they usually account for about 30 per cent or more of a given population.

### *Temporal innovativeness (innovation reaction time)*

The dominant measure of innovativeness is the speed between you encountering the innovation and your purchase and use of the product. There's a bit of debate between measuring innovativeness in terms of product release date (speed from market entry) or product encounter date (internal innovativeness measure). Either way, it's based on reacting quickly to the new idea. Faster response times move you from proto-laggard into innovator (fastest), early adopter (faster), early majority (slow) or late majority (really slow). The biggest flaw with externally measured temporal innovativeness is that it tries to ignore factors such as financial resources which are often the barrier between desire and action. If you've seen something new, wanted it instantly but had to wait until the money came together to buy it, you're still displaying all the important temporal innovativeness indicators.

### Domain-specific innovativeness

Domain-specific innovativeness is the consumer's relative innovativeness within a specific product class (Goldsmith and Hofacker, 1991; Goldsmith and Flynn, 1992). This explains the apparent paradox of people who can be incredibly innovative in one aspect of life and exceedingly conservative in other areas. Someone who is forever trying out new software on their computer could be content with a veritable antique of a mobile phone. Similarly, a voracious appetite for the latest Flash or Shockwave game title can be paired with a music library that's still played on a CD player that's not built into a computer. Domain-specific innovativeness respects the complexity of modern life and doesn't require innovativeness to be a universal personal trait that must apply to all parts of life to apply to one aspect ('one for all and all for one' only applies to the Musketeers).

### External factors

There are a few consumer-centric elements, such as availability of the innovation, purchase price (with subscription fees, etc.) and loyalty to pre-existing products, that can take the edge off the actual adoption of an innovation even with a strong desire for the newest, latest and/or greatest devices. One of the advantages of the Internet in this respect is the diversity of low cost, low involvement novelty that exists within sites such as Shockwave (www.shockwave.com), YouTube (http://uk.youtube.com) and Facebook (www.facebook.com). The interest-driven nature of the Internet allows for the novelty prone to load up on new content through tools such as Google Reader (google.com/reader) that can be set to draw down new blog content as it happens. However, the innovativeness of the consumer is only one part of new product adoption and the part where marketing has the least say in the matter.

## Novelty seeking

Novelty seeking is where the consumer prefers the new, interesting and different over the established, repeated and conventional. This is a sliding scale between a craving for newness and a preference for the established. Preferences for the established are the central selling feature for most cable television and the reason behind increased DVD sales for popular television series after they've finished their free-to-air television run. Whilst

process – the customer's willingness to take social risks. Unsurprisingly, co-creation is much more likely to appear at the innovator and early adopter phases and slightly less likely to be present around the early and late majority phases. Keep in mind that the notion of use innovation, which is the process of coming up with new ways to use an old product, is a form of co-creation, so it's not the exclusive domain of the innovative. It's also worth considering the extent to which the co-creation behaviour can be ritualized, observed and easily mimicked to enable the consumers with higher levels of social awareness to co-create value in the 'proper' manner. Co-production is a factor to consider when designing the value offer (Chapter 6), setting the position of the product in the marketplace in the minds of the consumer (Chapter 7) and engaging the customer in ongoing relationships (Chapter 8).

## Generic site visitor types

While each marketing segmentation strategy can draw from the existing literature and findings, the final strategy will be based on a unique set of variables determined by the product and the organizational goals. The market typology presented here, developed by Lewis and Lewis (1997, in Breitenbach and van Doren, 1998), is an illustration of the types of market segments that can be developed to outline broad market needs, which ties into strategy (Chapter 3), tactics (Chapter 4) and product development (Chapter 6). The five generic visitor types include:

1. *Directed information seekers*: people who search for timely, relevant and accurate information on a specific topic or set of topics. Wikipedia, Google, the International Movie Database and Amazon are their home grounds.
2. *Undirected information seekers*: the classic 'web surfer' model of the users who follow a random interest-driven path, clicking on links of interest and information that looks new, interesting or different. These are the people who power social bookmarking services such as StumbleUpon and Delicious, and who love any site that has 'Link of the Day'-style content.
3. *Bargain hunters*: who are there for the shopping, discounts and cheapest options. In addition to searching for discounts, giveaways and free samples, they are most likely to be the downloaders of shareware or freeware programs. They've got Google alerts on 'brand name' plus discount, subscribe to newsletters offering sales and deals, and probably have automatic searches saved at eBay as well. They'll be members of one or more coupon-trading sites.
4. *Entertainment seekers*: who are in this for the fun and tend to see the Internet as a very large toy box (whilst having a small number of sites they heavily frequent). You'll know this type if you've friended them on Facebook – you'll be getting invitations to play various Facebook games, and whilst they seem to be starting a new game every week, they're probably playing all the old games as well (we don't know where they find the time either). Also in this category are online gamers, YouTube fans, movie trailer downloaders, online radio listeners and anyone else in pursuit of a hedonistic outcome from their Internet experience.

5. *Directed buyers*: who are the hard-core shoppers of the online world. They're not in this for the pleasure of the hunt that drives the bargain hunters, rather, they're consumers on a mission, and once they've hit the target, that's it. They are online to find the product they want to buy, rather than to research it, play with it or take home a sample version of it. They're much more likely to buy direct from the manufacturer, although they can be found on Amazon as well as eBay.

## Product use positioning

Back in Chapter 4, one of the available positioning strategy techniques involved focusing on the way the product was used by a specific market segment. The following section outlines a set of uses of the Internet, common user behaviours and ways of using a website that can be considered as segmentation and positioning variables.

This is the 'behaviour' end of consumer behaviour. Dann and Dann (2004) outlined a collection of different reasons for using the Internet as a prototype usage behaviour segmentation strategy for the Internet. The behaviours on this list aren't mutually exclusive – anyone may be motivated by one or more of these approaches as they make use of the technology at their disposal. In addition, we've also connected the consumer-side behaviours here back to the organizational objectives for using the Internet (Chapter 3). The list includes:

○ *Using the Internet to learn,* which includes searching for items of interest, learning new ideas and old ideas, and tracking down points of trivia (such as lyrics to songs, actors in movies and whether that childhood memory of a cartoon about a blue–green environmentalist was actually real). The Internet has the near-perfect framework for text-based information search and the idea of the semantic web is an attempt to develop a text index of images, sounds, video and experiences. Sites that support and encourage information seeking include the Internet Movie Database (www.imdb. com), Wikipedia (www.wikipedia.org), blogs, Flickr and others.

  • Related business objective: information dissemination, promotion

○ *Using the Internet to search*, which is an applied form of learning based on either answering a specific question or hunting down additional information for problem-solving purposes. Searching has a couple of interesting side issues in that it relies heavily on the consumer's ability to conceptualize keywords that describe their problem, top-of-mind awareness (Chapter 7) and unprompted recall (or semi-prompted recall if you're getting Google to provide you with auto-completed search terms).

  • Related business objective: information dissemination, promotion

○ *Using the Internet to communicate*, which is the use of the Internet for conversational purposes and to maintain contact over distance (or proximity if you've ever twittered to the person at the end of the dinner table). This is facilitated through voice over IP (www.skype.com), e-mail (Gmail), various embedded chat systems (Facebook), IRC channels, social media messaging (FlickrMail), instant messenger

and 2, the near-perfect replication of information changes the physical world model of scarcity-based pricing to the digital world of abundance pricing. Abundance pricing is where you charge based on the value gained from the use of common and shared resources rather than charge for restricted access to limited supply. Scarcity pricing still has a role in e-marketing – scarcity exists in terms of exclusivity of access based on time (pay more, go first), priority (pay more, get more), features (pay anything at all, get more) and social recognition (finite membership lists with associated social status of being the 'in-crowd'). Whilst scarcity isn't dead, it's becoming appropriately scarce in the abundance economies of the Internet. Meanwhile, abundance economics has definitely only just come to the forefront of online pricing (and is still relatively scarce as a price tactic).

### Everyone's an exporter

Secondly, the Internet is a genuinely global marketplace where the rest of the world can access your website. Passing comments on the US election on your blog will have American commentators show up and argue with you. You rarely have someone drop by for a quick backslap and virtual cup of tea. There's the usual pros and cons argument to be had here about globalization, cultural hegemonies and other not-quite-completely marketing related issues when the entire world can (technically) access any other part of the Internet (filters, firewalls and government censorship not withstanding). Just because you're in front of it, it doesn't mean the people who run the firewall can't see you.

Marketing has taken to the globalization of information and digital experiential products with much enthusiasm (and the occasional lawyer's nightmare) as the drastically lowered entry barriers into export markets means any website can operate on the international stage. Of course, this doesn't mean that the Internet is free from import/export duties, taxes and local customs officials when the physical goods do arrive on the doorstep. Whilst the primary barriers to export have dropped through cost-effective, simple distribution logistics over the Internet, and cost-effective international mail and courier services for smaller shipments of physical products, it doesn't necessarily mean that some of the more complex aspects of international shipping have gone away (Chapter 2). At the same time, whilst the world is at your disposal, your formerly geographically defendable target market is also available to everyone else with business intentions towards your customers. Competition rises in direct proportion to the lowering of access barriers to the outside world (Chapter 5).

Specific goal-oriented objectives should be developed to take advantage of the strengths of the Internet when it comes to the global marketspace. The most efficient use is to adapt those existing activities within the firm which best fit the strengths of the Web and organizational objectives. For example, if you're in the business of selling information that's reasonably transferable between countries (business advice, fashion, music criticism) then the Internet is well suited for information export. At the same time, if you're in the heavily regionalized information marketplace (tax law, regional insurance, local government) there's no real need to develop global distribution channels if your value offering is only relevant to the local market.

## Marketing mix for value creation

Building something of value for somebody else is the foundation of business and combines art, science and little bit more than that. The fundamentals of value creation are grounded in understanding consumer behaviour at the technical level (know the models, mechanisms and frameworks – Chapter 5) and understanding the specifics of how 'your' consumer is likely to behave. When we discuss target markets in this chapter, we'll occasionally refer to them as 'your' customers, since they're the group you are trying to address in your marketing activity. You don't own them per se, and competition says they're free to swap and choose their own solutions to meet their requirements. It's just easier for us to consider a basic market segmentation of 'yours' being the ones you're targeting, 'theirs' as the ones you're targeting who are with your competitors, and 'not thine' as the target markets you neither need nor want.

Segmentation is absolutely critical in guiding marketing mix decisions. You cannot make a universal product which is priced at the universal reference point and delivered through universal distribution (Chapter 3). What you can do through segmentation is make very precise decisions about the marketing mix aimed at triggering very specific responses from part of the market. Whilst we'll talk about generic decisions in the models in the rest of the chapter, you will need to make these decisions based on what you know about your current customers, potential customers and non-customers.

The marketing mix framework requires an upfront declaration – this section is about your product, your pricing strategy, your choice of distribution and your plans for promotion. Whilst the whole point of the exercise is to create a value offer for the marketplace, you'll be focused on what you can do with the resources at your disposal. It's vital to remember that the purpose of marketing is to meet customer needs profitably, which means retaining the balance between what the market wants (everything, free) and what you can provide (virtually nothing, expensively priced) so that you both win (something of value, reasonably priced for profit). Remember that the marketing orientation is customer centric, not customer dominated. With these caveats in mind, the remainder of this chapter is divided into the first three elements of the marketing mix: product, place and price.

## Product theory

A physical product is the total bundle of features and benefits that the seller offers the consumer. It includes the visible tangible product, any intangible benefits such as status and prestige, lifestyle benefits such as convenience, and ancillary services such as warranties and helplines (McColl-Kennedy and Kiel, 2000). The digital product is a similar proposition – a bundle of benefits that the seller offers the consumer (which exist in an electronic medium such as a computer, console or handheld device) that offer a series of intangible benefits based on their ownership and use by the consumer along with any ancillary services that augment the intangible digital product. Consumers buy the benefits they believe they will receive from the functionality, ownership and use of a product (Fojt, 1996). Rather than buying ¼ inch drills or ¼ inch holes, they buy the capacity to create ¼ inch holes when the mood takes them. Marketers, on the other hand, tend to sell the features of the drill, the range of drill bits and the variety of holes that could be made available in a wide range of substances as they look for the message that matches the need in the market with the product on offer. The trick is to find out whether the market wants a set of holes with precision (and thus requires your drill) or just wants a way to sink a boat (which opens up a range of other options). The more flexible you can be in presenting the feature set which you control to the market, the more likely the market is to figure out how your product can meet its requirements for drilling holes in things. This chapter introduces a suite of product theories to help you understand what it is that you're offering to your customers and what the customers are looking for from you.

## The extended product model

Kotler and Roberto (1989) developed an extended model of products to encompass the variations on products that assist social change. In their model the marketer has to consider which of the three elements (an idea, a behaviour or a product) should be the focal point of the change campaign. We've borrowed their initial concept and exported it across to the Internet where online products are faced with the option of being about an idea (content, belief, attitudes, values), a type of activity (one-off or recurring behaviours), can involve some object (physical or virtual, nothing at all) or be a combination of all three (see Figure 6.1).

In this model, 'idea' is the conceptual framework associated with the product experience and consists of:

○ beliefs, which are the consumer's understanding of the facts, knowledge and information associated with the product, and which can be generated by the product itself
○ attitudes, which are cognitive interpretations of positive and negative reactions to the product and which may incorporate emotional responses of liking or disliking a product
○ values, which represent the compatibility (Chapter 5) of the product with the consumer's personal view of the world in terms of ethics, morality and the sense of social appropriate conduct.

'Behaviour' divides into two categories based on one-off immediate actions and recurring activity. One-off behaviour covers a few different options such as the product being offline dominant so that the one-time event is the purchase for shipping and the rest of the associated behaviours are offline. Alternatively, the one-off behaviour can be the initial registration and set-up behaviour as experienced in the Introduction, where you registered for a range of services. The gap between one-off and recurring behaviour explains why a poorly considered recruitment campaign can result in massive numbers of people signing up to a service (Twitter) but failing to actually use the service

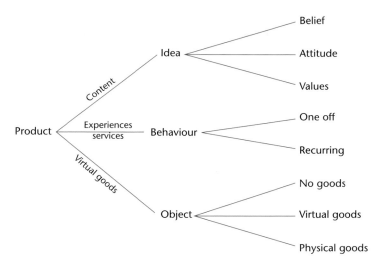

**Figure 6.1** Branching diagram of the product components
*Source*: adapted from Kotler, P. and Roberto, E. (1989) *Social Marketing: Strategies for Changing Public Behavior*. New York: Free Press

(60 per cent of accounts remain inactive – Martin, 2009). Providing the answer to the 'Okay, now what?' question is a case of supporting an ongoing behaviour. You probably experienced a set of these 'Okay, now what?' moments during the Introduction set-up-athon, and from this point, we can start demonstrating the behaviours that support the use of the services (some of you may have found inherent merit in the services, or worked out your own uses). Ongoing is the extent to which the product is either a facilitator of an activity or represents an ongoing set of behaviours in order to make the product valuable to you or your consumers. If you consider the phone for a moment – the one-off acquisition of a mobile phone is a 'Now what?' scenario. Using the phone to call friends and family is the ongoing behaviour, and the true value of the phone comes from the convenience it delivers through being used.

'Object' splits into three categories: absence of anything, a virtual object and/or a physical object. It's usually hard to combine the absence and presence of an object – tea and no tea being the rare exception noted by Adams and Meretzky (1984) – so for the purpose of Figure 6.1 either there is no object (virtual or physical) or there is some form of object which can exist as being physical and/or virtual.

The model can also be used as a way of considering how a product can reach the market by answering the following questions:

o What ideas do the consumers need to have to use the product?

- What facts do they need to know to use the product?
- How do we increase positive evaluation of the product and address any negative evaluations?
- Does this product contravene any ethical, moral or value positions in the world view of the target market?

    ○ What behaviours does the product require for use?

        ● Are we asking for a non-recurring behaviour initially?
        ● Do we require recurring behaviours to get the most out of the product?

    ○ What is the substantive nature of the product?

        ● Is this a physical product to be acquired online and supplied offline?
        ● Is this a virtual product that resides on the consumer's computer?
        ● Is this a non-corporeal virtual product that doesn't stay on the consumer's computer when they've finished with it?

## e-marketing product types

In Chapter 1, the virtual product diagram (repeated here as Figure 6.2) briefly introduced the concept of different forms of Internet-friendly products such as service, virtual goods, content and experiences (Figure 6.2). It's also worth remembering that these four product types are not 'real' in the sense of being tangible goods. However, they're real to the consumer in the sense of emotions experienced, money spent, knowledge gained or files acquired. Although home-based computers are fairly recent inventions, society has quickly transferred ideas of property and ownership from the physical world. Although the contents of an iPod are completely intangible, you want to ensure that if you replace the physical object, you also include the data content on the new device. From your perspective, you're most likely to be delivering either content (blogs, YouTube videos, whatever you put on MySpace) or virtual goods (audio, video or other files) for downloading at this point in your e-marketing career. This is a relatively easy starting point since a range of services exist to facilitate file

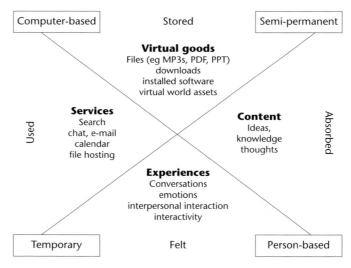

**Figure 6.2** The virtual product portfolio
*Source*: Chapter 1, Figure 1.4

delivery such as Slideshare (www.slideshare.net), Scribed (www.scribed.com), and Lulu (www.lulu.com).

### Virtual goods

Virtual goods are files that require virtual logistics to move from the point of production (the server) to the point of consumer (you) whilst being semi-tangible in that they take up storage space on your computer (or iPhone, iPod, Kindle, etc.). Virtual goods vary a bit in type and nature – whilst there's an argument to be made that a YouTube video can be a virtual good, we'd rather put the temporary cached files like streaming audio and video in the services category. Virtual goods can fill up a hard drive whereas virtual world goods fill up that virtual world's storage locker equivalent. For example, in an massive multiplayer game such as World of Warcraft there's a finite upper limit to the actual number of items an individual character can store within the game world. Consequently, the virtual goods occupy the nearest equivalent of physical space in that environment (Chapter 14).

### Content delivery

This is part service, part virtual good as you experience cognitive reactions to exposure to content online. It ranges from gaining new ideas (or reinforcing old ones) through reading content, active learning, passive learning and second-hand learning (new knowledge gained from mere exposure to the Internet – osmosis has never been so searchable) to thoughts had in reaction to online content (including 'When will I learn not to click links from that friend?'). As this is an internalized process, there's a need for customer co-production in that you have to play an active role in consuming the content (you can download a copy of the *Matrix*, you just can't learn Kung-Fu by installing it on your iPod). Content delivery can be relayed by virtual goods (podcasts, DOC, PPT files, the Introduction's PDF) although the emphasis is usually on content delivery through web pages, e-mail and other online content.

### Experiences

Experiences are different from content delivery in that these are the emotion reactions to the content you experience. These are the experiential elements of video gaming and the hedonic reactions to videos, music and online interaction. Experiences are personalized and internal, and subsequently require a bit of customer co-creation. As with the content delivery, these can be administered through virtual goods, although it's less likely that someone's going to get emotional over a WMV file versus getting emotional over the content of the film. Never underestimate the value of simple stimulus-response experiences that provide a constant stream of rewards and challenges (Figure 6.3).

### Virtual services

These are your interactions with some form of automated process on a server somewhere on the Internet and range from checking your e-mail, updating your Facebook status or

THE MOST POWERFUL GAMING SYSTEMS IN THE WORLD STILL CAN'T MATCH THE ADDICTIVENESS OF TINY IN-BROWSER FLASH GAMES.

**Figure 6.3** Flash games
*Source*: http://xkcd.com/484

adding dates to online calendars through to online banking, money transfers on PayPal, and more recently, cloud computing. Cloud computing is a remix of the ancient art of time sharing with contemporary Internet technologies such as file sharing, software as service and remote computer access. We've classified streaming audio, streaming video and online conversations as part of the services cluster which puts YouTube, Facebook and Twitter into the service delivery camp.

## Tangible to intangible

In terms of their suitability for online activities, products should be evaluated on the basis of a continuum from tangible to intangible. Few products are considered to be purely tangible (physical product) or purely intangible (pure service). Certain product categories, with their mix of tangible and intangible features, are particularly suited to online development and delivery. As mentioned in Chapter 2, a chief feature of information-based products is their ability to be sold and delivered through the Internet versus the physical goods which can be sold online and then delivered through conventional physical channels. Figure 6.4 highlights the typical relevant online content for a variety of product types. From this continuum it can be seen that while all product categories and organizations could potentially benefit from online activity, the relative importance of the online element varies considerably.

One area where the online–offline continuum is inverted from the standard is where the primary purpose of the site is to sell physical objects (for example, eBay: www.ebay.co.uk) versus a site which sells physical objects that are the result of virtual processes (for example, Zazzle: www.zazzle.com). The most remarkable of these processes is the avatar printing industry such as Fabjectory (http://www.fabjectory.com/), and Figureprints (www.figureprints.com) who create physical world copies of creations initially developed for entirely virtual environments. There are 3D-scanning firms that can reverse the process and put a copy of something real back into the virtual world. Fundamentally, the divide between the physical and the virtual creates two distinct end points

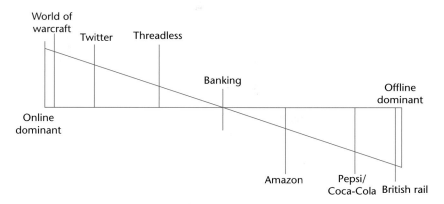

**Figure 6.4** Online to offline
*Source*: adapted from Dann, S. and Dann, S. (2004) *Strategic Internet Marketing 2.0.*
Brisbane: Wiley and Sons

on the marketing continuum: products that require a traditional distribution system to operate in conjunction with online activities (physical products) and products that do not require a complementary physical distribution system (digitized products).

## Offline dominant: physical products and the Internet

Given the nature of the Internet, the main interactions between physical objects and the Internet are covered by pricing or distribution. Physical objects that interact with the Internet in their own right (consoles, phones, children's toys) are generally divided into m-commerce (Chapter 13) and 'beyond the Web' (Chapter 14). For the most part, the more physical the product, the less likely you are to need an e-commerce product mix compared with the distribution mix.

## Intangible goods and digital rights management

If you're dealing with virtual goods, digital goods and anything that takes up permanent memory space on a hard drive (USB, iPod, DVD, etc.), you're going to need to balance out the customer's sense of ownership with any digital rights management system you plan on implementing as part of a digital rental scheme. One of the complexities of the abundance economy is that the ease of replication of data alters the consumer's and the marketer's perspective of its value compared with physical objects. Whilst renting a physical disc which you return at the end of the period has the hallmarks of temporary ownership (acquisition and return), having a software package that time expires feels different. It's still taking up space on the hard drive, it's there in the Programs menu and just doesn't work until you pay the next round of rental fees. Digital products have a semi-permanent state even when rented, and whilst those iTunes movies evaporate at the end of the rental period, they're still taking up hard drive space during the 30-day waiting period. Downloading a video rental from iTunes feels no different from downloading a permanently owned file from Gmail (time to download not withstanding).

One of the problems of the digital rights management (DRM) era has been the effort expended to reduce the ways and means by which digital goods can be owned by the consumer. When it comes to movies, music, data, images and other files, most users feel as if they own the data product with the same sense of 'real ownership' as they do for the DVD in its case on the bookshelf. If real ownership is a feature sought out by the market, sell it to them. DRM should be used by the e-marketer to favour the paying customer as a means for creating additional value over the lifetime of a customer, and could play a useful functional role in relationship marketing (Chapter 8). One of the benefits of DRM systems is the ability to track ownership of a digital good over the lifetime of a user account. This results in the compilation of a long history of purchases, cross-recommendations and direct sales from your database of product ownership and preference information. If your DRM system knows the customer bought the last three albums from a band, it should also be up to recommending the solo albums from the artistes and the new 'Best of' hits compilation. Not only that, but there's the capacity of DRM systems to work as digital product insurance that covers the end user against hard drive loss. Companies such as Valve have used DRM systems to create a form of insurance whereby the ownership of the right to download and install the software is tracked over the lifetime of the account – once you've bought it, you're assumed to be legitimately entitled to download and use it on any PC where you can install and run the Steam client. Whilst there are significant privacy issues to be addressed (Chapter 15), there's also market value to be created by treating the legitimate owner as the legitimate owner of their data. This contrasts with the current tendency of DRM systems to treat the paying user with suspicion and hostility as a temporary (and untrustworthy) lease holder of the digital goods.

The problem for e-marketing is that the use of DRM in its most restrictive manner limits the value and use of purchased goods (maximum numbers of reinstalls, limited numbers of re-downloads of the software). Whilst the business model of hitting the customer for multiple purchases of the data might fly with the accountants, it's poorly received with the general public and a very poor fit with the satisfaction of customer requirements. Few customers appreciate having to pay repeatedly for something they feel they already own. Having learnt the value of ownership from physical goods, there's an expectation of ownership in the virtual domain. Where DRM is used to restrict ownership through repeated verification, you also create an ongoing distribution cost for your operation. If the customer must validate their products on use each time, you're going to have to run validation servers and bear the costs of these being permanently available. As far as costs go, a second dissuading factor should be the need to maintain these DRM legacy systems to support older purchased DRM products or face class action lawsuits if you decide to revoke the ownerships of legitimately purchased goods because the validation systems cost you too much to run. Don't expect positive word of mouth and good brand outcomes if you decide to strip the consumer of their ownership of something they believed is their property. It doesn't matter how clearly you stated it was borrowed time in the End User License Agreement (EULA), these are rarely enforceable in the court of public opinion for your company's reputation. You may think of the data products as long-term leases, but if the consumer thinks they own it, be prepared to cop the fallout if you try to confiscate it from them later.

## Information as product

The product category for which the Internet is most suited, and for which it was designed, is information. Frieden et al. (1998) argue that information as a product has sufficient unique characteristics to differentiate it from both physical goods and services. They identify the characteristics of the information product as follows:

○ Information has a mathematical form (mode) regardless of the medium of transmission. In other words, information has the capacity to be digitized without any loss of content.
○ The mode of information refers to how the information exists symbolically as words, pictures, numbers or sounds.
○ The medium refers to the physical means by which information is delivered to users (i.e. print, broadcast, digital or visual media).
○ Information may be uniformly consumed by more than one person at different locations at the same time. While information is the same for all customers, individuals may choose to interpret and use it differently.
○ There is no theoretical limit to the supply of information from any single producer.
○ The consumption of information does not deplete or distort it.

The marketing implications of treating the information product as a separate category help to focus on its suitability in the online environment. Three elements are important here: the nature of information, the fact it is an inexhaustible resource and the ratio between production and replication costs.

1. The flexible nature of information, coupled with the ease of its distribution, removes many of the economies of scale issues for smaller producers. Conversely, some scaling issues exist when the demand for an information product exceeds the capacity of the server (reverse economies of scale).
2. Information can be replicated indefinitely without distortion and can be consumed simultaneously at multiple locations without being extinguished. This has resulted in the inversion of scarcity-based economic models.
3. Information is comparatively more expensive to create compared with the cost of replication. This places the product cost centre further back down the value chain into the hands of the creator rather than the distributor (again with economic consequences).

## Customer co-creation of value and product

Customer co-creation of value takes the benefits–features continuum and tilts the workload towards the customer because they're expected to put their own take on the product during the consumption process. With that in mind, it's often useful to offer the customer a modular framework (or open sandbox) in which they can make their own set of benefits, in preference to proscribing what you can (and can't) get out of the product with a long feature list.

Customer co-creation of value is a significant contributor to e-marketing customer satisfaction (Chapter 5) and the development of ongoing relationships between consumers and the marketplace (Chapter 8).

Customer co-creation has a significant impact on the extent to which you can produce self-service technologies within an e-marketing environment and entrust the customer with their own outcomes (Chapter 8). It's particularly noticeable in the Blank White Server (www.blankwhiteserver.com) concept, where the product is a digital shed with some basic tools and a squad of enthusiastic developers (BYO people). Similarly, games such as City of Heroes, World of Warcraft, EVEOnline and others have events, guilds and infrastructure that are generated by the players who are paying members of the game's community. NCSoft has taken this platform even further with the City of Heroes/City of Villains franchises which have player-created quests and tasks – an area previously reserved for exclusive use by the game's creator. This may or may not be the best way of handling such tasks. The system has been quite heavily exploited by the player base for maximum gain for minimum effort. This is a form of value maximization in the value creation process but not necessarily the form the creators had in mind when they built the system. From the e-marketing perspective, co-creation can arise at any point in the core, actual and augmented product as the consumer figures out how to make use of the offering to suit their own needs.

## Three levels of product (core, actual and augmented)

Finally, after considering a range of ways of dividing products into the sub-categories of services, ideas, digital goods and physical goods, it's important to at last consider the consumer's view of the product in terms of what needs it meets (core product), what features it has (actual product) and what else it offers to them (extended product). Core products are the benefits that the product will provide to the customer. These may vary significantly from individual to individual. Use your market segmentation from Chapter 4, and the motives list from Chapter 5, to develop higher-level generic core products for your target market. However, be aware that the core product is the co-created outcome of combining the actual product with an actual consumer in real life as they use it for their own purposes. As a marketer, you must cede control of the core product to the end user for them to feel that it's truly their solution to their problem. If you're Google and someone converts their Gmail account into a Getting Things Done system using the functionality you'd set aside for sending and receiving e-mail, shrug and move on with business (or hire them and open up a Getting Things Done service).

Actual product refers to the features, functions, style, branding, positioning and organization side of the product. Defining the actual product is a lot easier than determining value since it's your decisions that result in these elements featuring in the virtual good, tangible good, service or idea. You need to have a clear view of what the customer needs the actual product to have in the way of features to let them create their desired core product – and which of those features are central to the value offering that customers perceive. On the e-marketing front, it's the actual product that's often the most easily communicated – even Gmail focuses more on the storage space than the 'convenient communications' element.

Finally, the augmented product is the bonus level of the product which combines consumer-side elements such as perceived social prestige, word-of-mouth-based communications about the product and product positioning with the corporate side elements such as money-back guarantees, insurance and after-market service (tech support, roadside assistance). Since augmented products include the social messages associated with the product and brand, you can reposition the same actual product in the minds of the consumers to provide the rebellious option for the innovator and social compliance for the late majority. Augmentation of the product is driven through branding, promotion and online word of mouth (Chapter 7). An augmented product also depends on the availability of the product offer to provide add-on features such as convenience, which are governed more by distribution than the core or actual product itself.

# Distribution

The art of distribution is as old as the art of war itself. Careful management of supply lines between secured territories and advance portions of armies made the difference between success and failure for many military campaigns. In the battle for the consumer dollar, the management of supply lines is every bit as vital. The advent of the Internet as a legitimate and popular distribution channel for ideas, services and virtual products brings another supply line into consideration for marketers.

The Internet is a big place. The advantage of the Internet is that it can be accessed from just about anywhere without the need to physically relocate to it, through it or around it as is the case with interactions with places and spaces in the offline world. The disadvantage of the Internet is that the real world still exists alongside it in a linear, analogue and eminently physical format. Consequently, when the time comes for the results of Internet activity to arrive courtesy of the offline world, all the lessons learned over hundreds of years of shipping goods in the physical world can be applied. The true value of e-marketing is only really appreciated when you consider (and subsequently attempt to control for) dependence on the various delivery technologies Chapter 2). This includes adjusting your online e-marketing activity to maximize your search engine optimization plan in order to better adapt to the virtual supply lines that connect your content to the major search engines (Chapter 4).

There's also the sense that the search engines themselves become one part retail shop front for idea brokering and one part wholesaler of Internet content. Similarly, virtual geographies (Chapter 1) become locations for virtual retail shop fronts or supply lines for e-marketing distribution to make your product available in the same place as the customer (Chapter 2). Just to add complexity to the already complex – the management of virtual supply lines also needs to consider the mobile (Chapter 13) and non-Web (Chapter 14) marketspaces alongside (or instead of) mainstream web-based distribution outlets. Finally, the whole point of the operationalization of supply lines, virtual shipping, real world atom movements and distribution is to act on the AMA (2007) 'delivery and exchange of offerings that have value' and the CIM's (2005) 'satisfying customer requirements profitably'.

## Distribution overview

Distribution, often seen as the least glamorous part of the marketing mix, has hit the spotlight in e-marketing. Fundamentally all Internet activity is underpinned by the massive automated distribution processes of the Internet with the result that whilst the Internet is the best at what it does (and what it does ain't always pretty), most e-marketers take the distribution channel for granted since the product is usually 'just there' and it 'just works'. Distribution is only truly visible when something goes wrong.

### Distribution is old news

The marketspace technologies of distribution are old news in offline marketing with them having been the fundamental core of marketing as far back as 1937 (Dann and Dann, 2007). Distribution in the modern logistics management environment is heavily automated, data driven and technologically sophisticated. Supply line management technologies created entirely new genres of physical goods management such as just-in-time shipping. The speed of data exchanges between store and producer is getting to the point where you're practically using the retailer as a 3D world for interacting with the manufacturer (it's not quite that bad, and not quite that good at the same time). It's feasible that you could create a virtual grocery store that bundled together your groceries and shipped them to your doorstep – if it wasn't for the experience of retailers that the last mile of the delivery channel is the hardest mile. One hard learnt lesson of the DotCom1.0 era was the underestimation of the cost of last-mile delivery (shipping to the home) and how useful the consumer is when they cover those costs for you by popping down the shop for the pint of milk and packet of crisps at their own expense.

## Co-location and service delivery

Services still require co-location even in the era of the Internet. You have to be logged in at Gmail to send mail (although just like the Royal Mail, it arrives even if you're not there). Any online service that you have signed up for requires you to be at their website (or using their software, or third party software) in order to co-produce the service experience. Similarly, when you look at virtual worlds (Chapter 14), social media (Chapter 12) and cybercommunities (Chapter 9), the co-creation of these environments draws heavily on services marketing theory (Chapter 8), co-location and co-creation (Chapter 5). It's worth stating, and restating, the need for the customer to be at the point of service when considering your online product development. The level of disintermediation surrounding the Internet occasionally causes both customer and provider to forget they have to interact somewhere and somehow to make a service work for the both of them.

## Idea distribution

The distribution of an idea can also be the promotion of an idea, depending on where the idea is distributed and which arm of the mix claims the credit. Social marketing writers have long recognized that separating the distribution and promotion of an idea is largely arbitrary (Fine, 1990; Kotler and Roberto, 1989). Marketing information products that are dependent on the acceptance, use and sale of ideas also create a similar problem in determining where the online promotion of an idea ends and where the distribution begins. This raises the question of whether the content of a website counts as an idea product or a promotional message. To what extent does the movement of an idea from the mind of the originator into the mind of the recipient owe the journey to promotional techniques or idea distribution tools? For the most part, these questions are academic in nature, unless a practitioner wishes to take greater control over the movement and diffusion of their ideas. Determining the dividing line between promotional technique and marketspace distribution technique will become increasingly difficult as more ideas are promoted and distributed across the Internet. Chapter 7 examines some of the elements of merging promotion and idea products into the same delivery platform.

## Marketspace

Marketspace operates as a parallel to the physical world marketplace. It is the conjunction between ideas and exchange, where goods, services, ideas and money can be exchanged as items of value. The marketspace–marketplace continuum addresses how the value chains of product services, procurement, distribution and production can be developed and used in both the on and offline environments. Marketspace is the digital twin of the physical marketplace, where virtual value chains and virtual logistics are engaged to move intangible goods and ideas across data networks, with little or no recourse to physical environments. Marketspaces are an artificial, intangible market for information (Weiber and Kollman, 1998). A marketspace is defined by three parameters:

○ content: the idea or information being traded. It's no overstatement to describe content as the lifeblood of the Internet given that the only actual value of the Internet infrastructure is its capacity to bring content from creator to consumer (Chapter 1). Content also forms the backbone of the idea product framework and can be generated from within the Internet (data from indexes, website traffic reports) or provided by external parties (uploading videos, writing blog posts and web pages, interacting in virtual worlds).
○ context: which is the location in cyberspace where exchanges take place between producer and consumer and vary from a PayPal transaction on the Web (www.paypal.com), mobile phone screen (Chapter 13), Xbox console (Chapter 14), cybercommunity structure (Chapter 9), a vendor in a virtual world (Chapter 14), deal on eBay to payment through Twitter (www.tipjoy.com).
○ infrastructure: which is usually the Internet, although it can be any data network (mobile phone coverage, 3G) or proprietary network of shared information (Rayport and Sviokla, 1994; Pattinson and Brown, 1996; Weiber and Kollman, 1998).

The role and value of the Internet as a mediator of marketspace is based on the nature of the information product and the ability of the Internet to facilitate fast and effective movements of data. Information as a product is not subject to the lead times and shipping problems of physical goods. Multiple replications do not reduce or extinguish the original source and it can be instantly transported to any point in the production value chain (Mason-Jones and Towill, 1997; Jones and Vijayasarthy, 1998).

### Distribution for the virtual consumer in the marketspace

The Internet exists at two distinct levels. The first level is the physical representation of the network through computers, wires, cables and the second level consists of the human users of the system. Computers that use the Internet independently of human users are mostly employed by search engine companies and tend not to be engaged in online commerce. For the most part, computers have not yet been given authority to approve their own purchases over the Internet due to security considerations (and the general lack of enthusiasm towards letting computers buy parts for themselves. It never ends well.). We increasingly rely on sophisticated algorithms and arcane data-processing methods to determine *Google Page Rank* and other associated search engine constructs. Consequently, search engines are slowly becoming a distinctive market segment to address alongside your primary human market.

Annoyingly, Google's search engine robots (and their computer minders) use approximately 200 different variables to determine their ranking and weighting of the webpage and where it should sit in the search engine results. Not only is this uncomfortably similar to consumer behaviour theory, it also presents some logistical considerations for the e-marketing distribution of ideas. On the one hand, the more information that can be added to the Google, Yahoo! and Microsoft search engines, the easier it is to be found on the Internet. On the other hand, if the promotion of an idea is also the distribution of the idea, the first few lines of a Google, Bing or Yahoo! search result might be enough to answer your question without needing to load the original searched-for site. In this case, the information product in the search engine's cache effectively created, communicated and delivered value without any form of reciprocal exchange. It's the one advantage of the physical world over the search engine-based Internet environment – merely seeing the snacks cached in the fridge in a Boots store remains point of sales promotion rather than actual consumption of the product.

## How to set up a physical goods channel

Distribution channels online tend to assume that the customer will tolerate any form of distribution if the price is cheap enough and the product good enough. This assumption hasn't always been the fast track to success hoped for by many e-marketing managers. Satisfying customer needs includes questions of when, where and how the customer can access the product through the distribution channels. Thankfully, there's a fairly straightforward strategy outlined by Mols (1998) which covers three steps for identifying, anticipating and satisfying customer requirements for delivery. These steps are:

- ○ ask the customer first
- ○ assess if the customer's answer is feasible
- ○ work out the charges and price accordingly.

### Ask first

Put the question into the market research, talk to the customers and listen to requests on Twitter, Facebook or e-mail. Ask if the buyer is willing to trade price for speed (slower shipping at cheaper rates) rather than assuming anyone outside the country wants the product within 24 hours at triple the cost of the actual product. Use segmentation (Chapter 4), market research (Chapter 5) and competitor analysis (Chapter 3) to assess what expectations the customers have and if any reference prices exist for shipping (as they do for products). Always provide the maximum number of shipping options that the accounting department can handle if the customer is the one paying the bill for the postage and handling.

### Assess how to provide the distribution

Practicality and pragmatism need to be the dominant considerations for a marketing manager when arranging distribution channels based on market demand. It's also incredibly important to set reasonable expectations for delivery. The single most important facet in all of delivery is reliability. If you promise a reasonable time frame and deliver faster than expected, the customer will be happier than if you promise unrealistic deadlines and deliver later than promised. Be consistent, be reasonable and have some faith in the market being smart enough to realize that the laws of physics apply to the shipping of physical goods. You can't move objects as fast as you can move data (and even data has hard limits on how fast it can go). Provide the customer with a range of options that lets them trade speed for price and they'll feel more satisfied with the shipping as they exert greater control over their choices.

### Plus postage and handling

Work out how much this will cost and who's picking up the tab. 'Free' shipping isn't free (even data has download costs). The shipping cost comes out of someone's budget and the question is whether the customer pays for it openly at the end of the transaction or if it's a hidden charge bundled into the total costing calculations. Giving the customer options based on trading speed for price provides transparency, increases trust and gives you a sense of control in that you feel more satisfied with electing for either speed or cost savings. Providing a single, expensive shipping option that doubles or triples the price of the product takes away from the consumer's sense of empowerment and harms the potential transaction between customer and company. Understanding this is vital when you're dealing with physical goods distribution facilitated by Internet shopping. If you offer multiple shipping options in your domestic market, the international customers will feel ripped off if you offer a single high-priced 'choice'. Cross-check the total cost of shipping smaller units of physical goods to see whether or not you're pricing your lower-end products out of the market with excessive postage and handling costs.

○ shareware, which is a time-limited (or feature-reduced) version of a software product that offers sufficient functionality to allow the user to try it out before requiring a financial price commitment to continue using the service or software. There are several novelty flavours of shareware, such as postcardware (send a postcard to the author) or catware (pet a cat). These are usually classified as non-financial price costs (unless you have to buy a cat to comply with the licence agreement).

○ trialpay, which is a variation on the shareware concept. By introducing a barter system to the shareware model, you can exchange access to participating software products by taking up offers from other companies brokered by the TrialPay (www.trialpay.com) company.

○ donation-based pricing, which has been an established aspect of the shareware sector prior to its high-profile use by the band Radiohead (www.radiohead.com) in its decision to release *In Rainbows* with an open-end price – users could download the album for free or pay a financial price of their choosing through the site. This model has been replicated numerous times elsewhere before and since the Radiohead experiment although few have received quite the industry attention and speculation.

○ auction-based pricing, which is where the sellers set a reserve price and the buyers bid to determine the financial price. Although most classically associated with eBay (www.ebay.co.uk), standard and reverse auctions have been used to set prices for contracting, domain name sales and a range of business-to-business activity.

○ fixed financial pricing, which rounds out the far end of financial pricing through the use of set prices including sales, discounts and rebates (www.amazon.co.uk), volume pricing (www.zazzle.com) or structured costs depending on service levels (www.lulu.com).

It's important to separate licencing arrangements (libre) such as Creative Commons, Copyleft and Open Source from pricing strategies (Chapter 15). Although certain financial obligations may be imposed by various libre agreements (non-commercial use or the requirement to share-alike), libre agreements may also support financial pricing structures (Gnu Public License) whilst placing certain conditions on the product (code can be viewed, modified and modified versions redistributed). Similarly, setting a nil financial price (gratis) does not automatically invoke the libre status – financially free software may still have restrictive licence arrangements, copyright enforcement and closed source code.

## Price strategy and tactics

Pricing objectives are what you want to achieve strategically through the setting of a specific price level. Successful marketing practice dictates that these objectives should be consistent with the overall strategic, financial and positioning objectives of the organization. In other words, set your prices to support the overall positioning strategy (Chapter 7), marketing strategy (Chapter 3) and other tactical considerations (Chapter 4). The good thing about pricing objectives is their consistency – if you're online, offline or somewhere in between, you still can apply the same pricing formulae.

Rather than repeat the formulae here, we're going to focus on four e-marketing uses for pricing objectives. These are:

○ making money, which brings the CIM (2005) definition's 'profitably' aspect to life
○ market share, which is how price will be used for gaining and defending your territory
○ reference pricing, which is the pricing equivalent of a positioning strategy
○ mindshare, which is how price can be used for achieving certain psychological objectives through using price as a means to communicate with the consumer.

### Making money

Financial objectives are split into cost-based objectives and profit-oriented objectives. Cost-based financial objectives are literally the approach where you make enough money to pay the bills. As long as you've covered the immediate costs of production (and have a bit left over for unforeseen expenses), you're achieving your desired outcomes. Most e-marketing startups look to the cost-based model for their first few years of operation. Admittedly, more than a few blogs will be running cross-subsidized losses where the day job pays for the evening and weekend blogging operations. Most of the cost-based objectives either focus on unit-cost-plus-some pricing, where costs are covered and a percentage or a fixed dollar amount is added to each unit of output. Online intermediaries such as Cafepress (www.cafepress.com) provide fixed base prices for their custom-printed merchandise which you can raise either across the board on a fixed percentage or per individual item for the cost-recovery margin. Strictly, any gap between cost and revenue is profit. If you're cost-recovering, the gap isn't profiteering in nature.

Despite the conceptual simplicity, implementing a cost-plus objective has a number of limitations. First and foremost is the evaluation of your time costs. Many bloggers feel that they shouldn't charge for their services or feel that the time they commit to the blog isn't 'proper' work if they happen to enjoy their blogging. That's a bit like handing back part of the weekly pay cheque to the boss because you enjoyed being at work. It's vital to properly cost the actual expenditures such as domain registration fees, server rental space, Internet access (even if you're not thinking of it as a workspace) and any expenditure such as buying advertising space on other systems. Consider the non-financial aspects listed above in terms of non-financial costs of production (effort, psyche, lifestyle, time) when calculating your operating costs for cost recovery.

Cost price marketers are also faced with trying to predict an accurate measure of the final cost of individual items in advance – a difficult job given the flexibility of costs of individual components combined with the difficulty in attributing joint costs to specific items (Baker et al., 1998). Even where it is possible to accurately determine and allocate costs, further limitations of this approach include the fact that it ignores consumer demand, the influence of competitors, economies of scale as production increases and does not distinguish between variable and sunk costs (Winker, 1991). Attributing specific costs to intangible products is more difficult than attributing such costs to tangible products (Lovelock et al., 2007). Given that a large proportion of Internet-based products are services or information products, this limitation is of particular relevance.

| | |
|---|---|
| Facebook | www.facebook.com |
| Figureprints | www.figureprints.com |
| Flickr | www.flickr.com |
| Froogle | www.google.com/products |
| Gmail | www.google.com/mail |
| Google Adwords | adwords.google.com |
| Google Sketchup | sketchup.google.com |
| Livejournal | www.livejournal.com |
| Lulu | www.lulu.com |
| MySpace | www.myspace.co.uk |
| NCSoft | www.ncsoft.com |
| PayPal | www.paypal.com |
| Radiohead | www.radiohead.com |
| Remember The Milk | www.rememberthemilk.com |
| Scribed | www.scribed.com |
| Second Life | www.secondlife.com |
| Slideshare | www.slideshare.net |
| Tipjoy | www.tipjoy.com |
| TrialPay | www.trialpay.com |
| Twitter | www.twitter.com |
| Wikipedia | en.wikipedia.org/wiki/Gratis_versus_Libre |
| Wordpress.com | www.wordpress.com |
| World of Warcraft | www.worldofwarcraft.com |
| XKCD: Duty Calls | xkcd.com/386 |
| XKCD: Flash Games | xkcd.com/484 |
| YouTube | www.youtube.com |
| Zazzle | www.zazzle.com |

# Branding and promotion

By the end of this chapter, you should be able to:

- draft a basic e-marketing communication plan

- understand the use of integrated marketing communications for positioning and repositioning

- use branding and promotion to assist online service delivery

- understand the means and mechanisms of online promotion

- appreciate the value of genuine word-of-mouth communication for online promotion.

you'll want to post about how bad the communicator is on your blag or wobsite (Figure 7.2)!

- ○ *decoding*, which is where the customer interprets the channel message against what they know, understand and already have learned about your brand, product and previous messages (Chapter 5). Decoding is where a message will go right or wrong based on how well you've understood your recipient. Just as a side note: when you do miscommunicate because of a decoding issue, what you have to appreciate is that whilst you did not intend that message, the message that was decoded is the reality for that recipient. Apologize first, improve message encoding second and understand the market third. Don't disregard the recipient's complaint because that's 'not what you meant to say' – if you didn't mean to say it, accept responsibility for the message and don't keep saying the very thing you're trying to avoid by continuing with the faulty message.
- ○ *receiver*, which is the customer, viewer and anyone who encounters the communication message, who may or may not be your target market.

Connecting all these elements is feedback and noise. Feedback is the reaction of the market. Hopefully, as a result of a successful decoding process, it will be what you intended in the marketing strategy and manifest itself in improved brand image, better sales or increased site visits. To complicate matters, not all messages get through to the recipient as easily as the plan anticipates. Throughout the process both sender and receiver can encounter 'noise'. Noise is any process or activity that interrupts the flow of communication. It can be physical (server downtime) or it can be intangible (distractions). The results can be either missing the message altogether or misinterpretation leading to unexpected decoding or unanticipated feedback (Figure 7.2).

**Figure 7.2** Mispronouncing words
*Source*: http://xkcd.com/148/

## Idea products versus promotion

In the previous chapter, we introduced the concept of idea, behaviour and object as being three parts of the total product. The tricky part of the marketing mix is that the communications arm also involves the product. It communicates the idea of the product, provides information to form beliefs and shapes values and attitudes through persuasive message approaches. In addition, communication also impacts on the augmented product concept through the development of the brand and the social messages associated with the use and non use of the product. Finally, just to add a little more complexity into the mix, the promotion of an idea product is also its distribution, consumption and co-creation (Fine, 1990; Kotler and Roberto, 1989). Confused yet? When you read this page, you're receiving an idea product embedded in a physical good, the value of which (idea and book) comes almost entirely from what you do with it in this course, your daily life or your workplace. Since the mix is interconnected, we will bring in the idea element of the product because it fits into promotion, branding and positioning across the chapter.

Similarly, since drawing the line between the promotion and distribution of an idea may not be possible in the e-marketing context, it's worth cross checking your promotional campaign against promotional and distribution theory to see which models will be the most useful for the given circumstances. That's the beauty of marketing theory – not only is it circular, it's also very modular. The modularity of marketing is well suited to the blurred boundaries of the Internet. It doesn't matter if the Internet is a promotional medium, distribution channel or actual product at the end of the day. What matters is how you can use it to satisfy your customer's needs. Consequently, the Internet can be product, service, place and advertisement all rolled up into a single interactive package.

## Communications of offerings that have value

This section of the chapter steps back from the Internet as the Swiss army knife of marketing and focuses on using the interactive medium as the message platform. For the next few pages, we'll concentrate on the Internet as a communications tool which can be used to generate awareness, interest, desire, and activity (AIDA). The AIDA model is a standard issue marketing promotion framework that posits the four roles of any communication message are to create one of the following:

o *awareness*, which is where you help the consumer become aware of your product, help them form attitudes towards the product and trigger problem recognition by providing an initial understanding of what the product is and what it can do for them. This is where the PR elements of being discussed on Twitter, profiled on blogs or being the banner advertising at the side of the Facebook page come into play.
o *interest*, which is where you're getting the consumer to form beliefs, feel a need for the product and generally move from 'I've heard of that' to 'I wouldn't mind trying one'. Whereas awareness can be a dry, information-based, rational form of

that combines market research to understand the consumer and their current thinking about a product or service, and the use of IMC to communicate a message that your product is like or not like an existing one. It's partly related to innovation adoption theory in that the easier it is to position a product based on its familiarity, the more likely it is that the product is targeted to early or late majority and is in the later stages of the product lifecycle. This is also a technique that's heavily geared towards customer co-creation on one side (Chapter 8) and the anticipation side of the CIM's definition of marketing (Chapter 2) on the other. With a strong reliance on co-creation, positioning is also an awkward area to evaluate as you can only put the requisite visual cues, product experience and information into the marketspace. You don't have the final say on how the customer interprets your offering (Chapter 4).

### Five forms of positioning

There are five forms of positioning of interest to the online marketer. We've chosen to use the Kotler and Lee (2008) positioning frameworks from social marketing for their compatibility with the positioning ideas and behaviours.

○ Behaviour-focused positioning, which is where you position yourself, your product and the rest of the operation by emphasizing the behaviour you want the end user to undertake. If you're starting up a search engine, emphasize the use of the technology for specific types of behaviours – finding the best holiday deals or searching for a celebrity photo.
○ Benefit-focused positioning, which is where you position your product based on the specific benefits it will provide the potential user. In other words, the communications focus on the 'What's in it for you message'. These benefits are usually associated with the core product and focus on the intangibles such as safety, convenience or time saving.
○ Barriers-focused positioning, which focuses on setting yourself up as being similar to some other part of your customer's life. This way, adopting your product or using your website won't be perceived as too hard, too challenging or too complex to use. Barrier-focused positioning is a slightly misleading label as the strategy actually focuses on identifying and then reducing barriers to adoption. Once you know what's stopping people from using your product, you can place yourself in the correct context for their lives – if people aren't using your message service because they feel they've got nothing to say, position the service as a way to listen to their friends talk.
○ Competition-focused positioning, which allows you to position your site, service, idea or product in relation to your key identified competitors. This is a comparison-based strategy where the main communications focus on the 'We're just like Competitor X only faster/cheaper/cleaner/nicer' and so on. This strategy is usually underpinned by an overall market share expansion approach and is of most value in the highly competitive maturity phase of the product lifecycle.
○ Repositioning strategies, which are about trying to move from where you currently fit to somewhere else in the market. Repositioning may be desirable for any one of

a number of reasons. In some cases, a solid positioning strategy that has delivered success in the past needs to be revitalized to reflect new market realities. In other cases, the communications mix failed to deliver on the desired strategy with the result that the market saw you in a very different light to the one you saw yourself in. Brands which last the distance undertake regular brand audits to make sure that they are still where they want to be in the mind of the marketplace and that the marketplace still values what organizations in that position have to offer.

## The strategic elements of positioning

Positioning is the underpinning foundation of marketing success. The marketing mix exists to support the product's position so, without a clear idea of what that position is, the marketing mix will lack direction and inevitably will become inconsistent and ineffective. From a strategic perspective, the key point to remember at all times is that the desired positioning strategy developed in the organization is not necessarily the position that the product or firm holds in the marketplace. To differentiate between the two remember that the positioning strategy outlines the planned way that you wish your product, service, idea or organization to be understood by the target market relative to other players in the market. Your actual position is how the market interprets your messages, brands, products and services and how they evaluate you relative to the competing offers in the market.

As well as acknowledging the difference between a positioning strategy and a market position, it's also important to recognize that there are two core characteristics of positioning. First, positioning is a relative concept. A market position and a positioning strategy are both based on the notion of being faster, stronger, cheaper and so on. In other words, the description of your positioning strategy will be in comparative rather than absolute terms. Secondly, positioning is subjective not objective. Many better mousetraps have failed in the market because they assumed that the objective improvements would be understood and appreciated by the market. The 'better' product as far as the market is concerned is the one they perceive offers them the best outcomes on a particular criterion. It doesn't matter how often you demonstrate to Coke drinkers in blind taste tests that they actually like (and often prefer) Pepsi, they're still going to buy the product they want – which is Coke.

Understanding your market position requires a degree of detachment from the emotional investment you've made in your brand combined with some solid and objective market research. You may think that your product is a prestige-priced, sophisticated alternative to the everyday options – the market may see you as pretentious and overpriced. If gaps appear between how you see yourself and how others see you, the challenge is to change that perception. In some cases the discrepancies could be due to objective issues that can be relatively easily changed such as additions to product features or modifications to the distribution network. More often, however, the problem arises because of the failure to fully integrate the communications mix with the marketing mix. Ensuring that the market-perceived position of the product is the same as the marketer's desired position relies heavily on developing an appropriate and effective branding strategy, which in turn is supported by a quality IMC strategy.

The range of available advertising sizes is more limited than even the classified section of a newspaper. Some providers such as Facebook allow for additional text beneath their advertising, although Facebook has a narrow choice of size. While the acceptance (or, more accurately, active rejection) level of banner advertising has been changing with the evolution of the Internet market, the change drifts back and forth between the 'end of days for banner adverts' and their role as the saviour of free social networks. Despite over a decade of presence online, the banner advert has achieved neither dominance nor destruction and appears to be a fairly stable constant feature of the online terrain.

### Text-only advertising

The strangest development of advertising on the Internet has been the rise of 'retro'-styled text-only advertising. The best-known version of the system is Google AdWords, which started life as short text advertisements next to the Google search results and spread across to Google-owned services such as Gmail and Blogger. After establishing that AdWords didn't bring the downfall of blogging society, they've spread to a range of websites and can be easily added to blogs, websites and other areas.

Google AdWords act like a cross between a haiku and a note passed in class – they appear on the right-hand side of the page of results for a standard Google search, along with the Google Premium Sponsorships (which appear at the top of the page). In many senses, the Google AdWord restrictions require more poetry than marketing to develop key copy points – with an effective maximum of two lines (or a single sentence) per advert and no visual element, clarity and conciseness are vital. Similarly, the Premium Sponsorship Advertising simply places the URL and a short phrase at the top of the search results for the page.

Critical to the operation of Google's advertising system is purchasing keywords. Google AdWords works on the principle of purchasing a keyword which then triggers the display of the advert when a user searches for that keyword. If the user clicks on the AdWord banner, Google bills the advertiser. If, however, the advertising doesn't draw attention, the advertiser isn't billed for the space. While this means paying only for what works, Google's system gives you a (not very large) maximum number of searches to perform at a reasonable rate before suspending your advertising and requesting that you rework the message. As mentioned above, keyword purchasing has problems galore due to the Google system having no concept of nuance, context or subtlety. If you're running a pro-marriage website with Google AdWords, you could find an ambitious divorce lawyer's advert showing up beside the wedding cakes and prenuptial template files. Many activist websites covering topics such as politics, race, gender and other issues have found their site content triggering inappropriate auto-generated AdWord content. Consequently, whilst Google AdWords has its role, it's a developmental system despite having launched back in 2000 (the dark ages of the Internet).

### Offline advertising (the outside world)

The beauty of the Internet is that it provides an unlimited supply of paradoxes. Name a virtue of the Internet and it's just as likely to be a vice. That same open landscape which lets you speak freely is a boundless, seamless digital environment of shared voices of all those other marketers speaking freely. Your voice is competing with a lot of other voices, and some of those have some serious offline clout to back them up (@bbc, @aplusk, @oprah). Attracting people to your part of the Internet, be it Twitter, a blog, your Facebook page or website, is a specialist skill. The role of the promotional mix, in this context, is not to deliver customers to the site, but to deliver the address of the website to customers in a timely and useful way. The problem with offline promotion of the URL is that the offline world is a dead pointer (Dieberger, 1997). Dead pointer is a charming term which refers to any time a URL is displayed in a medium where it cannot be accessed by clicking or immediately interfacing with that medium. The dead pointer is the predominant form of media in the real world. Any website address seen in an offline context needs to be transferred into the online world. In order to make the jump from billboard to web browser, offline promotion of Internet addresses needs exceptionally high unaided recall or some form of supplementary media in terms of print or direct mail. Systems such as the QR code partially alleviate the dead pointer issue by transferring the consumption of the offline advert into an immediate experience on a handheld device (assuming the phone has the appropriate Internet access available).

## Direct marketing

Direct marketing refers to activities by which products and services are offered to market segments in one or more media at a personalized level. Usually, direct marketing is conducted by phone or mail with the attempt to either solicit immediate response (catalogue buying, phone shopping) or deliver promotional materials. It has an unsurpassed ability to be used by marketers for narrowly defined targeted marketing in that messages can be customized and mailed directly to the target recipient. The disadvantage of direct mail is a lower market profile in that mail-out campaigns do not get incidental viewing by non-targeted members of the audience. In addition, the propensity of direct mail to be used for unsolicited mail-outs has led to the medium gaining a reputation for being junk mail rather than a value-added service. For the moment, consider direct e-mail marketing to be an off-limit zone for standard advertising activity and restricted to only dealing with established customers who have requested updates from you as part of their ongoing relationship with your organization (Chapter 9).

### Why e-mail is not direct mail

E-mail is not a direct-mail channel, no matter how nice it would be if Internet users would accept the same level of digital junk mail as they do paper mail. Since the costs of e-mail are picked up by the receiver and the carrier networks, unsolicited mail is treated with the appropriate level of hostility as befits any form of resource leech. No matter how tempting a mass unsolicited mail-out may seem in terms of dollars per customer annoyed, the damage to the branding and image of the company will far outweigh any potential benefit. Similarly, there is no real point to purchasing an e-mail database list from a list reseller since users cannot tell the difference between unsolicited spam and resold mailing list spam. The Internet has ushered in an age of relationship-based direct marketing where the consumer has become empowered to invite direct marketers to become part of their lives and reject those who show up uninvited. Use e-mail once the transaction has been initiated by the customer and your e-mail message will be a valued part of the customer's inbox (Chapter 2).

## Personal selling

Personal selling is the hand-to-hand combat of marketing promotion, where personal communications techniques are used to sell a product to an individual in a personalized, face-to-face environment. Personal selling offers an unparalleled level of customization, interactivity, flexibility and feedback in a very specific and localized transaction. The disadvantage of personal selling is that it is one-to-one, rather than one-to-many, and is a very labour-intensive method of promotion. This in turn makes it very expensive per target reached. Personal selling is not usually associated with overt website promotions since it's a personal contact between sales and buyer, and usually conducted out of sight of the main market through VOIP, e-mail and direct messaging.

## Point-of-sale/point-of-purchase displays

Point of sale/point of purchase refers to in-store displays such as posters, signs, sampling and materials designed to influence the consumer's brand choice at the point of purchase. The advantage to promoting websites and the Internet is that the consumer gets given the direct relationship between the website and the product at the point of purchase, which can be valuable, particularly for post-purchase follow-up. Even for fast-moving consumer goods which are consumed immediately, traffic can be driven to the site via point-of-purchase promotions through the use of competitions based on registration of initial purchase. The downside to in-store promotions is that the customer leaves the website address behind as they leave the store, either with or without the product which the website was designed to promote.

Online point of sales can be the nemesis of a quick and pain-free transaction as you try to navigate your way through three or four pages of 'Special offers exclusively for you right now' text with the 'Skip to checkout' button hidden in the smallest font at the base of the page. This approach by the e-commerce industry to make the purchase button hard to find is the physical world equivalent of placing an obstacle course between the shopping and the checkout counter. Other online point-of-sales options occur within the website or shopping cart with the recommendations systems, such as Amazon's habit of advising you of what other products people bought to go with your current product and iTunes's recommendations based on your previous music purchases. The more accurate and less intrusive the recommendation, the more valuable it'll be seen by your customer and be perceived as a genuine 'Hey, if you liked that, you might want this as well' rather than an aggressive upsize-selling technique.

## Publicity

Publicity is any form of non-personal mass promotional activity that is not paid for by the organization. Most frequently this refers to news articles or editorial comments, but it can also be seen as incidental placements in films, video or television footage where the product or organization is an incidental, rather than paid, part of the background. The obvious advantage of this method is the low cost associated with the genuine publicity events that occur through media reviews of the website, or incidental featuring of the website in media coverage. The downside to publicity is the lack of control exerted over the use of the URL and the potential for incomplete or inaccurate reporting of the address and website. Advertising of URLs at sporting stadiums has the advantage of the incidental news coverage during the sports reports, although it is more common to see only half the address, or to have the address obscured by the sporting event it was sponsoring. Publicity also flows from the organic discussions on the Internet that spring up around events, news articles, or flow through from high-profile acts that generate conversation. Zappos.com rose from obscurity to having a fairly high Internet profile quite quickly simply through a conversation about how a single staff member being flexible and acting with a bit of compassion turned a potentially bad situation (customer late with their return shipping due to family tragedy) into an act of kindness (waiving late fees, sending flowers). The publicity generated from one genuine act of kindness multiplied quickly as it was blogged, tweeted and discussed as a genuine topic of conversation.

## Public relations

Public relations refers to the deliberate, planned and sustained effort to institute and maintain an understanding between an organization and any group with which the company needs to communicate, such as the government, citizen groups or the media. PR campaigns concerning websites are usually based around developing a stated corporate position on an issue and directing further inquiries to the website where greater depth of information can be made available. The advantage of this approach is that depth and clarity of information on a subject can be more readily accessed by the general public or media than through press conferences or other PR tools. Public relations has traditionally been seen as a subordinate support function in marketing although it is being used as a corporate positioning tool.

Public relations is having a fair degree of trouble adapting to the new rules of the Internet where bloggers aren't journalists, don't have fax machines and don't tend to have the established partnerships with PR companies. To some extent, this is a good sign for the PR industry as it has moved from a carefully crafted message to a targeted market into a mass broadcast model as technical capacity outstripped strategic thinking. If you want to engage in PR campaigns that involve bloggers, there are a few simple rules:

1. Be interesting. First, and foremost, understand that your role as the PR agency is to provide something of value to the blogger so they've got something they can write up on their blog. Do them a favour by being novel, topical and interesting and they'll reciprocate by doing you a favour in promoting your work to their readership. Public relations is the creation, delivery and exchange of communications that have value. Think idea product, think market needs and really think about what you can offer the writer to solve their problem (need for copy) before you attempt contact.

2. Do the market research. Read the targeted blog's current posts and as far back into the archive as you can find. Eliminate blogs that have negatively reacted to similar ideas to the one you're about to pitch. Check for conflicts of interest, histories of conflicts with the company and the type of audience to expect at the blog.

3. Segment. Use the same degree of care and consideration for targeting blogs, news outlets and other commentators that you would use for picking your target market. Your objective is return on time invested, with an emphasis on smaller numbers of higher quality contacts rather than a string of 'Dear Blogger' posts that will hit the spam filter (at best) or receive negative coverage (at worst).

4. Contact. Look for cues on the blogger's site about their preference for unsolicited comments. Some high-profile blogs have very specific instructions for making contact to suggest content – BoingBoing.net uses a specific web page and structure for content suggestions (http://www.boingboing.net/suggest.html). This is a relationship between you and the blog author, so start with a positive impression by taking the time to know their preferences.

5. Communicate. Build the relationship with the blogger by talking to them, cultivating them as a contact and generally treating them as you would a paying customer. They're making money for you indirectly by cutting your promotion costs and hopefully generating credible endorsements and conversation starters.

6. Disclaim and own the message. Transparency is a critical issue with bloggers and sponsored messages. Openness, honesty and transparent conduct will increase the likelihood of repeat message business as the blogger and their audience are less likely to react negatively towards the presence of a commercial message in their community space if it's handled appropriately. Late 2009 saw the US Federal Trade Commission release a series of guidelines for sponsored blog posts, payola content and other disclosure requirements. Pay attention to the spirit as well as the letter of the laws that govern disclosure.

7. Don't Astroturf. If you can't build a genuine grassroots movement through honest contact, don't try to fake a string of blogs, blog comments and message board participation to push your message. You will get caught, you will be exposed and you'll be a topic of conversation that will feature the hashtag #fail quite prominently as your brand is associated with low-quality campaigning, dishonest behaviour and every other negative piece of publicity the Internet can muster. What little gain you could make from the deception won't be worth the brand damage to your company, and future campaigns from the same agency. Besides, if you're getting no traction with the public relations, it's probably a safe bet you're not moving products, so something's gone wrong at the core of the operation. Less cheating, more revision, and you'll do better next time.

### Search engine optimization: PR for computers

Search engine optimization (SEO) is an applied form of PR campaign with a very specific target audience consisting of the search engine ranking algorithm at one or more of the major search engines. As a specific and highly targeted form of communication, it comes with a couple of problems that need to be highlighted. First, for a variety of reasons, both legal and technical, Google (www.google.co.uk), Bing (www.bing.com), Yahoo!Search (search.yahoo.com) and the other thirty or so search engines will all use a different mechanism for ranking and rating your website. SEO strategies need to be targeted towards the search engine used by your primary market since if you've got an amazing search rating at a site your customers don't use, it's a waste of effort. Secondly, search engine optimization is an evolving art form that has to update and react to changes in the way in which search engines manage their indexes, ranking and priority ordering. For the most part, relevance, accuracy and value tend to win out over keyword stuffing backlinks and referral tricks at the end of the day. That said, because the search engine business is a very young industry, there's a lot of change and upheaval forthcoming as the major engines continue to research and develop new ways of handling the massive data set that is the Internet. The broad advice for search engine optimization for your campaign is fairly straightforward in that most search engines respect content over technique and prioritize their results accordingly. Make something of value for your customers and the odds are firmly in favour of that process providing a decent organic SEO score. Also, it's vital to remember that the point of being highly ranked in a search engine is to engage the human customer who comes to your website to see your offering of value.

## Sales promotions

Sales promotions are marketing activities conducted to stimulate short-term growth in sales through techniques such as coupons, prize promotions, competitions and free samples. The advantage to the sales promotion is that it encourages goodwill among consumers and tends to stimulate immediate sales. Offers such as 'buy two, get one free' encourage brand switching and immediate sales spikes. The major disadvantage of these elements is that the consumer market is becoming exceptionally sensitive to sales promotions and is willing to engage in brand switching to track the promotional offers. This is particularly rampant where switching costs are low, for example, websites, where the use of sales promotions to encourage visits to a website will not necessarily guarantee loyalty. It is far more likely a customer will track through the different sales promotions online and collect a range of offers from different websites. Sales promotions offer features in the non-Web world with discounted package deals, console or system-exclusive content, free demonstration downloads (within game links to purchase) or expansions through downloadable content (DLC) and in-world game items (Chapter 14).

## User-generated content

User-generated content is the point where marketing, co-creation and easy access to high-end authoring tools collide in a complex tangle of legality and authenticity. On the one hand, there's nothing more persuasive than a customer who's so keen on your work that they'll build their own advertising campaign to promote your stuff on your behalf. On the other hand, there's nothing more terrifying for an integrated marketing communication campaign than interlopers who don't have a grasp of the strategy, tactics and component style guides. It's a tough balance that currently is erring in favour of legal challenges, lawyers and copyright enforcement.

---

### User-generated content versus lawyers

From a marketing perspective a serious problem now arising is that the type of user who'll take the time out to make something on your behalf will be quite vocal when your lawyers show up with the cease and desist letters. The gap between the acceptance of user-generated content and the use of lawyers was most pronounced during the competition between the *Star Trek: The Next Generation* and the *Babylon 5* television shows back in the early days of the Web (1995 to 1997). Paramount Studios (*Star Trek*) would send carefully worded legal threats from their lawyers to shut down fan sites that were dedicated to spreading support for the *Star Trek* show. At the same time, the fledgling Warner Bros sci-fi series *Babylon 5* contacted the creators of the fan sites and offered them access to 'official' sanctioned fansite kits that allowed the site owners to continue promoting the new series as a semi-sanctioned operation. The result was the development of an active *Babylon 5* fanbase that was spending significant effort on promoting the show through word of mouth, whereas the *Star Trek* fans were periodically dedicating more effort to generating negative publicity over yet another heavy-handed shutdown of a site attempting to sell Paramount's show to the rest of the Internet.

---

User-generated content is an off-shoot of the word-of-mouth styles of publicity and promotion that simply arise because the user of a product tries to encourage those around them to share the experience. User-generated content is how fan clubs, user groups, reading groups and movie-watching events have all spawned around a core group of enthusiastic fans who use a combination of word of mouth and self-created content to connect with other fans to form a community (Chapter 9) and encourage non-fans to try the product.

Word-of-mouth advertising has also seen a major revamp having been recently repackaged as 'viral marketing', so named because the marketing message is spread through the community in a fashion not dissimilar to that of an infectious virus. While a more charming metaphor probably does exist, viral marketing has several elements that make it extremely valuable for the promotion of websites. Promotion by word of mouth and word of mouse is recommended where the site contains a medium to high level of complexity and engages in services that can be used as a topic of conversation or for which users would seek the opinions of their friends and family. From a marketing perspective, word of mouth is valuable at the point that the market is influenced by social pressures in terms of either needing to communicate their social leadership status (early adopter) or to conform to the conversation surrounding them (early and late majority) (Chapter 5). The rise of social media communication platforms has actually improved the quality, quantity and capacity of organic word-of-mouth campaigns as genuine experiences that can be relayed through a social group with limited or no loss of details. One blog post from a happy customer posted to Twitter can be re-tweeted rapidly with any number of endorsements.

Certain aspects of social media systems also provide opportunities for assisted word-of-mouth activities. These are predominately organic developments from the customers which are gently assisted by marketers. Back in the Introduction when you signed up for the social bookmarking site Delicious (www.delicious.com), you would have noticed the links to the hot topics and trending conversations. These are social cues that can form the basis for the first trigger to start a word-of-mouth conversation around a site, service, product or event. Similarly, Twitter provides an index of popular topics, tags and words that the general public are tweeting in a given period (www.twitter.com), which provides another set of social cues as to topics of possible online conservation for the early majority (Chapter 5). Finally, aggregator sites such as Slashdot (www.slashdot.org), Digg (www.digg.com) and Metafilter (www.metafilter.com) create environments where word of mouth can be generated from genuine (and slightly forced) conversations about sites, brands and products that appear in the popular trends charts.

## Principles and tactics

Once the general trend of your promotional campaign has been determined, next comes the details of what to say and how. Writing text-based copy for a website is significantly different to writing copy for traditional media. Similarly, decisions need to be made about the extent to which messages are fixed or fluid.

### Dimensions of a promotional message

The objective of all elements of the promotional mix is to say the right thing to the right person at the right time and have them receive, perceive and interpret the message in the right way (Kiani, 1998). In order to achieve this outcome, there are three main dimensions that a promotional message needs to balance:

1. message, which is the meaning to be transferred from the advertiser to the audience
2. format, which refers to the attributes of the advertisement that attract the audience's attention, such as relevance, timeliness and usefulness
3. context, which is the media platform used by the promotional message.

Context offers the message certain opportunities for audience attraction and message interaction through static (outside world), dynamic (reactive advertising such as red buttons on cable television) or interactive (conversations in social media) options. A good promotional message needs to balance its strength in each of the dimensions so that the message is supported by an appropriate format and the best use of the opportunities available in that context. The major contexts for promotion consist of online and offline locations where you can point someone at your online content (or somewhere else through your online activity).

### Static advertising

Static advertising includes the outside-world strategies of everything beyond the front door in the physical world such as sky writing (difficult but achievable), bus sidings, billboards, bus shelters and postcards stuck to phone booths. It also incorporates indoor advertising such as television, cinema, radio, direct mail, magazines and other printed or broadcast advertising materials consumed inside a private home or at work (or on the Tube, etc.). Sales promotion and point-of-sale advertising are also covered under the indoor advertising banner. If you can't click on the URL and get a response, it's a static advert. It may also include the product dot.com category where the URL is printed on the product, packaging or instructional materials.

### Dynamic advertising

Dynamic advertising occurs when clicking on the URL has some outcome that includes another page loading, a call to action, a purchase opportunity or related online activity. This is often conducted by contextual placement such as Google AdWords, banner advertising and the annoying advertising overlay on YouTube videos. It's also incorporating the calling-card approach, where the author of an e-mail, blog comment or bulletin board post casually includes the URL to their site as part of their signature file contact details.

### Interactive advertising

Interactive advertising is where you move from the computer-generated dynamic interaction and bring the communications to the interpersonal level. The rise of social media has created a duality where automated systems (web content, dynamic delivery) can create opportunities to escalate the promotional message to conversations between real people. This incorporates the classic one-to-one models of personal selling, direct e-mail exchanges, messenger chats and Facebook comments with the one-to-many-to-one dynamics of a conversation on Twitter or in blog comments. Interactive advertising requires people to be talking to people in order to incorporate word-of-mouth communications models, personalized responses in the communication and the sociable side of social media sites (Chapter 12). It's also the IMC nightmare scenario as consumer conversations are customized, interactive, fast and likely to be totally 'off script'.

## Six tenets of promotion

Aitchison and French-Blake (1999) argue that the best use of the promotional mix comes through an understanding of creativity as a subjective experience. This involves an understanding that no objective 'truth' exists in a trade that works in the realm of persuasion and that the role of good promotion is to reach the highest, not the lowest, common denominator with the target market. These statements can be translated into a six-point framework to guide the creation of effective promotion:

1. Promotion should be about empowerment. Positive promotions offer you information on how a product, idea, service or website will improve your life. Persuade through benefits rather than features.
2. Promotion can signpost social change. Promotion and the mass media promotion of Internet sites produce a constant stream of encouraging messages for the general public to experience the online world. Same rule applies for subsystems of the online world – celebrity, media and advertising use of Facebook, MySpace and Twitter raises their level of acceptance and adoption in the wider community.
3. Promotion can support and encourage. A good promotional campaign doesn't just add value through new recruits, it also reaffirms the brand loyalty of existing customers. Promotional campaigns based on relationship marketing – from online advertising to sending a thank-you e-mail to a recent user of the website – can go a long way towards the long-term success of a Web presence (Chapter 8).
4. Promotion should send news. It's okay to take time to spread a message rather than constantly be persuading a targeted audience member to perform an action. Sometimes, just raise awareness or increase likeability and let those two elements handle the call to action. Less rush, more consumer empowerment, and greater rewards await.
5. Promotion can be used to share experiences. 'If you get it, share it' is the mantra of social media. Promotion can be used to communicate shared meaning in a community. Honesty, humanity and emotional connections are central to the success of social media (Chapter 12), cybercommunity (Chapter 9) and ongoing relationships (Chapter 8). If your website is a shared experience for people just like the target adopter, it increases the sense of relevance, aids recall (Chapter 5) and improves the likelihood of the site breaking through the clutter to reach the targeted recipient.
6. Promotion can be used to answer a dream. The core business of marketing is to identify, anticipate and satisfy customer requirements. What if you went beyond core requirements and knew the customer well enough to tap into their dreams, needs and wants? You'd be delivering a higher level of product, gaining a greater level of recall, motivation and desire to access the site, and generally having a better time of it as you provide the customer with something they really want. If you do it in a sustainable way by making a profit, you'll ensure that you're still there next time they need you. This happens more than a few times in the social media and community orientated sites, and should be a required element of a user-generated content site (Chapter 6).

## Conversations and the share of voice

In Chapter 2 we mentioned the concept of the one-to-many-to-one model of interactive, hypermediated communication as the major game changer for interactive marketing when compared with the offline world. When Hoffman and Novak (1996) put this idea forward it was at the dawn of the era of connectivity, so their emphasis was on the ability of the consumer to e-mail a response to the marketer who could

means (promotion). Knowing your role in the larger operation makes the micro-level decision that much easier.

## The checklists

The aim of the checklists is to give you a sense of the different ways you can communicate with the market and the sort of answers you'll need to be able to generate to make best use of the promotional opportunities online.

### The content pitch checklist

The content pitch is the toughest in the communications plan. Brevity requires focus. Being able to deliver your central message, idea or product value in a single sentence takes practice and is a great way to determine if you really know your product well enough to take it to the market. Inside the content pitches, we've set up the requirements for some of the more common places you'll need to have a short, fast and mostly consistent response.

### 140 characters (tweet)

Even if you're not a fan of the Twitter approach to life, chances are someone in your marketplace is going to want to tell their followers about your product. Essentially, this is the concentrated version of who you are, what your product offers the market and what's in it for them. You'll need two or three Twitter responses that are shorter than 140 characters so you can fit the @ username into the reply to the question 'So what does it do?' Although brevity counts with Twitter, stay true to the personality of the brand – luxury goods tend not to talk in SMS text speech. If you're asking other people to re-tweet your product launch, sales or call to arms don't forget to include #hashtags in the message so you can track the participants and reward them accordingly.

### One sentence (Twitter BioPitch)

The one-sentence pitch is the hardest sales pitch on the Internet but surprisingly common for something so complicated. We've nicknamed it the TwitterBio pitch since they're a leading offender when it comes to asking for a one-sentence summary of who you are, what you do and what you have to offer to the world. That said, it's a lot like branding, positioning and good slogans – knowing yourself well enough to describe who you are in a sentence is a good skill to develop. It also expands quite nicely into the elevator pitch.

### Two sentences (elevator pitch)

The elevator pitch draws its name from the time you have between two floors in an elevator ride to explain what it is that you do, sell, have to offer or want from someone. The key to a successful elevator pitch is knowing the audience – if you're explaining to a prospective customer why they should give you money, then you'll need to talk about the benefits from their perspective. Your elevator pitch to the CEO, your manager or your boss's boss will be based on a variation of how your project is helping achieve the company's goals (i.e. profit, cost reduction, be awesome). As with the one liner, it's a great starting point to get into the bigger bio pitches that are needed in longer conversations (two, three or ten floors) and to fill out the 'about you' section of those websites we signed you up to back in the Introduction.

### Paragraph (website bio pitch)

The paragraph bio pitch is an exercise in self-promotion, self-description and marketing chicanery. The challenge for a bio pitch is that you have to discuss yourself (if it's a personal bio) and most people find that to be an incredibly challenging combination of self-reflection, embarrassment and self-aggrandizement. Thankfully this is where the marketing tricks come into play. First, head back to the product (core, actual, augmented) model to ascertain what you want to present in the bio pitch. Secondly, view this as an exercise in consumer-centric thinking – what do you think you'd like to know as a customer that would give you confidence in the company? Focus on mapping yourself against core product (Who am I to this customer?), actual products (What can I do for you?) and augmented products (What would you like to know about what I've done previously to build your confidence in me?) and you're on the way to the first draft of the bio. The paragraph bio pitch can be expanded up to any length required to fill out the 'About me' details on most websites, blogs and social media websites.

## The SEO plan

The problem with search engine optimization in general is that it's an inexact art and still a while away from being an inexact science when it grows up. Google has over 2 million hits for the letters SEO and goes thoroughly over the top with the search for 'search engine optimization' with 85 million hits. Much has been speculated, written and generated about the arcane art of Google wrangling, Bing stacking and Yahoo! stuffing without a lot of clear and certain outcomes.

Search engine marketing (SEM) and SEO both target the software infrastructure that underpins the various search engines. To that end, there's a whole array of complex tricks that will only be briefly appreciated by the search engine's software until Google, Microsoft and Yahoo! change the equations driving the rank order again. For the most part, the following aspects have been fairly clear-cut and consistent – SEO is a means, not the ends for marketing, and marketers who focus on customer needs in the development of a website are likely to score reasonably well on Google as the higher-quality content on the site also encourages word of mouth, links, referrals and happy customers.

There are two areas where e-marketing and the SEO tactics do combine. First, keywords are a central part of the SEO, SEM and e-marketing experience as these are the means by which your customers (current and potential) will seek out your website. Consequently, you'll need to ensure that the common words, phrases and language that your customers would use to describe your products, brands and sites are present somewhere on the website. With brands, this is strangely straightforward – you'll usually

| | |
|---|---|
| Bing xRank | ww.bing.com/xrank |
| BoingBoing.net | www.boingboing.net/suggest.html |
| Cafepress | www.cafepress.com |
| Delicious | www.delicious.com |
| Digg | www.digg.com |
| GIMP | www.gimp.org |
| Google | www.google.co.uk |
| Inkscape | www.inkscape.org |
| Metafilter | ww.metafilter.com |
| Photoshop | www.photoshop.com |
| Slashdot | www.slashdot.org |
| Twitscoop | ww.twitscoop.com |
| Twitter | www.twitter.com |
| @cnn | www.twitter.com/cnn |
| @aplusk | www.twitter.com/aplusk |
| @oprah | www.twitter.com/oprah |
| Will it Blend? | www.willitblend.com |
| Yahoo! Search | search.yahoo.com |
| Zazzle | www.zazzle.com |

# CHAPTER 8

# Services and relationship marketing

## Learning objectives

By the end of this chapter, you should be able to:

- describe the way in which the Internet operates as a service

- use services marketing theory and models to map out your approach to online service delivery

- understand how to build, maintain and assess online customer relationships

- appreciate the value of relationship marketing in e-commerce.

## Introduction

Services and relationship marketing provide an intertwined pairing of theory and practice which covers a large portion of online marketing activity. Any website that has a recurring interaction with the customer will be building a relationship with its users (even if site operator and site user aren't currently aware of relationship marketing). If your e-marketing is about delivering consumer interactions through applications, file storage or data access, you're in the service delivery business. There's a strong argument to say that the entirety of e-marketing is services marketing (except the bit where it's about physical goods). e-marketing service products covered in this chapter are those sold and/or distributed via the Internet. While you can accompany them with an offline activity, we're interested in the Internet-delivered options. Online banking is a service that's attached to offline activity (banks, physical money) while Google Calendar (www.google.com/calendar) handles the documentation and co-ordination of offline activity (classes, parties). The online element is of interest here rather than the offline activity to which it is anchored – Google Calendar doesn't actually attend the party (even if you're carrying a Nexus One).

This chapter covers the basic principles of services marketing in relation to the Internet and service offerings based around e-commerce. (If you've not taken a services marketing course, it's worth picking up the full semester of study since services are vital to the global economy. Plus it's fun, and helps if you want a career in consultancy.) The discussion of services marketing is followed by a review of the principles of relationship marketing, which itself arose out of services marketing research in the mid 1990s and examines how the ongoing use of a site or web service can develop into a mutually beneficial relationship.

## Services marketing

To appreciate the benefits of shifting service delivery online, it is necessary to have a detailed understanding of the differences between goods and service product delivery, and the components of the traditional service product. Online services marketing has an advantage over the offline counterparts since time dependency and one-on-one interpersonal interactions between service staff and customers are significantly reduced or completely eliminated through technology.

### The e-service product

The e-service product requires a variation of the product model from Chapter 6 (Figure 6.1) because services tend towards a combination of three approaches: services to people, services involving people and services involving goods (Figure 8.1).

'Services to people' products result in temporary person-based experiences (Figure 1.4, Chapter 1) that cover entertainment (www.shockwave.com), educational videos (www.youtube.com) and instructional materials (www.instructables.com). 'Services involving people' products require interactions between individuals and cover

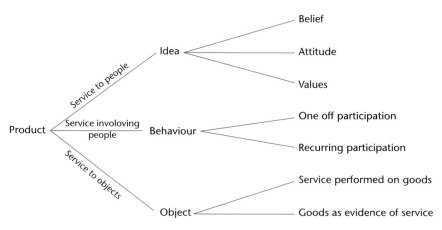

Figure 8.1  Service product model

a large amount of social media activity (Chapter 12), person-to-person e-commerce (www.ebay.co.uk) and using the Internet as a brokerage medium for direct interactions with other people. Finally, 'services to objects' products involve those products where the purpose of the service is to modify something (physical or virtual) in some way with the assistance of the service provider. This broad and vague definition lets us put Zazzle's (www.zazzle.com) product customization in the same category as e-banking (www.lloydstsb.com), augmented reality applications (Chapter 13) and downloadable PDF reports from Dopplr (www.dopplr.com). In short, if the service gives you a document, file or physical item at the end to prove that something happened (this doesn't include the receipt) then it's 'a service to objects, with physical goods as evidence' whereas if you're manipulating (or hiring someone else to manipulate) an object, then it's 'a service performed on objects'. The distinction is real and important as it determines whether the physical objects are secondary proof of service (augmented product) or the central element of the process (core product). For the purpose of the Figure 8.1 diagram, objects and goods includes virtual products, physical goods, electronic content and other stuff covered by Figure 1.4 (Chapter 1).

Defining the service product involves understanding elements of observable consumer behaviour and linking these to the underlying motivations which spur a consumer into action. This is because service products put a lot more responsibility on the customer to contribute to the final outcome compared with physical products which are usually purchased ready made and assembled. The inseparability characteristic of services means that, for most, the quality of the overall outcome from the customer's perspective is due to a combination of the skill of the service provider and the information provided by the customer. For example, if a client books a hairdressing appointment online and asks for a haircut, they may come away from the salon thrilled or furious depending on what the hairdresser does to their head. If, however, the client takes the time to talk to the hairdresser about their motivation for getting a new style (going for a job interview) they are far more likely to come out with a haircut that they like and which is appropriate to their circumstances. This process is referred to as customer co-creation and is a key feature of the services sector and one which has expanded significantly in importance with the development and adoption of Web 2.0 and social media technologies.

Whilst the same principles which underpin physical product models can be used to understand the service value offering, it's a little more complex when the service process is intangible. That said, it's quite rare to find an offline service that's a 'pure' service without any tangible elements. All products exist on a continuum, with the majority of products combining elements of the physical (e.g. a computer) with the service product (e.g. helplines and repair warranties). Similarly, it's always worth considering that whilst the e-marketing services of cloud computing, data storage, online banking or Google are intangible, they're accessed through physical objects, and those objects can influence how people think about the online service.

### Distinguishing between goods-orientated and service-orientated products

On the Internet the distinction between goods and services is more difficult, given that the Internet itself is intangible. Most e-commerce is related to the provision of a service or retailing event rather than the transference of a physical good. However, Langford and Cosenza (1998) proposed that a service/good analysis should focus on determining the extent to which each element of a service process can be seen as being more like a tangible product as opposed to an intangible one. Their method uses a holistic approach to examine product and associated strategies to determine whether services theory or tangible goods theory is best suited to each step. This is illustrated in Figure 8.2.

The process of analysis begins with establishing the product benefits that the customer buys and how these product benefits are perceived. These benefits are then classified using the four traditional points of differentiation between goods and services to distinguish those which are primarily service elements and those which are goods

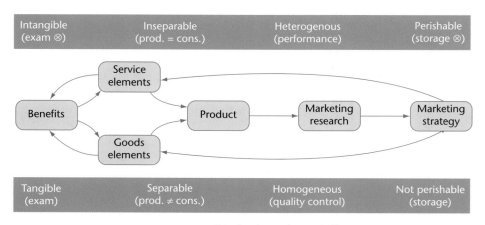

Figure 8.2 Service/goods analysis

elements. For example, conventional wisdom would see online ordering and using a remote-hosting service as being a pure service which has the product benefits of:

o hosting on a remote computer rather than the customer's own computer
o 24/7 access to the website for the general public (rather than access relying on the owner of the site being online)
o economies of scale, whereby a series of sites can share a larger and more powerful single computer and connection than each could afford separately (Reedy et al., 2000).

## Defining the service product

As is the case for all marketing strategy, the key to developing and communicating a position in the market is having an intimate knowledge of the 'product' that you are offering. Differentiating between the core and augmented product, and understanding how each is interpreted and used by different market segments, is critical to the design of a services e-marketing plan.

### Core product

Core service products involve the transfer of knowledge and temporary access to skills rather than the acquisition of any physical object. Consequently, services do not result in the ownership of anything. In most cases, for example medical services or legal advice, service purchases involve the right to use or access a service or service personnel for a specified period. With respect to online services, again, purchase doesn't result in ownership but rather the right to certain provider attributes. Features such as security, convenience, access and portability often form the core of the pure Internet services developed as part of the Web 2.0 economy. Web 2.0 systems are based around the development of multiple core product offerings which are differentially interpreted and valued by different target markets. For example, Flickr is simultaneously a photo library, a keyword-searchable image database and a personal photo album. For each user of the site, the core product will depend on their particular needs at a given point in time. Extended families can share photos with each other around the world (convenience), local interest groups can form around collections of photos from documenting a common event (community) and visitors to the site can find key images (database).

Significant challenges arise for services marketing as a result of the co-creation of products which occurs due to the input of customers into the service process. From the perspective of the company, co-creation can lead to the existence of multiple unplanned service products as individual consumers customize their experiences. Unless the organization stays in constant two-way communication with its customers, it won't have a full appreciation of the interpretation of its core product from the market's perspective.

### Augmented product

Internet-based services have been fitted into the augmented service product by an increasing number of physical goods and services marketers. Given the surprisingly large number of products with websites and community and social media engagement, producing a website that can enhance the end-user experience by providing a service element is a commonplace technique. The secret to effectively using a website or social media presence as an augmented service involves providing a value-adding service rather than simply using this as an advertising add-on. Putting together a web presence (site and social media) that offers something genuinely useful can create and maintain a good relationship with the consumer. Examples of value-adding services include sites which provide product assistance (www.kelloggs.com/recipes), regular updates on progress made (developer diaries) or news of forthcoming releases (Steam, Team Fortress 2). Other uses of online services as part of the augmented service product are to provide:

- o a venue for entertainment in a bid to create and sustain brand loyalty by giving the end users a chance to engage with each other – for example, Pop Cap Games's one-minute Bejeweled game (apps.facebook.com/bejeweledblitz) provides a competitive community environment for Facebook users and a platform for Pop Cap to be able to talk to its fans about new product releases that would suit enthusiastic Bejeweled players
- o reinforcement of the decision to purchase from the organization in an attempt to reduce post-purchase cognitive dissonance which can be seen through the fan pages on Facebook, or through the membership of community forums
- o additional services which complement existing products, such as the iTunes site and its ability to create an ongoing value for the iPhone and iPod (www.apple.com/itunes). Other functions such as ongoing updates and patches for registered software owners (windowsupdate.microsoft.com), extended downloadable content (Xbox360) or the use of search facilities for online versions of back issues of magazines (www.wired.com).

## Four pillars of services marketing

There are four classic points of differentiation between a service and physical good: intangibility, inseparability, inconsistency and perishability. Intangibility is where the service products are performances that have none of the physical characteristics of goods in that they cannot be touched, tasted, seen, heard or observed before performance occurs (Langford and Cosenza, 1998). Intangibility is a defining point for the Internet (since the Internet isn't real), which means there's opportunity for service theory to assist e-marketing.

Inseparability is the simultaneous consumption and production of the services that require the consumer/recipient and the service delivery mechanism to be in close proximity during the service (Bateson, 1996). Inseparability works for the e-marketer as you tend to need to be present at the computer for your Internet service experience. (Circumstances such as automated downloading or similar advanced systems allow the user to leave to eat or sleep while the computer handles the transaction at which point it becomes inseparable from the service transaction.) Services such as Dropbox (www.dropbox.com) have elements of inseparability – you, the computer, the Internet and the Dropbox server all need to be linked for it to really work (offsite backups are only as useful as the timeliness with which they get you out of trouble for losing the current working copy of a document).

Inconsistency relates to the way in which no two services encounters will be identical due to the human influence of the service, and the high level of variability between consumer, service provider and service environment (Woodruffe, 1995). A common criticism of both service and the Internet has been the tacit acceptance of inconsistency as an excuse for poor standards. Inconsistency is a factor that needs to be addressed, either through service roles or through service design, rather than used as an excuse for poor delivery. On the Internet, inconsistency occurs in a range of areas, including website design, changes in site navigation, variable access speeds to popular sites and changes to addresses of popular sites.

Perishability is the way in which services cannot be stored, stockpiled or used once the service opportunity has passed (McGuire, 1999). It is not possible to send a client back to last Thursday to use the spare seat on an aeroplane or take advantage of the empty hotel room. (Resolving service perishability will be one of the first major commercial applications of time travel. Extensions to deadlines for university assignments will be the second.) Services marketers needs to address the issues of load sharing, managing demand and levelling out peaks and troughs in demand.

Taking each of these traditional services elements in turn, it is clear that the Internet has had a significant impact on not only the delivery of services, but also on the way in which services marketers can use the unique characteristics of the Internet to overcome many of the problems which persist in face-to-face service encounters. This is not to say, however, that the Internet has solved all of the problems of services marketing. There are still grey areas of intangibility which will always be open to consumer interpretation.

### Intangibility

The nature of service products is that they're intangible, can't be directly evaluated using any of the physical senses and lack a physical object as the central part of the deal. That said, intangibility is not entirely clear-cut since the extended product model indicates that there's significant overlap between the tangible and intangible elements of a product. Core products tend towards the intangible (satisfaction of a need), actual products have more physicality present (hence the 'actual' rather than virtual) and you're back at intangible when dealing with the extended product (brands, warranties, social prestige). From a consumer perspective, intangibility makes it difficult to objectively evaluate one service relative to another. Unlike physical goods which can be compared on the basis of size, colour, material, durability and so on, services have no clear, externally observable points of comparison. Problems associated with intangibility include added difficulties in defining and communicating the service product, particularly in terms of quality. To overcome this issue, services marketers rely heavily on tangible cues associated with the positioning of the service and its delivery.

### Inseparability

A second key feature of services is that for all personal and many other services, production and consumption occur simultaneously. For example, a haircut cannot take place if the client and hairdresser are not in the same place at the same time. The higher the level of inseparability based on the interaction between the customer and the skills of the service provider, the less likely it is that the service can be delivered across the Internet (within reason). This means that the method of service production is as important to the consumer as its delivery because the producer is present when the service is used (McGuire, 1999).

Most consumers have little interest in the personality, working conditions or general demeanour of the factory worker who produced their computer (despite Dell's chirpy advertising campaigns). The personal characteristics of the service creator become much more vital when you're the consumer who's present as the service is produced, and even more important when that interpersonal service can be stored in data and passed around the Internet for all to see. The inseparability criterion derives from the importance of people in the services marketing mix (McColl-Kennedy and Kiel, 2000). The people performing the service are, to the consumer, an integral part of the product. In many cases they are the product or, at least, the human face of the organization they represent. In e-commerce, the website replaces the person as the first impression. Most people are not concerned about the EDI systems that support the transfer of their money from their bank account to the store's account during an EFTPOS transaction, but in an online banking transaction, the look and feel of the site become an important aspect of the transaction.

Inseparability also adds to the perceived risk experienced by consumers. Instead of the usual evaluate–purchase–consume sequence of consumer buying behaviour, services require a purchase–consume–evaluate approach. The higher the service is in terms of intangibility and inseparability, the lower it is in search characteristics such as size, style and weight, which can be objectively compared prior to purchase. Because services are essentially experiences, it is not possible to evaluate a service until after it has been both purchased and consumed (Lovelock et al., 2010).

### Inconsistency (heterogeneity)

Due in part to inseparability and the person-to-person interactions characteristic of services, it is difficult to guarantee consistent service from one delivery to the next even with high technology (or especially with cutting-edge technology). Variations in the performance of the service provider, changed expectations of the customer, the mood of the client, or the performance of the bandwidth renders no two e-service interactions identical (Zeithaml and Bitner, 1996). Online service delivery is subject to the vagaries of the Internet, including Internet-wide congestion (sometimes referred to as 'Internet weather'), site-specific traffic loads (Slashdot effects) or congestion at the local ISP, capped Internet connections, poor 3G coverage and the ambient capacity of the computer. Internet services are vulnerable to inconsistency due to factors well beyond the control of the e-marketer, just as extraneous factors impact on real-world service delivery. Perceived service quality is largely based on service providers consistently meeting the expectations of customers over time rather than any specific objective measures.

Internet-based services offer the opportunity to provide heavily scripted features and functions while giving the illusion of variability and interaction. Intelligent systems which are programmed to respond to 'if–then' statements concerning consumer questions will consistently produce the same path if the same answers are given. This increases consistency although occasionally this can be at the expense of accuracy – the site can consistently offer the wrong answer. While this may be appropriate for mass-consumption services such as fast food, certain types of retailing and routine financial transactions, the variability or inconsistency of service delivery between customers is one of the major strengths of key service industries.

Customization is both expected and demanded for services such as legal advice, psychological counselling and complex financial advice (Woodruffe, 1995). Inconsistency in the services marketing strategy is both its greatest strength and potentially its greatest weakness. Achieving the optimal balance between customization and consistent service quality is one of the major challenges facing service managers. Cybercommunity structures offer the greatest opportunity to develop inconsistency as a saleable point for services which require a large amount of human interaction (Chapter 9). The important factor to remember in determining the extent to use the Internet to attempt to eliminate inconsistency is the extent to which this inconsistency is a part of the benefits sought by the consumer in terms of personal service, customization and human interaction.

### Perishability (storage capacity)

Services are time dependent and cannot be manufactured, stored off-site and dropped into place once required, even with the increased digitization of the world. This is particularly true of personal services and entertainment. Once the opportunity to experience a show, football game or other event has passed, it is lost forever (Fisk et al., 2000). Similarly, it is not possible to store all the spare rooms a hotel may have on a quiet night for use at a later date when bookings exceed the number of rooms available. Internet sites which suffer from fluctuating demand cannot transfer the demand curve backwards in time to use the stockpiled bandwidth from last week.

From a managerial perspective, the major implication of this time dependency is the need to manage demand through pricing and promotional activities to ensure the effective use of resources within the organization. If demand is not managed adequately, two problems arise. First, the fixed costs of equipment, staffing and facilities become disproportionately large in relation to overall costs, with the result that total capacity is underutilized. Secondly, customers who are either unable to experience the service during peak times or are given substandard service due to resource constraints are likely to become dissatisfied with the service provider and switch to an alternative supplier (Lovelock et al., 2010).

While the differences between physical goods and services impact significantly on the way in which services-oriented marketers develop and implement strategies, it is important to recognize that most products combine elements of both of them. An effective goods–service analysis in which similarities and differences are explicitly identified is essential if optimal strategies are to be developed (Langford and Cosenza, 1998).

## e-service advantages

The online environment is well suited to the delivery of quality e-service products since they're essentially intangible and information based. Service delivery technology has

○ providing constructive feedback, participating in beta tests and making suggestions or giving advice, for instance, about new products. It can include the development of user-generated content and fan content for the product, brand or company, the use of innovations and much higher levels of customer co-creation.

Taken to the logical extension, many loyal customers of software products will produce materials, patches and other associated materials for the company. The enthusiasm and loyalty that can be exhibited online is occasionally unsettling for companies (particularly with trigger-happy lawyers) that are not used to the user-generated responses. Valve Corporation (owners of Steam, Half Life, Team Fortress and other games) capitalize on the user-generated content that comes from loyal customers by releasing tools and equipment (software development kits, level editors) for their games. They work on the assumption that working with a loyal customer base (rather than suing them) can build incredibly strong loyalty to the organization.

## Principles of relationship marketing

Relationship marketing operates on the foundation of three principles: trust, commitment and reciprocity. Trust is the willingness to rely on an exchange partner in whom one has confidence, and this includes a belief in the trustworthiness of the partner and a reliance on the other partner to perform (Moorman et al., 1993; Grönross, 1994). Commitment is the perceived need to maintain the relationship, either because of the inherent value of staying, or because of the costs associated with leaving the exchange (Geyskens et al. 1996, in Wetzels et al., 1998). Reciprocity is basically the notion of equality, mutual obligation and Bagozzi's (1975) exchange theory.

### Trust

Developing trust is a major issue facing the online marketer. Trust is a particularly interesting aspect of the Internet – social media requires trust (without or without verification), and ease of access to unverified account generation creates a fertile market for fake accounts, impersonators and imposters. At the same time, the nature of social media as a communication platform between real people tends to force the fakes into the background as they're either revealed due to errors, old friends or being hunted down by zealous media types. In marketing terms, trust is one of those multifaceted issues where there's the human language version (faith in others) and the commercial language variation (willingness to rely on others who you believe will deliver). For the most part, even when the commercial language version of trust is in place, there's usually more to be gained through honesty, humanity and emotional connections for successful, ongoing relationships than merely sticking to the letter of the legal definition of trust (Chapter 7).

The commercialized version of trust comes with instructions on modifying levels of trust up and down (pushing trust downwards is a form of demarketing that can be used to interfere with a rival product idea). Downplaying trust is also a tactical decision that may be used to remove certain categories of users (innovators) because their demands on the service (high-end use, complex requests) may exceed their value (small number of heavy users). Every couple of years, Livejournal (www.livejournal.com) provides a working example of breaches of trust as a means to lower the barriers for paying users to leave the service (Chapter 6) through its propensity to forget that the paying customers stick around to interact with the people on the free accounts. When the service provider breaches the trust of the free account holders, it also has an impact on the paid account holders' view of the firm, so caution must be exercised with trust reduction as a demarketing tool.

Doney and Cannon (1997, in Jevons and Gabbott, 2000) outlined five processes to form trust in business relationships. These are:

1. calculative processes, which is where you try to second-guess the value of cheating or defrauding the relationship. This theory is derived from economics and comes complete with a set of complex mathematical equations (and the assumption of impossibly rational behaviour) that indicates that if the benefits of cheating do not outweigh the costs of being caught, then the parties to the transaction will be honest. It also says a lot about economics that this form of 'What's in it for me to betray you?' behaviour is even considered to be a type of trust.
2. prediction of future intent based on past behaviour, is where you trust based on verification of the other person's past trustworthy activity. It's one part economics (risk calculation based on history) and one part precognition as you try to guess if you'll be the one ripped off (if they decide to go to the Dark Side this time). There's some difficultly with this method online where no transaction history exists, but it can be a very positive method where transaction histories can be accessed. eBay (www.ebay.co.uk) offers access to transaction histories of bidders/sellers through ratings systems, and offers the opportunity to contact participants of past transactions (Arunkundram and Sundararajan, 1998). Searching Twitter or checking Google's Blog Search (http://blogsearch.google.com) will provide some history to transactions where you think something is suspect.
3. credibility, which is where trust is derived from the capability and capacity of the other party to deliver on its promises. Websites which offer sample downloads, trial products, peer reviews and user ratings all provide indications of the credibility of the organization to deliver on its promise. Plus, there's a certain level of effort that indicates the economic costs of cutting and running on your £5 purchase just isn't worth the apparent set-up costs (economic motive).
4. motive assessment, which is based on interpreting the motives of the transaction partner. This assumes that the exploitative party will be obviously exploitative, will look like trouble and will be recognized for not having the transaction partner's interest at heart. This is a difficult method of trust, since the operation of any commercial exchange should have an equal split between offering the customer what they want (consumer's interest) and gaining the best deal for the company (self-interest).
5. transference process, which works on the principle of word of mouth, third-party referral and trust by recommendation. Word of mouth on Twitter, positive blog posts, large numbers of people indicating they 'like this' company on Facebook

○ The customer enters their credit card or other payment details (trusting behaviour).
○ The organization ships the goods and services, and bills the correct amount, and the customer's credit card details are kept secure (keep the promise).
○ The customer feels satisfied with the organization and increases their trusting beliefs towards the specific site they've just shopped at, and e-commerce generally.

Improved communications are at the core of this approach. Undoubtedly the Internet has increased the capacity of organizations to communicate and interact with their customers on an individual level. The interactivity and customization possible through Internet transactions means that a greater level of information transfer is possible and in many cases is occurring. Whether the capacity of the Internet to create customized

**Table 8.1** Determinants in trust development on the Internet

| Stage | Strategic guidelines | Operational objective | Web mechanism |
|---|---|---|---|
| (1) Identify | Start with customers<br>Exploit unique properties of Internet technology | Compile information on what an individual purchases or may want<br>Create a profile of the customer | Incentivised online questionnaire |
| (2) Improve | Exploit unique properties of Internet technology<br>Build relationships with customers | Improve aspects of the service that are not meeting or exceeding the expectation of customers | Customised online questionnaire<br>E-mails |
| (3) Inform | Exploit unique properties of Internet technology<br>Build relationships with customers<br>Leverage existing business | Increase the knowledge of customers about the hotels and the loyalty scheme to enhance brand loyalty | Direct e-mailing<br>Electronic newsletters<br>Online noticeboards and updates<br>Online information centre |
| (4) Tempt | Exploit unique properties of Internet technology<br>Build relationships with customers<br>Leverage existing business<br>Build a service, not a Web site | Persuade customers to try new service, product or sector<br>Persuade customers to purchase more through personalised contact | Direct e-mailing<br>Special electronic promotion leaflets<br>Automated cross-selling |
| (5) Retain | Exploit unique properties of Internet technology<br>Build relationships with customers<br>Leverage existing business<br>Build a service, not a Web site<br>Think radically | Develop new loyalty building schemes aimed at retaining and reinforcing the link with customers | Exclusive Web site and services for loyalty scheme members<br>Online members' magazines<br>Online members-only customer services |

*Source*: Gilbert, D.C., Powell-Perry, J. and Widijoso, S. (1999) 'Approaches by hotels to the use of the Internet as a relationship marketing tool', *Journal of Marketing Practice: Applied Marketing Science*, 5(1): 21–38.

strategies translates into a corresponding increase in trust, which in turn leads to better relationship development, remains to be seen.

## Should you be thinking transaction or relationship marketing?

Gilbert et al. (1999) established six points to determine when the relationship marketing paradigm is most suited for application.

1. The customer has an ongoing or periodic desire for the service.
2. The customer controls the selection of the service supplier.
3. An alternative choice of suppliers exists and the alternative suppliers offer similar enough products to make switching viable.
4. Brand switching is a common phenomenon since it's feasible for the customer to move from one provider to another.
5. Word of mouth counts as a valuable form of communication about a product.
6. You can cross-sell products.

One of the most important factors to consider in electronic customer relationship management (eCRM) is that relationship marketing is an optional extra on the transaction and is not the transaction itself.

As Feinberg and Kadam (2002) point out rather bluntly, consumers consume stuff, not eCRM. Many relationship marketing experts have lost the plot in this regard and often place the value of customer relationship management and relationship marketing over that of the actual transaction. If the buyer wants to purchase and leave (transactional), holding them to ransom and refusing to release them until they have a business relationship with you is ludicrous. If the aim of the relationship is to give the customer what they want, then perhaps the relationship marketers might want to consider giving the customer their freedom. Not every person will want eCRM, and some will be actively opposed to having to form a complicated relationship with a website just so they can make a one-off purchase.

## Conclusion

The defining characteristic of services is that they are intangible. Not only are Internet-based products predominantly intangible, many of the commercial products available online are themselves services. Consequently, there is a significant overlap between the issues that need to be addressed by both e-marketers and services marketers. Core to the success of online services marketing is a thorough understanding of the 'product', or in other words, the benefit that your online presence is providing for the consuming public. Is the online presence the prime focus of the organization or a value-added extra for a more traditional marketing campaign?

Whilst the dual intangibility of services and online marketing make this a more difficult proposition than occurs in traditional goods-based marketing, without this understanding, effective marketing is not possible. Related to, and emerging from,

| | |
|---|---|
| Thinkgeek | www.thinkgeek.com |
| Twitter | www.twitter.com |
| @bbcnews | http://twitter.com/bbcnews |
| @big_ben_clock | http://twitter.com/big_ben_clock |
| @Number10gov | http://twitter.com/Number10gov |
| Windows Update | windowsupdate.microsoft.com |
| Wired | www.wired.com |
| Wotif | www.wotif.com |
| XKCD | www.xkcd.com/523/ |
| YouTube | www.youtube.com |
| Zawinski's Law | www.catb.org/~esr/jargon/html/Z/Zawinskis-Law.html |
| Zazzle | www.zazzle.com |

# CHAPTER 9

# Community and networks

By the end of this chapter, you should be able to:

- explain the role and value of cybercommunities

- understand the fundamental principles of community development

- discuss how communications operate in an online community environment

- appreciate acceptable behavioural norms and standards in online community engagement

- understand how online communities and social networks interface with the firm's marketing activities.

## Introduction

Community has always held a significant place on the Internet. From its inception, and its precursor bulletin board systems, the Internet has had a history of using the communication capacity of networked computers to gather like-minded people together in virtual spaces. Whilst the Web began life as a complex footnoting system for a thesis, the success of e-mail, USENET and IRC grew out of the recognition that the true value of the Internet lay in its capacity to connect people with similar ideas and mindsets into communities of thought even if physically they were widely dispersed across the world. The rise of social networking sites and the development of a community infrastructure on the web is a public recognition that the best application of the Internet is its ability to facilitate access to other people (Bray, 2007). Whilst Internet use can still be a solo sport, it's increasingly being used for group participation through Facebook (www.facebook.com), Twitter (www.twitter.com), Google Sidewiki (www.google.com/sidewiki) and a host of other social media and social networking services.

Chapter 9 focuses on the consumer behaviour and marketing aspects of social media through the cybercommunity structure, whilst Chapter 12 looks at the technicalities of different sites. This chapter is about how people form community, groups and shared understanding around social systems and the roles that these communities can play in e-marketing. Cybercommunity is where communications theory, consumer behaviour, personal identity and technology combine to create an environment that is both enticing and threatening to the online marketer. Communities online are subject to less physical restrictions than their offline counterparts. Whilst most of the rules of the community including laws of libel, fraud and misconduct exist in both environments, there's a sense of liberation from certain traditional community infrastructure requirements when the community develops online. Whilst traditional communities rely on proximity and need for physical co-location before social bonds can develop, a key feature of online communities is that they are free of these physical constraints.

Online marketing has made brave, sometimes misguided and occasionally successful forays into the online community environment. In order to fully understand the benefit of the cybercommunity to marketing, it is first necessary to understand the concept of the cybercommunity. This chapter overviews the foundations of the cybercommunity concept and the construction and use of identity in the community environment before examining the role and value of natural and artificial communities to online marketers.

## Cybercommunity

Cybercommunity structures can generate environments, social norms and practices far removed from what is possible in the real world. To some extent, the virtual community is a movement towards niche segmentation based on self-interest, where you're represented as how you see yourself rather than how marketers see you based on measurements on psychographic and demographic profiles. The relevance of the cybercommunity, and the reconstruction of self-image in the online worlds, is that it represents a new level of market segmentation which goes beyond psychographics.

Traditional market segmentation breaks users into strictly defined categories based on who you are, what you earn and what the aggregate of those scores means for your postcode area. Psychographics and lifestyle segmentation group people according to what they do and how they live relative to others. Cybercommunity allows for an environment where individuals act out their self-images and for segmentation based on self-representation; that is, how people see themselves rather than how marketers see them based on the application of key market research variables and scales.

## Background to community

Although there's a slew of anti-Internet articles written in any given year proclaiming the death of community, society and friendship (as we know it) because we're talking to strangers over the Internet instead of shunning strangers in the street, every social media mechanism (from USENET to Twitter) has spawned numerous meet-ups, social events and face-to-face activities. In effect, the Internet provides a time and space independent mechanism for the StreetCar Named Desire model of community – friends/followers are just strangers you haven't met yet. Cybercommunities arise where a group of individuals engaged in computer-mediated communication move beyond basic exchange of information into the formation of a community structure based on the exchange of shared goods of value (Dann and Dann, 1999).

Dichotomies are the foundation of most good typologies, and cybercommunity typologies are no different in this respect. Cybercommunities take one of two basic forms: natural communities and constructed communities. Natural communities arise from human interaction where the exchange of emotional support augments pure information transactions. Constructed communities are created with the purpose of facilitating emotional support transactions. The purpose of the distinction is largely arbitrary – for a community to succeed, it needs the presence of the same factors whether it evolved from people swapping notes on science experiments or from an intention to establish a cancer survivors' support network. Either way, the importance of the dichotomy is to recognize that evolution and construction are two methods of establishing a community.

Recent developments in social media community platforms have delivered a new measure for community structures as being either symmetrical or asymmetrical communities. Symmetrical communities occur where the structure requires a mutual recognition of the membership of a group. Facebook's requirement that you acknowledge the friend request from someone before they become part of your community structure is a common example of a symmetrical community in action. Asymmetrical communities such as Twitter, World of Warcraft or blogging allow for non-reciprocal community structures and unilateral 'friendships' where you follow someone who doesn't follow you (also known as being a fan when it's done offline).

Just to add to the fun, there's also the question of transient–permanent fixtures for the cybercommunity. Transient communities are those cybergroups whose presence is only noticeable when the group is active, such as members of an IRC channel or e-mail chat list, participants on a game server, people at a concert or attendees at a conference. Permanent fixtures are those cybercommunities which use dedicated Internet locations, such as virtual worlds (Chapter 14), Facebook groups (Chapter 12), web forums and social media sites such as Orkut, Facebook, Twitter and MySpace. It's worth noting that the only reason to consider permanency and transiency as features of a community is to understand where the consumer is likely to be found – the infrastructure is of far less value than the individuals and marketers who can be easily caught up with the prettiness of a venue (on and offline).

None of the three dichotomies (artificial–natural, symmetrical–asymmetrical, permanent–transient) has inherent merit or inherent negative connotations. Nor are they unique to the Internet. The decision as to which type of fixture to select for the cybercommunity depends largely on available resources, which format best suits the needs of the community and what already exists on the Internet. What distinguishes cybercommunities from other elements of the Internet is that the cybercommunity combines elements of content and communication into a value-added function (Barnatt, 1998). Websites usually offer a choice between communications interaction or content and, even where the two elements are found in conjunction, it is often generated by the objective of forming the basis of a transaction rather than a community. Cybercommunities offer the opportunity to turn the Internet consumption experience away from solo existence into a shared experience between geographically diverse people.

To explain the cybercommunity phenomenon, it is necessary to first examine the three elements that distinguish it from other Internet functions. First, the nature of communications on the Internet is reviewed to demonstrate how it has led to the formation of the cybercommunity. Secondly, the concept and construction of community is overviewed to outline the key characteristics of the process. Finally, the consumption of the cybercommunity experience through the use of avatars and the reconstruction of identity is examined in relation to the notion of community as a value-added experience.

## Communications

Online communication happens at three levels: the individual level, group one-to-many level, and group one-to-many-to-one level (Hoffman and Novak, 1996). Individual-level communications relate to the exchange of information through mediated or unmediated communications between two individuals (MSN, Facebook chat, e-mail, SMS, Twitter direct message). Communications at the one-to-many level describe the publishing–broadcast paradigm where a single message is sent to multiple recipients (mailing lists, Facebook status update, Twitter comment, blog post). Communication at the one-to-many-to-one level on the Internet occurs where interactivity, publication broadcast and mediated communication merge to create a new range of communications options (Twitter replies, Facebook comments, blog comments, Google Sidewiki). All three models are discussed in further detail in this chapter, however, it is important to recognize that they are a series of indicative models rather than absolute descriptions of how communications function on the Internet. Other models not covered in this book can be equally valid when describing the Internet communications function and communications models.

## Individual level-mediated communications

Mediated communication has been occurring since humans determined how to encode messages into a storable format (cave walls are much like early hard drives in that they're reliable, still hold the data and there's no modern way to read them accurately). Figure 9.1 illustrates the basic message communications technology that describes everything from medieval messengers and carrier pigeons to the (less than) contemporary telephone.

The mediated communications model is applicable at any point at which the message communicated is carried by a third party (device, person, pigeon) rather than received through direct face-to-face contact (this includes voice over IP, telephones and videophones). It's robust, reliable and functional.

Expanding on this basic paradigm is the concept of computer-mediated communications, which represent a specific method of communications technology. Kaye (1991) defines computer-mediated communications (CMC) as the use of computers as communication tools by people who are collaborating with each other to achieve a shared goal which does not require the physical presence or co-location of participants and which can provide a forum for continuous communication free of time constraints. The message is the message, and the medium is the home computer. Usefully, CMC predates the mass popularity of the Web 2.0 movement, and much of the developmental work on the idea was at the core of the foundation of the Internet in the 1950s since computer-facilitated communication was valuable for multipoint communications between university, military and government institutions. It's also an accepted aspect of society that is remarkable from a technical level, yet wholly unremarkable from the public's point of view. General use of the computer as another form of letter writing, an alternative to phone calls and a means for group collaboration is part of university, school, corporate and home life as CMC has proved to have a relative advantage over each of the competitor options.

Following on from the basic level of computer-mediated communication is the more complex form known as hypermediated communications. Hypermediated communications (HMC) are communications transactions that are conducted through the medium of the Web. Where CMC has a greater sophistication than basic mediated communication, HMC introduces newer elements related to the hypermedia environment. Due to the more complex nature of the hypermedia systems, HMC recognizes that it is even possible to exit the environment without actually having completed the

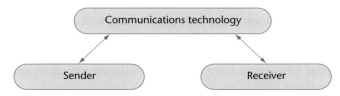

**Figure 9.1** Mediated communications model

*Source*: Hoffman, D. and Novak, T. (1996) 'Marketing in hypermedia computer-mediated environments: conceptual foundations', *Journal of Marketing*, 60(3), July: 50–68

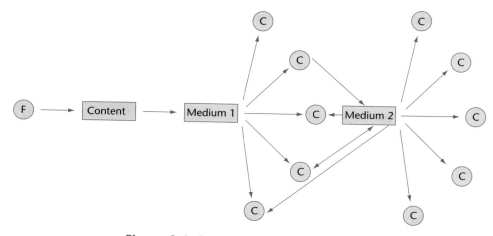

**Figure 9.4** One-to-many to many-to-one

Source: adapted from Hoffman, D. and Novak, T. (1996) 'Marketing in hypermedia computer-mediated environments: conceptual foundations', *Journal of Marketing*, 60(3), July: 50–68

person reached. The main disadvantage of the model is that it does not allow for direct feedback from the recipients. This weakness is amplified when the audience can use an alternative medium for their feedback. Twitter tends to be the real-time response channel for television audiences to comment, re-tweet and pass judgement on the viewing offerings. This effectively creates a new model of one-to-many-to-many-to-one, where the original message sender is left out of the communications loop that emerges between the people consuming and discussing the original message.

This structure provides opportunity for communities (artificial and natural) to build around mass media events, discussion threads on blogs about *The X Factor*, Facebook groups which lie dormant until the opening credits of *Great British Menu* start, and television-specific community forums that light up with each screening of new (or old) episodes. The problem for the marketer in this situation is that the community is well beyond their control and is an event that's not there for the capturing as a commercial opportunity (historically, attempts to commercialize the organic venues of cybercommunities usually result in the discussion disappearing at the same speed as work chat disappears when the boss sits at the lunch table). From a marketing perspective, these natural communities either need to be observe-only situations, where you watch the commentary and take the feedback to the organization, or thoroughly ignored if the community is talking about you rather than trying to talk to you. If they're talking to you (or posting open questions), then that's your cue to engage and to close the feedback loop (Figure 9.4).

### Group level-mediated communications: computer-mediated one-to-one

The major development between broadcast models and CMC was the capacity for interaction between sender and recipient. The new mediated environment allows for immediate and/or delayed reaction to the transmitted content. Figure 9.5 illustrates the machinations of computer-mediated communications.

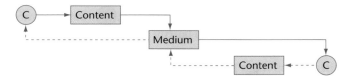

**Figure 9.5** Computer-mediated communications

Source: Hoffman, D. and Novak, T. (1996) 'Marketing in hypermedia computer-mediated environments: conceptual foundations', *Journal of Marketing*, 60(3), July: 50–68

In this model the sender–receiver dichotomy is a temporary rather than permanent state as is the case in broadcast models. Content is generated by the sender–receiver, transmitted through the medium, received and acted upon by the receiver–sender and returned through the medium to the originator. A customer sends an @comment to a store on Twitter to ask about the price of a product, the store owner responds with an @ or direct message with the correct price. This potential for interaction is the basic building block of the cybercommunity as it represents the capacity for interaction and exchange. Community does not exist in isolated communications between two individuals. In order to develop a cybercommunity, the third level of mediated group communication needs to be present.

### Group level-mediated communications: computer-mediated one-to-many-to-one

Computer-mediated communication was designed to take a single message to a single recipient. This basic concept was subsequently upgraded into the computer-mediated one-to-many-to-one system. Group level-mediated communications merge the CMC time-independent personalized message with broadcast's multiple recipients and includes the capacity for direct interaction or indirect broadcasted responses. Figure 9.6 illustrates the operation of the one-to-many-to-one model.

One-to-many-to-one is the dominant communication style of the cybercommunity as it allows several people interested in a single topic to view the original post, comment or tweet, and to respond to that and other responses. The users play an integral role in the medium, and the message exchange can be categorized in any one of four ways:

1. original broadcaster
2. receiver–broadcaster
3. receiver–sender
4. receiver.

Original broadcasters can send messages in a one-to-many style to the medium. Unlike traditional broadcast models, other users of the medium can respond, either directly as receiver–senders or indirectly as receiver–broadcasters. Receiver–senders apply the CMC one-to-one model in that their messages return to the originator rather than the broadcast medium. Receiver–broadcasters send their messages to the medium as a

environment, community access is based on the communications ability of the membership and their access to the tools of communication. Access using communications skills creates a literacy barrier that will inevitably exclude some people from being able to fully access the community. Although some multi-user environments are experimenting with bilingual systems, it would still require users who interact within the bilingual environment to be able to converse in multiple languages to interact with other bilingual speakers.

Despite the language barriers, cybercommunity structures which predominantly depend upon word-based communication also bring about a unique socialization process where the human body is effectively discarded in the first instance, and members are represented as collections of ideas and written expressions. The physical body, and the social cues associated with it, are removed and replaced by the perception of the individual as a transmitter of ideas, feelings and communications (Coyne, 1998). Part of the effect of the conversion of humanity into the written identity has been the lowering of many cultural and physical barriers resulting from physical cue-based stereotypes.

Cybercommunities exist through the strength of their members and the resulting social network capital that's generated by a cohesive group of shared interests, social support and other goods of collective value with a critical mass of members to support and share it. All communities share the economies of increasing returns in that the community needs a critical mass for value to occur. In addition, for the most part the marginal returns improve for all members, as more members join, to a point of critical overflow, where diminishing returns occur as the community becomes too big to manage.

Cybercommunities take time to establish, grow and strengthen, although fast burn, single issue or limited lifespan communities can and do exist (and can be huge fun). Communities have a propensity to develop in a natural cycle of birth, growth, maturity and decline (and look suspiciously like product lifecycle curves). For commercial operators seeking to engage in the support and the development of cybercommunities, this long-term focus in an apparently short-term environment frequently leads to difficulties in reconciling short-term goals with the community's potential long-term value. Many operators attempt to take short-term gains by implementing access fees, subscription rates or other charges in order to make a short-term profit with the result that, unless there's some extremely compelling value in the community, members leave to find low-cost/no-cost alternatives that meet their needs.

### Concepts of community 6: Communities of self-expression

Since 1999, the term blog has become synonymous with self-published online journals, which are effectively public diary systems for individual writers. (The terms 'blog' and 'webjournal' are used interchangeably – 'blog' is the shortened version of weblog; webjournal is more encompassing of the diary-style online journals). While the concept of an online diary may not seem to automatically top the list of methods of community creation, these webjournal structures have resulted in a new form of online community – the community of self-expression.

## Fitting community into e-marketing and e-marketing into communities

The existence of spontaneous gatherings of target market members in a shared space of mutual value is a dream for marketers seeking to reach key market segments. Successful engagement of members within online communities, however, remains rare. The failure of commercial marketers to effectively penetrate online communities is based on a fundamental misunderstanding of both the role and value of the community to its members and a lack of appreciation of the protocols and etiquette of online engagement.

### Protocols for engagement

The widespread access to the Web 2.0 style of communication has developed a consumer class of active communicators who expect and demand interaction with the companies they buy from over a range of issues. The demand for conversation and conversational engagement can be daunting for marketers who are more comfortable with the monodirectional broadcast model or the bi-directional e-mail exchange. The one-to-many-to-one-to infinity of a good social media debacle is also enough to have the company's lawyers wanting to vet every single exchange and place the most bland statements into the very space the consumer wants a decent conversation. While basic principles of marketing and communication are the same online and in traditional settings, the manifestation of these into appropriate behaviour varies considerably.

### *Rules of engagement 1: Conversation and community are not the same*

Community does not equal conversation, and conversation does not equal community. (Neither are strictly marketing activities in their own right either.) Merely talking to (or at) a group of customers is not the same as those customers forming bonds of community with each other. Community is what the consumer makes from the shared goods of value, the sense of belonging and the rest of the factors, and may or may not involve marketers at all. Conversations and conversational marketing is more relationship marketing (Chapter 8) through social media (Chapter 12), and the two shouldn't be mistaken. If you're only having bi-directional conversations with individual users, and the users aren't interacting with each other, then you don't have a community.

### *Rules of engagement 2: It's not your community*

The hardest aspect of using a cybercommunity for most marketers and companies is letting go of control since the community approach to communication is in direct conflict with the principles of integrated marketing communication (IMC). IMC dictates control over the message by a limited number of voices who speak in unison to establish and maintain a consistent brand. Community operates by a range of diverse voices rambling on about whatever the community finds interesting, and may or may not reflect

Permanent community environments can also play host to transient communities such as gaming servers (Xbox Live, World of Warcraft, Second Life, City of Heroes) holding specific theme night events such as a Halloween contest, 'Meet the Developer' or similar.

Although IRC is an older platform, it's worth considering the value of a web-based or classic IRC channel as a means for real-time group conversation environments without the physicality or graphics requirement of a virtual world. IRC has experienced a resurgence in popularity as a common ground or community hall approach for political groups, voluntary organizations and others looking for a live venue. It has the bonus of being text based so conversations can be archived for later access, analysis or publication. The nature of the chat is such that it's a good venue for social interactions offering immediate gratification to users but can become unwieldy and difficult to read where large groups are engaged in conversation. The IRC channel is similar to a party in that multiple conversations can coexist in the room, but it takes a skilled user to handle the conversational traffic and follow the separate threads of conversation. Alternative real-time environments in virtual worlds are discussed in Chapter 14. Using a virtual world gives a sense of physicality to the event, whether it's a conversation hosted on a Halo map or a chat in Second Life, the virtual world provides objects, rooms and location-based interactions. Using a virtual-world space allows users to experience proximity and separability and interact with a level of proximity in a quasi-realistic environment (depending on your environment).

Web-based communities can exist at the macro level (Facebook, Plurk, MySpace, Orkut and Livejournal) at the mid level (Facebook groups and Livejournal communities) or somewhere in between (FriendFeed rooms, Twitter friends' feeds and related aggregated community conversations). They can also function at the micro level of individual posts, blogs, pages or discussion threads. Each of these aspects functions around a similar physicality of a specific location where the community members can be found in discussion with each other. The mechanisms are less interesting in the context of cybercommunity because the dynamics of the human interaction are the determining feature of whether a community exists. That said, the mechanisms of these approaches are outlined in Chapter 12 if you're planning on building the physical foundations for a cybercommunity.

## Community infrastructure: community

A cybercommunity needs to have a sense of community before it will be more than a series of well-published good intentions. While the other elements of the Rheingold checklist are important, it is essential that the feeling of belonging exists, otherwise a community will not succeed. To create the community environment, the organization must understand that the community itself is the point of the exercise and the creation of the community is going to be an investment cost in the long-term future of the organization.

One of the most important things to appreciate when creating and establishing a cybercommunity is that it is a long-term process. A cyberRome cannot be installed in a day. The community structures are a process of evolution and development, meaning in blunt terms, long-term costs and investments for long-term gains. Companies need to focus on the big picture of the gains that community can bring rather than the narrow view of the costs that it incurs. Every aspect of establishing and maintaining a cybercommunity will cost either time or money – usually both. Twitter's 'overnight' success occurred three years after launch and Facebook's position as a dominant social gateway to communities has taken at least a decade to establish as it began life as an exclusive community for US college students and grew outwards.

It also has to be recognized that the community must give benefit to the user meaning that the organization will have to give something before it can expect to receive. To access most communities the user has to give away a range of demographic and psychographic data, so having already incurred the cost, they expect a reciprocal benefit.

### Aiding and abetting a community

If you build it, the search spiders will come. If you want people rather than search arachnids as the dominant users of the site, you'll need to provide some assistance and support in a few critical areas. First, take the pressure off the community to be a direct revenue source. People have come to this environment to interact with each other, not to click on your Google Adwords or whatever advertising funding model you think will work. If you can't afford to run it, then don't set it up in the first place. Community is a long-term investment in people, their satisfaction, interaction and eventual use of your products, because your products are what got them chatting with each other in the first place. Many commercial communities wind up too quickly as part of cost-cutting measures before any return on investment is remotely calculable or possible. Communities which are accessed for free do not preclude the organization from charging for premium value-added services that extend upon the free service offering. Flickr successfully converted from a free community to a structure of free and paid accounts. Livejournal periodically attempts to remove the unpaid accounts without considering their value to the paid users, which usually leads to the organization apologizing and reinstating the part of the site the paid users thought was most useful – access to other people.

### Getting out of the way

The community exists for the benefit of members of the community. This has to be logged and noted in any and all aspects of the community's planning phase, implementation and review. If at any point you're going to balk at the community not being for your benefit, don't set up a community. It's possible to benefit from a community, but it's only going to happen if the community members are getting something out of the bargain in the first instance. Focus on the community members first and the incidental benefits for the organization (market research, product information) will flow from there. Alternatively, if you can't take this approach, look for the organic communities that are relevant for your operations and engage with them.

Remember, a community is not a focus group nor is it a controlled laboratory environment. Communities need to be given free reign to develop and create their own environment, leaders and structures. Companies which give freedom to their community structures while focusing on providing for some of their needs have greater success than those who feel a desire to treat the community like a lab experiment. The natural environment of the cybercommunity is also an important aspect that needs to be carefully observed and maintained by commercial hosts. In any group of people natural leaders will emerge and social dynamics will take place to create factions, allegiances and similar psychological groupings within the community. Support should be given to the leaders of the communities and to those members who provide value-added services to the community. In many cases, recognition and a note of thanks can be sufficient reward for a community member providing services that would otherwise have been the responsibility of the company hosting the community. The company needs to support or at least passively ignore any spread of the community beyond the boundaries of the hosted cybercommunity.

One of the key mistakes that can be made with a cybercommunity is to try to force it to stay within a company's allocated domain so that it can be probed, measured and watched by corporate members. If a community is growing to the point of natural expansion beyond the limits provided by the host organization, it is a sign of an extremely successful community and should be encouraged, or at least not actively discouraged. Tacit approval for unofficial sites that support official functions can also lower the costs to the organization. If a community member sets up a website to support your commercial cybercommunity, that is a maintenance and development cost that is being provided free in return for the benefit the user has gained from being a member of your community. It is a display of brand and community loyalty that promotes a positive image for the company hosting the cybercommunity.

Another major issue in hosting a community is to remember that for a community to survive it needs to be monitored and supported. A good healthy cybercommunity will be self-supporting and (hopefully) self-generating sufficient content to keep the members interested. However, they are not perpetual motion machines, and as with all human gatherings, there will be peaks and lows and points at which the communities are no longer of value. Cybercommunities which have exceeded their useful lifespan should not be propped up simply to meet a preset budget line expenditure or website design charter. Similarly, communities that are thriving should not be terminated because their six-month time frame has expired. Their value is in that they are living environments which need to be reviewed and monitored over time.

### Caveat: moderation

Cybercommunity structures require moderation in the form of active participation by one or more teams of community managers. Community management a combination of the grounds maintenance, building security and emergency clean up crews insofar as they need to have authority and responsibility to maintain the order and functionality of the host community site. This includes removing the inevitable spam content, enforcing community standards, setting the norms for respectful behaviour, and removing users who persist in breaching the site's terms of use or codes of conducts. Unmoderated hosting venues tend to fall victim to automated spamming systems, noxious behaviours and are counterproductive to the purpose of developing relationships with the customers.

## Destination marketing: cyberspaces as tourist places

There is more to having people clicking down a path to your website than building a better mouse trap. Cybercommunities are not self-evident benefits to most users, and certainly in the crowded market of the Internet, many users will never get to see more than a fraction of the virtual worlds on offer. If this sounds vaguely familiar then it is because it is the permanent dilemma of tourism marketing. Tourism marketing deals with how to get people to leave their homes for a brief virtual community stay at a tourist destination. Many of the problems, issues and solutions that tourism marketing has used over the years are applicable to the issues faced by cybercommunities.

In order to apply tourism marketing to the cybercommunity structure, one key assumption must be made – to conceptualize cyberspace as a place. This philosophical assumption has been variously mentioned explicitly or implicitly throughout both this chapter and other aspects of this book. The key to treating cyberspace as a location is to recognize the terminology used to describe behaviour within the environment. People conceptualize cyberspace as a location, due in part to the influence of authors such as Gibson (1984) on the terminology used to describe the Web. The importance of recognizing the assumption of locality and physicality in cyberspace is that it is a conceptual environment. There are no physical boundaries in the Internet and nothing physical exists within this environment. So, why then do we adopt the assumption of physicality in a cybercommunity?

Cybercommunities can be places within the Internet and recognized as such by their boundaries. For example, virtual worlds exist only on their home servers or by means of their websites. Facebook exists predominantly at www.facebook.com, whereas Twitter is housed at Twitter.com and is extremely accessible from a range of third-party sites such as Socialoomph (www. socialoomph.com), software such as TweetDeck (www. tweetdeck.com) and mobile phone interfaces such as Twitberry (www.orangatame. com/products/twitterberry). Whilst you can access Facebook via a mobile phone and through Tweetdeck, it's not the full Facebook experience of applications (including stray farmyard animals and random mafia war announcements), other people and the full feature set.

People constitute communities, whether they are real, virtual or cybercommunities. Gibson's (1984) 'consensual hallucination' clause in the description of the fictional cyberspace matrix indicates it only ever exists as a place because the users agreed that it is a place. Similarly, the idea of virtual goods, virtual products and virtual services in Chapter 1 and Chapter 6 depends in part on the acceptance of a string of binary as a real 'thing' whether it's a sword in World of Warcraft, an MP3 on an iPod, or a PPT file from the class. The 'real' nature of the products is based entirely on our agreed acceptance of them as real.

### Using destination marketing for the cybercommunity

Destination marketing is the amalgamation of tourism products under the brand name of a location and which offers an integrated experience to consumers (Buhalis, 2000).

Cyberdestination marketing takes the amalgamation of the cyberenvironment and the services, community, community members and experiences which are offered under the banner of the cybercommunity name, location or brand. As part of destination marketing, Buhalis (2000) outlined six key factors (the six As) for bringing people to a location:

1. attractions
2. accessibility
3. amenities
4. available packages
5. activities
6. ancillary services.

## Cybercommunity attractions

Attractions refer to the reasons for going to a region, be it a natural environment, a heritage location, a purpose-built venue or a special event. Usually the attraction is closely associated with the region and recognized as the primary draw card for the area. In the cybercommunity, the attractions are the people (hence people as the killer app – Bray, 2007). However, virtual worlds offer other aspects as well – World of Warcraft is a gaming environment with specific quests, puzzles and challenges for the players as well as interaction with other people. YouTube has videos, Flickr has photos, Facebook has games and MySpace has glittery graphics. Each of the communities brings some attraction that draws people to that location in the first instance for the formation of the community.

## Cybercommunity accessibility

Accessibility in the real world depends on available transportation system (roads, rail, air, sea) to access a specific location (beach) combined with the capacity to move around within that environment (on foot or on a horse). Online, it is related to the degree to which the community can be reached by the ordinary user without the need for special software downloads (Introduction), the convenience of having the cybercommunity located at an obvious access point and the access to the service on a specific device (Twitter on the Xbox, mobile or PC). World of Warcraft, Xbox Live, City of Heroes and similar spaces usually require monthly access fees and specific hardware requirements. Within certain environments such as Steam, games which rely on specific servers located somewhere in the Internet tend to function like tourist bureaux by providing easy access to the desired location.

Accessibility also covers issues of technical skill (software operation), literacy (text-based environments), alternative access (transcripts for videos, descriptions of photos for vision impairment), physical access (geographic limits on broadband, time zone differences), and whether the community constitutes a safety space for the individual (inclusiveness, non-exclusionary language, non-triggering content).

## Cybercommunity amenities

Amenities for tourism destinations represent the physical facilities of accommodation, catering, retailing and ancillary tourist services. Cybercommunity amenities are features and functions of the environment such as direct chat, URL posting, image uploading, video hosting or file sharing for web-based environments. Virtual world video games have a recruitment stage where you learn the basics of the game coupled with various checkpoint locations that operate various in-game services (mail, banking or shopping). For transient groups such as IRC, amenities include functional elements such as 'ops', which represent a set of key powers to change topic, exclude or remove users and provide 'ops' to fellow users. Other functions such as the Facebook and Twitter list, or YouTube playlists, would count towards the amenities. Basically, amenities cover anything that makes life easier but isn't the core feature that would be listed under cybercommunity attractions.

## Cybercommunity available packages

Available packages in destination marketing tend to be controlled by tour mediators such as travel agents or airlines offering pre-arranged packages and conditions. Cybercommunities can offer levels of membership, ranging from the basic level of use to levels associated with control, management and, often, the capacity to create and modify elements of the environment. Subscriber-based cybercommunities may include free systems with low levels of access and varying levels of access depending on subscription fees. Livejournal offers four access levels: permanent accounts with full features, paid accounts with enhanced features for annual subscribers, advertising-sponsored accounts with a limited group of sponsored-enhanced features and the basic free accounts with just the core feature set.

## Cybercommunity activities

Activities incorporate all events, activities and related services that will be consumed as part of the tourism experience by a visitor to the destination. Some of these functions are beyond the control of the travel agency and local tourist board and others are established for the express purpose of attracting tourists, for example, festivals and special events. Cybercommunity activity can include regular conversation events (open threads to discuss *Top Chef*), date-specific activities (Halloween events in virtual worlds), expansion packs (World of Warcraft), downloadable content (Grand Theft Auto), web previews and reviews (Flashforward) and various contests. Cybercommunities also involve various activities, some official, some unofficial, as attractors to the group. Successful cybercommunities tend to have activities that extend beyond the core community structure into other venues, such as face-to-face meetings or involvement in other group-oriented projects. Some communities will enter teams into online competitions or gaming environments as part of the community group activities. This is particularly prevalent where there is a strong set of shared interests which form part of the shared goods of value.

### Cybercommunity ancillary services

Ancillary services for offline destinations relate to the services used by tourists – services such as banks, post offices and similar services. Cybercommunities can offer second-stage services, such as e-mail addresses, basic web hosting or environment-specific systems such as chat channels, applications (Facebook), auction houses (World of Warcraft), direct messages (Twitter), or event scheduling and shared calendars (Xbox Live).

Not all principles of destination marketing can be applied to each type of cybercommunity structure. Most of the functions outlined are primarily focused towards the more permanent structures, although the use of support websites can give permanence for transient mailing list-based groups. Overall, these six functions represent additional services that can be implemented by group members, or the host organization, at minimal additional cost to the host.

## Conclusion

The Internet provides marketers with a previously unheard of level of access to consumers. In particular, marketers have the potential to observe and interact with their consumer base through their engagement with online communities. Despite the potential for mutual benefit for both marketers and users, the effectiveness of community-based engagement to date by commercial marketers has been less than spectacular. Partly this is due to the conflict between the need for marketers to demonstrate short-term gains and returns on investment to the company, and the reality that community creation and development takes time. If marketers are to take full advantage of the potential of the Internet for consumer engagement they need to understand three things. First, marketers need to understand the development and use of contemporary models of communication, in particular hypermediated communications, and appreciate how these vary from traditional broadcast or personal interaction models. Secondly, marketers need to understand the different types of community which exist online and how the activities of different communities can add different levels and types of value to the organization. Finally, there needs to be an appreciation of the appropriate use of community, including an understanding of the cultural dimensions of community development and engagement. Unless these are understood, any attempts to create and engage online communities for commercial benefit will be doomed to failure (or at least suboptimal results).

## References

### Books and journals

Barnatt, C. (1998) 'Virtual communities and financial services – online business potential and strategic choice', *International Journal of Bank Marketing*, 16(4): 161–9.
Bray, T. (2007) 'The Intimate Internet', http://www.tbray.org/ongoing/When/200x/2007/10/04/Intimate-Internet (accessed 8 July 2010).

Brogan, C. (2009) 'The Plastic Human Problem', http://www.chrisbrogan.com/the-plastic-human-problem/ (accessed 8 July 2010)

Buhalis, D. (2000) 'Marketing the competitive destination of the future', *Tourism Management*, 21: 97–116.

Cothrel, J. and Williams, R.L. (1999) 'Online communities: 'helping them form and grow', *Journal of Knowledge Management*, 3(1): 54–60.

Coyne, R. (1998) 'Cyberspace and Heidegger's pragmatics', *Information Technology and People*, 11(4): 338–50.

Dann, S. and Dann, S. (1999) 'Cybercommuning: global village halls', *Advances in Consumer Research*, 70(25).

Gibson, W. (1984) *Neuromancer*. New York: Ace Books.

Hoffman, D. and Novak, T. (1996) 'Marketing in hypermedia computer-mediated environments: conceptual foundations', *Journal of Marketing*, 60(3), July: 50–68.

Kaye, A. (1991) 'Learning together apart'. In A. Kaye (ed.) *Collaborative Learning Through Computer Conferencing: The Najaden Papers*. Berlin: Springer-Verlag.

Rheingold, H. (1993) *The Virtual Community: Homesteading on the Electronic Frontier*. New York: Harper-Collins.

## Web references

| | |
|---|---|
| Facebook | www.facebook.com |
| Google Sidewiki | www.google.com/sidewiki |
| Socialoomph | www. socialoomph.com |
| TweetDeck | www.tweetdeck.com |
| Twitberry | www.orangatame.com/products/twitterberry |
| Twitter | www.twitter.com |
| Twitter (mobile site) | m.twitter.com |
| XKCD.com | www.xkcd.com/438/ |

# Implementation

## Introduction

Chapter 10 covers the often glossed over sections of e-marketing – implementing the ideas in practice and putting the e-marketing out into the marketplace. To do this, we're going to draw on elements from the previous chapters, link them together and develop a set of checkpoints on the road from objectives to implementation. The problem with marketing (and business generally) is the sheer volume of options available in any given scenario based on the combinations and permutations of markets, consumer needs, company resources and competitors. This means there's no real hard and fast specifics that can be given that will prove equally effective in all situations. That said, all it means for you as a marketer is that the models we're presenting are the starting point, and not the end in themselves. Merely being able to fill out a chart, a 2×2 matrix or a spreadsheet doesn't mean you've implemented marketing – it does, however, mean that if you've covered all of the parts in this chapter, you've thought about the wide range of issues you need to address when the time comes to turn the plan into reality.

## Implementation

Implementation involves combining the objectives, plans and strategies with the hard yards of actually doing the work listed in the tactics to-do lists. There are two key tasks to undertake before embarking on the final implementation of your product strategy or plan. First of all you need to go back and revise where you started from and where you want to go to. You will need to ask how the e-marketing elements of your plan fit into the broader business objectives of the whole of the organization (and if they don't, start revising your plans or look for a new organization). This involves a final assessment of the objectives to ensure that they are measurable and that the marketing metrics will be in place to actually collect the data necessary to demonstrate success or failure.

The second area that needs to be examined prior to going ahead with the implementation of the plan is the extent to which you have correctly interpreted and gauged the product–market fit. This will involve an examination of how the total product is interpreted by the market along with the necessary modifications needed before developing a relevant and effective positioning strategy.

### Packet mix objectives (Chapter 3)

Back in Chapter 3 we introduced the generic packet mix objectives, which make their encore performance in the implementation phase. Essentially, as you're implementing each aspect of the e-marketing strategy, you need to ask yourself 'How does this particular activity link back to achieving the overall marketing plan and corporate objectives?'

#### Cost-oriented objectives

The aim of e-marketing in cost oriented objectives is to produce the same bang for less bucks (pounds, euros, dollars, yen). This means paying greater attention to the documentation of the implementation process, better timekeeping records and a much greater focus on the dollars per hour metrics for time spent in social media activity.

- ○ Does this e-marketing approach lower overheads for the organization?
- ○ Are the resources you're redirecting into this e-marketing effort producing higher levels of effectiveness and/or efficiency and/or return on investment than they are where they are currently deployed?
- ○ Are the savings in print costs equal to or greater than the time costs of employed social media workers?
- ○ Are the customers benefiting (or at least not suffering noticeably) from the cost saving changes?

### Sales-oriented objectives

This is a single minded, single focus approach to e-marketing that examines every action against sales data. Update a blog, post a Twitter status or do anything much more than check your e-mail and you'll be checking the sales figures to see if it had an impact. The key here is to focus on making it easier for the customer to make the purchase, for the website to close the sale and to reduce the shopping cart abandonment rate. This is the scientific end of marketing, and it's all about the pre-test (old sales figure), intervention (site update, content release, sales promotion, fresh cup of tea) and post-test (new sales figure).

- ○ Does this activity lead to a direct sale? Is there a difference in response between offering a 20 per cent discount using a specific coupon code on Twitter versus a direct link in an e-mail to subscribers? Are people claiming cashback offers? Did they use the coupon code?
- ○ Does this activity lead to indirect sales? Is there a detectable pattern between non-sales activity (responding to customer feedback) and later sales spikes?
- ○ Are there obvious roadblocks appearing in the customer purchases? Sales cart abandonment at the shipping page indicates something's going wrong with the distribution channel. Abandonment at the payment options means you're not offering the right means for the customer to give you their money. (It's PayPal, Visa, Mastercard, Bartercard, direct debit, SMS credits, cash-in-an-envelope, livestock and international bank cheque in that order of ease of sending for the customer.)
- ○ Can you draw a path from your e-marketing activity to a sales outcome? Don't forget lead times and lag between interventions and outcomes. Scour the historical data for patterns, reaction times and impact information and don't always expect an immediate response from the market.

### Behavioural change objectives

These are the really fun parts of the business where you're able to demonstrate success based on people showing up and taking part in a specific behaviour. It's clear cut – either

ascertain if the customer is going to care about the entertainment long enough to get to the sponsor's message in the opening credits (forget about the closing credits).

- ○ Can this activity become community centric? Will people want to talk about it, brag about high scores, challenge friends to battle and post updates to their Facebook page about random farm animals?
- ○ Will user-generated content be accepted and acceptable as part of the entertainment?
- ○ Who's looking after the moderation of the content, community and work-flow of materials?
- ○ What is that cat doing in that photo and how do we caption it for maximum hilarity?
- ○ Are we having fun yet?

## Measuring the objectives

Once you've refocused your objective(s) in your mind (and the implementation plans), the next step is to start making notes on the metrics you'll need. Metrics are much easier to establish at the start of the process when you're setting up than trying to find some proof after the plan is well on its way to completion. Measure what you're doing, do what you plan on measuring and do the other bits that are neither measured nor planned but will ultimately help achieve the final outcome. Just because you can measure something doesn't make it worth doing and just because it's worth doing doesn't mean it's measurable. Get things done and measured in appropriate doses to satisfy the needs of the market (sales!) and the organization (accountability!) for maximum traction within the organization.

Consider what existing benchmarks exist, have been measured and were highlighted during the internal analysis of the organization (Chapter 3). Working with the internal analysis benchmarks (unless you're starting from scratch) helps you to identify variations from previous metrics, benchmarks and plans, and to draw conclusions about the impact of your marketing activity. It's also useful for seeing what the organization values interms of corporate knowledge – if the prior figures are financial (expenditure v return on investment), it's a safe bet the accountants will want more of the same data next time. Table 10.1 outlines a couple of sample metrics for each of the previous objectives.

Table 10.1 Metrics for objectives

| Objective | Sample metric 1 | Sample metric 2 |
|---|---|---|
| Cost-oriented | Internal accounting balance sheets | After-sales revenue |
| Sales-oriented | Sales | Payments to affiliates |
| Behavioural change | Increases in desired behaviour | Decreases in old behaviour |
| Information dissemination | Ranking in Google on keywords for the content | Traffic data (hits, downloads, views) |
| Promotional | Sales coupons redeemed | Conversations on Twitter |
| Entertainment-oriented | LPC (LOL per click) | Are we having fun yet? |

## Business model: expenditure to revenue

The second part of implementation is the money. Money is one of the problematic areas of business as most cultures tend towards regarding the open discussion of price, income, revenue and the rest of the pay-cheque generating activities as socially inappropriate. Artistes who disclose revenue from sales, merchandising and concert tours are deemed to have 'sold out' despite usually having sold very little. Movies are more likely to brag about costs ('the most expensive flop ever made'), books have nothing to write home about and bloggers periodically need to post 'Donations wanted'. Money changes everything insofar as if you've got money, you'll be encouraged to spend it, if you're spending it, you'll be encouraged to cut back, and if you're focused purely on cutting back, you're in danger of forgetting that I in ROI stands for investment. You've got to spend something (time, money, effort) to make returns (money, time, reward).

### *Budgeting*

Budget allocations for Internet-based marketing activities are frequently regarded as difficult to predict and can be subsumed into the overall marketing budget. A dedicated Internet marketing budget helps managers to evaluate what the total investment in this activity is, and what sort of returns they are getting. There are a number of different methods for determining a budget for online marketing. They include:

○ last year's budget plus an allowance for cost increases and new activities (valid only where the activity existed last year)
○ a percentage of company sales (assumes a sales orientation for the activity to continue providing its own revenue stream for survival)
○ a percentage of the overall marketing budget (integrated element of the mix)
○ a reallocation of the existing marketing budget (assuming that the increase in Internet activity will lead to a decrease in offline marketing activities)
○ competitor budgets and activities (reading the competitions' annual reports from their websites to determine their budget allocations)
○ needs for creating an effective e-marketing presence (investment cost plus running costs) and/or
○ graduated plan linked to results (more success, more money).

In e-marketing, there are the legends of the industry who can apparently raise venture capital at will with no readily visible or discernable business models or revenue stream (Facebook, MySpace). Others clearly have something up their metaphorical sleeve, since they're raising money selectively and not cashing in on reasonable to ludicrous buy-out offers (Twitter), or have hit the magic formulae in their secret mountain lairs (Google). Unless you're confident of being able to clean out a legitimate National Lottery or National Credit Union on command, it's much more viable to sort out how your e-marketing activity will spend money (and thus be paid for by something else), raise some money (and still be paid for by something else) or turn a profit (and pay for itself).

Table 10.8  Definitive options: Be new or improved in one or more category product

| Consumer motives | Idea | | | Behaviour | | Object | |
|---|---|---|---|---|---|---|---|
| | Belief (B) | Value (V) | Attitude (A) | One off (O) | Recurring (R) | Virtual good (VG) | Physical goods (PG) |
| Learn (Le) | LeB | LeV | LeA | LeO | LeR | LeVG | LePG |
| Search (S) | SB | SV | SA | SO | SR | SVG | SPG |
| Communicate (Cm) | CmB | CmV | CmA | CmO | CmR | CmVG | CmPG |
| Convenience (Cn) | CnB | CnV | CnA | CnO | CnR | CnVG | CnPG |
| Community (Co) | CoB | CoV | CoA | CoO | CoR | CoVG | CoPG |
| Anonymity/pseudonymity (An) | AnB | AnV | AnA | AnO | AnR | AnVG | AnPG |
| Escapism (E) | EsB | EsV | EsA | EsO | EsR | EsVG | EsPG |
| Recreation (R) | ReB | ReV | ReA | ReO | ReR | ReVG | RePG |
| Social pressure (SP) | SPB | SPV | SPA | SPO | SPR | SPVG | SPPG |
| Inherent awesomeness (IA) | IAB | IAV | IAA | IAO | IAR | IAVG | IAPG |
| Vending (Ve) | VeB | VeV | VeA | VeO | VeR | VeVG | VePG |
| ATM (A) | AB | AV | AA | AO | AR | AVG | APG |
| Self-expression (SE) | SEB | SEV | SEA | SEO | SER | SEVG | SEPG |

Table 10.9  The augmented history tourist application

| Consumer motives | Idea | | | Behaviour | | Object | |
|---|---|---|---|---|---|---|---|
| | Belief (B) | Value (V) | Attitude (A) | One off (O) | Recurring (R) | Virtual good (VG) | Physical goods (PG) |
| Learn (Le) | LeB | LeV | LeA | LeO | LeR | LeVG | LePG |
| Search (S) | SB | SV | SA | SO | SR | SVG | SPG |
| Communicate (Cm) | CmB | CmV | CmA | CmO | CmR | CmVG | CmPG |
| Convenience (Cn) | CnB | CnV | CnA | CnO | CnR | CnVG | CnPG |
| Community (Co) | CoB | CoV | CoA | CoO | CoR | CoVG | CoPG |
| Anonymity/pseudonymity (An) | AnB | AnV | AnA | AnO | AnR | AnVG | AnPG |
| Escapism (E) | EsB | EsV | EsA | EsO | EsR | EsVG | EsPG |
| Recreation (R) | ReB | ReV | ReA | ReO | ReR | ReVG | RePG |
| Social pressure (SP) | SPB | SPV | SPA | SPO | SPR | SPVG | SPPG |
| Inherent awesomeness (IA) | IAB | IAV | IAA | IAO | IAR | IAVG | IAPG |
| Vending (Ve) | VeB | VeV | VeA | VeO | VeR | VeVG | VePG |
| ATM (A) | AB | AV | AA | AO | AR | AVG | APG |
| Self-expression (SE) | SEB | SEV | SEA | SEO | SER | SEVG | SEPG |

approach focuses your attention on matching consumer motives with product elements to create the conditions necessary to either anticipate and satisfy the market (CIM) or present an offering that has value (AMA).

## Task 2: Design the fit

The second task in the product–market fit model is the business end of the process where the ideas, notes and plans from the background market research (Chapters 3 and 4) are combined with the marketing mix elements (Chapters 6 and 7) to create

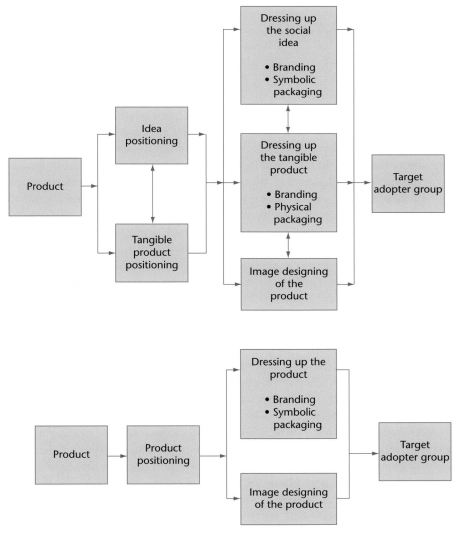

**Figure 10.1** Designing the fit for physical and non-physical products
*Source*: Kotler, P. and Roberto, E. (1989) *Social Marketing: Strategies for Changing Public Behavior.*
New York: Free Press

an offer that's going out to the marketplace. Designing the fit is alluded to in the CIM definition of marketing as the anticipation and satisfaction of customer requirements (Chapter 2), and relies heavily on both the substantive features of the actual product (capacity to solve a problem and/or meet a need) plus the position this product offer occupies in the mind of the consumer (Chapter 4). The aim in phase 2 is to design an approach that communicates the features of the product definition (phase 1) in a way that fits with the expectation of the market and the capacity of the organization to deliver.

Designing the fit involves three steps: positioning the product (Chapter 7) in the marketplace and mind of the consumer; 'dressing up' the product offering so that the IMC, user experience and other elements of the product are consistent with the positioning strategy and designing the overall image including the use of pricing, distribution and product features to communicate to the market (Figure 10.1).

### Positioning

Positioning consists of the consumer's interpretation of your product, price and branding efforts as you attempt to place your brand, product, reputation or ideas into a specific location in their mind (product is more like X, less like Y and not A). This means that it's one part customer generated and one part marketer created, and once more there are no hard and fast sure-fire success strategies (Chapter 7). e-marketing is at the more complex end of the positioning strategy, with the mix of intangible products (services, ideas, experiences), virtual goods and the occasional collection of real-world objects. Consequently, we're using both the single and split product models here – single product is where there's no physical product, and split product has both ideas and goods to be positioned, dressed up and addressed to the end user. There are five positioning strategies that integrate into the design of the product–market fit.

1. Price-based positioning. Table 6.1 introduced a nine-item grid of relative market prices (under, over and equal non-financial and financial costs) that can be revisited for selecting the appropriate market position based on price (or price based on market position).
2. Behaviour-focused positioning coincides with the organization's behavioural objectives as the offer is positioned based on the behaviour you want the end user to undertake. This links into the idea of the product being either a one off or a recurring activity.
3. Benefit-focused positioning tends to ally with the organization's promotion and information dissemination objectives in that position of the product is based on the specific benefits it will provide the potential user. This draws on the idea side of the product, and places an emphasis on creating strong belief and attitudes on the part of the consumer.
4. Barrier-focused positioning ties into behavioural change and promotional objectives where the aim is to show the compatibility of the product with some other aspect of the customer's life. This usually draws on the belief, value and the recurring behaviour elements of the product model.

5. Competition-based positioning is used where sales, price and direct head-to-head contrasts are needed to position the product offer in relation to your key identified competitors and rivals. This can feature comparison of objects (physical and virtual) through lists of features, although it's best achieved with idea positioning of attitudes and belief associated with your product *vis as vis* the opposition.

Repositioning is excluded since once you've decided to reposition, you'll be using one of the five positioning strategies for the new position. Table 10.10 summarizes the connection between the positioning strategy, organizational objective and the product model.

## Positioning and innovativeness

The Internet is the single largest new product development activity in existence. Every tweet, blog post and piece of content can be graded on the sliding scale of innovation from the really new ideas, products or content to quite new or well established.

New products are arranged across a three-point scale ranging from really new products (discontinuous innovation), quite new products (dynamically continuous) and less-than-new (continuous products). Really new product (RNP) is a term used by Aggarwal et al. (1998) to describe an innovation that is ground shaking, revolutionary and extremely likely to fail to be adopted. RNPs usually require a significant shift in consumer behaviour and an effort on the part of the consumer as they learn what the innovation is, how it might benefit them and how to actually use it. Since most PR firms don't have a solid grounding in innovation adoption theory, they like to present everything they're pitching as the most revolutionary of developments without considering whether that position is supported by the broader marketing activity, the desires of the consumers or reality.

**Table 10.10** Links between positioning strategy, objectives and product

| Positioning strategy | Objective | Product |
|---|---|---|
| Price | Cost-oriented | Belief |
| | Sales-oriented | Attitude |
| Behaviour | Behavioural change | One off |
| | | Recurring |
| Benefit | Information dissemination | Belief |
| | Promotional | Attitude |
| | | Value |
| Barriers | Promotional | Belief |
| | Behavioural change | Attitude |
| Competition | Sales-oriented | Belief |
| | Promotional | Physical goods |
| | | Virtual goods |

The sequel to the RNP is the quite new product (QNP), which builds on an existing set of products and behaviours. Whilst the RNP sets the benchmark for a whole new way of solving a problem, the QNP is developed with the second-mover advantage of being able to respond to the market's newly recognized needs. The RNP sets the initial standards and the QNP follows up on the marketplace reaction to those standards. Consequently, the QNP is much closer to the needs of the market and is the more successful as it starts from an established base of people knowing roughly what it does (it's a phone that takes pictures, it's a camera that makes phone calls), and can focus developing a relative advantage (clear photos, cheaper calls) over the RNP.

Following up the field is the less than new product (LNP), which is the staple of most businesses and the lifeblood of any developed marketplace. These are the minor customizations, tweaks and variations that proliferate during the growth to maturity phase of the product lifecycle. The LNP comes with a trifold advantage – economies of scale from market experience, greater exposure to the market with the subsequent ability to recognize and adapt to the needs of different segments and access to the early and late majority market places (70 per cent of any given market). This is why Call of Duty 6 is a sure bet, along with iPod Touch Generation 3 and Windows 8 – less-than-new additions to the existing product stable offer that not-quite-so-innovative certainty to the early and late majority marketplace.

Twitter provides a compact case study in the continuous innovation factory approach to online life. Original tweets are usually new ideas, content or concepts (and even if it's a statement of breakfast consumed, it's not something you knew before the tweet). Replies to existing comments are quite new products since there's an existing context for the commentary (QNP), and a re-tweet is a continuous idea (LTN) since it's repeating an existing tweet entirely. Depending on your personal innovation style, you may find the constant flow of new content to be a bug rather than a feature (laggard). Alternatively, you may follow opinion leaders who re-tweet and recommend existing ideas (early majority) or you could be the chatty one who's providing all of the new content (early adopter) instead of the person who reads about celebrity tweets in the newspaper the following day (late majority).

Value consideration from a consumer-centric view focuses on whether to develop new product offerings (RNP), upgrade existing versions (QNP) or offer minor repackaging of an older concept (LNP). In part, this can be determined by the type and nature of the target market and where they fit into the innovation adoption framework (Chapter 5) and Rogers's (1995) innovation features list. Rogers's (1995) five-point checklist asks:

1. What's the relative advantage of this offer over the competition?
2. Is the value offer compatible with everything else the customer does?
3. How complex is the value offering? Is complexity a positive feature or does it raise the time and effort price?
4. Can you try the product out without having to commit to it?
5. Is it obvious if you're using this product? Is the observability of product use a cost to minimize or a feature to sell?

Table 10.11 Innovation characteristics, innovation adoption category, and strategy

| | Relative advantage | Compatibility | Complexity | Trial | Observable |
|---|---|---|---|---|---|
| **Innovator** (diversify) | Novelty | Limited | Maximum | In the alpha and beta test | Noticeable if it works |
| **Early adopter** (diversify, market penetration) | Trend setting | Leadership | Status symbol | In the invite-only beta test | Used to promote their own visibility |
| **Early majority** (market penetration) | Followership | Fashionable | Moderate | Upgraded from a free account | Important to be seen to be fashionable |
| **Late majority** (market development) | Compliance | Forced | Simplicity | Free account | Complains it's everywhere |
| **Laggard** (ahem) | No advantage | Not compatible | Too complex | Signed up, couldn't see the point, left | Noticeable by their absence |

Sample answers to these questions across the five different types of innovation adopters produce Table 10.11 as a starting point for considering your positioning strategy based on innovativeness.

## Dressing up

Dressing up the product is the implementation of a positioning strategy through the performance of the marketing mix elements. There are three essential elements that the e-marketer can influence in designing the product–market fit at this point:

1. Branding (actual product, promotion), which was introduced in Chapters 6 and 7 as part of the product the consumer purchases, the consumer's experience with the product's performance and marketing communication activities.
2. Package (core product, delivery), which includes the site design consisting of the user interface and user experience, and which represents the nexus between the core product (what benefit it gives) and the way the actual product performs in the hands of the consumer (actual product). User experience (UX) is a specialist skill set which incorporates art design, human interface, psychology, a touch of marketing and a lot of prototype testing.
3. Symbolic (augmented product, price, delivery), which includes the various meanings that the product has for the consumer (Chapter 5), the market (Chapter 7), and how these cues all tie together to constitute the augmented product. It also incorporates the impression created by the price of the product (luxury, standard, economy) and the availability of the product through various distribution channels (exclusive, selective, common).

*Image design*

Image design is the holistic approach of integrated marketing communications that addresses the communication of the proposed positioning strategy to the marketplace. It incorporates the classical elements of the promotional mix (Chapter 7) with the contemporary elements of social media (Chapter 12), visual design, organizational voice and communication style choices such as one to many, one to one, one to many to one. Image design is criticized as a spin-doctor approach and whilst it can be misused, the purpose of the activity is to ensure that the means and methods of communication meet the needs of the market every bit as much as the product does. As image design is partially responsible for the creation of the consumer's expectations, it plays a vital role in the product–market fit.

## Deliver the fit

This is the mission critical payload for e-marketing implementation. Delivering the fit is the art of bringing distribution to life through one of four possible generic scenarios. As usual, the 'one size fits one size' disclaimer applies to this framework, and it should be considered the start of the distribution planning instead of the end game. The four scenarios are tied to the extent to which there's a need for a person in the process and whether there's a tangible good involved somewhere (Table 10.12).

To understand the flow of these delivery situations, it is first necessary to understand each of the nine components. These are:

1. diffusion object, which is the idea, service or product that is being offered to the market for use
2. communication message and execution, which is the content of what you want to say to the market to encourage the adoption and use of your product offering
3. communication media, which is the method of getting the message to the market using interpersonal, mass or online communications methods or a combination of all three
4. generating availability/placement, which refers to how the product, service or idea is placed in the market so that it can be seen and accessed by the potential consumer
5. outlet field force, which represents the direct interactions between consumer and organization in the process of 'selling' the product for adoption and use
6. availability outlets/venues, which refer to the ease with which potential users can access the product or service
7. adoption triggering, which are those elements of the marketing mix and positioning strategy which strike a chord with the target market and move them along the innovation adoption process, from awareness to interest, desire and, ultimately, action and satisfaction
8. personal presentation, which represents the one-to-one communications between consumer and organization that can be either face to face or via personal responses to online questioning
9. target group, who are the people you are trying to reach.

Table 10.12 Delivering the fit: four possible delivery scenarios

| No tangible/no presentation | No tangible/personal presentation | Tangible/no presentation | Tangible/personal presentation |
|---|---|---|---|
| Diffusion object Communication message and execution | Diffusion object Communication message and execution | Diffusion object Communication message and execution | Diffusion object Communication message and execution |
| Communication media | Communication media Establishing availability outlets/venues | Communication media Availability outlets/ venues Outlet field force Generating availability/ placement | Communication media Generating availability/ placement Outlet field force Availability outlets/venues |
| Adoption triggering | Adoption triggering | Adoption triggering | Adoption triggering Personal presentation |
| Target group | Target group | Target group | Target group |
| e-marketing elements | | | |
| Self-service website | Cybercommunity | Online shipping, export | YouTube videos Virtual world |
| Idea/experience | Services Experience Idea | Virtual goods Physical goods | Services Virtual goods Physical goods |

How these different elements are combined most effectively will depend on the nature of the product or service being offered and whether the organization chooses to use personalized or mass communications to reach the market. This will also determine the extent to which different e-marketing elements are used to complement or replace more traditional marketing and communications efforts. The four key scenarios are represented in Figure 10.2.

## Service blueprinting for delivering the fit

One tool that is particularly useful in the design of implementation strategies is the blueprint. Just as any successful physical construction requires a detailed design plan and blueprint, online activities require similar techniques. The electronic marketing blueprint is a tool that helps bring together the organization's requirements for online and offline marketing activities and integrates these into the overall strategic direction of the organization.

Blueprints allow managers across the functional areas of an organization to determine the extent and level to which each section will be affected by the decision to adopt an Internet-based marketing strategy. It is important to remember that marketing as a strategic function is cross-disciplinary and its effects are not confined to the

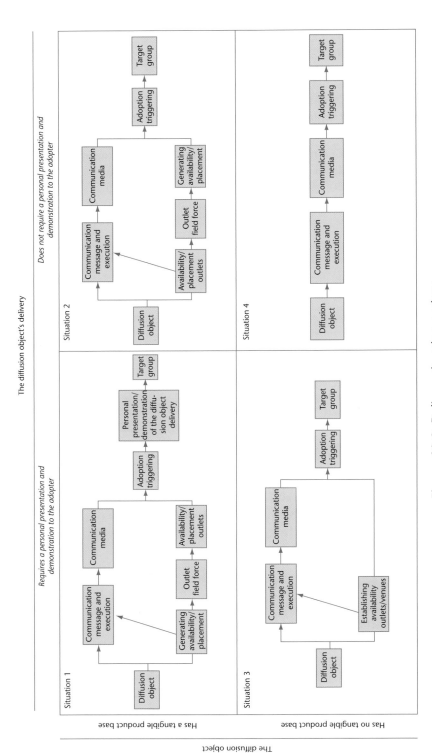

Figure 10.2 Delivery situation options

*Source:* Kotler, P. and Roberto, E. (1989) *Social Marketing: Strategies for Changing Public Behavior*. New York: Free Press

marketing section alone. Choosing a marketing strategy that turns the organization from a regional retailer to a global sporadic exporter will have an impact across the whole organization, and will require a holistic approach from the organization for it to succeed. Blueprinting decisions need the support and involvement of management in the development process because:

○ blueprint decisions are critical to overall organizational success. Full management support for the movement to an Internet-based marketing process is needed as changes to products for distribution online or from online ordering need to be addressed by logistics management.

○ they can cut across several product lines or divisional boundaries. Developing a website involves the co-ordination of IT divisions and marketing divisions. If the site development also requires the redevelopment of the product for digital distribution then engineering and production departments will also need to become involved in the blueprint.

○ they frequently require the resolution of cross-functional conflict. One of the advantages of blueprinting is that it maps out areas of potential inter-divisional conflict before the production (and conflict) commences. Once products are expected to be shipped, and customer orders have been taken, it is usually too late to decide who really should have been responsible for what function in the online marketing and distribution processes (Kalakota and Robinson, 1999).

The success or failure of internal marketing efforts to gain support for external marketing plans involving Internet activities will arise from how effectively the blueprinting process is supported by management. It requires leadership and co-ordination from the top as it is a dynamic process in which the organization's list of active projects is constantly updated and revised, projects are evaluated and, if selected, prioritized, and have impact on budget allocations. For an online marketing blueprint to be successful, it needs the involvement and support of the management from the start to the completion of the process.

## Delivering on schedule

Timelines are both critical to implementation metrics and planning. That said, they're also exceptionally variable in nature based on the task, resources to hand, people working on it and the vulnerability of the project to conservation of Ninjustu (TV Tropes, 2009). Many aspects of startup e-marketing scale about as well as ninjas do – one team member per task is effective, two is slightly less effective, three is adequate and four is the upper ceiling of team competence. Any number beyond four seems to be asking for the time to increase as the number of people added to a task increases the likelihood of delays.

Marketing has a series of lead time issues that need to be factored into the timelines (Figure 10.3). There's an instant and immediate reaction to a campaign when the target customer goes from awareness to action, and as such, the shopping cart and order forms need to be there waiting now. Editors at the meta-blog Boing Boing

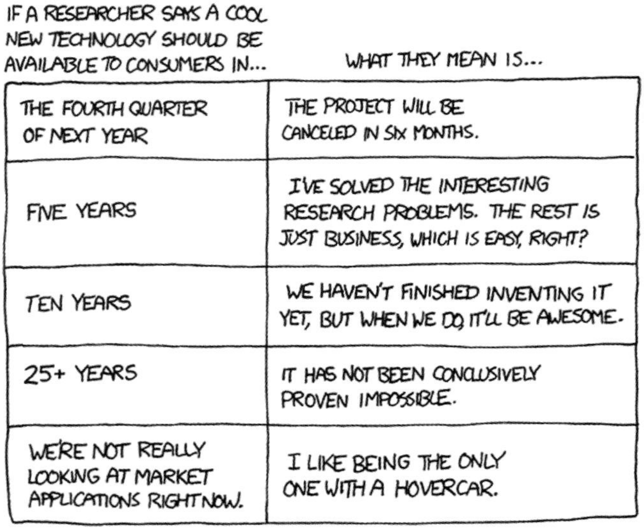

| IF A RESEARCHER SAYS A COOL NEW TECHNOLOGY SHOULD BE AVAILABLE TO CONSUMERS IN... | WHAT THEY MEAN IS... |
|---|---|
| THE FOURTH QUARTER OF NEXT YEAR | THE PROJECT WILL BE CANCELED IN SIX MONTHS. |
| FIVE YEARS | I'VE SOLVED THE INTERESTING RESEARCH PROBLEMS. THE REST IS JUST BUSINESS, WHICH IS EASY, RIGHT? |
| TEN YEARS | WE HAVEN'T FINISHED INVENTING IT YET, BUT WHEN WE DO IT'LL BE AWESOME. |
| 25+ YEARS | IT HAS NOT BEEN CONCLUSIVELY PROVEN IMPOSSIBLE. |
| WE'RE NOT REALLY LOOKING AT MARKET APPLICATIONS RIGHT NOW. | I LIKE BEING THE ONLY ONE WITH A HOVERCAR. |

**Figure 10.3** Translating timelines
*Source*: http://xkcd.com/678/

(www.boingboing.net) observed a distinct difference in the sales from books linked from their blog that were pre-order only versus immediately available for sale. Similarly, delays in production of the product can increase the vulnerability of the organization to an early peak (high interest, high desire, no option for action) that builds momentum for competitors.

## Issues in implementing e-distribution

Van den Poel and Leunis (1999) identified three distribution roles in marketing as the non-store information channel, non-store reservation channel with offline shipping, and online store purchase with online distribution and shipping. In very general terms, the capacity required for each of the three types of channels listed above should increase from 'non-store information channel' (just the data) to 'non-store purchase and delivery channel' (which is when it's a good idea to break out the Amazon S3 server farm). In order to meet these roles, Kostopoulos (1998) outlined a useful set of technical factors to consider in e-marketing – network access, server capacity and compatibility.

### Network access

Network access is the capacity to access the Internet (and includes m-marketing channels). It should not need to be said that the value of a website to a customer is only as good as the customer's ability to access the site, but it has to be said. Just because you can make a site inaccessible through Flash animations, video, high-resolution graphics and complex coding doesn't mean there's any economic justification for your excess.

If the aim of the site is to sell products, make the purchase process simple, painless and obvious.

## Server capacity

Server capacity is the ability of the technology to deliver the web presence and web delivery channel to the end user (and related to Chapter 1's Figure 1.2). Twitter periodically illustrates server capacity overloads (with the legendary Fail Whale graphic) that come from excesses of popularity. A chief problem for online distribution channels is balancing capacity reserve against wasted excess in that whilst excess capacity on the server is preferred to customers being unable to access the site, it's still a cost to cover. That said, in contrast to the physical world of the marketplace, capacity errors online result in people looking for an alternative method of satisfying their needs. You can turn fans away from a sporting event and have them queue up again next time. Turn people away from your website, and they will find another site to meet their needs – witness the number of people who update their Facebook status to comment on the Twitter service being down.

## Technical compatibility

Compatibility includes browser compatibility (IE, Firefox, Flock, Safari) and a broadened sense of technological compatibility with the end-user devices (mobiles, desktop, Xbox, fridge, iPods) in their various appropriate formats (Kostopoulos, 1998). Compatibility issues also cover how the digital information will be presented to the user (in terms of control, choice and how dependent the distribution channel is on proprietary software). This also extends to the provision of PDF, DOC, PPT and the nefarious DOCX file format of Office 2007 (a much maligned shift in format to decrease the interoperability of Microsoft's newer products with their older counterparts). There are five general rules for establishing compatibility to the widest market:

1. Use the widest accepted protocol. Security is through obscurity, compatibility is through open and widespread acceptance.
2. Remember the other formats – Windows, Macintosh, Linux and Unix users may also like to see your products as much as your primary market pick (Apple has a slew of Mac-only software. iPhones dominate but they're not the only mobile computing market.) Don't forget multiple browser compatibility as well – the whole reason we had you acquire the major browsers back in the Introduction was to give you the option to cross-check the performance of your site against the different alternatives. Also, be aware that Safari is the iPod Touch/iPhone default browser format, so if you're incompatible there, you're closing out the large iPhone mobile market (Chapter 13).
3. Forgo bleeding edge/cutting edge if you can use established protocols. The newest greatest thing is likely to have the narrowest part of the market (innovators) who are probably working for you in the design studio. The widest part of the user base is still using the older version of the software. Set it up for them, and you'll gain wider

marketshare at the start. If you can work with an existing format, that's one less cost for you and the end user.

4. Use Mols's (1998) guidelines for establishing a distribution format if there is no readily visible market standard. If a standard exists, use it. It's cheaper and easier than reinventing another wheel.

5. If you must establish your own protocol, give away the reader/viewer, hand out a functional but feature-sparse free encoder and charge heavily for the high-end corporate encoding software that does the really powerful stuff – corporations will both have the desire and the budget for the serious equipment.

There are other considerations for creating distribution channels that are compatible with the target market of the product. Most important of all is to understand that while technology is a major facet in making a successful digital delivery, it is the people behind the technology that determine the success or failure of the product.

## Defend the fit (metric)

The penultimate stage is the justification of the product–market fit, where you need to demonstrate how the e-element fits into the marketing strategy but also how they help achieve the organization's overall corporate objectives. If e-marketing is perceived as a cost rather than an investment then it becomes particularly vulnerable to cut backs in times of economic and financial stress.

Assessing the market fit and justifying why you have taken this particular series of actions is done in three steps:

1. Research the impact – ensure that your objectives are not only measurable, but also that they are measured. Conduct pre- and post-intervention research to see what, if any, impact your strategy has had on the target market and ensure that the research and objectives include measures that focus on both the tangible and intangible outcomes.

2. Use the research regardless of the outcomes (positive, negative or neutral). Knowing how the good, the bad and the mediocre occurs helps determine what to do next time. Unexpectedly positive results should be investigated as thoroughly as unexpectedly negative ones, since high short-term sales may represent a one-off peak from novelty-seeking consumers or the start of sustained business growth. Without knowing the reasons behind the success or failure, incorrect assumptions can be made which have a flow-on effect to the next measurement period.

3. Make the changes – if the market doesn't understand your subtle and witty campaign, change it. Research is only as valuable as the actions it motivates. After using the research to identify trigger points for action and/or inaction, adjust the marketing mix elements and re-measure to see if you have actually addressed the core of the problem.

## The metrics plan

Knowing what to measure and how to measure it is central to the metric plan. If you can't keep track of how far along the road to achieving your objectives you are then you're likely to run into the classic implementation problems of overspending in areas that are tracking well, underspending in those that need a boost and letting potential time bombs accumulate under the corporate radar. To develop an effective e-marketing metrics plan you need to be able to answer the following questions:

○ How will you know if you have achieved your objective?
○ What measurement instruments will you use?
○ How will you use these instruments to measure your objectives?
○ What market research will you do for your site?
○ What market monitoring will you use for your site?

### How will you know if you have achieved your objective?

The answer to this question goes back to the initial objectives formulation process. If your objectives are vague, multi-step and are not linked to benchmarks, the simple answer is that you won't know. An objective such as 'become an industry leader in online sales through improved company image' is virtually impossible to achieve as there is nothing to measure it against. On the other hand, if you had a clear objective of increasing sales by 5 per cent within six weeks of the initial launch of the campaign you have a start date (pre campaign), stop date (six weeks), initial sales benchmark and sales outcomes. It is easy to see in this case whether or not the objective has been met.

### What measurement instruments will you use?

Given the current tracking technologies available, combined with the trend in market research towards measuring tangible behaviours rather than intangible intentions or attitudes, it is tempting to rely predominantly on built-in systems to measure what people do when they get to your site. Whilst these technologies have many advantages, including improved accuracy, and they track actual rather than perceived behaviours, they are only useful in this context if they link to objectives and if those objectives add to the achievement of the overall corporate mission. Site visits are a popular metric as they are easy to measure and record. Similarly, online sales can be differentiated from traditional outlet sales, and the use of different parts of the site can be monitored, as well as the points of drop out. In addition to those metrics which can be collected and analyzed without the customer realizing that they are being observed, it is useful to include formal feedback forms onsite which address the less-observable elements of your objectives, such as asking where the customer found out about the site/company, which in turn can help determine the effectiveness of the traffic driving elements of the e-marketing strategy.

| | |
|---|---|
| Flashbang Studios | www.flashbangstudios.com |
| Flickr Pro | www.flickr.com |
| Flickr | www.flickr.com |
| Google | www.google.co.uk |
| Great British Heritage Pass | www.britishheritagepass.com |
| Is Gd | www.is.gd |
| iTunes | www.apple.com/uk/itunes |
| Jamendo | www.jamendo.com |
| MySpace | www.myspace.com |
| Off-Road Velociraptor Safari | www.raptorsafari.com |
| Problogger | www.problogger.com |
| ProWrestlingX | www.prowrestlingx.com |
| RemembertheMilk.com | m.rememberthemilk.com |
| Scribd | www.scribd.com |
| Slideshare | www.slideshare.net |
| Steam | www.steampowered.com |
| Twitter | www.twitter.com |
| World of Warcraft | www.worldofwarcraft.com |
| Xbox Live | www.xbox.com/en-GB |
| YouTube | www.youtube.com |
| Zazzle | www.zazzle.com |

# Applications

The third section of this book looks at the practical applications of a range of different Internet technologies and their suggested use for e-marketing. Chapter 11 covers the broad spectrum of 'things to do with technology, marketing and you' and looks at the different ways in which e-marketing has been used in business, non-profit organizations and society. Chapter 12 focuses on the applications and implications of using social media in e-marketing, including the need to engage in conversations with some types of customers (and not be quite so chatty with a few other types). Chapter 13 looks at m-marketing approaches, including the challenges of mobile marketing and the implications of Internet access that travels with the customer. Chapter 14 explores the options beyond the Web when it comes to e-marketing, with a specific interest in gaming consoles, virtual worlds and other defined e-marketing friendly (or hostile) spaces that use the Internet as their platform. Finally, the book concludes with a view of the impact of the Internet on society, the issues of culture, law, technology and innovation, and the current crisis of faith in intellectual property laws reflecting reality and how these shape the environment for e-marketers.

## Introduction

This chapter looks at uses of the Internet across three different approaches. First, are the general principles for classifying, categorizing and generally sorting what you can do with e-marketing into little self-contained boxes on a chart. Secondly, the chapter looks at the role of the Internet in international marketing and gives an overview of how the global nature of a medium means e-marketers have the option to target the local community, specific regions or the whole Internet-connected planet. Finally, the chapter ends with a set of checklists and strategies for putting the Internet to good use in any e-marketing context.

## Principles in application: frameworks for classifying the Internet

If there's one thing marketing loves more than a two-by-two matrix, it's a checklist of categories for assigning a wide range of diverse content on the Internet into neat little boxes. It's like market segmentation in that narrowing the world into a series of parameters becomes a means for focusing marketing activity. The trick is to remember that categories are just models and that these models help with figuring the world out insofar as they let you compare like with like but don't reflect reality as a whole. The Internet is a big, complex and weird place and any simple 'N+1 list' category scheme won't necessarily capture the essence of everything (even the ones with the 'other' and 'everything else' boxes at the end).

### Using the lists

There are five reasons to break open the bullet points on Word and start making categorical lists of websites, and clustering different parts of the Internet into boxes.

1. Segmentation, including general market segmentation and more specific use segmentation approaches (Chapter 4). Knowing the types of sites your customers will be visiting aids expectation management for when they're at your place and gives a good idea of what sorts of features, benefits and outcomes they'll be expecting.
2. Positioning strategies and the research needed to be able to explain your own Internet product as a 'cross between SiteX and ServiceY' (Chapter 6). Although final market position is in the mind of the consumer, it never hurts to be able to make suggestions such as 'Brand X is the Twitter of canned tuna' or 'Product Y: it's like Google for your best friends' to help align your desired position in the market with the user's actual perceptions.
3. Product features, including the market research end of ensuring that your relative advantage is actually an advantage (Chapter 6) rather than just another standard feature on the competitor sites. Offering e-mail with your search engine isn't a relative advantage in the age of Google. Similarly, if you've promised compatibility with

various other services, it's worth creating a category of services where the promises come true, plus handy lists of the non-compatible sites.

4. Promotion, including cross-promotion, site alliances, collaborative ventures – and for the business model inclined – the types of advertising that appear on similar types of websites (Chapter 10). Blog rolls, alliances, web rings and other collaborative– competitive approaches require you to classify friends (and foes) into useful and publishable lists.

5. Identifying friendly community structures, including organic communities which discuss your service, product and brand and unfriendly ones that do more than just discuss the product. Community identification and classification (Chapter 9) also fits into the listening aspect of market research (Chapter 4) and the conversational end of social media (Chapter 12).

Lists and classifications can be useful when applied to answer a question, solve a problem or create a new view of existing information (Figure 11.1). The question for you as a marketer is not just when to use the lists, but also when to publish the lists you've used as a part of the site's content. One of the unexpected cultural phenomena of the early Web 1.0 website was the list of related links that provided a convenient exit from the site and directed traffic to other people's content. There's still value in the Web 2.0

Figure 11.1 The inter-blag
*Source*: http://xkcd.com/181

era in pointing people away from your site – either because you don't want to deliver what they're asking for in a product (audience selection) or because you've already met their primary need and you've developed an alliance with another provider to meet the secondary needs (hardware manufacturers linking to the software providers, movie information sites linking to DVD stores, blogs linking to Amazon for affiliate sales). Publishing and promoting your classifications can be useful as a form of promotional tool, PR source or public whitepaper document that can bring traffic and attention to your site.

## Classification 1: Types of online attractions

The principle of the online attractor list is to create the same sense in designing and developing an online product that you'd take in setting up a store, theme park or major public attraction (Watson et al., 1998). Attractors are designed to be sites with the most potential to interact with the greatest number of visitors from the target market and offer interactions that are specific to the objectives of the firm. This makes attractor sites something that meet a set need in the market and difficult for competitors to replicate (Watson et al., 1998). Attractors consist of two levels of design: the content level, which is the substantive part of the product (soccer content for FA Cup site), and the node level, which is the navigation and user-interface level (buttons, links, graphics and interactive elements).

The attractor approach is based on the service marketing principles for the design of a good service (Chapter 8) and uses distinctive differentiation involving hard-to-replicate value offerings that meet the needs of the target market by being integral to the product experience offered by the company. The twelve attractor types outlined below are based on the works of Watson et al. (1998), Wen et al. (2001) and the authors spending far too much time online playing with the Internet:

1. Entertainment parks
2. Content archives
3. Exclusive sponsorships
4. Town halls
5. Clubs
6. Gift shops
7. Retail outlets
8. Service sector
9. Freeway intersections
10. Customer service centres
11. Journals and blogs
12. Single-purpose sites.

### Entertainment parks

These are sites, services and products designed primarily to entertain through high levels of interactivity, contests, prizes and other rewards. They include gaming websites such as Shockwave (www.shockwave.com) and World of Warcraft (www.worldofwarcraft.com), most of the content for the Xbox and just about everything sold through Steam (www.steampowered.com). This type of offer relies heavily on telepresence and flow states, and makes heavy use of interactive elements to provide a near-constant state of challenge-stimulus-reward for the consumer.

At the web level, entertainment parks tend to be sponsored by advertising and commercialization is based on free demonstration versions that plug the full registered commercial option or paid features such as no advertising or extra content. Services such as World of Warcraft, Xbox Live content and iPhone applications tend towards the fully paid with either one-off purchase or recurring charges (or both). The purpose of the sites is to encourage repeat visits either to win recurring prizes or to continue playing with the digital toys on display. These sites are the digital Disneyland of the Internet, where fun and play have priority over information and sales pitches. Of course, having moved the visitor into a positive mind-set, the website may also try to sell a product or two on the way to recoup the cost of investment (usually through a gift shop set-up, see below). Design features include the use of easy-to-follow paths and predetermined event areas such as games, puzzles and contests. Node-level interactions feature a large number of interactive elements, most of which will take a certain period of time (up to five minutes) to load. The waiting time is frequently used to explain the rules or instructions of the game, or to promote the content sponsor's message.

## Content archives

Content archives are the online equivalent of libraries, video stores and museums in that they contain large amounts of special interest information around various topics. These sites focus on providing massive volumes of information in audio (www.jamendo.com), video (www.youtube.com), pictures (www.flickr.com), text (www.scribd.com), PowerPoint (www.slideshare.net) or some other format (www.legaltorrents.com) to provide users with historical information (www.waybackmachine.com) or other content (www.archive.org). Content design emphasizes logical structures based on hierarchy, topic category, timelines or tag clouds. Node-level design places a strong focus on interlinking related topics and information, forming a giant interactive database of interrelated content (www.imdb.com), cross-references (www.tvtropes.org) or taxonomical structures (www.wikipedia.org).

## Exclusive sponsorships

The purpose of these sites is to either showcase corporate involvement in an event or generate traffic for the sponsor's core business, with the consequence that the product design is purpose built to redirect interest from the application, site or content to the main game (e.g. the organization sponsoring the event or the movie being promoted). The content is short term in nature and tends to either disappear into the digital ether after the event or be left as the technical equivalent of an archeological dig. Typically, sponsorship sites tend to be dedicated to the promotion of specific events, such as sports events, concerts and movies, software demonstrations or download sites. Exclusive sponsorship sites often integrate a range of features to reinforce the corporation's involvement with the event and might, for example, include free applications for the iPhone that promote one-off events such as movies, sports events and demonstration software for video games.

### Town halls

These types of website content and service represent the venues, meeting spaces and public forums of the Internet and are typified by their ability to allow share of voice to an individual through either registration or anonymous participation. Twitter fits into the town hall model as a space for conversation where the conversation is not guided by the site owners. This type of content can also be part of the infrastructure for a specific site or service. Examples include moderated forums – where invited guests are available for semi-public debate on topical issues – digital talk shows and even YouTube with its ability to post replies via text and video to other content. Town hall structures may also split their functionality between the live action areas and an archive of previous events. There is a strong degree of crossover between the node design of the archive and the site-level interactivity orientation of the entertainment park in town hall designs.

### Clubs

Club-style e-marketing content differs from the town hall insofar as the club is designed for membership and mingling, while the town hall is designed for broadcast and debate. These types of services are typically larger sites that are dedicated to supporting and hosting cybercommunities (Chapter 9) or smaller club-style arrangements of blogs that allow registered membership for frequent contributors and commenters. Facebook is the pinnacle example of a club-based site where the membership is more important than the broadcast and the purpose of the site is the connection between the users rather than the users' ability to promote content to a wider audience (Facebook can be used for that, it's just not as good at blogging as it is at poking friends). Cybercommunity structures exist either as the focus for the site (www.slashdot.org) or as an integrated element of an entertainment park. The distinguishing factor of the club site is the strong emphasis on either room-based groups or dedicated themed areas such as the Facebook fan pages.

### Gift shops

Gift shops are the free-content providers of the Internet and focus on the efficient and effective distribution of downloadable content and digital products. Gift shops differ from content archives in that they are set up to provide files to the user through a retail experience minus the cash register, whereas content archives prefer the 'look, don't download' approach. Gift shops can be found in operation inside the retail shop fronts of sites such as iTunes, Steam and Xbox Live. If you're able to download the product for free, you're in the gift shop, whereas if you have to hand over credit card or Paypal information, it's a retail outlet. Gift shops share similar design concerns with retail outlets and are frequently built alongside a retail outlet function.

## Retail outlets

Retail outlets are the revenue generators of e-marketing and offer physical goods, virtual goods, virtual services and payments for everything in between. This is a broad category which incorporates any site with a shopping cart, product categories and a range of online shipping choices from direct download to physical mail shipping. The highest-profile web-based retailers are Amazon (www.amazon.co.uk) and eBay (ebay.co.uk), with Steam, iTunes and the Xbox Live Arcade offering similar non-web retail functions (Chapter 14).

Content design is based around a central catalogue of products, offers or services functions, and a shopping cart function for the transactions. It's quite common to find a relatively complex taxonomical structure that mimics the content archive design elements as a means for sorting, classifying and categorizing the products into digital aisles and shelves akin to the supermarket. Digital retail outlets frequently use the 'Top 10', 'Best Selling' and 'Most Popular' sub-categories to encourage sales based on perceived peer approval (Chapter 5) and the 'Recently Released' category to appeal directly to the innovators. Retail outlets and gift shops are often built in parallel to provide free samples, bonus content and other reasons for the consumer to revisit the combined store front as part of a relationship-building approach (Chapter 8), and as a means to provide a specific advantage to this retail outlet (exclusive content, free offers) ahead of other online or offline outlets.

## Service sector

In addition to gift shops and retail outlets are the service sector elements of the Internet. Service sector element include the shopping carts built into the previous two offerings and represent aspects of the site design that allow consumers to either engage in a specific service exchange such as e-banking (www.lloydstsb.com), bill payment, subscription renewal, or customized membership options. The difference between the service sector and retail outlet is basically the outcome of the transaction – if the result is a physical or virtual good, it's a retail outlet; if it's a service, experience or intangible outcome, then it's a service. It's worth noting that these elements are frequently built into other attractor components. For example, the community site that has a range of subscription settings (e-mail notification, avatar customization) is offering a self-service control panel that enhances the community experience through a service sector element. Design issues for the service sector elements tend to involve complex back-end components that support large amounts of customer-focused customization of the site offering, plus a hefty dose of security since problems with virtual services are incredibly hard to undo (even compared with digital products).

## Freeway intersections

Freeway intersections are the portals, search engines and content indexes that exist to redirect you to somewhere else within the site (Yahoo! or MSNLive) or allow you to select bits of the rest of the Internet (Google, Bing). Portals are designed to offer gateways into specific content such as news-related services or a gateway to the rest of the product offerings. Portals can include a range of customizable information services such as news reports, weather forecasts and horoscopes, or can be a form of overview of the total services available (iTunes, Steam). These sites borrow heavily from the printed media design school by deliberately trying to replicate the look and feel of newspapers, or alternatively, are laid out like an electronic bento box.

Search engines are designed to search the whole of the Internet, a specific sub section (site-specific search) or a specific device (iPhone). These can either be simple search-only approaches or diet portals. Diet portals are search oriented sections that have added layers of portal-style content so that various common functions, features or searches can be accessed from the search page. Search-only systems are the exact opposite with sparse-looking input boxes and 'Search' buttons. Although Google was the past master of the simple search (one input box, two buttons), it's much more of a diet portal these days with the fifteen or so options available from the front page.

## Customer service centres

Customer service centres are content elements that are established for the purpose of providing after-sales support, updates, downloadable content or product-use information. These elements are commonly attached to retail and gift shop systems as the after-sales service areas. They can also be standalone after-sales service websites for physical goods or part of a corporate website which offers electronic versions of instruction manuals, help guides, product-use videos, information on warranties and helplines. The design of a customer service system may resemble the content archive or retail outlet as it tends to require complex taxonomies of products, product-related information and software. Functionality may also include elements such as the search engine, gift shop and even the community as a means of providing frameworks to find information, updates and support.

## Journals and blogs

Journal elements are collective online diary systems such as Livejournal (www.livejournal.com), Dreamwidth (www.dreamwidth.org) and Open Diary (www.opendiary.com). Journals represent the more personalized approach that deals with the writer's day-to-day life (Figure 11.2). Blog systems are more attuned to annotation of the user's web experiences and commentary on events, websites and issues, such as Vox (www.vox.com), WordPress (www.wordpress.com) and Blogger (www.blogger.com). That said, a webjournal and a blog can be used for either purpose. The distinction between them may seem an arbitrary categorization, although it's worth noting that the inherent community orientation of Dreamwidth and Livejournal loans itself more to collective socializing than can be found through the WordPress and Blogger sites. Similarly, the blogs tend to feel more like standalone publications and tend towards a different style of engagement with the reader-commentator-author dynamics. The blog can be used as a broadcast and community element of the site, whereby the corporation is the provider of the content and the blog is the conversation and communication outlet. Alternatively, blogs and journals can be offered as features of the broader product

**Figure 11.2** Bored with the Internet
*Source*: http://xkcd.com/77

offering, as is the case with the journal and notes function in Facebook or Windows Live's blog function that you acquire by default when you sign up for Windows Live Messenger (the artist formerly known as MSN Messenger).

### Single-purpose sites

Kottke (2008) identified the phenomena of 'single serving sites' which are task-specific websites described by domain names such as Is it Christmas? (www.isitchristmas.com), which has one day of saying 'Yes', and the rest of the year saying 'No'. These sites can also include countdown timers to certain events such as New Year's Eve, product launches or elections. Single-serving sites are often set up for jokes, parodies or political commentary rather than for serious use in e-marketing.

## Using online attractors

Each of these elements is stackable and can be combined in a range of different approaches to create a total product offer of physical, virtual and digital goods, services and experiences (Chapter 6). For example, the Xbox360 console offers a series of service sector elements (Xbox Live renewal) alongside the Xbox Live Arcade (retail/gift) and the semi-permanent worlds of the Xbox Live-hosted game servers (clubs, town halls). iTunes offers a combination of gift-shop, service sector, content archive and retail out-let but currently (at the time of writing) lacks an iTunes-hosted community structure. Meanwhile, Google seems to have an ambition to offer one of everything on this list (and then start expanding the list into a whole new array of objects).

## Classification 2: Types of content

The second classification structure is derived from an examination of various content elements within a product and can be considered the ingredients list on the back of a website, a software package or an online experience. These classifications are based on Dholakia and Rego's (1998) typology of web page content, which illustrated the different purposes for which individual elements of a website could be used. It's worth noting that these elements are related to the online attractors, as the attractors focus on top-level design issues with the types of content being the component parts in the main design. By way of metaphor, a chicken tikka masala is expected to consist of chicken and the various spices in the tikka masala, so the presence of the site-level element (chicken) in the components list is both welcome and expected. Similarly, when you've decided to build a community structure, you'd expect to find community elements within the site contents as well as just the top-level design. There are ten broad types of content that can be found within an online attractor, including:

1. advocacy content, which is tailored to promote a position on an issue, such as human rights, political issues or ideological positions
2. brands and branding content, which includes classic promotional elements, branding, logos and other classic advertising elements
3. comparative information, which can be head-to-head comparisons between products or brands, such as a consumer choice guide, direct comparison advertising series or even a list of features similar to Table 11.1
4. corporate information, which promotes the organization, organizational goals and objectives (the dull legalese statements, copyright attributions and unflattering end-user licence agreements are included here)
5. direct response elements, which initiate communications or feedback to the company, server or other interactive elements. These can range from surveys, customizable music selections, high score tables and e-mail forms, or functions such as bookmarking a page through Delicious (www.delicious.com), to sending a shortened URL through a Twitter client (www.is.gd)
6. index pages, which provide the navigational components for sites such as content archives, retail outlets or gift shops. These pages are often detailed elements within a larger page or structure

7. political and lobbying content, which can range from the support for votes, causes, candidates and campaigns to requests to vote in online popularity contests such as the Webby awards

8. public service components, which are set up to support worthy causes or social campaigns rather than to encourage the reader to support the creator's point of view (advocacy or political)

9. Retail/sales pages, which are the order forms, price guides and related elements that are necessary for running a gift shop or retail outlet attractor

10. blogs/microblogs/life streaming elements that are the component parts of the journal and blog sites, and are the content from the individual diaries and journals.

## General application for the Internet

The Internet has four main applications: accessing other people (communication and community); accessing other information (knowledge, experiences, entertainment); being accessed by other people (markets) and mediated exchange (transaction, conversation, delivery). From an e-marketing perspective, the main value occurs in the people, markets and delivery, with information being an added bonus. For the average consumer, it's people, information and communication with marketplaces as the bonus element. Consequently, what we (marketers) see as the killer application (markets) is not what the customer necessarily cares about when they're online. This means that when we think of marketing applications for the Internet, we shift some focus away from the consumer orientation back across to the organizational goals.

At the forefront, the most obvious applications of the Internet are aspects we've mentioned previously such as:

○ market research into relevant markets and on competitors (Chapter 4)
○ promotional activities (Chapter 7)
○ conversations and communication (Chapters 9 and 12)
○ the websites, web presence and every other aspect of 'being online' (Chapter 14)
○ taking orders, sales and marketspaces.

In terms of generic applications, it's worth considering the use of the Internet from a company perspective as fitting into 'enhanced business process', 'cost centre/investment' or 'generating revenue'. If you spend all day on Facebook talking to customers, participating in groups and monitoring brand perceptions (yours and your competitors') then it's an enhanced business process (market research). The use of the Internet to improve business processes occurs through the facilitation or automation of specific functions. These can include inventory management, purchasing, project management, shipment tracking and inter-office communications. Thirty minutes on eBay and a half day on Wednesdays for auction management is 'generating revenue'. Alternatively, Internet applications can be more strongly located within revenue generation through direct sales, sponsorships, advertising, subscriptions and affiliate sales. Finally, buying PDF files, data sets and advertising space on YouTube can be classified as 'cost centre' or 'investment' but generally falls into the camp of 'spending money'. Knowing which category to fit the Internet behaviour into is vital so that the firm knows whether to expect direct revenue, reduced costs or outright expenditure.

## International and export marketing: putting 'world wide' into the Web

This section examines some of the issues associated with the global nature of the Internet, that is the fact that each and every element of the Internet is potentially accessible from anywhere on the Internet-connected planet. Rather than just assuming that global access = desire for export marketing, we outline the choices of being global, glocal or locally focused, and the key issues involved in going into the export e-marketing business.

### Going global, glocal or local?

By its very nature the Internet is international and global in its reach with the consequence that any marketing undertaken on the Internet could default into being international marketing. In reality though, there's a range of reasons such as product type, distribution issues and (in)ability to supply a global market that means choosing local or global as a focus of the e-marketing strategy makes more sense. This section covers the potential intentional applications of e-marketing with a bias towards export-oriented e-marketing.

When considering an international e-marketing strategy, there are four considerations to keep in mind.

1. The Internet is not a level playing field. Larger firms still have greater resources and, although everyone can access a website, it does not necessarily follow that everyone can deliver goods. Share of voice is infinite on the Internet, so it's a crowded market with big players from around the globe contesting for your market.
2. Physical products still need to be delivered which means logistics still count in the real world, even if they can be surmounted in digital world(s). Economies of scale in shipping may require regional agents, or the shipping costs could kill off the value of the product to the end user (Chapter 6).
3. Some smaller local markets are more valuable than larger international target markets. Just because mass communications on a global scale are possible, it does not necessarily mean that marketing to all countries is the most effective and suitable approach.
4. Attractiveness of international markets is determined by national characteristics such as access to technology, economic power, political stability, digital capabilities and freedom of expression.

All these characteristics need to be evaluated before a specific market can be considered sufficiently attractive to invest in through an Internet-based approach to international marketing. For example, Australia has just about everything a British marketer would want in terms of technology, economic power, political stability – apart from the continued tyranny of distance for physical and electronic shipping (Australia's distance from the UK is such that the physics of a data exchange automatically induces lag between server and client).

## Is all Internet marketing a form of international marketing?

Despite the global reach of the Internet, not all web-based marketing can realistically be classified as international. While anyone, anywhere, can access the promotional and information materials on a given website, actually accessing the full range of services and products offered by the company running the website may be limited by geographical or other constraints. As is the case with all aspects of the Internet, some companies choose to take full advantage of the range of benefits offered by the medium while others choose a more limited role. That said, the distinction between e-marketing and international marketing (marketing for export/import) is becoming increasingly tenuous with the 'Think local, download global' mindset of the consumer.

Facebook is nominally an American corporation, set up under US regulations, subject to US laws and with a population of 19,750,940 residents in the UK (being a US site, it doesn't understand there's a difference between England, Northern Ireland, Wales, and Scotland). Facebook is thoroughly confusing from the classic export/import approach. Content is hosted through the United States from various non-American regions, and Facebook feels like a local operation to the average user (particularly with the language options for Cymraeg, Gaeilge and UK English). By careful use of IP block identification, Facebook can also detect where you are in the world and offer localized language offerings (which must get very annoying for anyone backpacking across Europe with a laptop).

If you've elected to sell through Facebook advertising, you can be selective and regional in your approach. If you're delivering services through Facebook via applications, it's a little less selective (still possible, but usually ill-will generating when you lock out certain regions). One of the dual-edge benefits of the Facebook user's global/international network of friendships is their tendency to want to share certain applications and games (such as ones based on Scrabble) with others, and the users have a tendency to not want to have to put up with seemingly artificial barriers based on regions.

## International orientation

e-marketing content can be classified in terms of commitment to internationalization versus localization according to the following classifications:

o *Domestic orientation*: which is where the content, goods and/or services are intended for the local area (this is a local website for local people). Availability can be IP locked to region-specific domains ('This video is not available in your region') or unable to be ordered without a credit card from the appropriate geographic region. Domestic only may be a deliberate strategy based on limited capacity to supply a market, ideological commitment to reduced carbon footprint, technical limitations (power supplies, left-hand drive cars) or problems with licences, patents and trade embargos.

## *Think local, act regional*

Limit the geographic focus of a website or distribution strategy. Although the Internet can reach out to anywhere on the globe (including the International Space Station), acting regionally allows marketers to reap the benefits of the Internet while working within a confined territory. Whilst you can get eBay in space, the postage charged by NASA is astronomical.

## *Pay attention to government regulations*

Rugman's (2001) identification of the myth 'because it's the Internet, governments don't apply' can inform Internet marketers as to how to minimize their exposure to international court cases. Extradition laws can and do apply, and prohibited activity in one nation is going to remain prohibited even when you're providing the component parts from another geographic region. Minor issues such as the differences in local ratings for film, television and games can have serious consequences – Australia doesn't have the equivalent R18 rating for video games which means games in the adult classification which are on the shelf legally in the UK can't be sold into Australia by direct mail or digital download.

Zugelder et al. (2000) offer practical solutions to minimize exposure to legal risks in various countries by either stating the limited trading area (e.g. 'Products from this site are available to UK and European Union countries only') or actively rejecting trade from selected regions (e.g. 'Products not available for shipping to Antarctica'). Sites which engage in global trading can establish 'choice of forum' legal clauses in their sales contracts that indicate which nation's legal system will be used to settle any dispute. Overall, if you're going to go for the global market, be smart about it, and look at the legal risks associated with the countries where you expect to find your major markets.

## *Recognize the world trade blocs, regional limits and other geographic segments*

Observe trading blocs for the express purpose of dealing with regional trading areas rather than perceiving the world as a single marketplace. If nothing else, breaking the world down according to the DVD region codes means identifying which areas have machines that can read particular DVDs (and if a region 0 DVD strategy is the best for you). Similarly, regional variances in basic elements such as electrical voltage means thinking through whether your product needs an adaptor, different power plugs or different transformers in the main device. Right hand side and left hand side of the road driving can influence the design issues for GPS mounts, hands-free car kits and other devices (including the way the mapping software is going to be thinking through which lane is needed for turning). Other variations between regions include religious observation, strength of individualism versus collective orientation (sell as 'buy one and be unique' or 'buy one and fit in') and the role of innovation as a menace or advantage to society. Thinking in terms of trade regions in the first instance will also assist in developing the right mind set for developing the appropriate segmentation strategies within each bloc, region, country, geographic region or market cluster. Remember, you sell to individuals (customers) not to conglomerates of national averages (nations).

## Pragmatics of international e-marketing

If you've decided that your e-marketing strategy (Chapter 4) should incorporate an export element, then the next section is definitely for you (if not, you possibly could skip a few pages if you're confident exporting won't be in the exam). When considering international e-marketing, your strategy will vary depending on the type of exporter you want to become. This in turn will influence the type of entry mode and in turn, the respective barriers to exporting that can be influenced through the use of various aspects of e-marketing.

### Pick your exporter type

There are two main types of exporters based on the organization's commitment to internationalization and the effort invested in the process: regular exporters and sporadic exporters. Regular e-marketing exporters fit the mould of the traditional, offline exporter in that they have a clear commitment to developing an international orientation and are prepared to put in the resources to develop an international marketing programme. For these organizations export activity is core to their business, not just an add-on. To take a clear international orientation requires the firm to develop safe, secure, online ordering and payment systems. There must also be, for all physical goods, an adequate and appropriate method of delivery. Such systems require significant investments of financial and human resources and, in many cases, will also involve the development of strategic alliances with local partners. This would not only ensure delivery of goods, but would also assist in complying with local regulations.

Sporadic exporters are the 'international by default' class of e-marketers who have benefited from the online environment providing opportunities for a reactive approach to their international marketing orientation. Often small or niche businesses, these organizations respond to international inquiries and, where possible orders, but do not have the same investment in export infrastructure that is apparent with regular exporters. Their international activities tend to be opportunistic rather than part of an integrated strategy. Sporadic exporters are not always as planned as regular exporters and yet can can still be very profitable. Further, it is not uncommon for sporadic export to be a precursor to the development of an integrated, regular export orientation.

For many firms, the commitment and risk involved in developing a regular export orientation in the first instance is too great. Sporadic export activity provides an opportunity to develop an international orientation with relatively low risk. This is consistent with traditional stage-based or evolutionary views of the development of international marketing activities (Andersen, 1993). One of the key benefits of the gradual development of international markets is the experiential learning that occurs within the organization prior to a major investment in export or other international marketing

Table 12.2  Sample tactics

| Objective | Sample tactic | Likely social media site |
|-----------|---------------|--------------------------|
| Cost-oriented | Reduce advertising spent | Set up accounts with YouTube (youtube.com), Vimeo (vimeo.com) and other video-sharing sites |
| Sales-oriented | Create affiliate links | Have easy-to-use affiliate sales HTML code for inserting into Blogger and WordPress blogs |
| Behavioural change | Build and maintain a support group for participants | Set up a Facebook group and encourage people to 'Become a Fan' of the project |
| Information dissemination | Set up an emergency response donation account through PayPal | Use a Twitter keyword related to the disaster and a Bit.ly link to the donation page |
| Promotional | Hold a 'Products in use' photo contest with prizes for creative product use | Require photos to be tagged with a specific keyword on Flickr or Twitpic |
| Entertainment-oriented | Produce a Flash or Shockwave game based on criminal activity, farming, manual labour, hospitality industry or cleaning fish tanks | Facebook. There's nowhere else on the Internet that brings such inordinate love for washing up virtual dishes while the real ones are ignored |

social media. There's always a risk in e-marketing that the nature of the Internet as a communication device will focus thinking on promotion and distribution. This risk is further amplified when the e-marketing is conducted on a media platform known for its one-to-many-to-one broadcast capacity. Table 12.3 is a breakdown of the types of uses of social media according marketing mix elements for each of the major packet mix objectives.

The re-introduction of people into e-marketing is an interesting combination of existing technologies (e-mail, direct messaging, real time chat) with newer systems of social media sites (community structures), along with the odd bit of voice and video technologies. As part of social media tactics, it's also the point where you need to consider what technologies and tools you'll use to manage the social media (e-introduction: setting up for e-marketing). These break down into three categories:

1. *Direct management through the social media website*: Using the site directly will give you the same or similar end-user experience as the standard adopter of a social media site. Plus, certain aspects such as Facebook's advertising controls or Flickr's metrics can't be accessed outside of the site itself. Whilst this usually is an optimal operation for most social media sites, it does mean leaving the Flock web browser open all day at work versus using task-specific software for campaign management.

2. *Desktop software*: Running the social media campaign from a desktop client comes with a set of advantages insofar as software interfaces to the major social media sites usually allow for multiple account management, or come with a range of additional features that can be beneficial for the marketing. The downside to the software comes from it being a third-party access and thus not being able to access all of the social media site's features. TweetDeck (www.tweetdeck.com) allows for posting content to Twitter, Facebook and several other sites, but it can't view these sites (and therefore is mostly immune to the lure of Facebook's games).

3. *Mobile access*: This involves using the site through a specific purposed application on the iPad, iPhone, HTC Desire or Blackberry. Whilst most social media sites can be accessed through any web-enabled mobile phone browser, it's not worth considering mobile marketing access to social media if you're not running a dedicated smart phone. You'll want the processing power and easy keyboard access to make it worthwhile both financially and practically.

In addition to working through the nitty gritty of the resources, technical issues and tactics, you also have to ensure that what you plan on the social media front complements and supports the rest of the e-marketing game plan.

**Table 12.3** Objective, marketing mix and social media

| Objective | Marketing mix | Tactic | Social media activity |
|-----------|---------------|--------|-----------------------|
| Cost-oriented | Price | Higher margins per unit | Positioning as a luxury brand through social media exclusivity |
| | Product | Reduce production costs with user-generated content | Accept user content submissions through Flickr, Facebook or MySpace |
| | Promotion | User-assisted automated promotion | Automatically post application use to Facebook status |
| | Place | Affiliate re-broadcast | Shareable media, viral messages |
| | Person | Community advocates | Endorse fan-created social media groups |
| | Process | Use social media to talk directly to users | Track hashtags on Twitter, keywords on blogs, join Facebook fan pages and engage in conversation |
| | Physical evidence | Support fan art, fan content | Endorse quality fan-created virtual products |
| Sales-oriented | Price | Promotional discounts | Exclusive codes through Twitter |
| | Product | Exclusive content for social media users | Registering with a Facebook app gains access to in-game special items |

Table 12.3 (Continued)

| Objective | Marketing mix | Tactic | Social media activity |
|---|---|---|---|
| | Promotion | Promotional codes | Re-tweet with #hashtag for a special discount code for 15% off |
| | Place | Discounted shipping for social media affiliates | Followers of a Twitter account receive 5% discount on shipping |
| | People | Affiliate sales | Facebook referrals |
| | Process | Social media-linked custom products | Print Flickr photos onto mugs, mouse pads or business cards |
| | Physical evidence | Discounts for product-in-use content | YouTube videos and Flickr photos available for use receive loyalty points or discounted merchandise |
| Behavioural change | Price | Twitter hashtags | Reduce social risk by demonstrating mass adoption of the idea |
| | Product | Regular instructions on maintaining ongoing behaviours | Daily Twitter updates with links to blog or YouTube video of behaviour |
| | Promotion | Hashtags and bookmarks | Conversations on Twitter marked with #hashtag |
| | Place | Face-to-face meet ups by city | Facebook events |
| | People | Twitter accounts | Official staff accounts |
| | Process | Progress blog | Description of the behavioural changes document on a regularly updated blog |
| | Physical evidence | Badges for blogs | HTML code and image for inserting into blog posts to show progress |
| Information dissemination | Price | Visual guides to information | Graphical guides posted to Flickr |
| | Product | Detailed instructions | YouTube step-by-step videos |
| | Promotion | Submission of content to meta filters | Links on Delicious (www.delicious.com), Reddit (www.reddit.com) and Digg (www.digg.com) |
| | Place | Creative commons licensed content | Easy linked or re-uploaded content to be shared through blog posts |

| | | | |
|---|---|---|---|
| | People | 'Ask the Expert' chat sessions | Facebook chats |
| | Process | Social media outreach | Answering questions and responding to feedback through Twitter |
| | Physical evidence | Branded applications and content | Branded Facebook content included information applications |
| Promotional | Price | Temporary price reduction/special deals for affiliate sales | 24-hour online sales with bonuses for purchasing through affiliate links |
| | Product | Product reviews | Free products sent to review blogs |
| | Promotion | Internet-only advertising, product previews | YouTube-exclusive trailers for movies, games and products |
| | Place | Social media sharing buttons | 'Post to Twitter', 'Post to Facebook' short cuts attached to content |
| | People | Identified social media staff | Official spokesperson account |
| | Process | Official social media accounts | Verified Twitter account |
| | Physical evidence | Branded social media | Icons and images used on social media sites represent the brand |
| Entertainment-oriented | Price | Freemium games | Purchased with cash upgrades for Facebook games |
| | Product | Games | Facebook applications involving cows, mafia, vampires and baked goods |
| | Promotion | Film trailers | Embeddable content for blogs, YouTube uploads |
| | Place | Dedicated social network | Exclusive company-run network for 'insiders' |
| | People | Celebrity bloggers | Paid for/sponsored tweets by celebrity figures |
| | Process | Interactive demonstrations | YouTube video games, Facebook applications |
| | Physical evidence | Icons, avatars and branded content | Twitter backgrounds, Facebook profile pictures, Livejournal icons and event-specific sponsored themes for Blogger and WordPress |

## Positioning

Positioning in social media is based on a combination of matching the right voice for the organization in the way it communicates through a social media site with the right style of site. MySpace, Facebook, Google Sidewiki and Blogger each have distinctive tones, flavours and styles that can be determined by observation, experience and some slogging through Google looking at where your competitors are running their social media. Looking back at the generic positioning strategies from Chapter 4, social media can be used as part of the overall IMC approach to placing the company into a specific slot in the consumer's mind in some of the following ways:

o *Use or application positioning,* which is what the end user actually does with the product. Use positioning in social media lends itself to YouTube (product demonstration), Facebook (liking brands, products and activities), Delicious (tagged website) and Flickr groups for types of photography.
o *Product user positioning,* which is based on who uses your product rather than how it's being used. This is a little more awkward in many respects as finding the people who use your product may actually breach privacy laws or just make good customers feel uncomfortable that you're tracking them. Using some common politeness and a sense of distance can be useful (just owning something doesn't mean you want to friend the manufacturer). It's also worth developing affiliation markers (such as graphic icons or badges for blogs) that you put on your own site to allow users to self-identify with your company. Facebook pages for products and brands are the most overt of the user-positioning activities.
o *Attributes and benefits positioning,* which involves basing your positioning strategy on features and elements and means looking for keywords on Twitter, tags in Delicious and using Google's Blog Search. This positioning strategy is possibly the least effective since social media is more about people than product features.
o *Price quality positioning,* which involves using prices associated with the goods and services to influence perceptions. As such it will rely on careful selection of social media content to maintain the appropriate look and feel. Prestige pricing doesn't work well with MySpace, and generic priced goods wouldn't have their own exclusive social media network.
o *Cultural symbol positioning,* which aligns your position in the market through images, icons and wording which makes it near perfect for tapping into sectional interests in social media. This is where Facebook groups, Livejournal communities and niche blogs are viable means for social media positioning for your products. It's also worth using Delicious and other tagging services to see how people identify and cluster your content in their own words.
o *Product class positioning,* which is the corporate word association game where you align yourself against offers from outside of your own product category. Facebook offers a means by which you can purchase advertising related to keywords in the user's profile, so if you're looking for product class positioning, you can make use of the customer's self-proclaimed metadata where they identify their interests

(Xbox360) to pitch a product with product class positioning (It's the Xbox360 of phones).

○ *Competitor positioning,* which is done by focusing on a specific competitor and outlining the similarities or differences between you and them. This simply means being on the same social media services as your nearest and dearest rivals just so you're not noticed by your absence. It's probably the worst positioning strategy to take in social media because you'll inevitably start to show signs of not wanting to be on the service if you're only doing it to keep up with the Joneses.

The aim of the social media positioning strategies is to ensure compatibility with the larger IMC agenda within the organization, which in turn ensures consistency between your operations and the main company activity. Discrepancies between what you say in social media and what your organization does elsewhere tend to inflict high levels of brand damage in a relatively short space of time.

### Budgets and time allocations

Costing social media campaigns requires an assessment of financial spend on content (including re-purposing existing content from other areas), HR spend on staff and staffing numbers, and the time cost of assigning a staff member to the social media project. Time costs are variable based on levels of success and the peak demand periods for your social media teams. There's also an HR issue in that the peak discussion period for your product (particularly television shows) may be outside of regular office hours and may result in overtime or the need for flexible work schedules. This could also prove highly beneficial from a PR/publicity perspective if your organization is willing to engage in creative and flexible HR practices to ensure staff are available during peak social media demand.

Financial implications in social media are linked directly to the revenue to expenditure approaches listed in Chapter 10. For the most part, social media activity starts out as an outreach exercise in community engagement (Revenue 0), promotional activity and brand building (Revenue 1) before becoming subject to the return on investment requirements (which it should have from the first instance if you're doing your marketing plans properly). The type of revenue strategy is also heavily dependent on the social media site and the prevailing culture of the system – you're far more likely to bank direct revenue (Revenue 3) through Facebook if you make an entertaining game (entertainment objective) that can be enhanced through real-world cash payments via PayPal. At the same time, if you try to push direct sales links through Twitter, you're likely to fail (and be marked for spam or blocked) unless you're running a deal of the day arrangement with once-per-24 hour updates. Flickr is usually, if not exclusively, Revenue 0 centric, Google Sidewiki isn't conducive to direct or indirect sales and Livejournal is more community than marketplace with more value from unpaid and unprompted product testimonials. Just be certain to include your stated revenue expectations. If you're relying on Revenue 0, where is the money to support it coming from? Whose Revenue 3 are you using to cross-fund the activity? And what returns can the organization expect for its investment in this activity?

## Step 3: How are we communicating now?

Step 3 is another benchmarking process that encourages a critical review of the current operations of the organization before embarking on the social media activity. There are four areas to be considered.

1. *Market research*. How are you engaging with the marketplace directly to antici-pate and identify their needs? What approaches are being used for monitoring, observation and carrying out other research? (Chapters 3 and 4).
2. *Market feedback*. Is the market addressing the firm directly through unsolicited feed-back? Are you receiving e-mail testimonials, @mentions on Twitter, direct messages, snail mail, feedback on websites or nothing at all?
3. *Promotional plans*. What are you currently doing in the way of promotional activ-ity? (Chapter 7). Are you talking at the market through one-to-many broadcast-style communications (Chapter 6) or are you talking to the market through one-to-many-to-one techniques? Are you engaged with the existing communities associated with your products or similar products? (Chapter 9). The aim here is to document the existing communication approaches to see where you can augment and enhance the current IMC strategy and to avoid overlap or cannibalization of the markets.
4. *Frontline staff*. Who is currently talking to the customer on a regular basis? Services marketing theory identified the boundary spanner staff member as the gateway point between the organization and the customer. If you're using a mixture of offline and online means to engage the market, should you be allowing your frontline staff to use social media accounts as part of their day jobs?
5. *Knowledge management*: What systems are in place to track user feedback, customer requests and other key information about the way in which your organization talks to, at and with customers?

One issue with regard to the boundary spanner staff is the extent to which you intend owning their personal social media presence. There have been cases where newspaper journalists have been required to have work profiles on social media networks and have been prohibited by contract from owning or operating a personal profile on the same network to avoid 'brand confusion'. Sports stars have been instructed either not to have public profiles on Facebook or to have their management run the profiles to main-tain appropriate behaviour befitting a sponsor-owned sports media property. Knowing how you're currently communicating will also reduce the risk of a strategic blunder of radically altering how you conduct yourself online – if you've personally been updat-ing your own blog, Facebook page and Twitter account, you'll need to explain why you're suddenly transitioning across to an editorial team staffed with ghost Twitterers, bloggers and lawyers. If you do need to change style and voice, it's effectively a rebrand-ing and repositioning exercise (Chapter 6), and should be conducted with similar levels of planning and market monitoring.

## Step 4: Where is the conversation?

The fourth step is the first point where you shift focus from internal operations and start examining where you're going to set up operations in the social media field. There are two approaches to consider when selecting your social media site. The first is to view where your type of customer can be found through target marketing. The second is to assess whether the social media site you'd like to use will be conducive to the sort of activity you'd like to encourage amongst your target markets.

### Target markets

Once again, this section of the plan draws on pre-existing decisions from the e-marketing and broader marketing plans to identify your priority markets, and where the members of these markets can be found in social media. Key questions to consider are:

○ Who are you currently addressing with your marketing communications?
○ Who do you want to address?
○ Do you want them to have the capacity to talk back to you?
○ Why would they want to talk to you?
○ Do you really need to be their friend?
○ What value are you to them?

Simply being able to provide feedback and input into the firm isn't a value proposition. Whilst a portion of the social media early adopter crowd will expect to be involved in co-designing products, and seek out the co-production opportunities, you'll also have a large slice of early and late majority audiences who believe their role in the process stops at the purchase decision. Know your target market before heading into social media so you know if you're up for a conversation with the highly chatty innovator/early adopter, or just doing FYI announcements for the early/late majority.

### Social media sites

Picking a social media site should be done on the basis of whether the site is conducive for marketing activity (and permits it to take place), whether the target market is already there (or could be persuaded to join) and whether the organization is prepared to take this seriously and do the hard work required for this activity to be done properly (Figure 12.4).

In the e-introduction (setting up for e-marketing), we recommended a series of social media sites for you to join, explore and generally poke around with in the settings menus in order to familiarize yourself with the way the systems worked. (Those of you who didn't, go back to the e-introduction and set up shop. Come back when you're ready, we'll wait for you.) The idea behind exploring, playing and tweaking around with your personal accounts on social media sites is to gain an understanding of how you can use them for your own personal gain (fun, time wasting, life streaming, virtual racketeering, etc.). At this point, you'll want to return to these sites to look at them from a marketing perspective in terms of how the different mechanisms can be used for achieving your organizational objectives. Table 12.4 outlines several of the sites listed

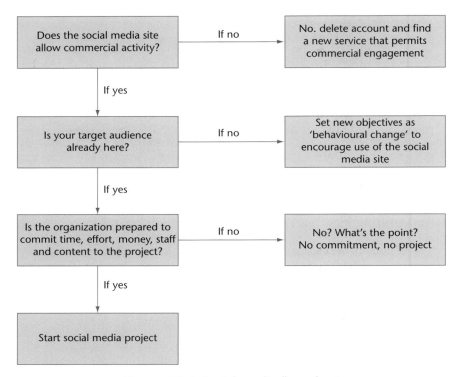

**Figure 12.4** Social media flow chart

in the e-introduction, together with sample purposes, objectives and strategies (there's more detail on each social media site later in this chapter).

Whilst it's tempting to sign up to every social media site you can find (and one of the authors did), it's also unrealistic to think that you'll benefit from a login at every spot on the planet (Figure 12.5). Channel exclusivity is an effective strategy for social media marketing and you're better off with one or two complementary systems that you maintain well rather than a dozen poorly updated sites.

**Table 12.4** Short list of recommended sites

| Site | Purpose | Objective | Tactic |
|------|---------|-----------|--------|
| Blogger/ WordPress | Social commentary | Conversational | Reply to posts about the product, company or advertising |
| Delicious | Self-organization | Metrics | Assess tags as positioning strategy metric |
| Facebook | Social identity | Promotional | Fan pages |
| Flickr | Photo sharing | Information | Sharing product-in-use photos |
| Google Sidewiki | Yellow sticky labels | Market research | See what people say about competitor sites |
| Livejournal | Self-documentary | Conversational | Monitor for problems with the product |
| Twitter | Life streaming | Conversation | Keyword monitoring |
| YouTube | Sharing video | Behavioural | Instructional video |

**Figure 12.5** You don't need to join every social media site
*Source*: XKCD (http://xkcd.com/146/)

## Step 5: What impact will this have?

There's no value in any marketing activity that doesn't have an impact on the organization, its competitors and the marketplace. One of the areas of frustration espoused by end users and social media commentators is the propensity of organizations to still view the conversation between customer and company as a one-sided affair. If you're going to talk to customers because you think it's worth listening to them, you'll need to specify how what you hear from the market is translated into some form of actual outcome in the firm. There's a line of thought that argues you're better off not asking for feedback if you don't intend to act on it than you are to invite engagement and snub the contributions. There are three areas that the social media campaign needs to feed back into the broader organization:

1. *Metrics.* Your campaign needs measurements, the measurement needs to take place and you've got to actually reach the goals that were set by the objectives and measured by the metrics. If you've come to social media to sell products and you're not seeing an increased number of sales or revenue, then the metrics indicate you're not succeeding. Social media is not a fluffy area where there are no measurable outcomes. (Don't mistake failure to achieve goals as a case of 'We couldn't measure success therefore we succeeded in an immeasurable way.')
2. *Organizational decision making.* There's no point asking for audience participation if you're not going to let the audience participate. Accepting user input into the process is the hardest part of the co-creation, co-production and relationship marketing aspect of social media activity. If the organization's decision-making structures are not going to want to listen to the input from the market, don't engage in conversations that won't lead to outcomes. Promising to change a product, deliver a better outcome or solve a problem with customer service in social media is a written obligation that the customer can easily repeat around the Internet en masse if you can't actually deliver on that promise.
3. *Knowledge management.* This is probably the hardest aspect to implement as most marketing operations consider market research and promotion to be almost unrelated fields of activity (and if you're outsourcing, you're probably paying for two separate firms). Social media marketing will result in market knowledge, informal market research and other organizational knowledge that needs to be captured, managed and fed back into the design, production and planning processes (Chapters 4, 6 and 10).

*Social media stakeholders versus non customers*

Whilst many marketers have heard of the mantra 'The customer is always right', it's not actually true. Marketing requires the selection and rejection of certain markets (segmentation, target marketing) for the purpose of seeking the optimal fit between the needs of the customer and the organization's capacity to meet those needs profitably. Some customers are a poor fit since what the organization is offering doesn't fit their needs, others aren't willing to pay the organization's asking price (or even the cost plus operating margin price) and others don't fit the organization's user-based positioning strategy. This applies to the social media environment as well as the rest of marketing – asking the wrong customer for feedback won't be as helpful as targeting the right type of social media user (your customer).

Before dismissing a market segment involved in social media, it's worth reviewing the stakeholder analysis frameworks from marketing strategy. Social media is a form of media, and treating social media participants as stakeholders in the broader marketing process is a valuable element for ongoing business survival. Remember that the purpose of marketing under the AMA (2007) definition is to create, communicate, deliver and exchange offerings that have value to customers, clients, partners and society at large, and marketing is vital for social media survival. Society at large is an influential field where media (print, television, social) impact is still a significant risk factor to mitigate. There's good publicity and bad publicity, and anyone arguing that all publicity is good publicity never lost a lawsuit, had regulations changed or received an angry mob on the doorstep.

## Social media plan

The final step in the social media planning process is the documentation that creates a social media plan. Plans are important as they're distillations of the planning process that you can use for metrics, benchmarks and the basis of the next planning phase. They're also artifacts as much as road maps since your average plan doesn't last that long once marketing operations hit reality. The five steps of the social media planning process could be done around a laptop and a whiteboard in the space of a few hours, and once the web browser closes and the whiteboard is cleaned, the details of the implementation of the plan could easily be forgotten. (Note: digital cameras and whiteboards are great allies. Shots of whiteboards are surprisingly good documentation systems during the planning phase.) To ensure that the plan is useful, it's necessary to turn some of the decisions into written commitments. This has three key purposes.

1. *Clarification of details.* Writing down an idea ensures that everyone in the room actually agrees to it, and that the fuzzy bits we gloss over in our minds are converted into concrete steps towards achieving the plan.
2. *Documentation for justifying budget allocations.* When you're going to ask for time, money or staff, you want to be able to step people through your reasons for investing company resources in your project.

Table 12.5 Convert the planning process to a documented outcome

| Section | Detail | Step |
|---------|--------|------|
| Background | History, details and notes on prior goals, objectives or social media campaigns | Step 0, e-marketing plan and marketing plan |
| Existing benchmarks (if any) | Current metrics including sales levels, revenue and related figures | Previous plan/metrics |
| Campaign objectives | Statements of objectives<br>Timeline for objectives<br>Details of objective | Step 1 |
| Overall tactics | Marketing mix<br>Positioning statement<br>Budget allocations | Step 2 |
| Social media activity (N) to Social media activity (N+1) as necessary | Target market selection<br>Social media site justification<br>Tactics for this site<br>Marketing mix for this market<br>Metrics for this site | Step 4 |
| Projected outcomes | Results (desired metrics by timeline by objective) | Step 1 and 5 |
| Planned metrics | Metrics<br>Impacts on firm | Step 5 |

3. *Professionalization of the process*. Written benchmarks with written metrics, timelines and deadlines add a necessary level of gravitas to the operation. It's easy to consider social media as an optional extra or a time waster if there's no plan, no goals or no idea if you're achieving anything solid. Put it in writing and it's as serious as the spreadsheets, legal contracts and engineering documents in the other divisions.

Table 12.5 is a generic documentation guide for the planning process. It's worth noting that Step 3 in the planning process isn't reported in this model plan document. Whilst it's vital to know where you're currently engaged with the market when you're planning social media activity, it's less relevant to the documentation. Step 3 produces content for the decisions in Step 4, and the outcomes of those decisions are reported directly within the plan document.

## Social media sites

In the e-introduction, you were sent off to sign up to a range of social media sites as part of the e-marketing equipment list. This time around, we're looking more at the application of the sites to marketing activity. Given this is a printed book, and these are still developing sites with a reasonable risk of changing, we're not going to focus on the individual buttons, settings and options you'd need to use in each site. The aim here

Table 12.6  The social media shopping list

| Site | Address | Function | Content |
| --- | --- | --- | --- |
| Blogger | www.blogger.com | Commentary | Hosted blogging |
| Delicious | www.delicious.com | Social bookmark | Meta tags, content discovery |
| Facebook | www.facebook.com | Social network | Groups, advertising, applications |
| Flickr | www.flickr.com | Image hosting | Images, tags, content discovery |
| Google Sidewiki | www.google.com/ sidewiki | Meta commentary | Tags and social commentary |
| Livejournal | www.livejournal.com | Life streaming | Personal experience |
| Twitter | www.twitter.com | Life streaming | Short messaging system |
| YouTube | www.youtube.com | Video hosting | Video (strangely enough) |

is to look at a site, assess the purposes that your customers could be using it for, that you could use it for, and what (if any) goods, services or ideas you could bring to the marketplace through it. Social media can be used for the whole of the mix, and should not be considered an adjunct to the promotional mix (Chapter 6). The recommended social media site shopping list is outlined in Table 12.6.

Blogging is counted as social media despite predating the whole Web 2.0 upgrade. There are authors (bloggers, 'pressers, Twitterers) who will vehemently disagree with the inclusion of, Blogger, WordPress and Livejournal in the social media/Web 2.0 category for a variety of fair and valid reasons. Our rationale for their inclusion is that the corporate behaviour surrounding the use of Twitter, YouTube and Facebook for commercial activity can be adapted for the older blogging and journalling sites and, as such, the elements of voice, interaction with community and not being a nuisance are useful lessons for those environments as well as the classically identified Web 2.0 sites. Similarly, YouTube (videos), Flickr (photos) and Delicious (bookmarks) are all reasonably limited behaviours which have specific purposes that are much narrower than those of Facebook (talk to friends) and Twitter (talk to strangers). Each of the following sections is broken down into a brief overview of the service and what can be done with it (since you've encountered them all previously in the e-introduction), a summary of how each service interrelates with the social media objectives, and how each site relates to the content-communication media – social interaction framework (Figure 12.3).

## Blogger

*Related sites*: WordPress.com, Vox and TypePad

Blogger was established in 1999 and bought out and amalgamated by Google in 2007. It operates as a combination of standalone and hosted blog services. Being part of the Google product suite means Blogger has a solid level of integration with a range of Google tools such as Google AdWords, Google Analytics and Gmail. It also provides an established and verified identity to use when commenting on other blogs running on the Blogger platform. Sites on the Blogspot network are usually (but not exclusively) hosted by individuals and independent bloggers, which gives a grassroots feel to many of the sites. Since the network is backed by Google, there's a high level of commercialization possible within the system, starting with the hosting of Google AdWords advertising on site (Revenue 2) and support for affiliate sales programmes through Amazon (Revenue 3).

### Blogger social media objectives

Blogger fits neatly into entertainment, sales, behaviour change and information dissemination objectives with the business orientation, commercialization-friendly and metric-heavy approach offered by the site (Table 12.7). Blogger has a 'Monetize' tab within the basic settings of the blog and has preset options for using Adsense and Amazon Affiliate sales.

It's worth noting that promotional blogs are less successful when hosted as third-party operations and tend to be more viable as self-hosted blogs. Similarly, whilst there's an opportunity to reduce costs through Blogger sites, it's not been a highly ranked priority use of the site.

*In-house metrics:* Blogger doesn't provide direct metrics within the main blogging platform. Instead, as part of the Google family, it has access to the Google Analytics frameworks (www.google.com/analytics).

*Alternate metrics*: Raw numbers of comment counts are less important than engagement, conversation and involvement with the right target markets. Numbers of blog posts, and the blog posts being picked up or back-referenced at larger sites, is a good measure of reaching the right audiences directly (and indirectly).

**Table 12.7** Objectives on Blogger

| Objective | Sample tactic | Use of the site |
| --- | --- | --- |
| Cost-oriented | Reduced-cost digital distribution | Press releases, new content and media release |
| Sales-oriented | Catalogue-style updates, direct affiliate links, advertising keywords | Sales announcements, affiliate links, Google AdWords and direct sales links |
| Behavioural change | Ongoing encouragement | Regular content updates to support challenges faced in behavioural change |
| Information dissemination | Content dissemination | Regular updates of key information, links to off-site content on Slideshare or YouTube |
| Promotional Entertainment-oriented | Press releases, PR and ad copy Entertaining content | Self-promotional content Short stories, serialized content, captioned photos |

### Social media triad

A Blogger-hosted site without comments enabled is little more than a frequently updated website, and doesn't qualify as a social media platform. It's not a conversation if you don't let the audience speak at the point where you're making your statements (which is why this book is a monologue rather than a dialogue). Blogs operate within the social media framework in the following manner:

○ Content: written content, some images and a limited array of embedded links. Can be used for cross-promoting other content and linking out to other social media sites
○ Social interaction: direct interaction through comments sections on individual posts and indirect interaction by linking to related posts via track-backs, links or related techniques
○ Communications media: third-party hosted sites.

## Delicious

*Related sites*: Digg, Reddit

Delicious is a social bookmarking site that allows for community tagging, organization and recommendation of specific sites and pages (Table 12.8). Social bookmarking is a relatively advanced user behaviour requiring both membership of the Delicious community and habitual bookmarking behaviour (Ctrl-D). There are two ways to use the site for social media marketing: as a discovery mechanism for developing content for your own products and as a tracking mechanism for existing web-based activity.

Discovery approaches to Delicious rely on the 'popular bookmarks' and 'explore tags' which can be used to either directly access the site or to see a list of other users who have bookmarked the site and the keywords that they've used to describe it. Popular content is displayed in a range of sections – popular keyword tags, most popular and most recent bookmarks, as well as an exploration option to find highly bookmarked archival content.

Table 12.8 Objectives on Delicious

| Objective | Sample tactic | Use of the site |
| --- | --- | --- |
| Cost-oriented | Nil | Research |
| Sales-oriented | Limited | Research other successful sales offers |
| Behavioural change | Find related content | Post bookmarks related to behavioural goals |
| Information dissemination | Create notable content | Benchmark number of bookmarks per content item |
| Promotional | Notable content, viral adverts | Sharing viral-capable advertising |
| Entertainment-oriented | Alternate Reality Librarian Game | Prizes for content tagging |

Tracking through Delicious can be done for individual pages and sites to assess the positioning strategy of the content in the eyes of the Delicious community members. The shared community nature of the tags is a useful market research tool for seeing the positioning that individual users have given a site in their own minds. For example, an article on logo design has the obvious common English tags of 'logos, design, logo' and the less obvious keywords of 'inspiration, creativity' (plus a range of non-English tags for those sites that want to expand into multilingual content positioning).

The site tends to be Revenue 0 focused as either an investment in raw materials (links of interest for blog posts) or as a metrics system where it's the quality and quantity of time invested in benchmarking and reviewing trends. From a Revenue 1 to 3 option, it's worth searching the tags for keywords of sale, discount and your specific product to see which offers and adverts caught the attention of the community (and were bookmark worthy).

## Social media objectives

Delicious is suited to information dissemination above all other objectives, although behavioural change and promotion can sneak into the line-up if the product-content you generate is sufficiently interesting for someone to want to save for later reading. Promotional materials that are standalone in nature (great adverts on YouTube) and which have a tendency towards viral re-distribution are likely to emerge on Delicious as bookmarked items. Social bookmarking is ill-suited to sales, cost and entertainment objectives (unless you're running an augmented reality game for librarians).

*In-house metrics*: Each bookmark on Delicious has a broad scope of the tags used to describe it, the number of members who have bookmarked the content, and the individual tags each member has personally used to provide a positioning and popularity benchmark.

## Social media triad

Social bookmarking can exist as a non-social media platform if there's no conversation or engagement with the other users (which is entirely possible). The site does have an integrated social network function under the 'People' button, whereby you can align yourself to other users (become a fan) or have other users attached to you (gain a fan). Mutual fan recognition creates a quasi-private network of shared bookmarks (useful for group assignments) that can be sent to each member in the network. For example, when bookmarking a specific site, you can nominate to send the link to a member of the network operating within the social media framework.

o  Content: annotated links to external content
o  Social interaction: access to self-created network of shared links, direct access to network member's bookmarks
o  Communications media: third-party hosted site.

## Facebook

*Related sites*: Orkut, Bebo, MySpace

Facebook is the largest, most robust and most populated social media site that you'll deal with in e-marketing and social media (Table 12.9). Originally designed as an interactive yearbook system for US college students, the site has developed into an almost standalone island in the broader context of the Internet. Changes in privacy settings and a change of strategic corporate direction, from the walled garden of the early 2000s to an open-by-default site, is altering the level to which individual users will feel 'safe' in their social network activity. As a closed system, where content defaulted to only being available to friends and members of the user's network, there was a user tendency towards greater social disclosure than would be found in open-by-default sites such as Flickr or YouTube. This is in a steady process of change as Facebook pursues more openness and exposure to drive its advertising revenue, and users become less comfortable with the level of exposure to their personal photos, friend networks and status updates. Facebook has four functional levels of operation that are available to each user as part of the default account. These are:

o *straight consumption*, which covers the classic Facebook consumption behaviour of playing games, chatting and generally interacting with your network of friends
o *meta collection*, which is where Facebook acts as a clearing and sorting house for other social media activity by allowing users to post from YouTube, Delicious, Flickr and other sites to their Facebook profiles. This also includes the use Facebook logins to comment on blogs (and a link in the Facebook timeline to the posted comment)
o *user-generated content*, which is through photo and video uploads, blog-style notes and the lower end of Facebook Groups and Pages
o *commercial content*, which is through Facebook Pages, Facebook Groups and Facebook Advertising, Applications and Developer communities.

The breadth of options on Facebook allow for Revenue 0 to Revenue 3 activity across the site. Facebook applications present the easiest path to income by providing an accepted

Table 12.9 Objectives on Facebook

| Objective | Sample tactic | Use of the site |
|---|---|---|
| Cost-oriented | Niche promotional messages | Pay-per-click keyword targeted advertising |
| Sales-oriented | Direct sales of virtual goods | Applications with paid bonus content, items or points |
| Behavioural change | Support groups | Facebook page and Facebook support group |
| Information dissemination | Information page | Fan page of the information |
| Promotional | Viral message and promotion | Facebook advertising and an 'Update your status message to pass this idea along' campaign |
| Entertainment-oriented | Facebook applications | Something involving fish, mafia, farming, vampires and Bejeweled |

platform for running an application (usually a game) that allows users to purchase additional in-game items, credit or points in cash (Revenue 3) or through engaging in deals with sponsors (Revenue 2). Similarly, Facebook Advertising offers indirect awareness-raising options for Facebook Groups or Pages (Revenue 1), ads for Facebook applications (Revenue 2) or direct links to sales pages (Revenue 3).

## Social media objectives

Facebook is a central nexus for social media activity and as such facilitates most of the social media objectives with varying levels of fit. Given the near ubiquity of the service amongst social media marketers (and that you were sent off to sign up for an account if you didn't already have one), there are a few uses for cost-oriented objectives that focus on the relative low cost for highly specified targeted advertising, community infrastructure and communications options. Sales-oriented options are one of the strengths of the site, particularly if you're able to develop an application as your virtual product offer (particularly one with add-ons and accessories for sale) or through direct-to-sale advertising. Behavioural change is probably at the weaker end of proceedings although moving people into Facebook to engage directly with the company and its representatives is probably the most likely use of the site. Information dissemination can be achieved through Facebook Pages and through the ability of the site to draw together external links to Delicious, YouTube and other places.

Promotional objectives are incredibly well suited to Facebook through the direct advertising mechanisms that allow for narrowly focused campaigns based on geography, keywords and other demographic elements. There's also a strong word-of-mouth community element through Facebook status updates, viral memes and the Facebook timeline indicating when a friend has liked a specific page or is using a specific application. Finally, entertainment-oriented objectives can easily be achieved through the applications and groups functionality of Facebook.

*In-house metrics:* Facebook accounts have basic metrics on the Profile page of the numbers of Facebook friends and a track record of user activity on the site including inter-account engagement (posting on walls, commenting on statuses). The advertising section offers detailed metrics of click through rates, views per click and other display metrics. Similarly detailed data options are available for the applications.

*Alternate metrics*: Engagement within the community, including numbers of fans of the product page, members of the groups and group activity. Raw numbers are less valuable although more easily available than measuring changes in attitude from direct engagement in the community.

## Social media triad

Facebook is the definitive social media structure through evolution and design and since it began life as a social network service, it operates as a definitive role model for the social media framework.

○ Content: Facebook content ranges from the presence of other people, photo galleries and video content to a wide array of applications, discussion forums and communications systems

○ Social interaction: social interaction is either private through the internal message and internal chat system or public in status update comments, wall-to-wall posts or groups postings and discussion.

○ Communications media: third-party hosted site. Applications, including external applications and mobile content.

## Flickr

*Related sites*: Picasaweb, Photobucket, Imageshack

Flickr is the peak social media photography and image-sharing site (Table 12.10). Established as an independent operation in 2004, it was purchased soon after by Yahoo!. Although it still operates as a distinct brand, users are required to be part of Yahoo!'s network to access the services, and increasing levels of Yahoo! branding are appearing in the site. Flickr offers a series of social media functions including a discussion thread per photo (and with approximately 4 billion photos logged at October 2009, that's a lot of places to talk), user set discussion groups and Web 2.0 tag clouds. The service operates on user-generated content, with each account holder providing photos into the mix under a range of different copyright options from 'full rights reserved' to less restrictive 'creative commons' options, and a commercial licence option for images to be sold through Getty Images (www.flickr.com/gettyimages). Each photo can be tagged with specific keywords to make it findable by search engines and other users, and clustered into content groups by the Flickr servers. The site also permits external linking, hot linking and image hosting of Flickr content, which allows for the photos to be embedded in blog posts and Facebook or linked directly through Twitter. The site operates under a freemium policy of free accounts and paid service options which include metrics, larger quotes and increased functionality. Flickr is predominantly a Revenue 0 or Revenue 1 style of site for the users (and Revenue 3 for Yahoo!) since it's a free (or low cost) photo-hosting server with a massive archival gallery of content.

### Social media objectives

Given the purpose of the site as a photo display and sharing service, Flickr is ideally suited to cost-oriented objectives for visual products as it can display images of just

Table 12.10 Objectives on Flickr

| Objective | Sample tactic | Use of the site |
|---|---|---|
| Cost-oriented | Photo hosting | Real-world printing services that draw directly from Flickr files |
| Sales-oriented | Limited | – |
| Behavioural change | Visual instructions | Photo illustrations of step-by-step guides |
| Information dissemination | Visual content | Maps, illustrations, diagrams |
| Promotional | Product-in-use gallery | Photos of products in use by real users |
| Entertainment-oriented | Acquire photo of cats, place caption | Caption Cat Photo Community |

about any size that can be linked either to a range of services that produce physical goods, such as Moo Card (www.moo.com), or directly from Flickr through Snapfish (www.snapfish.com). Flickr doesn't currently allow for the direct sales approach of selecting images and using them to create desired products, so sales objectives are less viable. Behavioural change, information dissemination and promotional objectives that require visual cues, instructions or personal demonstrations of information (Chapter 10) can make use of the photo-hosting approach. Flickr's also been valuable for camera manufacturers because the site can be searched by the metadata each digital camera stores in a photograph. As a result, users can see what types of photos are possible by camera, and the most popular cameras on the site. Finally, entertainment-oriented objectives that rely on visual elements (such as captioned photos) have both an archival resource to draw from and a hosting service to display their content.

*In-house metrics:* Paid users have access to a reasonably sophisticated array of account-level metrics including referrer information, top photos of the day by number of viewings, view counts and graphs of trends in viewing data. Each photo also has individual statistics of view counts, referrer information and tag information.

*Alternate metrics*: Activity on each photo can be monitored with Flickr being able to be set to notify you if there's a discussion on your image.

### Social media triad

Flickr was developed to host conversations around individual images and community clusters of shared goods of interest (Chapter 9). The site also provides a mailbox system for direct private exchanges and public networks of contacts:

o  *Content*: images, community, 10-second videos
o  *Social interaction*: comments per photo, inter-user mail inbox, community discussions
o  *Communications media*: third-party hosted site, application.

## Google Sidewiki

*Related sites*: Wikipedia, StumbleUpon

Google Sidewiki is the strangest addition to the social media line up as Google attempts to bring the power of yellow sticky label annotation to the entire Internet (Table 12.11). Sidewiki doesn't exist as a separate site like the other social media services listed in this chapter. Instead, the content is accessed through any web browser that has the Google Toolbar installed (which didn't include Google Chrome due to irony and technical reasons). Launched in 2009, Sidewiki provides the capacity to annotate any web page (or section of a web page) with user commentary or discussions between Sidewiki users.

### Social media objectives

Sidewiki has limited functionality as anything other than an information dissemination tool and a market research device. As an extremely new technology, and a novel form of interaction with the Internet, use of the site is limited and mostly dominated by

Table 12.11  Objectives on Sidewiki

| Objective | Sample tactic | Use of the site |
| --- | --- | --- |
| Cost-oriented | Limited use | – |
| Sales-oriented | No use | – |
| Behavioural change | User experience | Encourage Sidewiki participation to discuss or endorse site content |
| Information dissemination | Add meta commentary to related sites | Add additional information or endorsement to allied content |
| Promotional | Alternate Reality Gaming | Clues in the Sidewiki to other sites |
| Entertainment-oriented | Alternate Reality Gaming | ARG Player commentary on clues and meanings of site content |

innovators. However, opportunities exist for using Sidewiki for promotional and entertainment objectives as it could be integrated into a web-based alternative reality gaming program (Chapter 14). It's not worth using Sidewiki for redirecting users away from a site with cheap sales tactics because Google does monitor the content and will rank down or ban users who misuse the annotations.

*In-house metrics:* All Sidewiki comments are associated with a Google account and any related account such as Blogger. All Sidewiki comments are compiled onto a user profile page to allow other users to verify and validate the user's impartiality (or biases).

### Social media triad

Sidewiki is an experimental form of social media at the time of writing, with interactive communication between users being possible but less than common as the system is slowly developing. Consequently, Sidewiki sits within the social media framework in the following manner:

o  *Content*: Sidewiki content has two elements: the site being annotated and the annotation, which can be manually ranked as useful/not useful or reported for abuse
o  *Social interaction*: Conversation can take place between users, and the individual Sidewiki remarks can be shared with Facebook, Twitter or e-mail
o  *Communications media*: In browser, Google Toolbar specific access.

## Livejournal

*Related sites*: Dreamwidth

Livejournal began life when the original developer decided to share the website updating mechanism with his friends and, as a result, created a community structure around frequent site updates amongst interconnected individuals. Livejournal is a server-based system, where the journals are all housed inside a single server network (www.livejournal.com) and which emphasizes the community network of the system. Updates to Livejournal operate through two mechanisms: external clients and the web page update mechanism. Since Livejournal is also a community structure, it has a series of easy mechanisms to interlink journals with a dedicated 'friends' network where individual members can list other Livejournals that they consider to be worth reading to be displayed on their friends lists.

Livejournal has been bought and sold several times since its inception and has suffered major losses of community support through corporate-level decisions that failed to identify and respect the community's relationship with the service. It spans the boundary between the cybercommunity (how the site is used by individual members) and the social media platform (how the site is used commercially) and, as such, comes with a limited array of objectives that it can support compared with more commercial sites. For the most part Livejournal tends to be a Revenue 0 or Revenue 1 type of arrangement where the site is used to maintain engagement with a community of followers by individual artists, writers, performers or small groups. Journalling sites tend towards the personal and interpersonal rather than the commercial and, as such, should be respected as places where people, community and conversations take precedence over commercial activity. Livejournal has a specific community structure that allows collectives of users to share posts and content. These groups form around a shared frame of reference based on shared consumption of the same goods, services or even ideas. That said, it's incredibly easy to create an anti-brand sentiment if you mistreat the community since Livejournal users tend to share experiences rather than product functions/features.

## Social media objectives

As a predominantly personal space, Livejournal is surprisingly well suited to information, behavioural and entertainment objectives (Table 12.12). The diary-style format lends itself to a personalized blogging style that can include serialized content from novels and frequently updated additional materials (concept art for movies). As an opt-in community, individual users of the site can also use it for sales-oriented objectives if they've otherwise provided something valuable to their readers/followers. For example, authors and musicians frequently announce the release of new material on their Livejournal accounts without problems (problems will arise when you attempt to ambush someone else's journal by engaging in sales-oriented behaviour in the comments section). That said, the site is a poor substitute for a blog or WordPress account for cost-oriented objectives since it's a community and requires a high level of time invested in building interpersonal relationships in order to succeed.

Livejournal also offers a range of promotional opportunities for on-site advertising through DoubleClick (www.livejournalinc.com/sales.php) and site-specific promotional opportunities such as sponsored themes or Livejournal Gift Accounts. These are less driven by engagement than Facebook Advertising and a poor substitute for interpersonal relationship marketing by being an active community member.

*In-house metrics:* Livejournal provides basic metrics in terms of numbers of mutual friends, friends. The site provides page view statistics, guest views (non-logged in users), statistics on commentary and trends in friend acquisition/loss.

Table 12.12 Objectives on Livejournal

| Objective | Sample tactic | Use of the site |
|---|---|---|
| Cost-oriented | Limited | |
| Sales-oriented | Announcing new products | Links to personal site, sales site or Etsy sales page |
| Behavioural change | Diary of change | Updates on progression of change of behaviour |
| Information dissemination | Sequential/serialized content | Diary-style information releases |
| Promotional | Livejournal gifts | Event-specific gifts |
| Entertainment-oriented | Serialized content | Daily commentary on the world, amusing stories, being interesting |

*Alternate metrics*: The aim of Livejournal is to develop a community and the focus should be on the quality of the conversations (volume of comments to posts seeking comment, number of times you comment on other posts where appropriate). A smaller number of useful relationships beats a large number of relative strangers.

### Social media triad

As one of the precursors to the social media movement, Livejournal started with the key defining features of Web 2.0 engagement, particularly with regards to social interaction being a primary function of the site design. It operates within the social media framework in the following manner:

o *Content*: other people, other diaries and communities
o *Social interaction*: comments on posts, participation in community and direct messages within the site
o *Communications media*: third-party hosted site.

## Twitter

*Related sites*: Plurk

Twitter is one of the poster children of the shift from static web content to the dynamic interpersonal updates of social media sites (Table 12.13). Formed around the idea of sending SMS-style messages to a group or individual with equal ease, the company was established in 2006 and rose to more mainstream prominence around 2008 with the involvement of Twitter accounts in several of the major elections of the period.

Twitter runs on an open application programming interface (API) design that allows the core function (broadcasting of short messages) to be used through a range of sites, services and software packages. Whilst smaller in nature and user numbers than Facebook, it does a specific set of tasks sufficiently well for Facebook to have mimicked

Table 12.13  Objectives on Twitter

| Objective | Sample tactic | Use of the site |
|---|---|---|
| Cost-oriented | Create targeted list of influential followers | Providing useful, timely or valuable information for re-tweeting by others |
| Sales-oriented | Announcing limited time discount codes | Re-tweet sales offers and discount codes |
| Behavioural change | Specific #hashtag | Encourage participants to use a #hashtag for announcing their involvement in the behaviour change |
| Information dissemination | Time-sensitive updates | Announcements of delays in services or event start times |
| Promotional | Links to external content | Short link to new blog posts |
| Entertainment-oriented | Being entertaining | One liners, jokes and entertaining interaction |

the short message update in 2009. Twitter operates across the Revenue spectrum as a personal account (Revenue 0), sales advertising medium (Revenue 2) or direct sales link approach (Revenue 3). The strength of the system is based on the interactivity and ease of re-transmission of interesting information plus the open community and conversation nature. Overt commercialization is tolerated to being openly disliked, and spam accounts are deleted relatively efficiently by the Twitter management systems. Twitter has been previously recommended in other chapters as a source of market research and market information, and as a feedback mechanism for real-time market monitoring.

## Social media objectives

As a social media channel, the primary objective of a Twitter account should be engagement with other individuals rather than using it as a wire service, a fax machine, or for headline summaries. Due to the flexibility of the service, it covers all of the objectives with varying levels of success in that you can switch to Twitter as a distribution outlet for ideas as part of cost objectives, whereby you can also reduce time to market for ideas, feedback and responses by operating in real time. Sales-oriented objectives are possible, although it's recommended that the hard sell be left off the network and that content other than repeated linking to a sales page shows up in your timeline lest you be deemed a spam account. Behavioural change objectives are easily supported, first by encouraging users onto the Twitter service as a means of fast communication with your marketers, and secondly, using #hashtags to track activity such as fitness, New Year's resolutions or charity donations. Information dissemination and promotional objectives both rely on Twitter as a broadcast mechanism for short links (Bit.ly links) to larger information, or quick updates and knowledge patches. Public transport networks around the world have taken to using Twitter as an information channel for announcing delays to their services. Finally, 140 characters is an amazing amount of space for an entertainment-oriented objective if you're backed by good writers, distinctive characters and a sense of style. Several television shows, videogames and web comics have taken to providing Twitter accounts for their characters and having ongoing 'off-screen' conversations between the fictional characters as part of an overall entertainment package.

*In-house metrics:* Twitter provides a set of basic internal metrics in terms of following (those you follow), followers (those who follow you) and listed (number of lists featuring your account) scores that are a semi-relevant metric of popularity. The site also alerts you to mentions of your account (twitter.com/#replies), the lists you're featured on (twitter.com/*[username]*/lists/memberships) and which of your tweets have recently between repeated on the site (www.twitter.com/#retweeted_of_mine).

*Alternate metrics*: Sites such as Twitter Analyzer (www.twitteranalyzer.com) provide analysis of the use of your account which can be used to benchmark use of the service against proposed timelines and schedules. Other systems exist to measure the influence of your account (www.twinfluence.com), its reach (www.tweetreach.com) and the frequency of re-tweeting and being re-tweeted (wwww.tweetstats.com). Twitter is also measured in terms of how you intend to use it. For example, using it as a small communications hub would require low friend/follower counts and good relationship marketing. Using it as a metafilter (low follower, high following) versus mass broadcast (high follower, low following) requires radically different approaches and metrics.

### Social media triad

As with Facebook, Twitter is one of the defining sites of the social media movement and is well represented in the social media:

○ *Content*: other people, short messages, third-party content
○ *Social interaction*: direct messages, indirect observation (timelines), replies (@replies) and re-tweets (RT)
○ *Communications media*: third-party hosted site, applications and mobile devices.

## YouTube

*Related sites*: Vimeo, Dailymotion

YouTube is the second highest profile of the social media sites after Facebook (Table 12.14). Set up in 2005 and bought out by Google in 2006, YouTube has been the battleground for content owners, content creators and copyright lawyers since it started accepting user-submitted video content. YouTube's democratization of video content distribution has been a remarkable bonus for e-marketing in general, and the provision of commentary systems per film clip has provided a discussion forum for users. Unfortunately, YouTube's commentaries are universally recognized as some of the worst on the Internet, with an amazing array of awful grammar, worse punctuation and straight-out offensiveness. This is a significant downside to using YouTube as a social media portal – you'll have to read, filter and clean up the mess that will accompany your videos once people start posting replies to them. Installing YouTube Comment Snob as recommended in the Introduction only saves you from other videos. You still have

Table 12.14 Objectives on YouTube

| Objective | Sample tactic | Use of the site |
|---|---|---|
| Cost-oriented | Global reach | Distributing content via YouTube |
| Sales-oriented | Direct sales links in video | Click to buy on iTunes |
| Behavioural change | Demonstrations | Video of the desired behaviour |
| Information dissemination | Instructional materials | Videos illustrating ideas or teaching new concepts |
| Promotional | Advertising | TVC on YouTube |
| Entertainment-oriented | Comedy, short sketches | Muppets covering *Bohemian Rhapsody* |

to read the comments on your own videos if you're going to monitor and clean up the community.

It's worth noting that YouTube briefly introduced the suggestion in Figure 12.6 as a feature (http://blog.xkcd.com/2008/10/08/youtube-audio-preview). Unfortunately, it failed to have the dramatic behaviour-adjusting effect hoped for in the comic and whether it remains in widespread use is unclear.

Figure 12.6 YouTube comments
*Source*: http://xkcd.com/481/

377

| | |
|---|---|
| Delicious | www.delicious.com |
| Digg | www.digg.com |
| DoubleClick | www.livejournalinc.com/sales.php |
| Dreamwidth | www.dreamwidth.org |
| Facebook | www.facebook.com |
| Flickr | www.flickr.com |
| Getty Images | www.flickr.com/gettyimages |
| Google Analytics | www.google.com/analytics |
| Google Sidewiki | www.google.com/sidewiki |
| Imageshack | www.imageshack.com |
| Livejournal | www.livejournal.com |
| LOLCats 'n' Funny Pictures of Cats | www.icanhazcheezburger.com |
| Maru | www.youtube.com/user/mugumogu |
| Moo Card | www.moo.com |
| MySpace | www.myspace.com |
| Orkut | www.orkut.com |
| PayPal | www.paypal.co.uk |
| Photobucket | www.photobucket.com |
| Picasa | http://picasaweb.google.com |
| Plurk | www.plurk.com |
| Reddit | www.reddit.com |
| Sainsbury's Community Forum | www2.sainsburys.co.uk/yourideas/homepage.aspx |
| Snapfish | www.snapfish.com |
| Stephen Fry | www.stephenfry.com |
| Stephen Fry on YouTube | www.youtube.com/user/officialstephenfry |
| StumbleUpon | www.stumbleupon.com |
| Tweetdeck | www.tweetdeck.com |
| TweetReach | www.tweetreach.com |
| Tweet Stats | wwww.tweetstats.com |
| Twitter | www.twitter.com |
| @sockington | www.twitter.com/sockington |
| @stephenfry | www.twitter.com/stephenfry |
| Twitter Analyzer | www.twitteranalyzer.com |
| Twitter Influence | www.twinfluence.com |
| Twitter List Membership | www.twitter.com/[username]/lists/memberships |
| Twitter Retweets | www.twitter.com/#retweeted_of_mine) |
| TypePad | www.typepad.com |
| Vimeo | www.vimeo.com |
| Vox | www.vox.com |
| Wikipedia | www.wikipedia.com |
| Wordpress.com | www.wordpress.com |
| YouTube | www.youtube.com |
| YouTube Audio Preview | blog.xkcd.com/2008/10/08/youtube-audio-preview |

# m-commerce

e-marketing

By the end of this chapter, you should be able to:

- recognize the multiple types of distribution channels created by the range of features on handheld mobile devices

- outline where and when m-marketing fits into the e-marketing strategy and tactics

- marvel at the wonder of mobile phones that just make phone calls

- appreciate the increasing convergence between mobile phone, mobile Internet and other services.

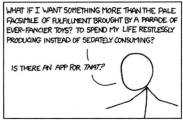

**Figure 13.2** iPhone or Droid?
*Source*: http://xkcd.com/662

started life as a command and control mechanism for loading/unloading iPods but has since transformed into a major e-marketing and m-marketing retail outlet

○ *custom-built phone-based web browsers* that were designed for sophisticated websites and heavy-duty web content. Apple's iPhone iPad and iPod Touch series use a cut-down version of Apple's Safari web browser (which doesn't run Flash or Shockwave, thus sparing its users from Facebook games) and Opera Mini (www.opera.com/mini) as a cross-platform smart phone web browser

○ *integrated camera functionality* that links the camera to other applications of the phone and which can be used for augmented reality applications, geotagged photography and Quick Response (QR) codes. Without anthropomorphizing the phone too much, the camera becomes the eye of the phone's operating system and can provide a range of data inputs to the rest of the phone – for example, with the QR codes, the camera can relay the visual information to the QR translation software which can react to the embedded information (e.g. loading a website)

○ *location awareness* through GPS (or a similar related technique) which is where the phone knows where it is geographically and can use this information in con-junction with onboard applications to record the location (Foursquare), access location-specific information (e.g. querying Google Maps for nearby coffee stores) or provide reference data to others (Apple's iPhone and iPad location information for weather applications)

This generation of technology represents a state of convergence between m-marketing and e-marketing and, as such, it's a question of where the emphasis is placed on practical issues such as designating a specific-purpose mobile site (http://m.facebook.com) versus the Internet site (www.facebook.com), or trusting the phone's browser to be able to deal with a single site. There's also a need to remember that this is a list of actual and augmented product features rather than a list of what your target consumer might actually do with their phone. There are a large number of iPhone users who own the leading-edge fashion in mobile technology but use fewer of the features than you'd find on a basic mobile device. At the end of the day, it's still about the market's use of the device more than the device itself (unless you're running behavioural change objectives). Having massively complex channels available won't encourage the early and late majority to use them (and you'll be hard pressed to keep the innovators out of the obscure ends of the options menu on any device).

## Too clever by half phones (TCBH)

The next generation of smart phone is described affectionately as the 'Too clever by half' phone. These phones will be building on the current smart platforms that already see fully integrated mobile communications, Internet and a functional suite of Word, Excel, PDF Reader and other office staples in the handheld devices. There are three distinct elements that are emerging in the next generation of phones (and related devices) that show significant potential for wide spread consumer adoption.

○ *Sophisticated augmented reality* applications take the ability of the smart phone's location awareness, camera, motion sensor and so on to create a device that can add contextual information about the world around it with minimal user input. Augmentation techniques such as contextual searching by pointing the camera at a barcode, QR code or physical object will present a wide array of marketing opportunities – not least of which will be in the services sector that will need to underpin the data acquisition, review and publication of augmented reality content.
○ *Mobile cloud-based computing* will see the combination of the cloud computing that underpins the netbook devices such as Google Docs, Zohoto and other platforms available by design in the mobile telephone networks. Currently, cloud-computing platforms can be accessed through phones in areas such as Gmail or DropBox on the iPhone and iPad (www.dropbox.com).
○ *Peer-to-peer telephony* (BitTorrent for phones) is where mobile devices can form ad hoc devices to meet their own needs for bandwidth, signal augmentation and other networked functionality. There are a few technical and business issues to address before it's a widespread phenomenon, but there's no reason not to have the mobile phones that are currently outfitted with Bluetooth, Wireless and 3G signals able to create ad hoc network structures that extend the range of mobile phone towers.

Although these technologies aren't in place at the time of writing, we've included them as a future set of channels and challenges for m-marketing. If the technology and market acceptance of sophisticated levels of augmented reality take off to the extent that basic augmentation has already been accepted (being able to communicate with anyone from anywhere you and your phone are standing is a basic augmentation of reality), then the marketplace for augmented reality content, service delivery and promotion should be quite profitable. If a mobile device can be used to overlay an additional layer of data onto the world, then the options for libraries (reviews on books), book stores (recommended reading lists), fashion (sizing options, colour choices), and food retailing (QR codes beside fresh ingredients that automatically generate shopping lists and cooking instructions) are extensive.

## Smart devices

The last category to consider is the increasingly diverse kit of smart devices that have thus far resisted the temptation to become mobile phones. For the most part, these devices rely on wireless network access and are technically part of the e-marketing portfolio. However, they're sufficiently mobile to count towards the m-marketing end of the activity rather than the computer-centric e-marketing side of things. There are seven broad device types.

○ *Standard issue MP3 players*. The Sony Walkman cassette deck was the original augmented reality device that allowed the user to overlay their own personal soundtrack on the world. As technology has upgraded, the non-wireless music device still remains a means to augment reality to by placing a layer of audio data over the real world, such as self-paced audio walking tours (www.walki-talki.com).

○ *Wireless-enabled MP3 players*. These can access various Internet hotspots to function as a phoneless iPhone (aka the iPod Touch and the wireless iPad), read e-mail, browse the Web and still remember to play music.

○ *Netbook computers*. These are a return to the early days of Internet access that relied on underpowered terminals linked to a powerful mainframe. These days it's under-strength laptop computers hooked into the cloud via wireless or 3G Internet access that present the cyclical nature of contemporary technology (a return to the good old days of the future).

○ *Handheld games*. This is an emerging area that could use both creative marketing thinking and product development to tap into the increasingly large number of portable gaming devices that have wireless capacity and the ability to form ad hoc networks. Devices such as the Nintendo DSi and Sony PSP are being touted as potential distribution platforms for digital comic books and magazines, in addition to game content.

○ *The next big thing*. This will be most probably something built by Apple, copied adequately by Google and almost copied (but just not quite right) by Microsoft that's touch screen, wireless, data oriented and doesn't cannibalize the MP3 player market whilst undercutting the e-book and wireless gaming device market (and isn't the iPad) that will feel strangely familiar (Figure 13.3).

○ *E-readers, e-books and e-magazines*. These include the Barnes & Noble Nook, Amazon Kindle, anything using e-ink and other devices which focus on the delivery of digital books and magazines as the primary platforms. These are distribution channels that the consumer buys outright before purchasing actual content to go with the device.

**Figure 13.3** A familiar technology
*Source*: http://xkcd.com/548

   o  *Descendants of the iPad:* including the upgrades, updates and changes to the iPad that spawn from software development, Flash for iPad, and the OS5.0 release. Odds are in favour of the iPad2 acquiring cameras, and almost-but-not quite telecommunications capacity to ensure that the iPhone retains a level of difference from its A4 shaped sibling.

Whilst each of these devices is interesting in its own right, and could produce a viable niche marketplace, they're outside the scope of the chapter as they predominantly depend on wireless access for their content, and that places them closer to the e-marketing end of the spectrum than the mobile phones.

## The m-marketing marketspace

Marketspace was first raised in Chapter 1 as the independent network of business connections, information and data flows that encompasses the entire electronic network commercial world. As the parallel universe for business connectivity, virtual value chains and virtual logistics are central to the success of the intangible goods and services network that makes up most of m-marketing and mobile telephony. The phone itself is physical, and most of the rest of the product ranges from the transmission of ideas as voice data across networks to virtual goods that reside within the phone's memory.

Mobile marketing's marketspace is represented at different levels of abstraction based on where the exchange of value takes place and who is the primary set of beneficiaries between consumers, content providers and the network owners:

   o  *Consumer to consumer*, which refers to communications, SMS and generally using a phone to reach out and touch someone
   o  *Consumers to content providers*, which is the exchange between the customer and marketers in the form of content for the phone (SMS, ringtone, m-service, application, streaming video)
   o  *Consumer to networks*, where the customer accesses the mobile phone network through a relationship with Orange, BT, Virgin Mobile or a similar phone provider. Whilst there's a lot of interesting marketing to be done in this space, it's not the focus of the m-marketing chapter
   o  *Networks to content providers*, which are the logistics and distribution functions that underpin the provision of content to mobile phones through phone provider-branded portals (e.g. Virgin Mobile content), dealing with the Apple iTunes AppStore policies or any other gatekeeper role the phone carriers play in the provision of content to consumers
   o  *Networks to networks*, which is the business-to-business engagement that allows for mobile phone carriers to communicate with each other and for calls from one phone provider to go through to another. (As with consumer to networks, this is another area beyond the scope of this chapter.)

The chapter will focus on the 'consumer to content provider', and to a lesser extent, the distribution network issues of 'networks to content providers' when looking at the structural issues associated with the m-marketing marketspace. As mentioned in Chapter 6, the marketspace operates across three parameters:

- Infrastructure: which are the data network (mobile phone coverage, 3G) and segmentation issues of the consumer marketplace such as technical demography, usage patterns and the audience match (Chapter 3)
- Context: which is the location where exchanges take place between producer and consumer
- Content: the idea or information being traded, which includes everything from SMS to application data, web pages, phone calls and embedded services.

## Infrastructure

The infrastructure of the mobile marketspace consists of the physical networks of mobile coverage including factors such as BT's wireless mesh that covers most of London, the 3G networks and the various mobile phone contract providers. From our perspective there are two areas of infrastructure that are largely out of the reach of the m-marketing approach: mobile networks and mobile carriers. The third aspect of infrastructure is the end-user market of mobile phone owners and their approach to the use of their phones. Mobile networks and mobile providers are best considered as adjuncts to the m-marketing campaign, retail outlets for distribution of content or services marketing case studies. The type of m-marketing that Virgin Mobile (www.virginmobile.com), BT (www.bt.com), Orange (www.orange.co.uk) or other telecoms providers can do with their own networks falls into relationship marketing, product provision and service delivery categories.

Two issues apply to the infrastructure requirements of the mobile network – first, the use and charging for data rates influences the ways and means in which the marketer can provide content to the end users and secondly, whether data is a primary feature of the package or a secondary consideration. The majority of smart phone packages operate with data as a core feature of the monthly service fee (with a range of responses to exceeding the data use quota in overrun charges or shaping) whereas the majority of mobile or mobile plus phone packages will have a limited data rate plan with expensive surcharges for excess content consumption. If you plan to provide significant volumes of content as an m-marketing product offer, it's worth checking with the target market as to what their plans and data limits are. You may need to negotiate with the service providers rather than end users for content to be included as part of the network's core service rather than as an add-on particularly if you plan to stream video such as short television commercial style serialized content. The phone providers probably need content for their own portals and there could be a more useful indirect market approach than going straight to the consumer on a pay-per-use basis.

The second critical aspect of the mobile networks is the mobile phone user and their preferences for the core, actual and augmented use of their mobile devices. As with social media, and most of the rest of this book, the first port of call is to look at the influence of the innovation adoption characteristics on the mobile phones and what this means for the marketspace. Mobile phones have been a popular topic for innovation adoption researchers over the years because they're a surprisingly high visibility product (particularly if you've got a very loud ringtone at a very embarrassing time) and there's an odd social propensity to lay mobile phones on tables when dining, holding meetings or generally sitting down at a desk (as this chapter is being written, the authors' mobile phones are sitting beside the computers as if to supervise the process). Table 13.1 outlines the match up between the innovation characteristics, types of devices and innovation adoption category.

From a marketing perspective, the mobile phone sector has one of the singularly shortest half-lives of any technical device (and a positively slow decay compared with cinematic movie releases) as the product lifecycle per phone leaps from introduction to decline in a period of months. This has the consequence of placing devices that are well suited to innovators into the hands of the late majority simply because of the speed at which a fashion (namely the iPhone) sweeps through the marketplace and people upgrade rapidly to avoid being seen with last year's phone. With that in mind, it's

**Table 13.1** Innovation characteristics by innovation adoption category

| | Device | Relative advantage | Compatibility | Complexity | Trial | Observable |
|---|---|---|---|---|---|---|
| **Innovator** | Smart phones TCBH phones | Novelty. Cutting-edge technology | The less the better | Maximum. They're writing applications for their own devices | Buying off eBay and unlocking | Noticeable for constantly playing with it |
| **Early adopter** | Smart phones | Trendsetting | Leadership. Integrated fashion statements (e.g. iPhone, iMac, iPod and latte) | Fashion and social message symbol. Used at least five of the Top 10 apps | Pre-ordering | Used to promote their own visibility |
| **Early majority** | Mobile phones plus Smart phones Smart devices | Followership | Fashionability. Owns an iPhone because they're popular | Minimum use of complex features. Sends SMS and MMS using shrtn wrds | Queuing for midnight releases | Ringtone set to overly loud |
| **Late majority** | Mobile phones | Compliance | Acquired by family wanting to stay in touch | Basic use of features. Might send an SMS once a year | End-of-contract upgrades | Complains about being sent SMS |
| **Laggard** | Landlines | Landlines can be left at home | Likes voicemail on landlines | Just wants voice calls | Work-provided mobile | Almost invisible |

worth then looking at the features of the phone in relation to the innovator categories, since m-marketing relies on people being able to use their phones as much as it relies on the phone having certain mission critical features (Table 13.2).

One of the key elements to consider is that whilst the physical device is highly visible, the actual use of the content on the device is mostly personal and invisible (even when you're sending an SMS, people can't always tell what you're sending,

**Table 13.2** Features versus users

| | Innovator | Early adopter | Early majority | Late majority | Laggard |
|---|---|---|---|---|---|
| **Application stores** | Submitting user-generated content to the store | Shops for items of interest | Buys from the Top 10 list | Resents needing to install it | Not installed |
| **Applications** | Writes their own/picks new | Relatively short lifespan | Large number of unused apps | Only the default apps | Puts numbers into the contacts list |
| **Basic applications** | Forgotten | Downloaded novelty applications | Downloaded games | Still trying to use the calendar | Uses the calculator |
| **Bluetooth** | On, enabled and useful | Headsets and accessories | Off by default since hearing bad stories from the news media | Nervous about breaking the phone if they change a setting | Factory default setting |
| **Camera** | Augmented reality, QR codes and lifestreaming | Uploads to Facebook, Flickr, MySpace and MMS | Photos of friends, family and pets on camera | Caller ID photos | Accidental photos of the inside of handbags and pockets |
| **Ringtones** | Personally created tones/silent | Favourite artiste's track | Top 40 hits | Chosen from factory defaults | Default ringtone |
| **Wallpapers** | Personally created | Own photo | Photo of partner/ children/pet | Children, partner or pet | Factory default |
| **Other downloaded content** | Jail break software, experimental code | Ringtones and MP3s | Back catalogue of no longer popular ringtones | Games selected by friends or family | Nil |
| **GPS** | Geo-tagging | Google Latitude | Maps and navigation | Argues with the map's instructions | Still uses a printed map |

| | | | | | |
|---|---|---|---|---|---|
| **Location awareness** | Mayor of somewhere on Foursquare | On and used for finding new places | Used to read reviews of new places | Says no when asked by apps | Isn't a feature on their phone |
| **MMS** | Uploads to the Internet instead | Sends to friends | Sends to family | Sends by accident | Can't receive on their phone |
| **Phone calls** | Stopped making them | Talks through the free quota allowance | Programmed speed dial | Some pre-programmed numbers | Still types in numbers by hand |
| **SMS** | Sends if the Internet access is down | Exceeds free quota | Mixes txt spk and full sentences | Uses txt spk | Misses the time before they were invented |
| **Storage space** | Replaceable | Nearing capacity | Been meaning to buy | Phone is still empty | Won't ever need |
| **Web browsing** | Extensive | Social media sites | Social media | Tries and the site times out | Sits at a computer |

using or if it's an SMS or a Google query). It's possible to be an innovator in one aspect of the mobile device's technology (SMS) and a laggard in another area (mobile photography). There's a discrepancy as well between the value-in-ownership of a socially popular device (compliance by appearance) and the value-in-use of the same device (disliked intensely for its complexity). It's also worth reviewing briefly the sort of functional motives that were considered for Internet use with regards to mobile devices. Revising the motives from Chapter 5 with the technical device categories from earlier in the chapter, Table 13.3 demonstrates the array

Table 13.3  Motives versus devices

| Consumer motives | Mobile | Mobile phone plus | Smart phones | TCBH | Smart devices |
|---|---|---|---|---|---|
| Anonymity | Knows where the nearest cell tower is located | Mostly location unaware | Shares location awareness | Knows where you and your friends are headed | Anonymous to location aware and location broadcasting |
| ATM | SMS purchase | SMS purchase | SMS purchase, banking apps | E-wallet | E-books, iTunes downloads |
| Communicate | Primary function | Primary function | Secondary function | Primary function | No |
| Community | Limited | Can send SMS to groups | Can link to social media | Phone has its own friends network of devices | Shared use of devices, aka the iPod earbud nod |

## Introduction

Chapter 14 explores e-marketing options beyond the Web with a specific focus on gaming consoles, virtual worlds and other defined e-marketing friendly (or hostile) spaces that use the Internet as their platform. Throughout the book (Chapter 13, m-commerce, notwithstanding), the e-marketing focus has been on delivering content, products and services through web pages. This chapter expands the framework of e-marketing from a web-based activity to one that can use any part of the Internet-connected physical world.

It's a chapter of marketspace, objects and interconnected places in the Internet that need specific hardware, software or other requirements for access. The underlying framework is very distribution centric since it's about the marketspaces, so the focus is less consumer centric than previous chapters largely because we're going to assume that if you're targeting a specific delivery platform, you're doing that to reach the customers who hang out there. That said, whilst we're looking at software vending machines such as Steam, iTunes, Xbox Live and Wii, we're also covering virtual worlds and the augmented virtuality service industry that benefits from understanding how the consumers behave online. Finally, in a tribute to New York theatre and the concept of Broadway and off-Broadway productions (the Premier League and First Division of theatre), we refer to the broad array of outlets, locations and platforms covered in the chapter as 'off web' (because Premier Internet and First Division Internet just doesn't sound right).

## The off-web environment

Distribution theory is rarely regarded as a glamorous part of the industry. With the focus on logistics, shipping and the bistro mathematics required to ensure that supply meets demand at the right place and at the right time, distribution is perceived as a lot less fun than advertising, calculating prices or building product offers (you know it's bad when economical modelling in pricing wins the popularity contest). With that in mind, we've drawn most of the theory being used in this chapter from the previous chapters to firmly place the off-web products, services and goods well within the core of the e-marketing framework that you've already encountered. Just because the virtual goods are downloaded to the Wii, or the service is delivered in World of Warcraft, or the behaviour needs an Xbox controller to take place, doesn't mean that they are isolated from the same frameworks that underpin the keyboard and mouse regime of e-marketing (and the keypad and phone approach of m-marketing).

### Complications and challenges in the off-web channel

The off-web environment presents some additional complications for e-marketing, such as exclusivity, consumer engagement, various business risks and channel limitations.

The first serious consideration when using off-web channels is to determine whether the content (product, good, service, behaviour) is transferable between various devices or if it is ideally suited to one specific channel. Channel exclusivity was raised in

Chapter 3 as a means of objective differentiation between products, platforms or companies. Channel exclusivity is often a feature of off-web channels which either provides an exclusive service (virtual world environment), or has content exclusive to that domain (exclusive game releases for Xbox or Playstation 3) or requires specific hardware only available for that device (WiiFit step boards, the Wii controllers, Xbox Kinnect controller).

Secondly, the nature of the channels being virtual worlds, video game consoles and self-service devices requires a level of consumer engagement in the service delivery. This can lead to significant social price costs in terms of the consumers' investments of their time, effort, pride and opportunity costs to co-produce the service. Depending on the platform, there's also opportunity for co-creation of content to become a feature of the service. Playing a multi-player online game (Team Fortress 2, World of Warcraft) presents opportunities for positive co-production (good gameplay, sportspersonship) and the opportunity for service disruption (ganking, griefing, ex-Counterstrike players). It's worth noting that the Entertainment Software Rating Board (www.esrb.org) specifically states that its ratings for multi-player games do not apply to online environments (www.esrb.org/ratings/ratings_guide.jsp). There's a load of services marketing theory that examines how to manage customers in physical environments that's largely based on the acknowledged presence of the service provider. It becomes a lot harder when there's no physicality, and you're not always going to have a service provider present. World of Warcraft has a player account population approaching 12 million spread over approximately 240 servers, thus making it two and half times the size of Ireland when it comes to population. All things considered, Blizzard does a surprisingly good job at maintaining civility in that environment without requiring a seat at the UN or an elected parliament.

Thirdly, the off-web distribution network is a relatively high-risk proposition for the brand, company and marketer insofar as picking the wrong platform for your exclusive release can be devastating and platforms may not prove as popular with the people as they did with the press (trade or mainstream media). Second Life (www.secondlife.com) was predicted as being the supposed super platform of the future – business, education, life and shopping were all supposed to move from the physical world into that specific three-dimensional avatar world. It failed to happen, and companies that invested heavily in creating content failed to see expected levels of return on investment (where expected may have included 'Pot at the end of the rainbow' revenue levels). Other problems occur when the platform fails to deliver to the expected marketplace – the relatively sluggish sales of the Sony Playstation 3 when compared with the Nintendo Wii, and the positioning of the Wii as a casual gaming device versus the position of the Sony Home Entertainment Portal, drove different crowds to each of the markets.

Finally, the last point to consider is the relatively restrictive nature of the platforms, insofar as you're not going to be in control of the channel and you have to comply with the requirements of the channel owners in order to play on their levelled playing field. Apple's iTunes store is usually the go-to candidate for heavy restrictions (discussed later), but it's also important to remember that Apple, Sony, Microsoft, Valve and Nintendo all have business rationales for protecting their content distribution channels in terms of brands, exclusive relationships and market dominance for their own products. There's

○ *Revenue 2*: These are the indirect returns that come from brokering sales, taking commissions and generally receiving a cut of the action without charging a subscription fee to access the service. This places Steam, iTunes on the PC and even Amazon's PC-based Kindle software into the indirect camp. If the consumer manages to navigate carefully, they could use these channels almost exclusively to access free content, thus indicating that there's no certain (just highly probable) revenue structure. It is an arbitrary line to distinguish free channels (Revenue 2) from paid subscription channels (Revenue 3). Similar is the need to purchase a device to access the channel in a Revenue 2 indirect approach (e.g. Xbox, Kindle, iPad) since there's no guarantee that ownership of the device will lead to revenue from the device's related channel.

○ *Revenue 2.5*: These are the channels that are cross-funded by product sales which are used to augment the value of the initial product and drive up the sales. Alternatively, these are channels that are part of the relationship marketing approach and are investments based on reciprocity (exclusive rewards for loyal members) and consumer satisfaction through ongoing service delivery. From an e-marketing perspective, this is the Windows Update, Adobe Updates and other software that checks the Internet for upgrades. Since it's funded for the purposes of maintaining an ongoing relationship, it's a form of indirect revenue. This also covers where virtual currency can be purchased within the software (Zynga Facebook games) or additional content bought from within the software package (Adobe Bridge, Poser 8, anything Zynga produces for the iPhone).

○ *Revenue 3*: This is the where the channel has an immediate direct revenue stream in the form of a subscription. Subscriptions may provide free content, access to exclusive content or opportunities to shop at the in-device store (Xbox Live Arcade). It's the "cover charge at the night club where you're also buying from the bar" approach to off-web distribution.

In addition to the approaches that can be taken for raising revenue from sponsorship, advertising, paid product placement and related approaches, there's also the old-fashioned method of charging a fee and receiving a payment. As mentioned previously, there's the monthly subscription approach (World of Warcraft), direct product sales (Steam), product and subscription combined (Xbox Live) or virtual currency (Zynga). There's also the iTunes approach to presenting an array of pricing structures for music which covers buying one track (single), two to three related tracks (EP), twelve or more tracks (album), and the 'completing the set' price discount for buying up the remainder of a partially complete album the store detects in your collection. (Genius does more than make playlists. It also generates shopping lists.) In terms of actually acquiring money for virtual goods and services, there are a few different approaches we've identified:

○ *Direct credit card*: which is the preferred method of Steam, iTunes, Nintendo, Xbox and a few other services where recurring billing is an option, or where you want your service to remember the details for instant purchasing from shopping cards or applications. iTunes is particularly good at storing credit card details to enable purchases on the iPhone to come from the established credit details set up within the desktop store front. This requires a bit of offline logistics with banks, business accounts and other set-up arrangements although it comes with the distinct advantage of being credit card to bank account for payment speed.

○ *Direct debit*: which is where you're probably on eBay as you're taking payments from casual users via direct deposit. It's been replaced with PayPal for most services that offered it in the early days.

○ *Prepaid/offline credit vouchers*: which is where you buy the network credits (Xbox Live Points, Wii Points) or real money equivalent (iTunes cards) as gift cards. This is a useful (albeit complicated to establish) method if you're likely to deal with an audience that doesn't have its own credit cards.

○ *PayPal* (www.paypal.co.uk): which is the international money vendor of default for a wide range of services. Although PayPal is one of the largest non-bank financial operations on the Internet, there are problems with the service freezing assets if it feels the account is subject to unusual traffic patterns – which has occasionally been triggered by a successful sales campaign producing a faster than expected rate of sales (or where a new product launch captures the market's imagination when the previous sales were mediocre). If you're looking for a long-term relationship with PayPal as a provider, it's probably worth establishing a pattern of advising of possible sales spikes or predicted 'unusual' activity. PayPal is surprisingly tetchy about short bursts of high-volume sales which often come about from offering a sales discount on Twitter or a short run of exclusive content.

○ *Third-party wallets* such as Amazon Payments (payments.amazon.com): which allow stored account details at Amazon to be used for payments at a range of places around the Internet, and thus turns Amazon into a B2B finance broker as well as the mega hypermarket of the Internet.

○ *Mobile phone payments:* which are hosted by providers such as Boku (www.boku.com), Paymo (www.paymo.com) or Dao Pay (www.daopay.com) where the user charges their purchase to their phone bill (thus highlighting the convergence of mobile phone and credit card financing). (See Chapter 13 for premium SMS and other details.)

○ *Virtual currency exchanges* such as PayByCash (www.paybycash.com): which apparently accept any legitimate or known form of financial payments to their accounts which they broker as cash payments from your customer to your accounts. PayByCash is an amazingly global operation given it offers popular payment mechanisms that are unique to various nations (it's big in Belgium isn't usually a unique selling proposition), and some of the more common (credit card, PayPal, direct debit) approaches.

○ *Virtual piggy banks* such as Spare Change (www.sparechangeinc.com): which allow users to top up their accounts with cash, credit, PayPal or mobile, or to receive payments from market research companies that can be used for purchasing virtual goods.

○ *Advertising brokers* such as RockYou (www.rockyou.com): who provide the brokerage and sales of advertising content to other services looking to promote on social media sites, and pay direct revenue to the content creators.

in generic terms about the principles of cloud computing, and point to a few examples rather than go into depth with device-specific channels. Overall, the features of the cloud can include:

o *Social media integration*: which, as discussed in Chapter 12, refers to interconnection between content, users and communication technologies through platforms such as Facebook and Twitter
o *Content creation networks*: which are supported by the entire array of shared content creation systems which range from collaborative file editing in Google Docs (www. google.com/docs), through shared whiteboards in Inkscape (www.inkscape.org) to Google Wave (www.googlewave.com/wave)
o *On-machine store*: which includes the ability of certain cloud-based systems to provide retail functions to buy content, hire services or purchase freemium content that becomes available anywhere the user is – as opposed to being allocated hard drive space on a specific computer somewhere
o *Intra-software store fronts*: which includes the ability to purchase virtual goods and services for use within the cloud application (e.g. rights to archive image use within a cloud-based image editor)
o *Mobile interface*: which is basically the entirety of how the 3G iPad is designed to operate, covers most of Kindle's operations and handles a fair amount of any time you read your e-mail on the phone without actually downloading the e-mail to the handset.

*Marketspace analysis*: Cloud computing is a developing application of the Internet that has been enabled by the simultaneous growth in network speeds and decline in server space costs. However, its limitations are based entirely on the network accessibility and bandwidth capacities of the user. For example, DropBox offers 50GB of online storage space which is larger than most monthly download quotas that don't include the word 'heavy' somewhere in the title. Similar problems exist when you're looking at the network congestion and bandwidth restrictions of trying to implement mobile 3G-based cloud computing. However, as a promising development for the future, it's worth the investment in exploring further in terms of the following:

o *Content*: just about everything
o *Context*: Internet based servers, some local hard drive space and a lot of in-browser applications that can't function in an offline mode
o *Infrastructure*: computers. Netbook users can consider the Jolicloud (www.jolicloud. com) operating system as an operational framework for cloud computing
o *Social interaction*: e-mail, chat, direct message
o *Attractor types*: Technically, everything can feasibly be supported in the distributed computing environment, although we've preferenced a set of options in Table 14.2 as the most appropriate use of the framework.

*Generic business objectives*: Cloud computing has been introduced in a range of operations (including the writing of this book) on the basis of its capacity to apply distributed access to content, files and services. The best fit between the platform and the generic business objectives will vary according to the type of objective.

○ *Behavioural change objectives*: which includes changing the way we use technology to see software as something we borrow or access rather than something we own; moving towards a collaborative virtual environment for document sharing and editing
○ *Information dissemination objectives*: where collaborative access to shared ideas is a lot easier if you've all logged into Google Docs and can read the same file (and edit live whilst discussing the changes amongst yourselves – try it with a group assignment sometime)
○ *Cost-oriented objectives*: which are a mixed function of reducing costs by using freemium services for e-mail, document handling and archival storage rather than investing in corporate IT infrastructure
○ *Efficiency objectives*: which is where the authors used DropBox to allow for the chapter drafts to be instantly available between authors, editors and production teams rather than relying on e-mailing files (and remembering which was the most recent version) or carting them around on USB sticks (and not being able to work on the file because you left the stick at home).

*Product user positioning*: Cloud computing is still a new concept, and it's really early days, which means we're in the innovator and early adopter phases. The most likely product user position that the average consumer would associate with this platform would be 'waste of time' since most people aren't doing collaborative work that can't be solved by someone typing and someone else leaning over their shoulder. However, for those with offices in multiple locations (or university assignment groups), cloud computing's collaborative environments, online file hosting and other options lend themselves to convenience, ATM and vending, and a certain level of inherent awesomeness of having the file you're working on be instantly accessible to someone the other side of the world. It certainly made the writing, editing and proofing process for this book considerably easier.

### Facebook games

We've isolated Facebook games as one of the more interesting uses of augmented virtuality insofar as the games themselves augment the Facebook user experience through engaging in community gameplay (assisting friends in activities in the applications), community development (encouraging sharing of rewards and gameplay engagement to build shared goods of value) and overt selling thoroughly virtual services and products (paying cash for in-game rewards). The key features of this type of Facebook game include:

○ *Social media integration*: which is the games' integration into Facebook, MySpace and the rest of the social media fleets. Zynga Games (www.zynga.com) operates on Facebook, MySpace, Bebo (www.bebo.com), Friendster (www.friendster.com), Tagged

As providers of third-party content to these worlds, there's a level of business-to-business (B2B) relationship marketing and management with the world owners to be considered – effectively, don't annoy the people who can ban the use of your product, and don't try to break their world through exploits, gameplay imbalance or other actions.

Virtual worlds have a moderately consistent set of features of interest to e-marketers, which include:

o *Social media integration*: which is where you provide a third-party link between the game and social media sites such as the in-World of Warcraft Twitter client (www.tweetcraft.codeplex.com)
o *Content creation networks*: which is where the games permit, sanction or ignore the sale of third-party plug-ins for real-world money (US$5 PayPal donations appear to be the base entry price). Alternatively, this is where your product will rely on user-generated content for the provision of core services such as mapping, auction house monitoring or other live data streams from within the game. As long as the customer gains from contributing to the data pool, most game players will assist with user-generated content community oriented applications that run as part of their game experience
o *In-game store*: which is where ideally you want to operate if you're selling in an environment that permits virtual goods, virtual asset trading or virtual currency exchange
o *One-way virtual currency*: which is most of the MMOs that don't permit or condone currency trading. Second Life and the Sony Network sanction real-world cash trading (money in, money out) through their official exchange rates and brokerage services. Other games such as EVE Online and World of Warcraft will hunt down and ban players if they suspect them of untoward currency trading
o *Mobile interface*: which is a developing market of on-device applications, store fronts and other services that allow the smart phones to be used for serving information to players whilst those players are in-game. Any iPhone application that can provide useful real-time data to an MMO player provides an augmented reality of a physical compass/dataset for augmenting the virtual gameplay experience.

*Marketspace analysis*: This is a variable marketspace due to the wide range of attitudes held by the MMO producers. At the far end, MMO owners may believe that third-party applications are an unwelcome intrusion into their game environments and can use copyright, end user licence agreements and other enforcements to prevent their use, thus wrapping up any desire you may have had to sell to their customers. In the middle, there's the sanctioned, permitted and largely ignored if it's not commercially exploiting the game's IP type of augmentation which doesn't necessarily provide a good Revenue 2 or 3 opportunity. At the other end, there are the games that actively encourage augmentation to create a customer co-production environment that gives their users increased incentives to continue paying the monthly subscription fees.

o *Content*: virtual world augmentation from maps, compasses, databases, knowledge, virtual objects and virtual currencies
o *Context*: virtual world servers (services, virtual goods), PDF files and mobile devices for information products
o *Infrastructure*: Game clients software, some additional third-party accessories
o *Attractor types*: Entertainment parks, content archives, clubs, service sector, customer service centres, town halls, and single-purpose sites.

*Generic business objectives*: Producing augmented virtuality products is either going to send your organization in search of good coding skills or be a means to convert the time you've invested in these worlds into something that mixes knowledge management software, training and instruction manuals. The best fit between the platform and the generic business objectives tends towards the following areas:

o *Entertainment-oriented objectives*: which involve augmentations that make the virtual worlds more fun by improving the overall experience
o *Behavioural change objectives*: which include training guides, technique improvements and other information that alters the way the user interacts with the virtual world
o *Information dissemination objectives*: which involves the production and distribution of insight into the virtual world, tactics and other insights gained from in-world experience
o *Sales-oriented objectives*: which are about converting your own in-game experiences or personally developed augmentations and selling them to the other members of your community.

*Product user positioning*: Virtual world augmentation attracts product users from across most of the spectrum and can be narrowed into different types of product offerings for each category of user.

o Learn: which is where you're producing instruction manuals, training guides, maps and ancillary support materials such as YouTube videos
o Search: which is the development of in-world knowledge management databases that can be used to assist the players in quest completion or in understanding the challenges they're facing as well as actual in-world search functions that help find places, people and things through maps and in-world compasses
o Communicate: which is where your accessories either offer intra-game communications such as voice over IP or extra-game communications such as embedding Twitter, MSN or Facebook into the virtual world
o Convenience: which is where you're aiming to improve in-world experiences with your products or services
o Community: which is where you augment a game with a guild structure that operates within the game and may be hosted on a separate web forum, Facebook group or similar arrangement

o Inherent awesomeness: which is where you do something spectacular that improves the virtual world either by exporting it to real life (3D custom figure printing, posters of game avatars) or producing an in-world experience (in-game radio stations)

o Vending machines: which is where you sell virtual goods in sanctioned environments

o ATM: which is where you're brokering cash in virtual world environments

o Self-expression: which is where your systems improve the avatar creation process, or provide additional accessories for the in-world experience such as the improbably large fashion industry in Second Life.

## Desktop vending machines

Desktop vending machines refer to any applications that are purpose built to provide self-service sales combined with automated product delivery without needing to load a web page. The two highest profile vending machines are iTunes and Steam. Amazon has begun to experiment with PC-based Kindle software packages, and other software vending machines are being developed for content delivery (video on demand, pay-per-view television). For the most part, vending machine software usually also provides other services such as community engagement (multiplayer games on Steam), data management (Blackberry phone synchronization software) or a direct interface to physical hardware (iTunes for loading iPods).

### iTunes

iTunes is the poster child for the wheel of retailing in a digital format. Starting life as a data-management tool for loading iPods, progressive iterations of the software have added the ability to purchase and download directly from the Apple iTunes library, subscribe to periodic updates from podcasts and rent time-expiring digital video content which can either be played on the computer or handheld device. With the advent of the iPhone, iPod Touch and iPad, the store also offers direct-to-device applications that can only run on the mobile devices (there's a way to create a virtual iPhone, but that's well outside of the average use of the system). As the definitive digital distribution platform, the iTunes store accepts direct credit card orders and prepaid charge cards. Since Apple has a large array of distribution networks in place to sell iPods, it's no real challenge for the company to also sell pre-paid charge cards to the offline marketspace. Features include:

o *Social media integration*: iTunes has the option to post a link to store content to Twitter or Facebook

o *Content creation networks*: Apple store content can be brokered through third-party providers such as Tunecore (www.tunecore.com) for MP3 distribution, direct submission for podcasts (www.apple.com/itunes/podcasts/specs.html) and direct submission for iTunes Apps (http://developer.apple.com)

o *On-machine browser*: iPod Touch, iPhone and iPad all run the Safari web browser (without Flash)

o *On-machine store*: Available on the iPod Touch, iPhone and iPad for direct purchase
o *One-way virtual currency*: iTunes pre-paid credit
o *Intra-game store fronts*: apps can sell virtual goods directly from within the application using iTunes account details
o *Mobile interface*: integrated in the iPhone, iPod Touch and iPad devices.

*Marketspace analysis*: The entry barriers for iTunes range from incredibly complex B2B relationships through third-party brokers to direct B2B channel negotiation with Apple. Apple maintains a fairly strict level of control over channel content to preserve the brand integrity of its iTunes store and its positioning as a relatively family-friendly environment equivalent to the local video store or magazine shop. Video and television footage suitability can range from general audiences (U) to restricted adult content (R18), whereas the application store operates on an iTunes-specific age index (4+, 9+, 12+ and 17+).

o *Content*: applications, videos, audio, television, movies, e-books and audio books
o *Context*: within the iPhone, iPod Touch and iPad; within the iTunes software; external hosting providers (podcasts); Apple's servers (all other content)
o *Infrastructure*: Apple computers running OS X and licensed developer kits for application development plus iPhone, iPod Touch and iPad as a testing environment (app development is not supported in Windows or Linux); third-party hosting for podcast distribution; iPhone, iPod Touch and iPad for application use
o *Social interaction*: iTunes provides limited feedback functions per sale item and limited sharing of content to Facebook and Twitter. No direct iTunes to iTunes communication (it has thus far resisted Zawinski's Law)
o *Attractor types*: content archives, exclusive sponsorships, gift shops, retail outlets, service sector customer service centre.

*Generic business objectives*: iTunes is the distribution channel for audio content (if you don't mind DRM and having to have content approved by a faceless process run somewhere in Apple). With the dominant share of the MP3 player market and despite the fact that Apple sells its music in the MPEG4 format (m4a file extension), iTunes is the best distribution outlet for audio content. It's worth remembering that the term podcast tends to be considered a portmanteau of iPod and broadcast, since iTunes was one of the more successful podcast directories to be widely adopted. The best fit between the iTunes and the generic business objectives is as follows:

o *Entertainment-oriented objectives*: which are the core business of providing audio, music, video and games. This is the channel and this is the platform for delivering digital entertainment content to a wide audience
o *Behavioural change objectives*: which can be supported through podcasting, behavioural tracking applications such as exercise programs (Runkeeper), e-books and audio books. If you have a virtual product that can support a behavioural change objective, it's worth ensuring it can be accessed by iPods and delivered through

iTunes. Similarly, any behavioural change objectives that require repeat behaviours can be enforced and assisted with iTunes apps that perform push reminders, play alarms, or have large reassuring check boxes with green ticks to register task completion

o *Information dissemination objectives*: any information-based objective that can be recorded in audio or video can use this channel. Apple releases its keynote addresses, product launches and budget meetings through iTunes

o *Cost-oriented objectives*: once you clear the various hurdles, fees and charges associated with product placement on iTunes, it's a lower cost channel for comparative reach than most physical media distribution options

o *Sales-oriented objectives*: iTunes is well suited to sales objectives that encourage free samples, product bundling, bulk discounts and, surprisingly, premium pricing for individual objects. The ability to sell virtual goods and additional content intra-application through iTunes is a valuable addition to the market penetration strategy portfolio

o *Promotional objectives*: theatrical movie trailers have their own category in movies; free apps can be used to encourage sales of paid apps and/or as promotion for offline products such as movie tie-in games, or physical goods and services.

*Product user positioning*: iTunes serves a wider market than just iPod, iPad and iPhone users insofar as the channel software runs on a PC and a Mac and tends to show up and be installed if you're not paying attention when you're installing QuickTime or Safari (and Safari shows up unannounced once QuickTime and iTunes are around). When it's used intentionally and willingly by end users, it's a reasonably competent media management tool, a good retail outlet and a useful means for wrangling iPods into order (and mandatory for iPhone activation and use). The most likely product user positions that the average consumer would associate with iTunes include escapism (movies), recreation (games, music), convenience (in-computer purchasing), learning (iTunes genius music recommendations), search (finding music), social pressure (Top 10 lists), inherent awesomeness (there's a music store in my computer), vending (buying music, video and apps) and a touch of self-expression for customizing the personal experience of the iPod devices (public goods for the devices, private goods for the apps, music and videos – Chapter 13).

## Steam

Steam is a Mac and Windows-based software client that is equal parts DRM system, consumer marketplace and community. Designed initially as a command and control mechanism to allow Valve to validate ownership of Half Life 2, it meets the wheel of retailing criteria as a progressive series of upgrades introduced a full-scale retail store, a community infrastructure, media and game management plus a series of community content-creation tools. The system supports a range of distribution options for supplying paid premium content, updates, expansions and exclusive in-game items to specific players as loyalty incentive rewards. The core features of the site include:

o *Social media integration*: limited, largely due to Steam having its own community infrastructure that includes player profiles, live chat and direct messaging (it's the Facebook of First Person Shooters)

o *Content creation networks*: extensive support for user-generated content including official content-creation systems (Tools menu), Steamworks which is a dedicated development network (www.steampowered.com/steamworks), plus capacity and organizational encouragement of community content. Valve periodically releases community-generated content for products such as Team Fortress as part of its official update strategy

o *On-machine browser*: technically, the Steam client runs a cut-down version of Internet Explorer to provide dual access to content within the game client and on the web

o *On-machine store*: yes

o *One-way virtual currency*: no. Steam accepts PayPal and credit cards but doesn't have its own currency bank

o *Intra-game store fronts*: limited but developing. Most intra-game content is sold through the main Steam virtual shop front

o *Mobile interface*: no.

*Marketspace analysis*: If you're looking for a PC-based video games distribution channel, Steam is one of the best resourced in terms of reach, accessibility and willingness to support independent games production. Valve openly publishes market research data on the performance of their own flagship games plus the results of the opt-in player hardware survey (http://store.steampowered.com/stats). The Steam platform provides a DRM system that ties ownership of the content to the user account rather than their devices through Custom Executable Generation (www.steampowered.com/steamworks/publishingservices.php). This approach differs from the device-centric nature of iTunes and other DRM platforms that tie ownership to machine rather than person. Valve has also integrated a cloud-computing approach to key aspects of the game set-ups such as save files, customization options and keyboard modifications so that distributors can make their games relatively portable, ensuring the experience at home or at a netcafé is relatively similar.

o *Content*: video games, video game trailers, virtual tool kits

o *Context*: Valve-hosted game servers, independent game servers, Steam software client

o *Infrastructure*: computer running Windows XP, Vista or Windows 7 and Mac OSX

o *Social interaction*: games can include direct voice chat, messaging and 'friends list' of allied players; Steam has an intra-software messaging system for real-time chat, messaging, groups and community

o *Attractor types*: entertainment parks, content archives, exclusive sponsorships, town halls, clubs, gift shops, retail outlets, freeway intersections, customer service centres

*Generic business objectives*: Steam is a dedicated retail outlet for game content at present although its extensive reach and ability to distribute video files for gameplay trailers

- *Social interaction*: short messages between consoles
- *Attractor type*: entertainment park.

*Generic business objectives:* E-marketers using the Wii as a distribution channel would need to dovetail with Nintendo's objectives and probably would be well suited to engage in the following areas:

- *Entertainment-oriented objectives*: focusing the marketing efforts on delivering entertainment goods and services to the platform
- *Behavioural change objectives*: including encouraging users to engage in the more physical games such as the Wii Fit and Wii Sports to achieve personal fitness goals
- *Sales-oriented objectives*: which include providing content to the service directly, and encouraging on-console purchasing.

*Product user positioning*: The positioning of the Wii has been based around the core benefit of the games console as a platform for escapism and recreation. However, there's a lot to be said for the inherent awesomeness that comes from controlling a video game character through the Wii controllers and the volume of social pressure that's formed up around the widespread diffusion of the console as a non-gamer's gaming platform.

### Microsoft Xbox

The Microsoft Xbox 360 is a video game and entertainment console designed for Internet connectivity and content downloads (for consoles with hard drives), and is built with a set of multi-purpose media and home entertainment options within the actual product. Backed by a history of hardware development from the original Xbox series, the 360 has been designed for networked interactivity, with local and network multiplayers built into the fundamental infrastructure. Similarly, the New Xbox Experience (aka the console screen) features interactive elements that link players to their friends, and notifications when an Xbox friend logs into their console (and sometimes when they start playing games). The system has player-community development embedded into the core services, with hosted events (Rockband Mondays, Halo Thursday), a calendar of gaming events and the ability to set up 'Xbox parties' which are user-created events that allow players to invite their friends to an intra-Xbox event. From point of purchase for the book research to time of writing, the Xbox console software has seen a series of upgrades and feature releases indicating an active interest by Microsoft in using the wheel of retailing on its console platform. Currently, the features include:

- *Social media integration*: including the ability to update Twitter and Facebook from the console (and if you plan to do that, buy the messenger keyboard for the Xbox controller if you like Blackberryesque small keyboards or plug in a real USB keyboard)
- *Content creation networks*: which include the XNA network (www.xna.com) for community and professional developers
- *On-machine browser*: it's possible to install a web browser via Windows Media Centre although the Xbox doesn't support web browsing as a default function

○ *On-machine store*: which includes the retail and gift shop modes that sell just about everything from fully downloadable games, expansion content (DLC) and in-game items (virtual goods such as specialist cars for Burnout Paradise) to parts for avatar customizations (virtual hats, shoes, shirts)
○ *One-way virtual currency*: Xbox Points
○ *Intra-game store fronts*: The Xbox platform supports intra-game content purchasing to allow for in-game virtual goods (cars, weapons, hats) and additional game content (songs, levels, maps). The Rockband and Guitar Hero franchises have just about perfected the integration of the store with the gameplay
○ *Mobile interface*: Limited mobile content through the Microsoft Zune.

*Marketspace analysis*: The Xbox supports a relatively wide range of age groups with its mix of hardcore gaming capabilities and additional supporting services such as a media centre, DVD player and home entertainment unit. Games such as Rockband, Guitar Hero and related music games have expanded both the user base and the marketspace mechanisms that are active within the console.

○ *Content*: games, social networks, entertainment media
○ *Context*: Xbox network, some limited crossover into the Windows Live web-and PC-based environments
○ *Infrastructure*: Xbox 360, Microsoft Windows Live (Games for Windows) accounts
○ *Social interaction*: voice chat whilst in game, between console messaging systems (including voice and video), Twitter and Facebook
○ *Attractor types*: entertainment parks, content archives, exclusive sponsorships, clubs, gift shops, retail outlets, customer service centres

There are three items to note with the Xbox. First, the use of standard USB ports in the device allows the USB Xbox controllers to be linked with desktop PCs. Since that means the console does accept USB keyboard input, it hints at the prospect of an 'Xbox as family computer' future. That said it's still really awkward to even consider Microsoft Office for the Xbox in its current format. Secondly, there's a distinct lack of a music store within the on-console shopping options, which is either the legacy of the failure of the MSN Music store (or a vague hope of an iTunes deal once Apple stops laughing at the Zune's attempts to dethrone the iPod). Thirdly, the marketspace for independent video and television content has remained relatively untapped compared with the level of independent gaming content available on the platform. There's an opportunity for pay-for-view (or ownership) content delivery via streaming and/or downloaded video with a solid infrastructure in place that could use a lot more content options.

*Generic business objectives:* When your target market owns an Xbox, there are a lot of advantages to be had from working with Microsoft's content delivery networks. The best fit between the platform and the generic business objectives are:

○ *Entertainment-oriented objectives*: where video, audio and gaming content can benefit from providing content into the platform

Whilst off-web platforms provide a targeted distribution channel for e-marketers, they are not without risk. Key amongst the potential downsides of engaging in off-web channels are the risk of being enmeshed in a platform which has limited reach and success, the potential for, and right of, those who control the platform to move the goal posts at any stage, and limits to the extent that content can be transferred between existing platforms and infrastructures.

# References

## Books and journals

Zawinski, J. (1995) 'Zawinski's law', *Jargon Manual*, http://www.catb.org/jargon/html/Z/Zawinskis-Law.html (accessed 2 July 2010).

## Web references

| | |
|---|---|
| Bebo | www.bebo.com, |
| Blizzard Store | http://blizzard.com/store |
| Boku | www.boku.com |
| Curse | www.curse.com |
| Custom Executable Generation | www.steampowered.com/steamworks/publishingservices.php |
| Dao Pay | www.daopay.com |
| Entertainment Software Rating Board | www.esrb.org |
| ESRB Ratings Guide | www.esrb.org/ratings/ratings_guide.jsp |
| Friendster | www.friendster.com |
| Google Docs | www.google.com/docs |
| Google Wave | www.googlewave.com/wave |
| Inkscape | www.inkscape.org |
| iTunes Apps | http://developer.apple.com |
| iTunes Podcasts | www.apple.com/itunes/podcasts/specs.html |
| Jolicloud | www.jolicloud.com |
| NCSoft | www.ncsoft.com |
| PayByCash | www.paybycash.com |
| Paymo | www.paymo.com |
| PayPal | www.paypal.co.uk |
| RockYou | www.rockyou.com |
| Second Life | www.secondlife.com |
| Spare Change | www.sparechangeinc.com |
| Spugnort's World | www.spugnortguides.com |
| Steam Game Play Stats | http://store.steampowered.com/stats |
| Steam Hardware Survey | http://store.steampowered.com/hwsurvey |
| Steamworks | www.steampowered.com/steamworks |
| Tunecore | www.tunecore.com |
| Wii Shop | www.wiishop.net |
| World of Warcraft Twitter client | www.tweetcraft.codeplex.com |
| XNA network | www.xna.com |
| Zynga Games | www.zynga.com |

# CHAPTER 15

# Social impact

## Learning objectives

By the end of this chapter, you should be:

- at the end of the book (apart from index)

- able to outline the ways that e-marketing and the future interact with each other

- painfully aware of the end-of-semester deadlines

- conversant in a range of new and interesting ways to license ideas, intellectual property and copyright for mutual social and commercial gain.

## Introduction

The final chapter contains the inevitable forward-thinking, future-gazing sections on how the Internet in the future might operate, who's likely to be trying to run it and what might happen next. This chapter is a summary, a review and a call to action for those who plan to be involved in Internet marketing. Most of the predictions are based around observations of historical cycles and emergent trends. However, some are just guesswork with a touch of personal opinion. Your mission, should you decide to accept it, is to work out which of these is most likely to be of benefit to your e-marketing career (and which bits will make it onto a 'Mispredictions' or 'Future Fail' blog post).

The future of the Internet is dependent on those who choose to shape its direction and functionality and on the actions of those who use it. Privacy and anonymity are issues of concern that constantly need to be addressed, and marketing needs to look beyond the narrow walls of e-commerce to aid in the defence of key issues of Internet freedoms, to defend open speech and to protect the freedom of publication and access to the Internet. Without these freedoms, e-commerce will wither and die as the diversity of the market succumbs to the monopolies and oligarchies that control the traditional print, television and radio media. The boom times for marketing come from competition, open standards and the good dose of humility that comes with being one of many choices rather than the only option.

### Brief note on the future

Anyone who can accurately predict the future normally never does it in a popular culture format. Those with that level of insight can usually be found discussing the outcome of horse races with the punters who just lost – if there's one professionally accredited fortune-telling society, it's the teams behind Ladbrokes (www.ladbrokes.com) and Centrebet (www.centrebet.com) who have a remarkable and profitable track record in picking the future. Publicly predicting the future is also fraught with obvious problems – if we know what will happen next, we can change the script. That said, everyone in the Internet game spends a portion of their life predicting the future (and another portion tinkering with that future to alter the script to suit their desired outcomes).

### *The future's alright*

The future is what it used to be. It's always been fast-paced, scary and subject to rapid change and development. We've usually had fewer resources than we would have liked, less time than we needed, and media that tells us that the advent of talking movies or its contemporary equivalent will be the death of civilization. Plotting the development of 'the future' over time indicates an incredibly steep curve from the discovery of fire to the registration of fire.com. Taken incrementally, the rate of change and the major social upheaval caused by fire is remarkably similar to that of the widespread diffusion of information technology (though information technology has less crispy outcomes).

Accept that the world will continue to change, evolve and generally not be like the good old days. Meanwhile, it's worth noting that at some point in the near future,

**Figure 15.1** Abstraction
*Source*: http://xkcd.com/676

people will be discussing 2010 in glowing terms as 'the good old days'. The future 2010 as predicted by the 1950s and 1960s hasn't materialized (less jetpacks than expected, no meals in a pill, no lunar holidays, no underwater cities and no Pan American Airways either). What has emerged is a present of highly accessible information, heavily interconnected people, and the ability to distribute ideas, services and goods across the Internet (Figure 15.1) in a way that allows the world to share the joy of a cat jumping in and out of a cardboard box (www.youtube.com/user/mugumogu).

## Surviving the future

Given that the world has survived for as long as it has everyone on board has the capacity to adapt to the changes that the future will bring (just as we did for the changes that the past brought along). Change is a constant that has to be factored into the equation of business life just as it gets factored into the day-to-day life of the consumer. At some point in your life, you have had to change brands, switch stores, use an alternative product or accept that a preferred product choice is no longer available. Then, just as now, you had to adjust to the change that occurred, and you did this willingly, reluctantly or without much consideration. In the development of the future of the Internet, changes will be greeted much in the same way – willingly, reluctantly or without anyone really noticing the difference.

The capacity of the individual to cope with change has, if anything, been improved by exposure to change. Since first forming consciousness as an individual, the average human still had to learn about fire (less the discovery, more the application) and from there learn about the Internet and what to do with a computer, keyboard and mouse. It took early humans a long time to come to grips with fire, yet many small children can operate a mouse more easily than their parents (both parent and child have also mastered fire on the way). YouTube provides instructional videos on just about everything from starting fire with an iPhone (there's probably an app for it) to unboxing an Xbox which means that the average Internet user has a wealth of other people's experience to use for reducing a really new idea (using an iPhone) to a quite new idea via vicarious learning. Old ideas can find a new lease of life since you can find blacksmithing instructions on YouTube alongside footage of personal jet packs. Nothing's ever really that far out of date anymore.

### Changes in society

People face the challenge of mastering technology and readjusting to the new format (Kostopoulos, 1998). Technology mastering is the ability of a person to increase their skills to a level where they can adapt to changes and new technologies, and whilst it's a learnt behaviour (Introduction), technology is speeding up in direct response to the widespread capacity of people to learn the old ropes. Just make it more entertaining – the breadth of technology available in the (relatively) mature marketspace of the Internet is far wider than any single person can master in totality. You have to pick your preferences, train up in those areas and bring in backup when you're out of your depth. Since this is a person-centric activity, the usual rules of innovation adoption (Chapter 4) apply, so if you're looking to train staff, the innovators are already self-teaching, the early adopters need to be taught (and taught how to teach the next generation) and the late adopters are quietly waiting for the class to start.

The second problem (benefit, feature, challenge) of new technology is that it invariably involves some form of content restructuring. Twitter turned the blogger into a copywriter focused on headlines or a conversationalist focused on snappy retorts. Blogging opened up the techniques of the daily columnist and newspaper journalist to the wider market (not that bloggers and journalists are automatically interchangeable). Prior to blogging, Web 1.0 introduced online self-publishing to a world that had only discovered desktop publishing a few years earlier. Each change of technology introduced a new format, a new way of delivering content and the desire to recast the old words into the newer frameworks.

## Roadblocks on the way to the future

Whilst the present is pretty amazing, and the future looks like it's got serious potential, there are some barriers on (or just over) the horizon that will need to be removed, routed around or generally dealt with in a socially productive manner. There are nine big picture issues that have been identified as having a potential impact on the future developments of the Internet and e-commerce. These are:

1. *Bandwidth*: The ongoing 'last-mile' issues of delivering content from the server to the end user. As the capacity of the networks increases, the volume of content

consumed on the networks has risen to match it. Developments in broadband, wireless and ADSL have improved the availability of high-speed solutions for the home user, although as with any channel system, as bandwidth has increased, so has the demand for higher quality, faster and better applications increased the strain on the system.

2. *Information flood*: The 'information for information's sake' aspect of web publishing. In part, this is a feature of the Internet's open nature, free standards and the ability of anyone with a computer and time to publish a website. The downside is that the amount of information on the Internet is enormous, frequently unverified and often replicated to the point of overkill. Automation of re-tweeting keywords, illegal (and economically pointless) rescraping of blog content into rebroadcast fake blogs and a range of other practices are muddying the waters of information clarity.

3. *Data integrity and data veracity*: The extent to which the information that is on the Internet is a true, accurate and a recently updated reflection of reality. This includes the break down of intentionally misleading content that's politically motivated or the use of fake grassroots movements (astroturfing) and downright misleading content for illegal but profitable ends (generally anything that involves teeth whitening or stomach flattening). There's also the problem of dead data resurfacing with a quick polish, update and retag. Snopes (www.snopes.com) has a huge database history of Internet scams, fake offers and urban legends which are dusted off periodically and recycled into the system by well meaning (or not) people passing on false information. Finally, there are the attribution errors that plague every form of media. Content is rebroadcast without the appropriate attributions, new attributions are applied to content that looks like it should be from a specific author, or someone showing off somewhere attempts to claim content as their own. (Plagiarism remains a dumb move. We've got Google. We'll find you and the other twelve copies of your 'original' work.)

4. *Equity of access*: The extent to which the Internet is available to all people, regardless of age, gender, nationality or physical capability. Equity of access is set to become the most critical flaw in the development of the Internet as improved bandwidth increases the visual element of the Internet at the expense of the text. This limits the accessibility of the Internet for the vision impaired and also reduces the extent to which automated translation systems can assist in lowering the language divide. Additional problems such as the digital divide between the 'info-rich' and everyone else (info-poor and info-middle class) is often the subject of debate and still holds a top-of-mind presence in the development of the Internet. Other problems exist in the global spread of the Internet to countries with restrictive regimes that deny access to technologies and services based on gender or race. This issue will become progressively more significant as businesses and governments move more services online and curtail their offline availability.

5. *Information exile*: Plans mooted by various governments, copyright agencies and other corporate lobby groups to crackdown on illegal file sharing by cutting off Internet access will create isolated individuals, families and communities who will be effectively exiled from the digital mainstream. The fundamental flaw with this type of proposal is the level of convergence in Internet, telephone, television and societal

activity – if you can be banned from the Internet for three alleged (and unproven) offences, should this also include a ban on mobile phones, interactive SkyTV and net.cafe attendance? Exiling people from the digital society for unproven allegations is a poor substitute for actual justice when the government is simultaneously trying to encourage greater online civic participation and e-government initiatives.

6. *Security*: The extent to which the Internet is a safe place to conduct business, government and daily life. Crime is an inevitable aspect of the Internet. Since the Internet mirrors the offline world, there was no reason to think it was ever going to be crime free. Security issues such as identity fraud (real and relatively low risk), hacking (real, medium risk), viruses (real, medium risk) and malware (far too real, high risk if you're not thinking before you're clicking) are the new weapons in a cold war arm races.

7. *Problem exists between keyboard and chair*: Helpdesk slang for situations where the computer problem lies in the lack of sophistication of the user. The Internet is a complicated place and the level of complexity available in the world is rising steadily. At the same time, the average level of education of Internet users is declining steadily as access to the Internet moves out of academia and becomes more widespread. This represents the hardest challenge for Internet marketing – at what level of sophistication do you draw the line and say 'You must be at least this smart/trained/educated/experienced to use our product'?

8. *Standards and compatibility*: The growing conflict between the open nature of the Internet and attempts by businesses to capture proprietary shares of the Internet for the licensing fees they believe could be generated from holding the Internet to ransom. If there's ever a choice between the use of an open agreed standard or trying to invent your own wheel, go with the open standards. Open shared standards (shared alphabets, common meanings for words, generally agreed speed limits) are common features of everyday life and make the world a lot easier to navigate for everyone.

9. *Silencing the share of voice*: The efforts, intentional or otherwise, of large corporations to capture control of the publishing and distribution mechanisms of the Internet through proprietary standards, modifications to copyright laws and establishing digital rights management systems. Marketers need share of voice to be open, loquacious and vibrant for our business (marketing) and for the ongoing survival of innovation, new products and new organizations.

## Dealing with the future present: preserving the ethos of the 'old Internet'

The Internet is a strange place. On one hand, it's a giant network of networks spanning most of the globe, offering access to an incredible volume of data, content and other people. On the other hand, it's full of photos of cats (captioned or otherwise), isolated niche communities and vast echo chambers of common agreement amongst like-minded communities.

Since its foundation as a gigantic backup plan for the military-academic complex, and a design infrastructure that was theoretically secure against mass being nuked from orbit (and even then you couldn't be sure), the Internet has played host to a range of sub-cultural trends, social traits and ideological commitments (Chapter 1). The Internet was designed with two fundamental flaws for e-commerce and online marketing. First, it was designed to be able to withstand a nuclear strike by treating a block in the system as damage and figuring out a path around the damage to the information and back again. Secondly, it was designed by engineers, scientists and academics who (originally) never considered it to be more than a mechanism for sharing information. This led to a cultural acceptance that open information sharing was more valuable than closed information hoarding.

These features of the 'old Internet' are worth considering if you're new to the system and worth preserving if you've been online for an extended period. There are two main elements of the Internet ethos to consider as an e-marketer:

1. *The gift economy*: which is a hybrid between karma, information sharing and reputation as a proxy for a currency economy. This area also has strong ties to co-creation of value, co-production and use innovation.
2. *Blockage as damage*: which is a fallback to the network's self-adaptation and survival mode that assumed that one central nexus control point made for a great military target (see nuking from orbit), and 500 distributed control points meant the military's accountants would balk at the requisition order for that much fire power.

## Gift economy

The gift economy is the concept of producing a product, service, idea or other piece of content (code, art, artifacts) then making it widely available to the marketplace for no financial, and usually minimal, social obligation costs attached. The gift economy seems to be an antithesis to the role of marketing at first glance (until you remember that marketing has this huge investment in consumer satisfaction, product development and social pricing). From a marketing perspective, it's often easy to see the gift economy as a problem or a competitor – for just about everything that marketers can create, there's a good chance that there's a gift economy producer providing similar options for free. Then again, since competition is a core part of capitalism, and that's a central philosophy of marketing, this isn't a problematic issue that needs solving – it's a challenge that needs addressing.

Gift economies arose from the initial competitive-collaborative environment of the Internet. Academic and programming cultural values place a strong emphasis on the acquisition of status and reputation based on how much value you give to the society by giving things away (Raymond, 1999). Respect is earned by freely distributing the fruits of personal labour, creativity, time and skill through publication, contribution and engagement in the community. While respect is not always directly bankable, many of the individuals involved in the gift culture still receive financial reward from the work they gave away for free, either through later software registration (freemium pricing, Revenue 0–1) or leveraging their gift culture reputation in other commercial ventures (Revenue 2–3).

The notion of the gift economy hasn't always sat well with the e-marketing community, particularly where the big, expensive, commercial production numbers are beaten to the marketplace by the smaller, faster and more robust gift economy competitors. Similarly, there's a major conflict between the two cultures in terms of type of reward and return on investment: gift culture trades in social price rewards in contrast to the money focus of the pay-per-use culture. Although both cultures respect the ownership of an idea and the value of an idea as being a commodity for exchange and transaction, it is the price of the exchange that differs. If you're facing a return on investment debate on the value of contributions to the gift economy, argue your case on Revenue 1 or Revenue 2 grounds with a focus on goodwill, brand building, credibility and community engagement (Chapter 9). Next, build a set of products that augment what you're giving away and make them available for commercial sale. To take a common example, hand out the core software for free and bill for the training, technical support and individual customization jobs (Revenue 3).

The gift economy and the tradition of routing around damage often means that providers of pay-for-use services face stiff competition from their free counterparts. In order to survive in this environment, the pay-per-use systems must provide greater value than the free competitor, in effort, utility, reward or outcome, as they cannot compete on financial price. If the service, product or good is of sufficient value, the consumer will be willing to pay a financial price for it. Further, the gift economy can be an immensely valuable element of e-marketing strategy – particularly where there's a strong trend towards co-production and user-generated content. The video gaming community has a long history of collaboration between consumers and producers of user-generated content. Companies such as Valve and Id Software make a point of releasing specific community toolkits for modifying their original games as a means of relying on the gift economy to create additional value for their core products. Further, when the gift economy providers are considered allied sources of customer value, you can encourage greater commitment to standalone distribution mechanisms (such as Steam) by providing distribution for the community-created content.

Similarly, it's always worth checking into the open source community for software solutions when you're setting up your marketing activities (the Introduction mentions a few open source community applications). As marketers, we are uniquely placed to contribute to the gift culture through our understanding of social price (and our ability to reduce the social cost of adoption of new products), distribution channels and our communication skills for contributing to documentation, wikis and help guides. Even if you feel you can't contribute to the core or actual product, there's always work to be done on the augmented.

It must be noted here that neither culture believes in intellectual theft, even if some people mistakenly tout the banner of gift culture when they engage in intellectual theft (they're wrong). At the core of the gift movement is the right to choose to sell or give away the idea, and that right is predicated on the basis of the assignment and license of the copyright which is inherent in the intellectual property. Illegal redistribution of content, either through reselling open intellectual property as a closed system or releasing closed content without permission, gives no value to the community. Stealing or trading stolen efforts of others is not producing anything new or valuable in the eyes of the gift culture.

## Blockage as damage

e-commerce tends to create blockages between users and data on a regular basis. The decision of major print newspapers to periodically seal off their archives (or current issues) for freemium or premium access is routinely described as a form of damage. As these blockages are subscriptions or some other form of paid service, login details or site memberships, there's a sense in the business world that they are both viable and valuable. This only holds true where you're either in the scarcity economy or providing significant levels of value that are unique to your enterprise – pay-walling a community works if there's no competition from free communities, and those free communities aren't significantly better than your paid product. Competition usually kills pay-wall arrangements because the freely available content is often easier to find in Google, and easier to build up over time as gift economy prone people put content back into their networks. There's a certain resistance to paying a monthly subscription fee to provide free content to a network so that the network owners (apparently) continue to benefit financially from your unpaid labour. User-generated content exploitation is only ever a short-term success on the Internet (if it works at all).

The problem for the people charging the subscription fees is that many users of the Internet treat subscription-based sites as damage and look for alternative methods to access the same information. When it comes to news media, it's often easier to find a free version of the information in print, on the television, radio or through links in the social media network. The mindset of the Internet culture is not against people receiving value for services offered, money for information or reward for effort. It's just that if you have a choice between two equally useful pieces of content, you're going to probably take the free one that you can get to immediately through the clicked link rather than the paid content that requires registration, payment, validation and time costs for access. Effort costs of searching the Internet are still cheaper than the financial and non-financial costs of subscription (especially if you have to get up, leave the computer and find your credit card somewhere in the house).

### *Censorship as damage*

Censorship and age-based content restrictions are useful in society and often work to the advantage of marketers who can communicate a lot of information about the expected target market and product content by picking the appropriate rating level for their content. An iPhone game with a U rating versus a 15 rating indicates a fair bit about expected content. The problem for e-marketing is where content rating is auto-mated and censorship protocols are based on broad sweeping algorithms – for example, several corporate firewalls contain a 'flesh tone' filter that attempts to automatically detect pornographic images by the level of light skin tone in a jpg. This automated approach ignores actual content in favour of a maths equation that ignores darker skin tones and bans images of manila folders as they cross the magic marker threshold in the software. Similar problems of keyword filtering led to breast cancer pages being banned (and double banned for word and flesh tone image failure). Other systems lock out entire domains for the transgression of a single page, which could see the entire Google

of neutrality would put a serious dent into the ability of e-marketers to use market development, diversification and/or product development were the bandwidth to be pre-allocated to an established market leader. Understandably, this is a bad thing for marketers and e-marketing generally (and an unwelcome additional operating cost for the market leader). Currently, marketing depends on the neutrality of traffic for its success – advertising content isn't charged more, product content isn't slugged with surcharges and tariffs, and technical innovations that led to financially valuable services such as Skype (www.skype.com), BitTorrent (www.bittorrent.com), iTunes (www.apple.com/itunes) and World of Warcraft (www.worldofwarcraft.com) aren't stifled by a lack of bandwidth.

## Clash of cultures: scarce versus abundant

In the early days of the Internet, there was a misguided sense of freedom from local laws and a belief that since the Internet was international, it was also inter-jurisdictional (and not bound by local restrictions). This proved to be a particularly optimistic and wrong interpretation of how the world's legal systems work. Far from being liberated from the laws of the land, the Internet is technically subject to everyone's legal limits. In practice, the offline rules of jurisdiction and extradition treaties limit the extent to which any one nation will be able to pull off a territorial grab for legislating and regulating the Internet, but that's not to say that the offline world doesn't hold some serious clout online.

All of the criminal laws that apply offline still apply online (if it's void in Utah in physical space, it's still void if you're on the Internet in Utah). There are distinctive borders in the Internet's infrastructure that result in a stepped rather than level playing field – the most overt being the Great Firewall of China (and the Rabbit Proof Internet Fence in Australia). There are other areas where the offline world's laws take effect.

○ Misleading trade practices include false advertising, fraud, deceit and the rest of the inappropriate behaviours available to the unethical business types. The Internet sometimes makes it harder for restitution as the bad guys hide out in some obscure places or run operations with hard-to-track offline operations.
○ Defamation, libel and slander all apply online in various shades of effectiveness based on the locations of the parties in dispute, their territorial restrictions and extra territoriality. Slander usually refers to spoken statements (think before you YouTube in anger) whereas libel covers the published written word (including SMS, Twitter and Facebook status updates) except in Scotland where both written and spoken statements are covered as defamation. The length of the content is immaterial to the nature of it being defamatory – there are court cases involving libel over Twitter status updates (140 characters of legal nightmare).
○ Audience controls (aka You must be X to Y) usually require credit cards to enter different sites or selecting your age from a pop-up menu (which presumes numeric illiteracy by the under-eighteen crowd) to view 'restricted' content such as alcohol websites, trailers for 15-rated films and/or anything to do with Modern Warfare 2 (Chapter 2). Spectacular failures of audience control mechanisms usually lead to news

coverage of the evils of the Internet, calls for mandatory filters and greater Internet censorship.

o Whilst the Internet is a global network, laws governing copyright tend to be regional and licence agreements for content are limited by physical world boundaries. Streaming video sites often have IP blocks to prohibit content from being viewed outside a restricted geographic area and DVDs are cursed with the mostly useless region codes (whereas the economy of scale for producing one DVD player for all regions beats the individual region-coded device. Cheaper DVD players are more likely to be multi-region by default as a cost-saving measure.)

o Income taxation laws are particularly ugly and make accountants rich and tax lawyers employable. The UK has complicated requirements for declaring income based on a variety of tax treaties with other nations which you'll need to consider if you're going into the casual or formal export business (www.hmrc.gov.uk/leaflets/c9.htm). Internet-based product sales and services are mostly tax exempt due to the fact that the medium reaches across national and international borders. That said, buyers are usually liable for the import duties or customs charges that their purchase would normally encounter, so real-world boundaries still produce Internet-related taxation issues.

## Intellectual property

There are two major areas of interest for e-marketers when it comes to intellectual property and the Internet: copyright and digital rights management (DRM). Copyright, trademark protection and the means and mechanisms of distributing protected ideas across the Internet were first raised as an issue in Chapter 2, and they're dealt with here with regards to two functional areas: how to use copyright for marketing and how not to let DRM get in the way of marketing activity.

Intellectual property tends to be an uncertain area of the law with an increasing level of effort being expended on creating ever-increasing copyright terms that are headed towards infinity (and beyond). Fundamentally, most of copyright law reform is centred around three issues: protecting ownership, extending the life of copyrights and punishing transgressors.

o Protecting Disney's ownership of Mickey Mouse is the reason why most of the significant changes to intellectual property laws occurred roughly near the end of Disney's projected copyright hold on Mickey Mouse. Without these changes there was a vague threat that the Mouse would have entered the public domain (and by vague threat, it meant that if Disney failed to register its trademarks, re-register copyright or create something new with Mr Mouse, then he'd be public domain).

o The lifespan of existing copyright has been increased from the original domain of twenty-eight years to fifty years (plus re-registration periods) into the current automatic copyright of the lifespan of the author plus seventy years. As authors, we depend on copyright for our revenue stream from this book, however, given it's expected to have a lifespan of less than a decade we probably don't need nearly a hundred plus years of protection on the manuscript. We certainly don't need it on every e-mail we've written (and yet it's automatically there irrespective of whether it's useful or not).

○ Penalties for copyright infringement are of increasing interest and have started at the unrealistic (penalties exceeding damages and lost revenues) and moved to the unreasonable (digital exile) for individual infringements through file sharing. Where this becomes problematic is when the rules for copyright infringement are applied to the logical conclusion of penalties for forwarding e-mail or re-tweeting (reproduction of copyrighted material without permission). It's a matter of time before the first multi-million pound copyright case is centred around 140 characters of reproduced content.

The consequence for marketing is that there is a need to maintain an interest in scanning the legal environments (Chapter 4) surrounding copyright, permissions for reproducing work and automatic penalty infringements. This is vital if your e-marketing strategy relies on either viral marketing (the constant reproducing and copying of your copyrighted adverts) or user-generated content that remixes existing marketing materials (fair use limits or straight copyright breach). The last thing that any marketer needs is the negative publicity associated with your viral advertising campaign being the reason someone loses their access to the Internet for copyright infringement.

## Copyright, Creative Commons and licensing

Copyright is the backbone of intellectual property issues involving e-marketing, Internet distribution and the use of appropriate licensing arrangements to protect both marketer and consumer. Related issues such as patents, trademarks, registered designs and the like are reserved for intellectual property law textbooks. As mentioned previously in Chapter 6, it's important to separate licensing arrangements such as Creative Commons, Copyleft and Open Source from pricing strategies since copyright exists automatically irrespective of commercial intent or whether you're charging a fee for the content.

Offline marketing is probably most conversant with conventional copyright allocations and restrictions such as the model release forms in advertising shoots that allow for the reproduction, re-purposing and reuse of the images for promotional purposes. Similarly, if you look at the fine print of competition entries that involve '25 words or less' contests, there's always some assignment of copyright from contestant to organizer. Copyright as it currently operates is well suited to physical media and scarcity-based environments where it's unlikely that anyone's going to be copying and reproducing your marketing material (they're more likely to pass the one print catalogue around a group if they're doing shared or bulk orders).

Marketing in the era of information surplus faces a few more problems than its offline counterparts when it comes to copyright issues. First, there's the minor inconvenience of the way information is copied and reproduced on the Internet being at odds with the default restrictive licences of scarcity-based copyright. It's not that you can't allocate surplus mentality permissions to copyrighted content, it's just that the current array of laws that govern copyright assume that it's supposed to be used in a restrictive manner such as protecting the IP of a corporation, authored content or recorded music. Where marketers plan to rely on the widespread replication and diffusion of their content through file sharing, re-tweeting, re-blogging and similar surplus economy activities, they're going to also need to ensure that their best customers (the reproducers) aren't about to run into serious legal problems.

Secondly, the age of surplus combined with the ease of copying, access to massive distribution channels and global networks open the doors to the temptation to ask for forgiveness rather than seek permission. This is a bad idea, since permission is cheaper than infringement and brand damage never helps sell products (Revenue −1). However, marketers may also find themselves facing off against their legal departments when the lawyers do their jobs (protecting the brandmarks, IP and trademarks) whilst stomping on the relationship marketing plans of the marketing department (customer co-creation, fan pages, user-community wikis, product-in use videos generated by users).

It's worth taking a look at how Lucas Art Films converted a growing legal problem of *Star Wars* fans' films into a marketing coup. It allocated fans specific permission licences to reuse intellectual property for films that preserved the integrity of the franchise (up to and including parodies) and which didn't exploit the opportunity for financial gain (starwars.atomfilms.com). Allocating specific content licences also created a strong legal environment to protect the fan film community participants from overzealous Lucas Arts lawyers and people considering 'borrowing' the fans' work for their own financial gain. It did wonders for maintaining community investment in the film franchise and for providing an ongoing stream of new user-generated content with minimal investment.

Finally, for the marketing department that wants to outsource a lot of the heavy lifting to the consumer community, it's worth investing in Creative Commons licensed content that's openly licensed for reuse by default (www.creativecommons.org/international/uk). Creative Commons is a form of copyright attribution which ascribes set standards of accessibility, reuse permissions and attribution licences to content by default with the consequence that material can be reused (for those permitted purposes) without needing to seek an initial copyright waiver or licence agreement. The idea of Creative Commons is based on the principles of 'Some Rights Reserved' versus the all-encompassing 'All Rights Reserved' approach of copyright law. Creative Commons has developed six licensing arrangements that exist in three formats: the unported copy (which is based on the Cerne Copyright Convention) and globally applicable, and a set of regional specific human language and legal code versions (Creative Commons, 2010). We're focusing on the six unported licences in the first instance, with links to regional licences to follow.

o *Attribution (cc by)*: www.creativecommons.org/licenses/by/3.0/
  This is the most open licence and allows users to do whatever they feel with the content as long as it upholds the basic elements of the agreement (moral right, fair use, publicity and privacy rights) and attributes the source material back to the original owner. It's probably the best type of licensed content to seek out for

content and infrastructure for commercial projects that want to tap into Creative Commons-licensed resources.

o *Attribution Non-Commercial* (cc by-nc): www.creativecommons.org/licenses/by-nc/3.0/

This licence allows for the same principles of remixing, modifying and building on your existing work although it doesn't permit commercial use of the results. It's a great licence to use if you want to encourage users to create content to contribute to the community through various creative works. This allows for a set of value-in-use rights to be preserved by the consumers in their co-creation/co-production process whilst avoiding creating complicated legal issues over IP ownership of the core properties. It's the ideal licence to support an active and legally safe community for fan fictions, user-generated content such as game maps, skins or other properties that can enhance the community's perceived value of your core product without causing the Accounts Department to have a heart attack at the thought of lost revenue (since there isn't lost revenue to be had by making a product more desirable to a larger market share).

o *Attribution Share Alike* (cc by-sa): www.creativecommons.org/licenses/by-sa/3.0/

Much like the Attribution licence for what it permits, this licence also brings with it the obligation to continue the Creative Commons licensing approach by stipulating that content created from your works must share the same licence arrangement. The amazing aspect is that if you've set this for commercial use, all derivative products are permitted to be available for commercial use.

o *Attribution Non-Commercial Share Alike* (cc by-nc-sa): www.creativecommons.org/licenses/by-nc-sa/3.0/

This licence is designed to allow for non-commercial work to be openly available for re-use and to be preserved from moving into a commercial arrangement later in the redistribution lifecycle. To some extent, this is a defensive licence that prevents minor modifications being used to lock free (gratis) Creative Commons-licensed content into commercially charged ventures.

o *Attribution No Derivatives* (cc by-nd): www.creativecommons.org/licenses/by-nd/3.0/

This is a licence for sharing the original materials in an unchanged format as long as the original source is credited. Unaltered original material may be used in commercial and non-commercial ventures, and can form the basis for compilations and other collections of content arrangements (think museums).

o *Attribution Non-Commercial No Derivatives* (cc by-nc-nd): www.creativecommons.org/licenses/by-nc-nd/3.0/

Affectionately dubbed the 'free advertising' licence by Creative Commons, this is the highly restrictive version that permits the sharing, redistribution and general promotion of the work without allowing changes, commercial gain or derivative works. This is the perfect licence for marketing communications, catalogues and other word-of-mouth centric marketing materials that you hope your customers want to share around.

Table 15.1 summarizes the licences, permissions and the appropriate text and visual logo to use to state your Creative Commons arrangement.

Table 15.1 Creative Commons licences

| Licence | | Logo | Derivative | Attribution | Non-commercial? | Share-alike? |
|---|---|---|---|---|---|---|
| Attribution | cc by | | Yes | Yes | No | No |
| Attribution Share Alike | cc by-sa | | Yes | Yes | No | Yes |
| Attribution No Derivatives | cc by-nd | | No | Yes | No | No |
| Attribution Non-Commercial | cc by-nc | | Yes | Yes | Yes | No |
| Attribution Non-Commercial Share Alike | cc by-nc-sa | | Yes | Yes | Yes | Yes |
| Attribution Non-Commercial No Derivatives | cc by-nc-nd | | No | Yes | No | No |

In addition to the human language version of the agreement, there's also a nationality specific set of legal documentation that's tailored for the specific requirements of each jurisdiction, and includes:

o England and Wales (www.creativecommons.org/international/uk)
o Scotland (www.creativecommons.org/international/scotland)
o Ireland (www.creativecommons.org/international/ie).

## Digital rights management

Digital rights management (DRM) systems are technologies in hardware and software that are designed to restrict the viewing of software to only those items which contain appropriate and valid registration codes. In broad terms, DRM is an electronic system for the management of intellectual and other property rights. More specifically, DRM has been introduced into the marketplace through the successive roll-out of new technologies such as Windows Media Player 9, numerous upgrades to WindowsXP, and, most blatantly, DVD region encoding.

There are some good marketing uses of DRM that provide genuine value to the end user and then there are the other ways in which these systems are anti-marketing in nature. Valve's SteamPowered digital distribution store is a DRM platform that incorporates rights and responsibility into a functional system. The key value provided by Steam is a mutual acknowledgement of the ownership of the products. Steam attempts to limit piracy by requiring online validation of the ownership of any game before it's playable. At the same time, the game is permanently assigned to the Steam account holder so that they are granted a global access licence – if the game is installed on a Steam-validated computer, the account holder will be recognized as having legitimate access. Providing a two-way rights and responsibility framework also builds a trust relationship between Valve and the consumer in that verification serves both player and producer.

Unfortunately, Valve's case is relatively rare as DRM is usually seen as a means of artificially raising the market value of a company by extracting maximum revenue from a single item. Using DRM against the customer is problematic from a marketing perspective for a range of reasons, including:

o *Undermining relationship marketing*: Trust, commitment and reciprocity is a two-way street, and the current propensity of DRM systems to treat the paying user with suspicion and hostility as a temporary and untrustworthy lease holder of the digital goods fails to deliver trust.

  • Solution: Treat the legitimate owner as the legitimate owner of their data.

o *Limiting or removing legal usage rights*: DRM systems are usually hostile to copying, reuse or inclusion in other formats which are legal and protected acts of fair use under various copyright acts around the world.

  • Solution: Manage legal rights the old-fashioned way – in a court of law.

o *Interference with the doctrine of first sale*: This is where you're only getting an extended licence to use the objects when you thought you were buying something. This usually exists to prevent the very legal second-hand market for used goods or to allow the manufacturer an unnatural level of control over your device (since you're only 'borrowing' it).

  • Solution: Sell rather than lease.

o *Transitory ownership of purchased digital content*: The Amazon Kindle and the Apple iPhone have a tendency towards this form of licence which allows the manufacturer the right to remotely delete content from your device.

  • Solution: Digital licence leases should be marked as 'Rent', 'Lease' 'Borrow until we take it back' and prohibited from saying 'Buy', 'Purchase' or 'Own'.

From the consumer perspective, most of the introductions of the DRM systems have gone unnoticed as consumers purchase their new CDs inclusive of rights management systems. There are occasional high-profile incidents with new release CDs having adverse effects on Macintosh computers (one artiste's CD had a particularly bad effect of totally crippling the Macintosh it was played on – to the point you couldn't even open the CD drive). Destroying the computers owned by the customers who just paid for your product is a dumb business strategy. Sony Music attempted the worst business case of DRM by using a highly dangerous malware strategy of installing a root kit software packages without the permission of the computer's owner. Placing unauthorized and unwanted content on a computer is a malware strategy, and once again, anyone unfortunate enough to buy a Sony-infected product suffered for their loyalty and their legal purchase.

As more of the consumer market switches to online entertainment and the PC becomes a more significant media vehicle (usually through broadband access), DRM software will have a greater impact on society. Whilst much of the contemporary (at the time of writing) debate concerns itself with the ramifications of freedom of speech, privacy and consumer rights, most of these concerns are from the consumer's perspective, rather than looking at the potential impact on business.

## How DRM works (an overview)

Iannella (2001) in a relatively technical article describes the three tasks of the DRM as being:

- *Intellectual property (IP) asset creation*: which is where the creator assigns rights to the use of their product and where the product itself determines whether it was created from acceptable content (assuming that this content is also part of a DRM system). For example, a song can be created from a range of existing music samples, each of which has a digital signature allowing it to be used for creating new music. From there, the IP asset owner can set what permissions they accept for their product (free to share, payment required, etc.).
- *IP management*: which is where the property can be traded and where the information concerning the creation is stored (artiste, title, DRM permissions). Part of the process of IP management includes the steps that the property has to take to authenticate that it can be used – and this is a major part of the complexity of the DRM process with regards to privacy, data collection and rights management.
- *IP use*: which consists of permissions management and tracking management. Permissions management dictates how the property can be used by the consumer – for example, a text document may be set to read only, prohibiting printing. Problems with permissions management are outlined below. Tracking management is the implementation of the authentication routines stored by the IP management. Tracking management has raised several serious questions regarding the consumers' rights to privacy and anonymity, which are also raised below.

In theory, the purpose of DRM is to provide digital permissions to use electronic files in order to preserve the creators' intended wishes for their products. In reality, the problem with DRM is that there are a limited number of organizations with the capacity to set the IP management, which essentially is beginning to set the scene for an IP rights management monopoly.

## Permissions management and the consumer

The first major problem for marketing and the consumer involving the DRM system is the redevelopment and re-education of the market as to what it is that they buy when they buy your product. One of the key, and for many of the major DRM proponents most important, aspects of the system is that you can allocate the number of uses of the product. Apple has integrated this particular habit into the iPhone and iPods with the idea that there are only a limited number of times you can reauthorize an iTunes account which presumes that your iPod won't die, the computer's hard drive won't die and that you're not going to upgrade technology that often. Try not to be an innovator who buys lots of new technologies if you're going to get a licence deal like this.

There are pros and cons for the use of DRM for the assignment of a limited number of uses for a product, and these are:

○ *Rental pricing*: which has traditionally been associated with a time period (weekly, overnight, three-day) for the rental of entertainment such as videos. Whilst the re-education of the consumer market is possible, it will require the existing market acceptance of time-based purchases to be converted to use based. Apple has made considerable in-roads into the digital rental market space with iTunes offering short-term leases of movies and television series, but self-deleting movie files are still quite creepy.

○ *Physical goods with limited uses*: which is potentially the worst aspect of the DRM system, whereby a physical device will be set to only function for a limited number of times before it must be re-authorized and paid for again. This concept is based on the idea of licensing limited use rights to goods – for example, a portable licence for the use of a desktop computer based on DRM systems would make for a useful hotdesk system. However, there's also the idea of creating defective-by-design systems that will become single use or limited multiple use objects that can't be reinitialized after the expiry period. This is a bad idea on several levels starting with the value-in-ownership arguments through to the environmental, sustainability and green issues of building made-to-be-broken and disposable products.

○ *Trade practices acts, misleading advertising and implied ownership*: which will be the legal minefield of advertising and promotion once limited-use DRM products become widespread. Consumers will need to be informed as to whether the product they are buying is a rental product (pay per access), limited-use product (ten uses, then recharge), full ownership (all yours) or some hybrid combination based on how much they paid originally for the product.

○ *Lock out codes*: which have been the bane of DVD customers across the world as the DVD devices are fitted with the ability for the DVD to refuse permissions for the fast forward, pause and/or rewind buttons to work. Mandatory infringement warning videos, compulsory trailers and generally treating the audience with contempt is not a grand plan when it comes to driving demand for DVD sales. If they've bought the disc, they're not about to steal a film (unless you make watching the DVD so unbearable they're better off downloading a pirate version).

In general, the implementation of DRM poses a problem for marketing in that it will require the rethinking of the nature of the DRM physical product and digital product, and who owns the product once the consumer has paid for it.

## Problems and issues with DRM and marketing

In theory, and as the creators of these technologies will argue, the purpose of DRM is to prevent unauthorized copying, piracy and similar intellectual property crimes. Unfortunately, a situation is being created where the widespread adoption of the DRM technologies means that unsigned works (legitimate software or media which does not include a DRM-licensed code) will not be able to be played on the DRM software or equipment. The rationale is quite obvious and simple – if non-DRM encoded data can be played, then piracy only needs to strip the DRM coding to be able to continue unabated.

The problem for marketing is extremely significant. DRM represents a restraint on the ability of the consumer to play materials on their personal equipment – potentially including your advertising materials. In order to have advertising signed by a DRM system, there will most likely be an additional proprietary royalty fee which will have to be paid to the DRM managers. It's not going to take a genius to figure out that difficulties will arise in getting DRM signatures for any advertising for a product that circumvents the DRM system. The advent of these forms of proprietary control standards risk the ability of business to conduct free trade without needing to seek publishing permissions from a non-government quasi monopoly system.

### Tracking management, DRM and privacy: We know what you watched last summer

The prospect of a global, unregulated marketing database of everything everyone ever did, bought, browsed, watched or listened to was supposed to just be the subject of science fiction. It wasn't supposed to be a blueprint as much as it was supposed to be a warning. Now, with the current rapid development of database marketing and the acquisition of masses of data from disparate sources – such as online purchase preferences, website choices, Facebook's Beacon program, Google's retention of search data, Yahoo!'s geolocation information from Flickr photos, retail data collected through Amazon, Sainsbury's loyalty programmes, iPhone applications using locational information, and Twitter updates with geotagging – it's possible to develop a moderately sophisticated profile of an individual consumer in terms of who they are, where they are (now, and recent past) and what their friends are likely to recommend they download to watch tonight.

With the widespread deployment of digital rights managed goods, services and products, any pretence of privacy simply disappears as soon as a central registry somewhere knows exactly how many times you've listened to Bob the Builder, and how many listens you have left. All it will take is for a database merger of DRM usage rights (what the consumer has listened to and what they're authorized to listen to) with any existing profiles (such as a tax file or social security number), and there will be no effective privacy for the consumer.

What does this mean for marketing? On the cynical end it means unprecedented access to market research data on actual usage patterns – until the market figures out a way to block or mask their consumption and still meet the DRM authentication requirements. It also means a violation of the privacy of the consumer (the readers of this book) in a way that even George Orwell's *1984* couldn't have imagined. The inappropriate use of data collection and profiling based on the DRM technology will drive privacy-conscious consumers away from the new technologies and, if the market feels sufficiently unhappy, may drive legislation that will prohibit this form of database marketing. Overall, marketing may find itself heavily regulated to restore a sense of privacy to the marketplace. The balance between what the market will tolerate in the name of market research and what the DRM technology will deliver as an incidental part of the authorization/verification processes needs to be carefully monitored and the benefit of doubt should go to the preservation of the consumer's privacy ahead of the collection of data for commercial ends. If it doesn't, then sufficient consumer resentment may cost more to marketing (generally) and the offending company (financially) than the possible benefits they could have gained from the extra, often irrelevant, data.

### Marketing information wants to be free (as in movement)

The most valuable element of the Internet for any marketer is the share of voice that cannot be dominated by one player. This is the feature that so many marketers have craved for decades as their campaigns languished outside of the price range of big media events, popular television shows and overpriced peak timeslots. Now that freedom of voice has come to the marketers, many of them fear the very thing they wished for.

With the fragmentation of the marketplace that has occurred with the introduction of the Internet, marketers need to find places to voice their message where it can meet their markets. Freedom of speech on the Internet is vital to the development of e-commerce, as regulation and control of content on the Internet will mean regulation of the marketing message. The widespread adoption of DRM is potentially the greatest threat to marketing messages and the freedom to communicate in a competitive marketplace. Once DRM systems are embedded into commonplace technologies such as televisions, radios and computers, marketers are at the mercy of the companies who hold the keys to the DRM software. And there's a fairly strong chance that the DRM rights managers aren't going to see any major ethical problem with selling exclusive advertising DRM rights to the highest bidder, thereby closing down an avenue of expression for other marketers.

Marketing already bears the cost of buying advertising space on television, radio and any other paid placement. Imagine being forced to pay royalties to a central authority for the privilege of producing a piece of content that you still have to pay to have broadcast. Proprietary standards that lock the user into a limited set of choices controlled by the equipment manufacturers can endanger the freedom of the marketer. Any system which can potentially limit competition and reduce channels for the distribution of dissenting ideas (such as advertising for rival systems) will have a negative impact on marketing. Marketing needs the Internet to be as free as possible so that it can never be squeezed out of the game by proprietary standards that reduce competition and create monopolies. Share of voice and freedom of expression are the reasons why the Internet has such low entry barriers and is so valuable to small- and medium-sized enterprises.

In order to prosper in the digital economy, marketing needs to ensure that the freedom it requires to operate effectively is preserved. This will mean that, occasionally, marketing will have to make some sacrifices for the greater good of society, including easing up on copyright protection and trademark suppression. In particular, the current battles over intellectual property online are a complicated balancing act between preserving the right of the business to profit from their own property and the rights of the consumer. Normally marketing would be looking to the preservation of the rights of the business, however, in certain instances, marketing needs the consumer's rights to freedom of choice to be maintained, even at the expense of the rights of businesses. Once dominant industry players have the power to dictate how and where a consumer is permitted to view various media (including television, videos, music and Internet content), then these entrenched players can block the marketing messages of their smaller rivals.

### DRM and the product lifecycle

The last and most significant legal and marketing issue associated with the use of restrictive DRM systems is the phasing out of an existing DRM system. Microsoft acknowledges that the DRM system that it uses may suffer from errors if you change certain elements of your computer's hardware (support.microsoft.com/kb/891664). Thankfully it also provides step-by-step instructions to solve that problem. That said, there's also the business issue of legacy support for existing DRM systems once the primary market has reached the decline phase of the product lifecycle. Unlike fixed licences (CD keys) or property assignment (actually owning the stuff), products that need to contact a DRM server to authenticate ownership are vulnerable to critical failure if the DRM server ceases to operate (Figure 15.3). Rather than being a hypothetical case, this was demonstrated when Microsoft elected to discontinue the MSN Music DRM servers in 2008 (with revised server shutdown dates for 2011). Customers who had purchased from the MSN digital store discovered that they were going to lose access to their purchased product. Discontinuing a product is a fairly standard protocol for marketing decision making if you've ever used a GE finance matrix or the product lifecycle. However, when discontinuing scarcity economy products (aka physical goods), shutting down the manufacturer doesn't destroy the existing products. It may make it significantly more

**Figure 15.3** Steal this comic
*Source:* http://xkcd.com/488

challenging to source spare parts but that's very different to what happens when the DRM master server ceases to function.

The prospect of confiscating paid products from loyal customers should be seen as a commercial disaster and a relationship marketing nightmare. When you consider that DRM files are a relatively new technology and prone to adoption by innovator and early adopter customers, then you're looking at burning the markets who were most likely to back your new products, pay premium charges to access your innovations and take the social risk of supporting your brand at the start. Hurting them with restrictive licences, confiscating their paid goods and generally treating them with contempt isn't a great business plan.

## Dealing with the new

If your first reaction to any new Internet or e-marketing technology is to ask how it can be used for promotion, then you're not cut out for a life as a good e-marketer. Throughout this book we've emphasized the marketing mix as a holistic device and pushed for the integration of consumer behaviour into strategy and practice. As a final step, we present five steps for developing strategies for adjusting to the future. These steps are:

1. *Follow the people*: Consumer behaviour will drive the Internet and determine the outcomes of many of the current issues. Security and privacy will be resolved by market demand as the market either requests (and receives) improved security or just does not care enough for it to affect their behaviour. Controls on the Internet that annoy consumers will be repealed by populist governments seeking social approval and re-election. Even at the business-to-business level, the individual is ultimately responsible for the decision of yes or no in the transaction.
2. *The old Internet is not the new Internet*: The current Internet is an evolving medium which will change, adjust, develop and gradually form into something different from the Internet of today. The best analogy is to look at the evolution of television and television content, from its first broadcasts to the current products. However, the permanence of Internet culture will continue to flavour the development of the medium as the systems mature and develop over time.
3. *Be radical*: Take Apple Corporation's advice and think different (www.apple.com). Be prepared to try new methods and techniques on the Internet, and be prepared for success and failure as it comes, whichever way it comes. The greatest danger facing the novice Internet marketer is not being willing to back their new ideas in the new medium for fear they might fail. Take heart from the fact they probably will fail, but at no greater or lesser extent than they would have failed in the offline world. However, being radical does not mean discarding past lessons or ignoring existing theory and practice. Radical marketing is about applying best practice that suits your products, your markets and the combined needs of your company and consumer, irrespective of whether it is new or old. Doing what fits best, rather than what has always been done, is the radical approach advocated by the Internet.

4. *Be robust*: Take the hits on the chin, get back up and keep going. The Internet is about long-term focus with short-term adaptability to rapid change. Many businesses that have succeeded in online marketing did so by being aware of the causes of their success and adapting to support those features, whilst being willing to take the set backs as they occurred on the way to establishing their long-term success. Adapting to where the markets are and what products are in demand is a necessary survival trait.

5. *Focus on the niches*: This advice should be redrafted simply as 'Focus on the markets'. The Internet offers unprecedented access to niche markets by allowing the interested consumer to find the interesting producer. However, the current mindset of the marketing discipline is hung up on believing that this can only be used for niche products when it clearly indicates that the consumer can find the marketer, if the consumer wants what the marketer has to offer. Study the needs, wants and desires of the market and see where your product can match up with what the consumer wants, within the constraints of what the company wants to produce. Focus on the markets, find out where they are, what they want and offer it to them online, and the customer will be able to find you every bit as much as you can find the customer.

A sixth and final point which does not derive from Randall's (1997) examination of survival strategies for the future, but rather from the observation of the best methods of dealing with the changing future, is:

○ *Have fun*: The world is an inherently interesting place. The Internet is an unstable climate of chaotic change and the ever-shifting sands of the consumer marketplace makes for a rollercoaster ride of a lifetime. Has any period of marketing ever been this much fun? This is one of the most exciting times in the history of civilization, with more on offer for the individual, company and marketer. Take the opportunities as opportunities, not threats, take the threats as challenges and take the risks as necessary. Enjoy the Internet as a wildly chaotic landscape while it lasts, before it settles down, grows up and becomes as staid and sober a medium as television or radio. We are living in interesting times, and marketing has the opportunity to have the time of its life by being part of creation of the future.

## Conclusion

Predicting the future is always a risky business and when it comes to the Internet, where change is rapidly created and diffused, the risk is even greater. That said, there are a number of key emergent issues and trends which are likely to shape the near to medium future on e-marketing. Depending which way the issues develop, the nature of the Internet as we currently understand and use it has the potential to be fundamentally changed.

Change in itself is not a bad thing but it's never been a good idea to throw out the baby with the bathwater. There are a few key philosophies of the original Internet culture that can stand the test of time and which should be preserved regardless of the changes in infrastructure and technology. Flowing from the Internet's foundation in the military and academia, the notions of the gift economy, open standards and treating blockages as damage characterize the old Internet and still underpin the new. Operating in an environment of plenty when it comes to information rather than taking the 'knowledge is power' approach is a challenge to many traditional businesses. Attempts to undermine these key concepts have seen the failure of many online commercial ventures.

However, the open environment of the Internet is only safe all the time that users are vigilant. Attempts by commercial interests to make online more like offline and restrict the flow of information through various means such as restrictive use of digital rights management are on ongoing issue. From a marketing perspective, information flow restrictions, whether they are the result of technical, commercial or government policy initiatives, diminish the potential value of the Internet as a key marketing channel. Despite over a decade of discussions there are still critical ongoing issues impacting on the efficacy of the Internet in marketing, including privacy concerns, preservation of anonymity and security. All the time the Internet continues to develop and evolve, new issues and concerns will arise. Marketers will need to keep abreast of the changes, respond to the issues and, most important of all, keep to the fundamental philosophy of marketing – the centrality of the consumer – if they are going to succeed in the ever-changing online world.

## References

### Books and journals

Creative Commons (2010) 'Licences', http://creativecommons.org/about/licenses, (accessed 11 July 2010).

Genieva, E. (1997) 'Legal aspects of the Internet', *International Information and Library Review*, 29: 381–92.

Hoffman, D. and Novak, T. (1996) 'Marketing in hypermedia computer-mediated environments: conceptual foundations', *Journal of Marketing*, 60 (July): 50–68.

Iannella, R. (2001) 'Digital rights management (DRM) architectures', *D-Lib Magazine*, 7(6) (http://www.dlib.org/dlib/june01/iannella/06iannella.html – accessed 11 July 2010).

Kostopoulos, G. K. 1998, 'Global delivery of education via the Interne', *Internet Research: Electronic Networking Applications and Policy*, 8(3):257–65.

Randall, D. (1997) 'Consumer strategies for the Internet: four scenarios', *Long Range Planning*, 30(2): 157–68.

Raymond, E.S. (1999) 'The jargon manual', version 4.2.0, http://www.tuxedo.org/~esr/jargon/ (accessed 11 July 2010).

Wilson, S. (1999), 'Digital signatures and the future of documentation', *Information Management & Computer Security*, 7(2): 83–7.

### Web references

| | |
|---|---|
| Apple | www.apple.com |
| Attribution | www.creativecommons.org/licenses/by/3.0/ |
| Attribution No Derivatives | www.creativecommons.org/licenses/by-nd/3.0/ |
| Attribution Non-Commercial | www.creativecommons.org/licenses/by-nc/3.0/ |

| | |
|---|---|
| Attribution Non-Commercial No Derivatives | www.creativecommons.org/licenses/by-nc-nd/3.0/ |
| Attribution Non-Commercial Share Alike | www.creativecommons.org/licenses/by-nc-sa/3.0/ |
| Attribution Share Alike | www.creativecommons.org/licenses/by-sa/3.0/ |
| BitTorrent | www.bittorrent.com |
| Centrebet | www.centrebet.com |
| Creative Commons UK | www.creativecommons.org/international/uk |
| HM Revenue and Customs | www.hmrc.gov.uk/leaflets/c9.htm |
| iTunes | www.apple.com/itunes |
| Ladbrokes | www.ladbrokes.com |
| Maru | www.youtube.com/user/mugumogu |
| Microsoft DRM support | support.microsoft.com/kb/891664 |
| Skype | www.skype.com |
| Snopes | www.snopes.com |
| Star Wars fan films | starwars.atomfilms.com |
| Twitter earthquake and tremor tracker | www.twitter.com/USGSted |
| World of Warcraft | www.worldofwarcraft.com |
| XKCD: Abstraction | http://xkcd.com/676 |
| XKCD: Approved content | http://xkcd.com/129 |
| XKCD: Steal this comic | http://xkcd.com/488 |

# Index